Public Private Partnership Contracts

This book provides a comprehensive overview of the law surrounding PPPs in the Middle East and North African region.

The significance of liberalized and integrated Public Private Partnership contracts as an essential component of the world legal and policy order is well documented. The regulation of PPPs is justified economically to allow for competition in the relevant public service and to achieve price transparency, thus resulting in significant savings for the public sector. In parallel to the economic justifications, legal imperatives have also called for the regulation of PPPs in order to allow free movement of goods and services and to prohibit discrimination on grounds of nationality. The need for competitiveness and transparency in delivering public services through PPPs is considered a safeguard to achieve international standards in delivering public utility services. First, it assesses the compatibility of the current PPP legislation and regulation in the MENA region with the international standards of legislation and regulation prevalent in many other countries, including the UK, France and Brazil. Second, it compares the practices in the MENA region with those of international bodies such as the OECD and World Bank. Comparisons are then made between MENA countries and those in Europe and Asia with regard to the influence of culture, policy and legal globalization.

The book will be of interest to scholars and students in the field of international contract law, public law and state contracts, finance law and private law.

Judge Dr. Mohamed A.M. Ismail, LLB, LLM, PhD; FCI Arb (UK) is Vice President of the Conseil d'État and Judge at the Supreme Administrative Court, Egypt.

Routledge Research in International Law

For a full list of titles in this series, visit https://www.routledge.com/Routledge-Research-in-International-Law/book-series/INTNLLAW

Available:

Backstage Practices in Transnational Law
Lianne J.M Boer and Sofia Stolk

International 'Criminal' Responsibility
Antinomies
Ottavio Quirico

The Future of International Courts
Regional, Institutional and Procedural Challenges
Edited by Avidan Kent, Nikos Skoutaris and Jamie Trinidad

The Far-Right in International and European Law
Natalie Alkiviadou

International Law and Revolution
Owen Taylor

The Responsibility to Protect in International Law
Philosophical Investigations
Natalie Oman

The Responsibility to Protect in Libya and Syria
Mass Atrocities, Human Protection, and International Law
Yasmine Nahlawi

Public Private Partnership Contracts
The Middle East and North Africa
Mohamed A.M. Ismail

Public Private Partnership Contracts
The Middle East and North Africa

Mohamed A.M. Ismail

LONDON AND NEW YORK

First published 2020
by Routledge
2 Park Square, Milton Park, Abingdon, Oxon OX14 4RN

and by Routledge
605 Third Avenue, New York, NY 10017

First issued in paperback 2021

Routledge is an imprint of the Taylor & Francis Group, an informa business

© 2020 Mohamed A.M. Ismail

The right of Mohamed A.M. Ismail to be identified as author of this work has been asserted by him in accordance with sections 77 and 78 of the Copyright, Designs and Patents Act 1988.

All rights reserved. No part of this book may be reprinted or reproduced or utilized in any form or by any electronic, mechanical, or other means, now known or hereafter invented, including photocopying and recording, or in any information storage or retrieval system, without permission in writing from the publishers.

Trademark notice: Product or corporate names may be trademarks or registered trademarks, and are used only for identification and explanation without intent to infringe.

Publisher's Note
The publisher has gone to great lengths to ensure the quality of this reprint but points out that some imperfections in the original copies may be apparent.

British Library Cataloguing-in-Publication Data
A catalogue record for this book is available from the British Library

Library of Congress Cataloging-in-Publication Data
Names: Ismail, Mohamed A. M., author.
Title: Public private partnership contracts : the Middle East and North Africa / Mohamed Ismail.
Description: Abingdon, Oxon ; New York, NY : Routledge, 2020. | Series: Routledge research in international law | Includes bibliographical references and index.
Identifiers: LCCN 2019059034 (print) | LCCN 2019059035 (ebook) | ISBN 9781138343436 (hardback) | ISBN 9780429439148 (ebook)
Subjects: LCSH: Public-private sector cooperation–Law and legislation–Arab countries
Classification: LCC KMC748.7 .I83 2020 (print) | LCC KMC748.7 (ebook) | DDC 346/.149270668–dc23
LC record available at https://lccn.loc.gov/2019059034
LC ebook record available at https://lccn.loc.gov/2019059035

ISBN 13: 978-1-03-223686-5 (pbk)
ISBN 13: 978-1-138-34343-6 (hbk)

Typeset in Galliard
by Swales & Willis, Exeter, Devon, UK

Printed in the United Kingdom
by Henry Ling Limited

To my parents' souls

Contents

Preface		viii
About the author		xii
List of abbreviations		xiv
	Introduction	1
1	The constitutional framework of state contracts in the MENA countries	29
2	The substantive theory of states' contracts in MENA countries	39
3	The principles of *Le Contrat Administratif* theory in MENA countries	57
4	The trajectory of the legislative and regulatory intervention from MENA countries to permit PPP techniques	77
5	PPPs in MENA countries' public procurements	106
6	The international dynamics of PPPs	142
7	The main substantive mechanisms of PPP contracts in MENA countries	158
8	Arbitration as dispute resolution mechanism in PPPs in MENA countries	203
	Conclusions	227
	References	237
	Index	245

Preface

Public contracting has become an increasingly important form of administrative action, so much that the modern state has been characterized as a 'contracting state.' States' role and intervention in public contracts in the Middle East and North African MENA region[1] has changed in the current years as this role is confined to being a regulator and observer adopting Adam Smith's vision of the state's role. Yet, while public contracting increasingly takes place in globalized markets, the law governing it has been understood traditionally as a purely domestic matter. Conceptual approaches to understanding how public contracts law is transforming in globalized markets are still largely missing. This is particularly important as rules for public contracting in global markets emerge very differently from the domestic context.[2] The process of internationalization or transnationalization of public contracts has various stages in MENA countries through decades started with the new *dual*/hybrid legal nature of the international administrative contracts such as the international public works agreements.[3] The following step nowadays is the liberalization of the public utilities' concession agreements from being a pure traditional administrative law concession in the form of domestic administrative contract to being altered to great extent as it is currently a new modernized contract with a *dual*/hybrid legal nature for PPPs or BOT/BOOT with their various techniques.

Legal globalization plays a fundamental role in the current change of public contracts' norms in MENA countries.[4] Despite globalization movements and the flow of a new legal culture to the legal systems of developing countries, as well as to their socio-economic structure and social traditions, it is worth noting that some areas can still preserve their national original identity. The latter

---

1 The terms MENA countries and Arab countries are used interchangeably in this monograph.
2 Mathias Audit and Stephan W Schill (eds), *Transnational Law of Public Contracts: An Introduction, Transnational Law of Public Contracts*, Bruylant 2016, 3–20.
3 Mohamed A.M. Ismail, *Globalization and New International Public Works Agreements in Developing Countries, An Analytical Perspective*, Routledge 2011.
4 J.E. Stiglitz, *Globalization and Its Discontents*, W.W. Norton & Company 2004; J.E. Stiglitz, *Making Globalization Work*, W.W. Norton & Company 2007; B. Snowdon, *Globalisation, Development and Transition*, Edward Elgar 2007.

Preface ix

concept applies to most developing countries, particularly in the areas of family law and in social traditions in Middle Eastern societies as well as in other developing countries. Religious beliefs and social customs practiced in these countries are not influenced by cultural globalization in the socio-legal domain.[5] Regardless of minor religious and social controversy among nationals in developing countries in areas of family law, conservative legal social cultures in Middle Eastern societies impose the same traditions and customs on the domain of human family relations. Legal matters that are considerably influenced by legal cultural globalization, such as the Administrative Contract Theory (*Le Contrat Administratif*), maintain some of their basic features. It is true that penalties stipulated in the Administrative Contract Theory have not changed to date in civil law jurisdictions, even with the existence of new trends aimed at the modernization and internationalization of the traditional Theory of Administrative Contracts.

In MENA countries new patterns of state contacts have appeared following the legal practice worldwide. Those new patterns are different from the traditional administrative contracts. The most significant patterns of state contracts that have new and unique contractual stipulations are the PPP techniques. It is worth noting that PPP contracts in MENA countries existed in practice before the promulgation of PPP legislation in the MENA region. There is a *'décalage'* between practice and the legislature in MENA countries as PPP legislation promulgation delays for years. PPPs in the form of Build, Operate and Transfer (BOT) were used as early as 1858 for the construction of the Suez Canal, which is considered one of the oldest concessions in history.[6]

PPP techniques aim to encourage greater inward of investments and are a significant boost for the economy. MENA countries aim to enhance their investment ecosystem by implementing PPP legislation and incorporate it into their legislative and regulatory frameworks. PPP techniques in the MENA region provide a vision that is eager to continue ramping up inward of foreign investments by creating legislative and regulatory frameworks for PPPs that strengthen the business environment and promote a better threshold of protection to foreign investors.

MENA countries' PPP legislation is part of a package of legal reforms intended to strengthen the legislative climate for current and prospective investors in the MENA region and shore up the economy as a result. This legal approach is also consistent with the Sustainable Developments Goals (SDGs) as it increases the ranking of MENA countries in the international financial institutions' classifications. It is an attempt to achieve a real implementation of the vision of 2030. The PPP approach is part of a wider and diversified program of

---

5 Mohamed A.M. Ismail, Legal globalization and PPPs in Egypt, An Analytical and comparative perspective on the current legislative and judicial modifications to and enhancements of the administrative contractual regime on PPP transactions, *European Public Private Partnership Law Review*, 2010, 1, 54.

6 Duncan Cartlidge, *Public Private Partnerships in Construction*, Taylor & Francis 2006.

x *Preface*

ongoing reforms designed to create new opportunities for investors looking to access to the MENA countries' market. Reforms implemented in recent years have helped to increase the Inward of Foreign Direct Investment IFDI. PPP techniques in the MENA region enable experimentation and innovation by businesses and improve the outcomes of public services for end-users.

This monograph is the first in the English legal text that deals with PPPs in the MENA region and fills a gap in the English legal text by offering a product that has unique and distinctive features. It sheds light on the constitutional developments in MENA countries and how it is now accepting new economic ideologies to enhance public utilities' performance and public services to end-users through new contractual PPP patterns. MENA countries constitutions do not adopt static economic ideologies, but they adopt dynamic economic ideologies which enable legislation and regulation to adapt the new developments in state contracts' theories. The aim of the latter theories is to achieve the best practices in delivering public services. The constitutional framework has considerably changed in the light of Arab Spring revolutions. What has been achieved through adopting the dynamic approach of the economic ideology in Arab constitutions? It is important to compare the current trends in *'le contrat administrative'* substantive legal theory in the light of the new PPP legislation and regulation and its impact on the current PPP agreements in the MENA region on the one hand and the traditional theory of concession agreements in MENA countries that have been influenced during previous decades with the French legal system on *'le contrat administratif.'* There are remarkable changes to *'le contrat administratif'* theory in the MENA countries in the light of new PPP legislation and regulation.

This monograph provides the academic base line of the current remarkable changes to the pulse and dynamics of the state contracts through new PPP patterns in MENA countries and assesses the excessive clauses in the current PPP legislation and agreements and weather they are still existing and to what extent they are influential to the foreign investor. It provides an analysis to the *'value for money'* concept in PPP patterns in MENA countries and codifies all case-law concessions before the relevant Egyptian courts with reference to the underlying legislative and regulatory principles. The monograph provides a taxonomy of themes that have emerged through administrative contracts litigation and traditional concessions before the courts of Egypt, in particular the Conseil d'État courts as these courts have influenced the legal systems of MENA countries through decades.

The underlying monograph is an attempt to deliver an objective and in-depth critique and analysis of the reasoning and *ratione* of the decisions of the relevant courts of Egypt in concession cases, and the current significant improvements in the legislative and regulatory frameworks of public procurement in PPPs in the MENA region. Further, it illustrates the way PPP legislation and regulation have been influencing academia in MENA countries particularly of Egypt and the relevant MENA states. In addition, it shows the new substantive nature of the PPP contracts in the MENA region which signifies the liberalization of traditional concession contract when it adopts PPP techniques.

The main features of this monograph as a reference point in academia in PPPs in the MENA region are to strive in offering an authoritative insight of the significant development of *'le contrat administratif'* theory through PPP legislation and the remarkable developments of state contracts theory particularly PPPs in Egypt and the relevant MENA region. It also provides an in-depth analysis to the current trends in MENA countries to adopt the free market economy disciplines and to assess the emergence of the trends of the partnerships between public and private sectors in MENA countries and the current theory compatibility with the fundamental principles of the world leading economist Adam Smith, and other leading thoughts such as the Chicago school.

This monograph scrutinizes the current remarkable changes of the substantive excessive clauses of *'le contrat administratif'* theory in MENA countries, in the light of the current change in the economic ideology and its current impact on Arab constitutions, legislation, regulation and contractual patterns. It analyzes the current PPP procurement legislation and regulation in the MENA region. It envisages furnishing the reader with an inclusive, coherent and analytical approach of the relevant academic theories, and jurisprudence of the courts in MENA countries. It aspires to provide a comprehensive evaluation of the policies which underpin PPP legislation and regulation in MENA countries and its compatibility as a legal framework with the international standards of states' public procurements such as the OECD MAPS of 2018 and the World Bank Benchmarking Report of PPP Public Procurements 2017.

PPPs represent a specialist yet significant academic interest in the international academia worldwide, and an increasing practice in international business and commercial legal environment. The relative frequency of PPP business transactions between the public and private sectors, as well as new developments in the interface between public and private sectors amplify the need for an advanced academic contribution which provides theoretical and conceptual frameworks, based on an assessment of the relevant law and jurisprudence in MENA countries.

It is widely recognized that there is an essential need to increase the capacity of MENA governments at all levels to implement PPPs successfully and MENA governments are relinquishing their traditional role as the sole employer in state contracts. This monograph is an attempt to explore current PPP techniques in the MENA region.

About the author

Judge Dr. Mohamed A.M. Ismail, LLB, LLM, PhD; FCI Arb (UK), has been a vice president of the Egyptian Conseil d'État since June 2008 and is currently a judge at the Egyptian Supreme Administrative Court. He has been working at the Egyptian and Arab judiciary since October 1991. He is Senior Consultant for the Legislation and Legal Opinion Commission since September 2013, and to the Ministry of Industry, Commerce and Tourism since January 2018, Kingdom of Bahrain. He is a Fellow of the Chartered Institute of Arbitrators (UK), visiting professor and PhD examiner at the British, Egyptian and Arab Universities, in International States' Contracts and Arbitration, particularly on infrastructure projects. He is a lecturer at the Cairo Regional Centre of the International Commercial Arbitration (CRCICA), Bahrain Chamber for Dispute Resolution (BCDR-AAA) and arbitrator in the International Construction Contracts' disputes, particularly International Public Works Agreements. Dr. Ismail is the State Prize Laureate in Academic Legal Research for 2011. The prize, which is the highest academic award in the MENA region since 1958, was granted to him by the government of the Arab Republic of Egypt. Dr. Ismail is a lecturer at the Arab League. He is a member of the *Comité Française De L'Arbitrage* and was a visiting guest speaker at the University of London. He has been a visiting professor at Cairo University, Egyptian and Bahrini universities since 2000. Dr. Ismail is a member of the research network of 'Public Contract in Legal Globalization' in Sciences Po University, Paris. He has widely published in the UK, Germany, France and in MENA countries, and is among the few Arab scholars who have published in the UK, Germany, France and other countries in English and in Arabic. He has presented numerous papers on his specialization. Dr. Ismail has published regularly for the Arab press since 2001. He was a member of the Advisory Board of the *International Journal of Legislative Drafting and Law Reform (UK)* in 2012–2014, a law journal that started as one of the IALS, University of London, publications. Further, he is a member of the Editorial Board 'the executive editor' of 'Al Qanoniya' Law Journal. The latter law journal is published in English and Arabic by the Legislation and Legal Opinion Commission, Kingdom of Bahrain. This law journal is one of the leading journals in the MENA region, particularly in Gulf states.

He is a regionally and internationally renowned specialist in state contracts, public procurement, international arbitration in state contracts and public private partnerships, especially when it relates to MENA countries' legal systems. In 2014, Dr. Ismail was a visiting research fellow at Max Planck Institute for Comparative and International Private Law in Hamburg. Dr. Ismail publishes with Max-Planck Institute for Comparative Public Law and International Law, Heidelberg, in private-public arbitration. He was a professor in the master's program at the Royal Academy for Police, Kingdom of Bahrain.

Dr. Ismail was formerly a Senior Legal consultant to H.E. the Egyptian Minister of Petroleum and represented the Egyptian government in state international business transactions in the oil and gas industry, especially in the UK, with law firms such as Shearman Sterling, the International Counsel to the Egyptian Government, as well as Baker McKenzie Egypt, the local counsel. He was a Senior Legal consultant to H.E. the Egyptian Minister of Trade and Industry and formerly a Senior Legal consultant to the Investment Sector in Egypt. He represented the Egyptian Government at the United Nations Conference on Trade and Development (UNCTAD), Geneva, for the Bilateral Investment Treaties (BITs) negotiations where developing states were involved.

Abbreviations

AAA	American Arbitration Association
AC	Law Reports, House of Lords (Appeal Cases)
All ER	All England Law Reports
BITs	Bilateral Investment Treaties
BOO	Build, Own, Operate
BOOT	Build, Own, Operate, Transfer
BOT	Build, Own, Transfer
CA	Court of Appeal of England and Wales
CRCICA	The Cairo Regional Centre for International Commercial Arbitration
CIA	The Chartered Institute of Arbitrators
EC	European Community
EPC	Engineering, Procurement, Construction
EPPPL	*The European Procurement & Public Private Partnership Law Review*
EU	European Union
FDI	Foreign Direct Investment
FIDIC	*Federation International Des Ingenieurs Conseils*
GCC	Gulf Cooperation Council
HL	The House of Lords
ICC	The International Chamber of Commerce
ICLR	*The International Construction Law Review*
ICSID	The International Centre for Settlement of Investment Disputes
ICSID Convention	Washington Convention on the Settlement of the Investment Disputes between States and Nationals of Other States, 1965
IFDI	Inward of Foreign Direct Investments
MITs	Multilateral Investment Treaties
Model Law	UNCITRAL Model Law on International Commercial Arbitration adopted in June 1985 and amended in 2006

OECD	Organization for Economic Co-operation and Development
PC	Privy Council
PPP	Public Private Partnership
PPPCU	Public Private Partnership Central Unit
RCADI	*Recueil des Cours de l'Academie de Droit International de la Haye*
Rev Arb	*Revue de l'arbitrage*
SPV	Special Purpose Vehicle
State Council	Conseil d'État
UAE	United Arab Emirates
UNCITRAL	The United Nations Commission on International Trade Law
UNCITRAL RULES	UNCITRAL Arbitration Rules as Amended 2010
UNCTAD	United Nations Conference on Trade and Development
UNIDEROIT	International Institute for the Unification of Private Law
Washington Convention	Washington Convention on the Settlement of the Investment Disputes between States and Nationals of Other States, 1965

Introduction

What is PPP?

Facing severe and deepening budgetary restraints, the modern state must balance the rising demands for transparency and accountability with efficient and effective mechanisms for the delivery of public services at national and international levels. Infrastructure is a key component of the business environment, enables trade and commerce and generates employment. It is estimated that the Middle East and North Africa (MENA) region will need between USD 75 and USD 100 billion of investments per year over the next 20 years to meet its needs. Since public finances remain strained in many MENA countries, rising infrastructure needs will require the mobilization of private investment. Recourse to Public Private Partnership (PPP) can help to meet these goals.[1] PPP is a stronger tool that aims to close the huge infrastructure gap that exists, especially amongst the low- and middle-income countries. PPP aims at a broader concept that is not just *value for money* but also *value for people*, with five key outcomes: increased access and equity, replicability, sustainability and resilience, economic effectiveness and stakeholder engagement. PPPs are sophisticated contracts between the public and the private sector, which work in partnership in providing public goods, works, or services.[2] Features associated with PPPs include a long-term approach to contracting (i.e., contract lengths over 15 years), effective risk sharing between the public and the private partners, and project financing through complex arrangements involving the economic operator as a third party to the contract.[3]

The infrastructure shortage in developing countries is a major obstacle to improved living standards, enterprise development, and the achievement of the

---

1 OECD Publications, 2, *Private Sector Development Handbook, A Handbook for Policy Makers, Public-Private Partnerships in the Middle East and North Africa*, available at: www.oecd.org/mena/competitiveness/PPP%20Handbook_EN_with_covers.pdf, last accessed on 12 October 2019.

2 Laura Panadès-Estruch, Assessing public private partnership law and regulation in the Cayman Islands: opening gateways or closing loopholes? *Public Procurement Law Review*, 2019, 3, 108–119.

3 Duncan Cartlidge, *Public Private Partnerships in Construction*, Taylor & Francis, 2006, 1–2.

2 Introduction

sustainable developments' goals. This is especially the case in the MENA countries, where infrastructure demand has long been rising due to population growth, rapid urbanization, and economic expansion, and was further amplified as historic MENA-region transitions pressured governments to increase living standards and improve the business environment.[4] The high levels of investment required for infrastructure projects cannot be financed only from the governmental resources. Private investment is therefore an option that governments cannot ignore. Private investment goes beyond mere additional capital to mobilize private sector technological expertise and managerial skills for the public interest.[5]

PPP is a significant regulatory trend that has emerged as a result of the strategic role of the private sector and its long-term engagement in delivering infrastructure and public services reflects on the legal treatment of risk distribution between the public and private sectors within PPPs and, in particular, the allocation and pricing of *construction or project risk*, which is related to design problems, building cost overruns, and project delays; *financial risk*, which is related to variability in interest rates, exchange rates, and other factors affecting financing costs; *performance risk*, which is related to the availability of an asset and the continuity and quality of the relevant service provision; *demand risk*, which is related to the on-going need for the relevant public services; and *residual value risk*, which is related to the future market price of an asset.[6]

Still, a number of failed public private partnerships in the infrastructure sector attest to the challenges facing policy makers. Infrastructure investment involves contracts that are by nature complex and of long duration, and that must ensure financial sustainability whilst meeting user needs and social objectives. The challenges are more acute when foreign investors are involved, as is often the case where the infrastructure project exceeds a certain size. In addition, private infrastructure investment has become increasingly scarce, due to the global

---

4 Benedicte Bull and Desmond McNeill, stated that: 'Also, at various World Summits, a change towards a focus on partnerships was noticeable. The first important steps were taken at the United Nations Conference on Environment and Development (UNCED, the Earth Summit) in Rio de Janeiro in 1992, when the Conference's Secretary-General Maurice Strong invited the newly formed World Business Council for Sustainable Development (WBCSD) to write the recommendations on industry and sustainable development. According to Richter (2002) these replaced the recommendations made by the UN Centre for Transnational Corporations (UNCTC). This trend was strengthened during a series of subsequent summits. The report from the International Conference of Financing for Development in Monterey, Mexico, in 2002, stressed that greater cooperation between the public and the private sector was crucial for overcoming the shortcomings of development finance.' Benedicte Bull and Desmond McNeill, *Development Issues in Global Governance, Public-Private Partnerships and Market Multilateralism,* Warwick Studies in Globalisation, Routledge 2006, 9.

5 OECD Publications, 2, *Private Sector Development Handbook, A Handbook for Policy Makers, Public-Private Partnerships in the Middle East and North Africa,* available at: www.oecd.org/mena/competitiveness/PPP%20Handbook_EN_with_covers.pdf, last accessed on 12 October 2019.

6 Christopher Bovis, Risk in public contracts – the treatment and the regulation, *EPPPL*, 2019, 1, Editorial, 1.

economic crisis, commercial bank deleveraging, perceived increased political risk in some countries, and tightened bank prudential regulations.[7] PPP contracts assume that the private sector has a direct responsibility in serving the public interest, as part of its contractual obligations *vis-à-vis* the public sector. Over the past 25 years, more than 5,000 infrastructure projects in 121 low- and middle-income economies have been delivered through PPPs, representing investment commitments of $1.5 trillion.[8] PPPs have supported the development of crucial infrastructure such as roads, bridges, light and heavy rails, airports, power plants, and energy and water distribution networks.[9]

The significance of liberalized and integrated PPPs as an essential component of the world legal and policy order is one of the main features of this monograph. PPP legislation and regulation have been influenced by economic ideology developments, as an implied constitutional ideology, which identified private sector practices in infrastructure and various economic sectors in the MENA region. Economic justifications for regulating PPPs have pointed towards introducing competitiveness to the relevant public services to increase cross-border penetration of services destined for the public sector and achieve price transparency and convergence to the end-users, thus resulting in significant savings for the public sector.

As the eminent economist Adam Smith[10] pointed out, the state role must be confined to its basic functions and the private sector must increase its role in economic life, in Arab countries, particularly in maintaining acceptable and affordable public services to end-users.[11] The main tenets of the Chicago School are that free markets best allocate resources in an economy and that minimal or even no government intervention is best. The Chicago School includes monetarist beliefs about the economy, contending that the money supply should be kept in equilibrium with the demand for money. The Chicago School aims at the reduction or elimination of regulations on businesses. The impact of government regulation on businesses is a significant topic in Chicago School theories. The Chicago

---

7 OECD Publications, 2, *Private Sector Development Handbook, A Handbook for Policy Makers, Public-Private Partnerships in the Middle East and North Africa*, available at: www.oecd.org/mena/competitiveness/PPP%20Handbook_EN_with_covers.pdf, last accessed on 12 October 2019.

8 International Bank for Reconstruction and Development, The World Bank, *Benchmarking Public-Private Partnership Procurement*, 2017, *Benchmarking PPP Procurement: Assessing Government Capability to Prepare, Procure and Manage PPPs*, 14, available at https://ppp.worldbank.org/public-private-partnership/sites/ppp.worldbank.org/files/documents/Benchmarking_PPPs_2017_ENpdf.pdf, last accessed on 12 October 2019.

9 Mohamed A.M. Ismail, Innovation in public procurements in the Egyptian PPP legislation (with reference to PPP legislation in Dubai and Kuwait), Gabriella M. Racca, Christopher R. Yukins (eds.), *Public Contracting and Innovation, Lessons Across Borders*, Bruylant 2019, 567.

10 Adam Smith, *The Wealth of Nations*, Wordsworth Classics of World Literature 2012.

11 Mohamed A.M. Ismail, *Globalization and New International Public Works Agreements in Developing Countries, An Analytical Perspective*, Routledge 2011, 11, with a foreword by H.H. Humphrey Lloyd QC.

4   *Introduction*

School is libertarian and laissez-faire at its core, rejecting Keynesian notions[12] of governments managing aggregate economic demand to promote growth.[13] This leading economic ideology in Arab countries, nowadays, began to influence legal instruments such as the legislation and regulation of PPPs. The role of the modern state is fundamental as it underscores the scope of state intervention in infrastructure and public utilities' services and outlines the scope of private sector partnership. Competition is one of the main instruments that PPPs maintain.[14]

The links between infrastructure and economic growth are well established. They include the impact of the infrastructure on poverty alleviation, growth, and specific development outcomes. As economies face growing demand for infrastructure, PPPs continue to play a crucial role in improving efficiencies in delivering public services, one of the key elements to narrowing the infrastructure gap.[15] In parallel to the economic justifications, legal imperatives have also positioned the regulation of PPPs as a necessary condition for the accomplishment of principles such as the free movement of goods and services, the right of establishment and the prohibition of discrimination on grounds of nationality. The need for competitiveness and transparency in delivering public services through PPPs is considered a safeguard to achieve international standards in delivering public utilities' services.

The United Nations' Sustainable Development Goals (SDGs) recognize both the relevance of quality infrastructure and the role of partnerships with the private sector in the post-2015 developments agenda.[16] In particular, the quality of the procurement process is a driver of PPP efficiency. Corrupt procurement practices continue to obstruct the delivery of a quality infrastructure.[17] Moreover, the design of the procurement process itself has an impact on the ability of governments to take full advantage of the potential benefits of PPPs for

---

12 Keynesian economics is an economic theory of total spending in the economy and its effects on output and inflation. Keynesian economics was developed by the British economist John Maynard Keynes during the 1930s in an attempt to understand the Great Depression. Keynes advocated for increased government expenditures and lower taxes to stimulate demand and pull the global economy out of the depression.

13 For the Chicago School's main concepts see: Milton Friedman, *Capitalism and Freedom*, University of Chicago Press 2002.

14 As Adam Smith pointed out 'Every man, as long as he does not violate the laws of justice, is left perfectly free to pursue his own interest his own way, and to bring both his industry and capital into competition with those of any other man, or order of men'. See: Adam Smith, *Invisible Hand*, Penguin Books, Great Ideas 2008, 127.

15 S. Knight, *Dubai Embraces PPP Again*, Allan & Overy 2016, available at: www.jdsupra.com/legalnews/dubai-embraces-ppp-again-13626/, last accessed on 7 February 2020.

16 United Nations Sustainable Development Goals, available at: www.un.org/sustainabledevelopment/sustainable-development-goals/, last accessed on 12 October 2019.

17 OECD, Methodology for Assessing Procurement System (MAPS), 2018, available at: www.mapsinitiative.org/methodology/MAPS-methodology-for-assessing-procurement-systems.pdf, last accessed on 12 October 2019.

delivering infrastructure.[18] This includes their ability to identify which projects are best done as PPPs and to manage contracts in a transparent and efficient way.[19]

In the Gulf States, governments have long been using the high revenues from hydrocarbons to provide the needed funds for infrastructure projects in their annual budgets without the need for support from the private sectors. Until recently, the low oil prices have paved the way for the growing interest in PPP. The current low oil price environment has encouraged the Gulf States governments to revisit the PPP patterns. Dubai, Kuwait, and other countries such as Oman, Bahrain, Qatar, and Saudi have started to look at PPP structures for assistance in their infrastructure programs.[20] The reduction in oil revenues has a high impact not only on the government cash flows, but also on the capital reserves of local banks, which significantly affected their liquidity. However, this does not mean that the government should pay more, instead, it should encourage the public authority to focus more on *value for money*.[21]

PPP definition

Although PPPs are not new, there is also no universally agreed definition of the term.[22] The abbreviation PPP is currently being used in development discourse to identify very different types of arrangements. This generates an incredible amount of confusion and makes constructive debate about PPPs' contribution to financing development needs difficult. PPPs are described as: a medium- or long-term contractual arrangement between the state and a private sector

---

18 International Bank for Reconstruction and Development, The World Bank *Benchmarking Public-Private Partnership Procurement*, 2017, *Benchmarking PPP Procurement: Assessing Government Capability to Prepare, Procure and Manage PPPs*, available at https://ppp.world bank.org/public-private-partnership/sites/ppp.worldbank.org/files/documents/Benchmar king_PPPs_2017_ENpdf.pdf, last accessed 12 October 2019.

19 The World Bank, Procuring Infrastructure Public-Private Partnerships Report 2018, available at: http://pubdocs.worldbank.org/en/256451522692645967/PIP3-2018.pdf, last accessed on 12 October 2019.

20 Mohamed A.M. Ismail, Innovation in public procurements in the Egyptian PPP legislation (with reference to PPP legislation in Dubai and Kuwait), Gabriella M. Racca, Christopher R. Yukins (eds.), *Public Contracting and Innovation, Lessons Across Borders*, Bruylant 2019, 568.

21 S. Knight, *Dubai Embraces PPP Again*, Allen & Overy 2016, available at: www.jdsupra.com/legalnews/dubai-embraces-ppp-again-13626/, last accessed on 7 February 2020.

22 'The term public-private partnership (PPP) does not have a legal meaning and can be used to describe a wide variety of arrangements involving the public and private sectors working together in some way. Policy makers have invented an ingenious array of terms to summarize what they are trying to achieve. It is therefore necessary for them to be very clear about *why* they are looking to partner with the private sector, *what* forms of PPP they have in mind, and *how* they should articulate this complex concept.' See: The International Bank for Reconstruction and Development, *The World Bank, Attracting Investors to African Public-Private Partnerships, A Project Preparation Guide*, 2009, 7.

6 Introduction

company; an arrangement in which the private sector participates in the supply of assets and services traditionally provided by government, such as hospitals, schools, prisons, roads, bridges, tunnels, railways, water and sanitation and energy; an arrangement involving some form of risk sharing between the public and private sector.

In academia and practice, there is no single, internationally accepted definition of PPPs. The PPP Reference Guide takes a broad view of what a PPP is, defining it as:[23]

> A long-term contract between a private party and a government entity, for providing a public asset or service, in which the private party bears significant risk and management responsibility and remuneration is linked to performance.

A PPP can also be defined as a contract between a public authority or government and a private partner for provision of an asset that the private partner finances; designs, builds or rehabilitates and from which services are delivered to the public.[24] According to the type of PPP, this is paid for by the public authority by means of some form of fee over the lifetime of the contract or from service users' fees or a combination of both.

The project functions transferred to the private party such as design, construction, financing, operations, and maintenance may vary from contract to contract, but in all cases the private party is accountable for project performance and bears significant risk and management responsibility. PPP contracts typically allocate each risk to the party that can best manage and handle it – risk transfer to the private party is not a goal but is instrumental for full transfer of management responsibility and for the alignment of private interests with the public interest.[25] PPP projects aim, among many goals, at the first stage to achieve the development of infrastructure. The infrastructure encompasses economic, social, and government infrastructure, that is, the 'basic physical and organizational structures' needed to make economic, social, and government activity possible.

In PPPs, there are many risks for the private sector to invest and for banks to finance; for instance, there is demand risk, change of scope of service risk, regulatory risk, and political risk.

Typical sectors that use the PPP model are energy; transport, such as ports, airports, tunnels, highways bridges and railways; water and sanitation; and urban services including accommodation-based projects in education, sport, health,

---

23 The World Bank, The PPP Reference Guide, version 3, available at: https://pppknowledge lab.org/guide/sections/1, last accessed on 15 August 2019.

24 The World Bank, Procuring Infrastructure Public-Private Partnerships Report 2018, 10, available at: http://pubdocs.worldbank.org/en/256451522692645967/PIP3-2018.pdf, last accessed on 12 October 2019.

25 Christopher Bovis, Risk in public contracts – the treatment and the regulation, *The European Procurement & Public Private Partnership Law Review*, Lexxion, 2019, 1, 1.

Introduction 7

and prisons. There are two principal models of PPP. The first is referred to as an availability-based PPP and the second, a concession PPP.

Availability-based PPP[26]

Availability-based PPP has the following basic features:

- The private sector party contracting with the public sector will normally be a limited company set up specifically for the project by its funders/shareholders known as a Special Purpose Vehicle (SPV). It is also called the 'project company.'
- The SPV is required to design, construct, rehabilitate, operate, and maintain infrastructure or an asset which is the basis of a public service.The SPV will use private finance to fund the upfront construction costs. The usual split is around 80:20 to 90:10 in favor of private debt, with the smaller percentage coming from private equity from SPV members. In developing countries this may come from multilateral banks such as The World Bank, other international funding agencies, or development agencies.
- The SPV will be paid a periodic fee (the service fee or availability fee) by the public authority from the point at which the contracted asset is available for use. This is often called the availability fee. This will include principal and interest payments on the debt, a return to the private sector shareholders and an amount for the services delivered.
- The SPV's only income is the availability fee. This is paid according to the extent that the asset is available for use or services provided in accordance with contractually agreed service levels.
- It is recognized that in countries where PPP is a new concept, private investors will be unlikely to fund construction and operation unless the economic and financial business case is strong and the investment climate sufficiently mature. For example, where the returns on investment are difficult to assess or where the risks are perceived to be too high, consideration is being given to 'blended finance' where public funds, for example from the multilateral development banks, might provide the first layer of finance which gives the private sector confidence to invest themselves.
- The services will be provided against an output specification rather than an input specification. The output specification will have measurable standards against which performance is assessed with a right to apply deductions/

---

26 The Dispute Resolution Board Foundation, Fostering Common Sense Dispute Resolution Worldwide, UNECE Publication, April 2017, Guidance on the Use of Dispute Boards in Public Private Partnership (PPP) Projects, www.unece.org/fileadmin/DAM/ceci/docu ments/2018/PPP/Forum/Documents/White_Paper_Guidance_on_the_Use_of_Dispute_ Boards_in_PPP_Projects.pdf, last accessed on 15 August 2019.

8 *Introduction*

penalties where these standards are not met. These deductions are usually taken from the availability fee.

- The SPV will enter into a contract or series of contracts (which are sub-contracts, in effect) with the design and build contractor and the operator of the asset. These contracts sub-contract most of the risks that the SPV has assumed from the public authority to these parties and in turn any deductions in payment made by the public authority. That 'pass through' or sub-contracting of risk will be insisted upon by any lenders to the project. Historically, the sub-contracting of the services was to more than one company with a separation of services between, for example, hard services (such as maintenance of fabric and structure); soft (cleaning, security etc.) services; and lifecycle (replacement of parts of the asset in accordance with its life cycle).
- Multiple interfaces have the potential to produce disputes and therefore constitute a risk to the project. The trend in more mature markets is for the sub-contractors to jointly assume such risks with any issues as to where ultimate responsibility arises remaining between them rather than with the SPV. Alternatively, the SPV may sub-contract all services to only one services provider.
- The aim of the public body throughout is to divest itself of all risk in this structure to the SPV. The aim of the SPV is to divest as much risk as possible to the sub-contractors.

Concession PPP[27]

- In concession PPPs there is delegated to the SPV the full operation of a public service such as a highway; bridge and tunnel operation and maintenance; railways; urban public services; power production; stadium and arenas. The SPV is in direct contact with the end users of the services.[28]
- It in turn receives fees from the users of such services from whom it recovers its investment entirely or almost entirely, e.g., road tolls. The SPV therefore takes the risk of the sufficiency of such fees to recover and give it a return on its investment. It also takes the risk over the lifetime of the project that it can meet and adapt the changing demands/needs of the end

---

27 The Dispute Resolution Board Foundation, Fostering Common Sense Dispute Resolution Worldwide, UNECE Publication, April 2017, Guidance on the Use of Dispute Boards in Public Private Partnership (PPP) Projects, www.unece.org/fileadmin/DAM/ceci/docu ments/2018/PPP/Forum/Documents/White_Paper_Guidance_on_the_Use_of_Dispute_ Boards_in_PPP_Projects.pdf, last accessed on 15 August 2019.

28 The Dispute Resolution Board Foundation, Fostering Common Sense Dispute Resolution Worldwide, UNECE Publication, April 2017, Guidance on the Use of Dispute Boards in Public Private Partnership (PPP) Projects, www.unece.org/fileadmin/DAM/ceci/docu ments/2018/PPP/Forum/Documents/White_Paper_Guidance_on_the_Use_of_Dispute_ Boards_in_PPP_Projects.pdf, last accessed on 15 August 2019.

user, in a way that the availability-based PPP does not. In availability-based PPP it is for the public authority to require any changes of service from the SPV and the project agreement and sub-contracts will set out how that will be compensated.

Typical PPP contract framework[29]

- It is useful to understand the typical contractual matrix for each of the above models as the number of parties with interests in a PPP require a greater number of contracts than does a typical design and build or design, build and operate contract. This form of procurement is more complex than conventional public procurement, principally because of the public services that are being delivered, the length of the procurement, and the strong influence that lenders have on allocation of risk in these projects.
- The project agreement is the head contract between the public authority and the SPV. Its duration will typically be between 20 and 50 years. The design and build obligations within the project agreement are sub-contracted by the SPV to the design and build contractor. The service delivery obligations are sub contracted to the operation and/or maintenance sub-contractor.
- The public authority has no direct contract with the sub-contractors even although in practical terms it may have significant interface with them once the asset is operational.
- The public authority contractually looks to one party for delivery of the services, that is, the SPV. The project agreement will set out the standards against which the service delivery is measured, for example, in availability and performance terms. The project agreement will provide a mechanism for reductions in payment where these standards are not met. Where the problems are chronic or recurring, this can lead to early termination. Where private lenders are involved these reductions will be 'passed on' to the sub-contractors. The aim in that situation being that the SPV is 'held harmless' so it is not bearing any financial risk.
- In some availability-based PPPs, there will be an agreement amongst the sub-contractors, as referred to above, where they jointly assume liability for the reductions and then reallocate such liabilities amongst themselves in accordance with underlying liability. The contract that provides for this is known as the interface agreement.

---

29 The Dispute Resolution Board Foundation, Fostering Common Sense Dispute Resolution Worldwide, UNECE Publication, April 2017, Guidance on the Use of Dispute Boards in Public Private Partnership (PPP) Projects, www.unece.org/fileadmin/DAM/ceci/documents/2018/PPP/Forum/Documents/White_Paper_Guidance_on_the_Use_of_Dispute_Boards_in_PPP_Projects.pdf, last accessed on 15 August 2019.

10 *Introduction*

- In practical terms, the sub-contractor that is due payment by the SPV at the point that the SPV has a right to apply the deductions, will suffer the reduction from its payment.
- 'Step in' rights are very seldom exercised as any lender 'stepping in' must meet any pre-existing obligations, the extent of which may be unknown at the point of step in. However, a lender will insist on having such rights.
- As events that give rise to multiple deductions can constitute an act of default under the project agreement giving the public authority rights of termination, there remains significant risk to the SPV of non-performance by its sub-contractors. The SPV throughout remains liable to the public authority even although its role may only be to provide the financing.
- There are certain direct agreements between the SPV's lenders and the public authority and between the lenders and the sub-contractors. The lenders to the project will seek to ensure that all risk has been allocated clearly and that suitable remedies have been included in the project documents to protect their position. They will want direct agreements with each of the parties contracting with the SPV to ensure that the project agreement or sub-contracts do not immediately fall away if the SPV is in breach of its obligations under them. The lenders will have the right to step into the project agreement and/or the sub-contracts. For example, this might arise where the SPV is in breach or one of the sub-contractors has become insolvent giving rise to termination risk by the public authority. In those circumstances the lender has the option to 'step into' the SPV's place in the project agreement to preserve the asset.
- In concession PPPs, the contract structure is less complicated. The concessionaire is often the SPV and it is this company that retains responsibility for delivering the service. At most, these services may be sub-contracted to the SPV shareholders. Beyond that, the SPV does not 'pass through' the risk in the same way that the SPV does in an availability-based PPP.

People-first PPPs: principles versus the myth

The PPP model can be used as a transformative tool that can put people at its core to achieve the UN SDGs. PPP contracts can deliver a pipeline of projects to improve access and equity, invest in resilience and climate change, have economic effectiveness, and ensure that there is stakeholder engagement. Economic effectiveness means more involvement of women in an infrastructure where there is a better representation of women in projects and companies, more women-led companies becoming suppliers to PPP, private sector involvement in PPP helping young women in the community to become entrepreneurs, and making and operating an infrastructure in ways that are more gender sensitive. PPP techniques are not tailored for individual projects. For a PPP to become transformative it must be allied to a concerted infrastructure policy, a clear sectoral plan (for water, renewable energy, etc. … .), and an action-oriented plan with private sector mobilization as its goal. Therefore, governments should

Introduction 11

develop 'People First PPPs' as part of the comprehensive, scaled-up transformative program of action to deliver the SDGs and the various climate agreements. Capacity building is of fundamental importance; therefore, governments as a priority should use every way to scale up their capacity-building efforts based on an action plan at different levels, all targeting the creation of more effective people-first projects. Delivery of PfPPPs must be by public civil servants with public sector ethos and be stronger with good quality consultants. As a PPP contract is not just an agreement, a proper legal framework is required to focus on the social side, with zero tolerance of corruption, a level playing field for sustainable procurement, and easy recourse to international arbitration, which must be permitted through legislation, particularly in countries that have some rules prohibiting arbitration in administrative contracts and state contracts in general whether public or private contracts.[30] The legal framework has to create the balance between investors' rights and citizens' rights. It needs to achieve a reliable threshold of protection to citizens' rights in addition to creating better investment environment for investors through legislation, contractual patterns, and dispute settlement mechanisms.

Sustainable and successful PfPPPs require sustainable transparency and accountability at all stages. The private sector must accept a different risk/reward ratio, improved governance and predictability by governments in doing business, and to be a partner with the NGO community. Low-income countries have extra risks that lead to the private sector's reluctance to invest. It is fundamental for governments to exercise its best endeavors to persuade the private sector to take longer-term perspectives and to accept less returns in the short term.

Procurement must promote value for people, and to achieve this target, the criteria for project selection need to be broadened to include *value for people*, not just *value for money*. PPPs are needed in a resilient infrastructure because of the huge costs in climate change adaptation and new technologies are required. One of the main roles of PfPPPs is that they can provide technological innovation (e.g., solar). Innovative finance-impact investing has great potential for harnessing a new willingness of investors to do well. Impact investing is improving forward as sustainable financing becomes a serious trend in the banking industry. Better metrics are needed to show the real impact of projects in support of the SDGs.

It is clear from UN practice that PfPPPs are currently of fundamental importance.

---

30 Article 2060 of the French Civil Code, which prohibits public persons recourse to arbitration. However, this prohibition has some exceptions such as in PPP legislation in 2008 and in some other legislation. In MENA countries, Article 1 of the Egyptian Arbitration Act 1994 prohibits arbitration in administrative contracts without the concerned minister's consent, Article 10/2 of the Saudi Arbitration Act 2012 prohibits governments bodies' recourse to arbitration without the prime minister's consent. Article 2/2 of the Qatar Arbitration Act 2017 adopted the same vision. For more details, see Chapter 8 of this monograph.

12 *Introduction*

Why PPPs?

Value for money and value for people

In addition to the *value for people* principle, a fundamental concept exists behind adopting PPP techniques, which is the *value for money* concept. A PPP project yields *value for money* if it results in a net positive gain to society that is greater than that which could be achieved through an alternative procurement route. It is often considered essential to carry out a *value for money* analysis during the feasibility stage as part of the initial preparation of any PPP project. However, *value for money* analysis can be very subjective and heavily driven by underlying assumptions, which themselves can be unreliable, especially at a pre-transaction stage where little or no upfront analysis has been done.

The *value for money* concept has special significance in PPP contracts. It is a relative measure or concept. The Green Book on the British Government Guidance on Appraisal and Evaluation, HM Treasury, 2018 states that

> PPP options are about more than financial issues, although these are important. For example, PPPs are cited as potentially offering higher levels of specialist and operational management expertise, greater management flexibility and focus and improved risk management. These issues should be considered on a case-by-case basis to produce realistic and objective estimates of costs and benefits arising from an option involving PPP, to compare against alternative options. The bundling of design build and maintenance activities can create better value in the right circumstances, by creating an incentive for high quality design and build.[31]

There are numerous analyses and reports developed by (or for) governments and national audit offices as to whether PPPs are, in fact, delivering *value for money*. The majority of these reports conclude that PPP generates *value for money*. The United Kingdom studies indicate that government departments that implemented PPPs, registered cost savings of between 10% and 20%. According to the 2002 census of the United Kingdom National Audit Office (NAO), only 22% of PFI deals experienced cost overruns and 24% experienced delays, compared to 73% and 70% of projects undertaken by the public sector as reviewed in a NAO survey in 1999. The UK Treasury reported in 2006 that, according to a study for the Scottish Executive by Cambridge Economic Policy Associates (CEPA), 50% of authorities administering PPPs reported that they received good *value for money*, with 28% reporting satisfactory *value for money*. Australia's National PPP Forum (representing Australia's Commonwealth, State and

---

31 The Green Book, General Government Guidance on Appraisal and Evaluation, HM Treasury, 2018, https://assets.publishing.service.gov.uk/government/uploads/system/uploads/attachment_data/file/685903/The_Green_Book.pdf, last accessed on 12 July 2019.

Territory governments) commissioned the University of Melbourne in 2008 to compare 25 Australian PPP projects with 42 traditionally procured projects. The study found that traditionally procured projects had a median cost overrun of 10.1%, whereas PPP projects had a median cost overrun of 0.7%. Traditionally procured projects had a median time overrun of 10.9%, whereas PPP projects had a median time overrun of 5.6%.[32]

All investment projects should be prioritized at senior political level. As there are many competing investment priorities, it is the responsibility of the government to define and pursue strategic goals. The decision to invest should be based on a whole of government perspective and be separate from how to procure and finance the project. There should be no institutional, procedural or accounting bias either in favor of or against PPPs.[33] Investigate which investment method is likely to yield most *value for money*. Key risk factors and characteristics of specific projects should be evaluated by conducting a procurement option pre-test. A procurement option pre-test should enable the government to decide on whether it is prudent to investigate a PPP option further. PPP projects transfer the risks to those that manage them best. Risk should be defined, identified and measured and carried by the party for whom it costs the least. The procuring authorities should be prepared for the operational phase of the PPPs.

Value for money should be maintained when renegotiating. Only if conditions change due to discretionary public policy actions should the government consider compensating the private sector. Any re-negotiation should be made transparently and subject to the ordinary procedures of PPP approval. There must be a set of rules concerning clear, predictable and transparent rules for dispute resolution. The government should ensure there is enough competition in the market by a competitive tender process and by possibly structuring the PPPs program so that there is an ongoing functional market. Where market operators are few, governments should ensure a level playing field in the tendering process so that non-incumbent operators can enter the market.

Public and private sector actors have different incentives to engage in PPPs. Arguments in favor of PPPs may include the capacity of the private sector to deliver high-quality investment in infrastructure. Private sector participation may also reduce the need for the state to raise funds upfront. Instead of building an infrastructure with capital upfront, PPPs use annual instalments from revenue budgets or user fees to pay for the infrastructure. In this way, governments do not need to directly take loans, but costs will appear either in future periods (as governments assume a future debt) or be absorbed by users. Although PPPs

---

32 Kuwait Public-Private Partnership Projects, February 2008, Project Guidebook, Ministry of Finance, p. 15.
33 Recommendation of the Council on Principles for Public Governance of Public-Private Partnerships May 2012, www.oecd.org/governance/budgeting/PPP-Recommendation.pdf, last accessed on 20 July 2019.

14   *Introduction*

represent a form of borrowing, the difference in the timing of the cash flows creates a strong bias in favor of using PPPs. Current austerity measures and accounting practices also create perverse incentives as governments can keep the PPP project and its contingent liabilities 'off the balance sheet,' which means that the true cost of the project is hidden. PPPs represent a very attractive business opportunity for companies such as construction and engineering companies, service providers and banks. Despite the new risk sharing patterns that do not exist in the traditional concessions, PPPs offer a less risky way of investing for the private sector, as they guarantee an income for a long period of time, which is normally largely underwritten by the government itself.

PPP options may be relevant to consider alongside other options as part of public service provision in options appraisal. PPP options can offer alternative funding models for public schemes. They can also offer strategic partnering arrangements for the cost-effective delivery and operation of public services. These include different possibilities for construction, operation, delivery and risk sharing, all of which have the potential for different costs, benefits and degrees of complexity relative to public sector provision or funding. There are also different risks and specific issues to consider in an assessment of a PPP option.[34]

Short-list appraisal of PPP options should take place in the same way as other options. This includes calculation of social value, valuation of wider social costs and benefits, application of optimism bias, risk costing and sensitivity analysis. When part of a business case changes through the process that alters cost, distribution of risk across different points in time or the transfer of risk between participants, this should be included and updated as part of the Net Present Social Value (NPSV) and budget calculations. Changes to costs and risk that occur during contract negotiations, should be fed into the NPSV and public sector cost calculations. This means the appraisal of the preferred option is properly informed before a final contract is agreed. Some of the factors that allow PPPs to create greater *value for money* than public procurement is considered below. These factors may also be among the appropriate reasons to procure by PPP.

Prior to undertaking a public-private partnership, a government should explore whether a PPP will deliver better *value for money* compared to traditional public procurement. Four methods may be used to assess the relative *value for money* of the different delivery models:

- a complete cost-benefit analysis of all alternative provision methods available to both the government and the private sector – this method is the most complex among the four presented here;
- calculation of a public-sector comparator before the bidding process to assess whether PPPs in general offer better *value for money;*

---

34 The Green Book, General Government Guidance on Appraisal and Evaluation, HM Treasury, 2018, https://assets.publishing.service.gov.uk/government/uploads/system/uploads/attachment_data/file/685903/The_Green_Book.pdf, last accessed on 12 July 2019.

- calculation of a public-sector comparator after the bidding process to assess whether a PPP bid offers better *value for money*; and
- the use of a competitive bidding process alone without a comparison between public and private provision methods.

Some have contested the robustness of the public-sector comparator, claiming that it is constantly manipulated in favor of PPP. The United Kingdom, for example, has replaced the public sector comparator to incorporate quantitative and qualitative factors in a *value-for-money* assessment.

Quantitative factors include a reference project, and *value-for-money* and affordability benchmarks. Qualitative factors include project visibility, desirability and achievability.[35]

Some criticisms of PPPs are undoubtedly true. Interest costs faced by the private sector are higher than those faced by the public sector; PPPs involve the necessity of profit and arranging and structuring the transactions is complex and costly. However, when managed prudently and with a supportive legal and institution framework, PPPs have been shown to be potentially cost-effective and to create *value for money* for governments and citizens. This requires that savings from developer expertise, from combining responsibility for designing, building, operating and maintenance and from an optimal 'least-cost' risk allocation exceed the additional costs of investors' return on equity 'profit,' a higher cost of capital and transaction costs.

Governments should assess whether a project represents *value for money*. *Value for money* is a relative measure or concept. The starting point for such a calculation is the public sector comparator. A public sector comparator compares the net present cost of bids for the PPP project against the most efficient form of delivery according to a traditionally procured public-sector reference project. The comparator considers both the risks that are transferable to a probable private party and those risks that will be retained by government. Thus, the public sector comparator serves as a hypothetical risk-adjusted cost of public delivery of the project. However, ensuring the robustness of a public sector comparator can be difficult and it may be open to manipulation with the purpose of either strengthening or weakening the case for PPP (e.g., much depends on the discount rate chosen or on the value attributed to a risk transferred).

In addition to the quantitative aspects typically included in a hard-public sector comparator, *value for money* includes qualitative aspects and typically involves an element of judgment on the part of government. *value for money* can be defined as what a government judges to be an optimal combination of quantity, quality, features, and price (i.e., cost), expected (sometimes, but not always, calculated) over the whole of the project's lifetime. What makes *value*

---

35 OECD, Dedicated Public-Private Partnership Units: A Survey of Institutional and Governance Structure, OECD Publishing, Paris, 2010, available at: https://read.oecd-ilibrary.org/govern ance/dedicated-public-private-partnership-units_9789264064843-en#page10, last accessed on 12 October 2019.

16 *Introduction*

for money hard to assess at the beginning of a project is that it ultimately depends on a combination of factors working together such as risk transfer, output-based specifications, performance measurement and incentives, competition in and for the market, private sector management expertise and the benefits for end users and society.[36]

Assessing *value for money*

The UK National Audit Office (NAO) uses three criteria to assess the *value for money* of government spending, i.e., the optimal use of resources to achieve the intended outcomes:[37]

- 'Economy: minimizing the cost of resources used or required (inputs) – spending less;
- Efficiency: the relationship between the output from goods or services and the resources to produce them – spending well; and
- Effectiveness: the relationship between the intended and actual results of public spending (outcomes) – spending wisely.'

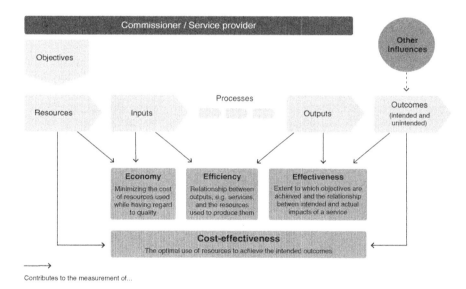

Figure 0.1

---

36 OECD, Recommendation of the Council on Principles for Public Governance of Public-Private Partnerships., available at: www.oecd.org/governance/budgeting/PPP-Recommendation.pdf, last accessed on 12 October 2019.
37 National Audit Office, UK, www.nao.org.uk/successful-commissioning/general-principles/value-for-money/assessing-value-for-money/, last accessed on 9 July 2019.

Introduction 17

The National Audit Office (NAO), UK[38]

Further, the NAO elaborates to illustrate that:
Besides these three 'E's, a fourth 'E' is applied in some places:

- Equity: the extent to which services are available to and reach all people that they are intended to – spending fairly. Some people may receive differing levels of service for reasons other than differences in their levels of need.

For example:

- The cost and level of provision of a service is more for one group of people than that for another group of people with similar needs;
- some people cannot reach, see, hear or use a service;
- the service may be unsuitable for some people's specific needs;
- a service is provided in a language that some people do not speak or terms they do not understand; or
- some people are unaware that the service is available to them.

In the UK, state organs play a fundamental role in distributing powers among the government and the parliament to achieve the best *value for money* practice in government contracts.[39]

Value for money and TSOs[40]

It is important that financial relationships with Third Sector Organizations (TSOs) are cost-effective, and that good *value for money* is achieved by the program or service involved. Poor *value for money* means either that:

- More needs to be spent to achieve the expected outcomes, leaving less money for other programs, services, users and outcomes; or

---

38 National Audit Office, UK, www.nao.org.uk/successful-commissioning/general-principles/value-for-money/assessing-value-for-money/, last accessed on 9 July 2019.

39 The interplay between state powers to manage public money is highlighted by the British government: 'The relationship between the government, acting on behalf of the Crown, and parliament, representing the public, is central to how public resources are managed. Ministers implement government policies, and deliver public services, through public servants; but are able to do so only where parliament grants the right to raise, commit and spend resources. It falls to the Treasury to respect and secure the rights of both government and parliament in this process.' Managing Public Money, UK, 2013 and updated version in 2018. Available at: https://assets.publishing.service.gov.uk/government/uploads/system/uploads/attachment_data/file/742188/Managing_Public_Money__MPM__2018.pdf.

40 National Audit Office, UK, available at: www.nao.org.uk/successful-commissioning/general-principles/value-for-money/value-for-money-and-csos/, last accessed on 9 July 2019.

18   *Introduction*

- The impact of the program or service is less: fewer users receive the expected benefits or outcomes; or all or some users benefit less than they should.

Those are high-level statements. What can you do to increase cost-effectiveness in actual financial relationships with TSOs? There are some areas to focus on:

- **Impact**. Make sure your program is really focused on outcomes, the impact on service users and communities that you are seeking to achieve, and not just on outputs, process or inputs. Not all outcomes will be obvious, direct or easily valued. You and/or providers may need to use evaluations and techniques such as Social Return on Investment (SROI) to establish the full impact of a program and its worth.
- **Priorities**. Make sure your program is focused on those outcomes that are priorities in terms of both:

  ○ analysis of greatest public need; and
  ○ the priorities of your governance group.

- **Take a long-term view**, where possible. You should seek the optimal combination of:

  ○ **whole life cost** – this is the cost, from start to finish, of the delivery of the agreed volume of the service you require to the agreed quality and timescale. It should include any start up and exit costs that you must meet as well as the direct funding to the provider for the service; and
  ○ **control of costs** – make sure you and your provider keep control of costs. Small, unnecessary or excessive costs can quickly snowball. It is easier to control a cost before it has materialized than after it has occurred.

- **Use competition**, where appropriate, to help you choose your provider. The Office for Government Commerce (OGC) says *value for money* 'should normally be established through the competitive process. A strong competition from a vibrant market will generally deliver a *"value for money"* outcome.' Competition can be used in procurement or grant.
- **Increase the efficiency of TSO providers**. Commissioners can play a role in this: through investments in capacity; through the use of competition; or through a targeted *value for money* study. Present this in the right manner and try not to make it sound threatening to the TSO.

The geographical scope of research

The geographical scope of this monograph covers the Middle East and North African (MENA) region, particularly Egypt, Morocco, Tunisia, Jordan, and Gulf countries. It is important to introduce the pulse and dynamics of PPPs in three countries that have the biggest investments in PPP projects in the MENA region. Those countries are Egypt, Dubai, and Kuwait as follows:

Egypt

PPP contracts in Egypt have started in practice before promulgating the PPP legislation in 2010 as well as many Arab Gulf countries such as Bahrain, which has many PPP projects but does not have yet PPP legislation. In Egypt before the promulgation of the PPP legislation in 2010, PPP contracts were subject to the previous state procurement law No. 89 of 1998, and in most MENA countries such as Bahrain PPP contracts are subject to the state procurement law No. 36 of 2002.

In 2006, the government of Egypt adopted a new long-term policy of pursuing partnerships with the private sector to expand the infrastructure investments. The government of Egypt has taken the initiative to introduce the PPP policy and program through the establishment of the PPP Central Unit (PPPCU) at the Ministry of Finance.

Egypt is perceived as one of the leaders in the PPP field in the Middle East North Africa (MENA) region. In Egypt, PPPs are key to the government's economic reform agenda and strategy to:

- Increase private sector involvement in public services through leveraging private spending against public spending;
- Provide a new source of investment capital for required infrastructure projects;
- Reduce government sovereign borrowings and associated risks;
- Drive the creation of local long-term funding market;
- Utilize efficiencies of private sector in running public services;
- Expand economy and stimulate job creation;
- Increase quality of public services to the Egyptian citizen.

Before the promulgation of the PPPs law in Egypt, the PPP policy framework was focusing on:

- The adoption and localization of international successful PPP models such as the UK;
- The promulgation of supportive legislative environment through the issuance of PPP law and its regulatory framework on one hand, and the standard PPP contracts, procurement documentation and procedures on the other;
- The creation of regulatory bodies for post contract implementation;
- Establishing a PPP central unit at the Ministry of Finance as well as satellite units in line ministries;
- Identifying projects that can use PPP techniques as part of line ministries' five-year strategic plan;

20 *Introduction*

- Finalizing budgetary and accounting practices to capture PPP transactions setting a 'best practice' precedence through pilot projects;
- Arranging for credit enhancement mechanisms;
- Stimulating a domestic banking sector to offer longer tenors and competitive pricing;
- Satellite PPP units have been established in various ministries and resources devoted to PPP projects.

Law No. 67 for the year 2010 was approved by Parliament on May 2010. The law is divided into four chapters containing 39 articles. Executive regulations were finalized and approved by the Cabinet in January 2011.

The PPP institutional framework consists of:

- PPP Supreme Committee chaired by the prime minister;
- PPP Central Unit Ministry of Finance;
- Satellite PPP units.

The most significant achievement in PPP contracts before the promulgation of the PPPs law was a contract that was financially closed during the financial crisis in 2009 for the New Cairo Wastewater Treatment Plant. The New Urban Communities Authority (NUCA), with the technical assistance of the PPP Central Unit of the Ministry of Finance of the Arab Republic of Egypt, invited bidders for the availability and operation of a wastewater treatment plant in New Cairo through a PPP. The project was for the design, financing, construction, ownership, operation, maintenance, and transfer of ownership back to NUCA after a period of 20 years or upon early termination of the contract, of a 250,000 m^3/day wastewater treatment plant in New Cairo, a new urban community.

The PPP contract was awarded through a competitive tender process open to both local and international bidders. The tendering of the project was conducted under the Egyptian previous Public Procurement Law No. 89 of 1998. The PPP contract set out the rights and obligations of the parties, including technical and output specifications, service and performance standards, methodology for periodic adjustment of availability payments, monitoring and reporting procedures, dispute resolution mechanisms, performance deductions, and termination and compensation procedures. The project broadly followed the United Kingdom Private Finance Initiative (PFI) model.

Tendering procedures were as follows:

- Invitation for expressions of interest in October 2007;
- Prequalification document finalized in February 2008;
- Opening data room in July 2008;
- Investors' conference in August 2008;
- Invitation to bid in December 2008;
- Announcing the winning bidder in May 2009;
- Contract signature in June 2009.

PPPs and the economic crisis 2008/2009

- Financing for new PPPs will be affected primarily on the debt side;
- Private developers will be more selective, demanding higher quality, more 'bankable' PPPs, with clearer forms of public support and risk-sharing;
- The infrastructure as an asset class will be preferred by many investors, compared to other investments;
- Donors should be prepared to play an increased (counter-cyclical) role in providing and facilitating financing for PPPs;
- Future PPPs in emerging markets will likely see an increase both in small-scale contracts (using local contractors) and in 'PFI-type' investment;
- Long-terms fundamentals remain: demand for infrastructure in emerging markets is large and growing and the financial and implementation capacity of governments is inadequate.

In 2010, Egypt promulgated PPP legislation stipulates in Article 1 that PPP contracts are subject to this legislation. It is understood that PPP contracts are subject to the party autonomy principle between the contracting parties without violation of mandatory rules in the PPP legislation or any other mandatory rule in the Egyptian legislative system.[41] It is worth noting that mandatory rules in private law contracts whether commercial or civil are rare in the Egyptian legal system.

Dubai

PPPs in the UAE or the wider GCC (the Gulf Cooperation Council countries, which are: Saudia Arabia, Qatar, Bahrain, Oman, UAE, and Kuwait) are not new. They have historically been undertaken under project-specific legislation or approvals. Mubadala Development Company initiated PPPs in the UAE with UAE University in 2007, Paris-Sorbonne University Abu Dhabi in 2008 and Zayed University in 2009. Dubai has also previously partially embraced PPPs in the form of operation and maintenance contracts (such as the Dubai Metro) rather than full PPPs. GCC governments have also had a successful history of quasi-PPPs in the electricity and water sectors (for example, the ADWEA IWPP program).[42]

First, the Dubai PPP law expressly excludes projects, works, services or supply of materials in the electricity and water sectors, as well as contracts exempted by the Supreme Committee for Financial Policy (the Committee) and, in line with general international practice and PPP legislation in other jurisdictions, it also excludes PPP contracts longer than 30 years.

---

41 In MENA countries legal systems, regulations do not contain mandatory rules.
42 S. Knight, *Dubai Embraces PPP Again*, Allen & Overy 2016, available at: www.jdsupra.com/legalnews/dubai-embraces-ppp-again-13626/, last accessed on 7 February 2020.

22 *Introduction*

The objectives of the Dubai PPP law are set out in Article 3 and these include:[43]

- Encouraging private sector participation in development projects;
- Increasing investment to serve Dubai's economic and social growth;
- Enabling the government to perform strategic projects efficiently and effectively;
- Using the private sector to enable the public to obtain the best services at the least cost;
- Increasing productivity and improving the quality of public services;
- Transferring knowledge and experience from the private sector to the public sector;
- Minimizing the financial risks to the government; and
- Increasing competition for projects (locally, regionally and internationally).

The law also enshrines the principles of equality amongst users of the services/ assets and (other than to the extent of an unsolicited bid) publicity, transparency, competitiveness, equal opportunities, equality, announcement of competition and the public interest (Articles 14 and 29).

PPP in the UAE or the wider Gulf States has been well known for many years. Instead of the need for significant infrastructure programs without having to pay for them up-front, Gulf States' governments have focused on bringing in new skills, better allocating risks to the private sector (including completion on-time and on-budget) and diversifying their economies away from carbon reliance. Nonetheless, the current low oil price environment has likewise encouraged the Gulf States' governments to revisit the PPP patterns. Dubai, Kuwait, and other Gulf countries such as Oman, Qatar, and Saudi Arabia have looked at the PPP structure as a pivotal tool to assist their infrastructure developments.[44]

PPP legislation in Dubai stipulates that a special committee for PPPs shall be formed, and it shall carry out and exercise all duties mentioned in Dubai PPP law. The investor selection shall be subject to the principles of publicity, transparency, fair competition, equal opportunity, equality, advertising for the competition, and public interests' considerations.[45]

PPP legislation in Dubai confirms that it will not apply the Procurement Law No. 6 of 1997 other than where the PPP contract contains no clear provision on a matter. Implementing PPP schemes in Dubai assumes that there is a new procurement system in Dubai for PPPs as the application of Procurement Law No. 6 of 1997 would create various unpredictabilities. The traditional procurement law in Dubai contains several requirements concerning tender conditions,

---

43 Adrian Creed, Dubai's new PPP law, *Construction Law Journal*, 2016, 32(7), 808–10.
44 S. Knight, *Dubai Embraces PPP Again*, Allen & Overy 2016, available at: www.jdsupra.com/ legalnews/dubai-embraces-ppp-again-13626/, last accessed on 7 February 2020.
45 PPP legislation in Dubai, Article 14/A.

timescales and contract terms, which do not sit easily with either the PPP procurement process or PPP contract. PPP legislation in Dubai contains provisions relating to the pre-qualification, tender and selection processes and PPP contract terms including bidding terms and conditions and financial security; conditions of the PPP contract, bid bond value, performance bond value calculations and means of comparing bids; and tender scoring and evaluation procedures.[46] These provisions provide the public juristic entity with a high degree of flexibility to specify the tender and contract conditions on a case by case basis. The overriding award criterion is the 'most financially and technically advantageous bid', but the government entity has discretion to specify the details of this, including the balance between technical and financial criteria, in the tender documents. PPP legislation allows private entities to make unsolicited proposals for PPP projects and allow the public juristic entity to contract directly with the entity that makes such a proposal. There is no requirement for such proposals to be put to tender.[47]

PPP legislation does not apply to electricity and water projects that are governed by the Electricity and Water Sector Law No 6. of 2011 or simple works contracts or supply contracts that are governed by Procurement Law No 6. of 1997.[48]

Kuwait

Kuwait has promulgated PPP legislation No. 116 of 2014, which contains a complete procedural and substantive framework for PPPs. PPP legislation in Kuwait considers the PPP pattern as an exception from the Public Procurement Law in Kuwait Law No. 49 of 2016.The proposal for the procurement and implementation of a PPP project may be submitted by the following entities: (a) public entities: a public entity wishing to propose a project that falls within its competences in accordance with the PPP Law shall submit a request to the public authority along with the comprehensive feasibility studies of the project in accordance with the law, its executive regulations and the guidebook. (b) The higher committee: the higher committee approves the request of the relevant public entity for the procurement of a PPP project in accordance with a PPP model, and it may propose PPP projects to public entities. (c) The private sector: the private sector may submit before the authority a draft concept along with preliminary feasibility studies, as per the authority's requirements, for the

---

46 PPP legislation in Dubai, Articles 14 to 24.
47 See Articles 12 and 14 of the PPP legislation in Dubai. See also: *Infrastructure Update, Dubai's New PPP Law*, DLA Piper, available at: www.dlapiper.com/~/media/Files/Insights/Publications/2015/10/Dubais%20New%20PPP%20Law.pdf, last accessed on 12 October 2019.
48 *Infrastructure Update, Dubai's New PPP Law*, DLA Piper, available at: www.dlapiper.com/~/media/Files/Insights/Publications/2015/10/Dubais%20New%20PPP%20Law.pdf, last accessed on 12 October 2019.

24   *Introduction*

implementation of a project and the approval of the procurement thereof in accordance with the provisions of the Law.

Methodology

The substantive approach of this monograph will be a threefold one:

i)   Comprehensive;
ii)   Innovative;
iii) Authoritative.

The approach is comprehensive in the sense that academic references shall encapsulate the current analysis of the developed theories of state contracts and the current trends of PPPs in Egypt and the Gulf States. Such an approach shall help the readers to formulate an inclusive view of an issue. The readers shall have a concrete view of an issue and the dynamics of its argumentation in academia.

The approach is innovative to the extent that the author intends to first provide the reader with the innovation in constitutional, legislative, and contractual theories in the MENA countries and second to combine those academic theories of PPP legal frameworks with its origins in litigation principles, identify litigation themes where relevant, and subsequently build up data-banks of arguments and consolidate their receipt by the court of Egypt and the Gulf States.

Finally, the approach is authoritative, by linking the relevant issues under discussion with the ever-important debate (academic and legal/current and future) on the role of PPP regulation in establishing a genuine competitive market in delivering public services. The courts of the MENA countries have always made clear references to case-law relating to the substantive theory of '*Le contrat Administratif*' and its developments on the one hand, and international agreements on the other, which support fundamental freedoms of commerce and trade. The authoritative approach of the book to the examination of public procurement in the relevant MENA countries will be augmented by the scrutiny of Egyptian law as a fundamentally influential factor and legal foundation to the procedural and substantive law and policy regimes of the relevant Gulf States, as well as the critical analysis of the MENA countries' arbitration practice in PPP dispute resolution.

The main characteristics of the MENA countries' legal systems

After World War I the Arab Middle Eastern and North African (MENA) countries were divided into British and French Colonies. In 1916 the United Kingdom and France signed the Sykes-Picot Treaty and the Arab world was divided into British and French colonies. The flow of English and French legal culture to the region then began despite some countries, such as Egypt, being influenced by the English culture, in general, as it had been a British colony since 1872. There was minor diversity within the Arab countries as some of them were directly influenced by the French culture and language such as the Maghreb countries (Tunisia, Algeria, and

Introduction 25

Morocco) in North Africa. The Gulf States were completely far away from French influence as they were British colonies. The real influence on the Arab civil codes began to appear in the late 1940s and early 1950s. By then, Egypt codified its civil code, particularly in 1948, which is based on French Napoleonic codes. Despite Egypt being a British colony until 1952, it was greatly influenced by the French legal culture. The influence of French Napoleonic codes spread from Egypt to all Arab countries, which codified their civil codes in accordance with the Egyptian experience. Libya, Syria, Lebanon, Sudan, Kuwait, Bahrain, Morocco, Algeria, Tunisia, Iraq, Yemen, and other Arab legal systems were directly influenced by the codification, doctrine, and practice of the Egyptian civil code. By that time, Arab countries did not recognize any other method of disputes' settlement except litigation and national courts.

The division of the Middle East into British and French colonies after World War I, and the influence of various legal cultures upon the Middle East

It is appropriate at this stage to refer to the leading role of the Ottoman Empire in the MENA region centuries ago and until British and French imperialism controlled the region for decades. The Ottoman Empire ruled the Arab countries through Islamic Shari'a law and the legal and judicial systems in those countries applied Shari'a law. The main sources of Shari'a law are the Quran and the 'Sunnah'.

The Arab world was divided into British and French colonies during the late nineteenth century and early twentieth century, after the deterioration of the Ottoman Empire. This division of the MENA region has diversified the character of the region in many aspects. It is true that the region still has its Eastern conservative character regarding family laws despite the forces of cultural and legal globalization, which are reshaping new patterns of state contracts in the region.[49] These patterns of public contracts were not recognized before in the MENA region. The division of the Middle East into French and British colonies had a minor influence upon the legal cultures in various Arab countries and also had a considerable influence on the language and some social and cultural habits (norms) due to the French influence on the Maghreb countries (Tunisia, Algeria, and Morocco). This French influence is not recognized in Egypt and the Gulf States. Despite this controversy, all Arab countries such as Egypt, Morocco, Algeria, Libya, Kuwait, UAE, and other Arab states are influenced by the French legal system in public law. These countries have written constitutions and were greatly influenced by the French system, not only in civil codes but also in constitutional law and administrative law. Some countries such as Egypt and Morocco have *dual* judicial systems like the French system. These countries

---

49 Mohamed A.M. Ismail, *Globalization and New International Public Works Agreements in Developing Countries*, Routledge 2011; and for the same author: *Public Economic Law and New International Administrative Contracts*, El Halabi Publishing 2010, 49 (in Arabic).

26 *Introduction*

have the ordinary civil, commercial and Ccriminal courts and another independent Conseil d'État for Administrative disputes. Among these administrative disputes are investor-state disputes according to the *Le Contrat Administratif* theory and practice. Pursuant to the Egyptian constitution the Conseil d'État is an independent judicial authority and an essential part of the judicial power in Egypt. It is widely respected in the regional Arab legal and judicial community as it is one of the democracy guarantees in Egypt protecting human rights, liberties and domestic and foreign investments through the state contracts court's circuit. Despite the differences in the British cultural influence on Egypt, the French cultural influence on Maghreb's three countries (Tunisia, Algeria, and Morocco) and the minor British cultural influence on the Gulf States, all Arab countries adopted Napoleonic civil codes.

The significance of the Egyptian legal system: why Egypt?

The Egyptian legal system is a special case in the international legal order. After the French invasion of Egypt (1798–1801) the Egyptian legal system was considerably influenced by the French legal system, through decades, in legislation, particularly when codifying the Egyptian constitutions and the Egyptian civil code. In recent decades, the influence of the French constitution of the Fifth Republic 1958 on the Egyptian permanent constitution of 1971 was clear.[50] The Egyptian Conseil d'État has built on the principles of the administrative contracts' theory[51] through the decades, because administrative law in Arab

---

50 Fathy Fekry, *Constitutional Law*, Dar Al Nahda Al Arabia, Cairo, 2009, in Arabic. The 1971 constitutional provisions in Egypt, particularly in the fundamental rights' section (core rights) and judicial power provisions, reflect this fact. The 1971 constitution was applicable from its promulgation in 1971 and until the Egyptian revolution of 2011. After the Egyptian revolution of 2011, the Military Council in Egypt issued a constitutional declaration of 2011. The latter declaration was applicable until 2012 when the 2012 constitution was promulgated. The current constitution of 2014 was valid from January 2014. The 2011 constitutional declaration, the 2012 constitution, and the 2014 constitution, have adopted most of the constitutional provisions of the 1971 constitution, except for Marxist ideology. For more elaboration see: Mohamed A.M. Ismail, *Arab Constitutions between Facts and Prospects*, Al Halabi Publishing Co. 2015, in Arabic.
51 The administrative contract (*Le Contrat Administratif*) in the Egyptian legal system is a contract between a public juristic person on the one hand, and a private person whether the latter is natural or juristic person on the other. The administrative contract must have three conditions, together, in the Egyptian legal system to be qualified as an administrative and not private contract. Those conditions are: (a) a public juristic person must be party to the contract; (b) the contract must concern the running and the management of any of the public utilities; (c) The contract must contain excessive clauses (*clauses exorbitantes*) that aim to achieve public interests. The aim of the administrative contract concerns public interests. The substantive nature of the administrative contract requires that the contracting state is not equal with the private person, so the state can achieve public interests through containing the administrative contract excessive and exorbitant clauses.

Introduction   27

countries is not yet codified through legislation.[52] Administrative law and administrative contracts' principles in Egypt and in Arab countries have been established through the Egyptian Conseil d'État decisions, which were influenced to a great extent by the decisions of the French Conseil d'État.[53] The substantive legal nature of the administrative contract has a special significance to this study, as in the past the Egyptian and MENA countries' legal systems did not recognize the new patterns of public contracts.[54] The administrative contracts thus are unique with their special substantive nature through implementing excessive clauses in favor of the contracting state aiming at the achievement of public interests and protecting public funds. Further, Arab legal systems have been considerably influenced by the French legal culture, through the Egyptian Conseil d'État decisions of the excessive clauses '*Les Clauses Exorbitantes*' of the administrative contracts, which was transferred from France to the Egyptian Conseil d'État jurisprudence.

It is worth noting that the influence of the cultural and legal globalization as socio-economic phenomena to the Egyptian legal system were among the main reasons behind the rise of private-public arbitration.[55] The flow of the legal culture from the Anglo-American common law jurisdictions to civil law legal systems was clear upon legislation, case law, and the new contractual patterns in Egypt. This flow of legal culture was one of the main reasons behind the rise of private-public arbitration in the Egyptian legal system.

The Egyptian legal system has greatly influenced Arab countries' legal systems and transferred French civil law legal culture to Arab countries as most of these legal systems were previously relying only on Sharia'a law. Further, Arab legal systems have been considerably indirectly influenced by the French legal culture

---

52 Sarwat Badawy, *Administrative Law*, Dar El Nahdah El Arabia, 1985, in Arabic, and for the same author see: *Administrative Contracts*, Dar El Nahdah El Arabia, 1988, in Arabic. See also: Soliman Al Tamawy, *General Principles of Administrative Contracts* 5th edn, Dar El Fikr El Araby 1991, in Arabic.

53 Sarwat Badawi, *Administrative Law*, Dar El Nahdah El Arabia, 1985.

54 Mohamed A.M. Ismail, *International Construction Contracts Arbitration*, Al Halabi Publishing 2003, in Arabic; and for the same author see: Ismail, *Public Economic Law and the New International Administrative Contract*, Al Halabi Publishing Co. 2010, in Arabic.

55 Cultural globalization is a cultural socio-economic phenomenon. Culture is influenced by globalization and it represents a set of practices, values, beliefs, and customs acquired by individuals as members of a distinctive society and resulting from interaction among people. Stiglitz highlights the problems caused by globalization in some parts of the world, as it generates unbalanced outcomes, both between and within countries. See: Joseph Stiglitz, *Globalization and its Discontents*, W.W. Norton 2004; Joseph Stiglitz, *Making Globalization Work*, W.W. Norton 2007. This economic approach is directly relevant to state contracts as, in most cases, this type of arbitration deals with state contracts which has economic and financial consequences to both contracting parties. The liberalization of traditional administrative contracts in Egypt and Arab countries, is a direct result of the cultural and legal globalization. See: Mohamed A.M. Ismail, *Globalization and New International Public Works Agreements in Developing Countries, An Analytical Perspective*, Routledge 2011 and 2016, 1–8 with a foreword by H.H. Humphrey Lloyd QC.

28 Introduction

in particular the French constitution of 1958 and the French Napoleonic Codes. The Egyptian Conseil d'État played a significant role in transferring the administrative law principles to Arab countries.

It is worth noting that both social and legal dimensions are interrelated in all Arab countries. The entire Arab region, whether Copts or Muslims, have the same social and cultural traditions as they are mainly Eastern conservative countries.[56] Cultural and legal globalization have a considerable affect upon international business transactions and disputes settlement mechanisms in the MENA region but do not influence the eastern social traditions that directly relate to culture.

---

56 Mohamed A.M. Ismail, *Supra* note 3, Routledge 2011; and for the same author *Supra* note 3, El Halabi Publishing 2010.

1 The constitutional framework of state contracts in the MENA countries

Introduction

Arab MENA countries constitutions have adopted significant developments and interpretations regarding state tools and mechanisms of contracting, whether through domestic or international contracts. As Adam Smith[1] pointed out, the state role has to be confined to its basic functions. In the light of Adam Smith's views, MENA countries' constitutions have not adopted a specific economic ideology. MENA countries' constitutions have adopted a dynamic economic ideology that enables states to change their economic model from a socialist model to a free market economy model to adapt the international market dynamic theories and practices as was the case in Egypt. Meanwhile, the political ideology in the MENA countries' constitutions is static. The legal framework of state contracts in the MENA countries has significantly developed whether in legislation, regulation, polices or in contractual patterns. The chapter explores the new developments in the constitutional framework of state contracts and PPPs in the light of the MENA countries' constitutions.

The constitutional framework of administrative contracts in the MENA countries

The constitution: the economic ideology in Arab constitutions

The influence of the French constitution of the Fifth Republic 1958 upon the Egyptian Permanent Constitution of 1971 was clear, in particular the fundamental (core) rights and liberties in the latter constitution.[2] The Egyptian

---

1 Adam Smith, *The Wealth of Nations*, Wordsworth Classics of World Literature 2012.
2 Fathy Fekry, *Constitutional Law*, Dar Al Nahda Al Arabia 2009, in Arabic. For more elaboration see: Mohamed A.M. Ismail, *Arab Constitutions Facts and Prospects*, Al Halabi Publishing 2015, in Arabic. Sarwat Badawy, *Administrative Law*, Dar El Nahdah El Arabia 1985, in Arabic and for the same author see: *Administrative Contracts*, Dar El Nahdah El Arabia 1988, in Arabic. See also: Soliman Al Tamawy, *General Principles of Administrative Contracts*, 5th edn, Dar El Fikr El Araby 1991, in Arabic.

30 *Constitutional framework – state contracts*

constitution of 1971 had four amendments since promulgation and until 2007. In the aftermath of the events of 2011 this constitution was replaced in February 2011 with the constitutional declaration of 2011, which was issued by the Military Council in Egypt. In 2012 and 2014 new constitutions were promulgated respectively and the 2014 constitution is still valid. The Egyptian constitution since 1971 and until the present stipulates that Sharia'a law is a main source for legislation. The 2011 Constitutional Declaration, and the 2012 and 2014 constitutions have adopted most of the constitutional provisions of the 1971 constitution, except for Marxist ideology.

The promulgation of the Egyptian constitution has several procedural steps, which end with a people's referendum. It was debatable whether there was a constitutional ban in the constitution of 1971 that prohibits PPPs and private public arbitration or not as this constitution had adopted Marxist ideology since promulgation in 1971 and until the 2007 amendments. Further, Article 172 of the 1971 constitution stipulates expressly the exclusive jurisdiction of the Egyptian Conseil d'État courts for the settlement of administrative disputes and administrative contracts.

The 1971 constitution in Egypt adopted socialist ideology as a result of the strong political ties between Egypt on one hand and the Soviet Union and the Eastern European countries on the other. Socialist ideology was the governing economic ideology in Egypt for decades after the promulgation of the 1971 constitution. Pursuant to this constitution, the public sector (whether public juristic entities or state-owned companies) was the owner of all tools for economic development pursuant to this constitution and the public sector has the lead in all economic activates with a restricted role in the private sector. The private sector during the sixties and until the mid-seventies exercised commercial activities, despite the nationalization of all economic sectors in Egypt pursuant to nationalization legislation by President Nasser in 1961, which considered severe economic crises that affected all economic sectors, and which had very strong negative impact on the Egyptian economy since 1961 and until the present.[3] Pursuant to Law No. 203 of 1991,[4] the Egyptian government started a new program for economic reform and privatization of the public sector entities particularly state-owned companies, with the target to fully privatize public sector companies.

Currently in Egypt, the constitutional declaration of 2011, the 2012 constitution, and the 2014 constitution have not adopted a specific economic ideology and left the door open to the parliamentary and presidential elections to determine the economic pattern that governs the economic life in Egypt during the presidential or parliamentary term. Egyptian constitutions left the elections' results to determine the economic ideology according to the presidential and parliamentary elections results and the candidates' political and economic programs.

In Gulf countries, and throughout the decades, constitutions have not adopted a socialist ideology but left the door open to a wide role for private

---

3 Law No. 117 of 1961 and its amendments.
4 Law No. 203 of 1991 for the Public Sector Affairs.

Constitutional framework – state contracts 31

sector participation in all economic activities and all economic sectors. This applies to the Kuwait constitution of 1962, the UAE constitution of 1996, the Oman constitution of 1996 and the Kingdom of Bahrain constitution of 2002 as amended in 2012. The same vision exists in the Morocco constitution of 2011, Tunisia constitution of 2014 and the Algeria constitution of 2016.

The Egyptian constitutional system has greatly influenced Arab countries' legal systems and transferred French civil law legal culture to Arab countries as most of these legal systems were previously relying only on Sharia'a law. Further, Arab legal systems have been considerably indirectly influenced by the French legal culture, in particular the French constitution of 1958 and the French Napoleonic Codes through the flow of the French legal culture from Egypt to Arab countries. The Egyptian Conseil d'État played a significant role in transferring the administrative law principles, in particular administrative contracts' principles to Arab countries.

The influence of the economic ideologies in Arab constitutions to state contracts

The economic ideology in Arab constitutions governs the concept of state contracting, particularly how can a state enter into administrative contracts with domestic or international entities? The question arises in both kinds of contracts; private contracts and administrative contracts as the latter contracts' constraints and exorbitant clauses exist in the MENA countries' legal culture. In the MENA countries' legal culture, public contracts, which are in the majority of cases administrative contracts, contain excessive clauses. The purpose of the excessive clauses in administrative contracts is to achieve public interest considerations. As administrative contracts aim at public interest, an important question arises: is there any constitutional ban that prohibits Arab states from entering into PPP contracts?

In the light of the Egyptian constitution of 1971, the public sector must lead all economic activities and economic developments in Egypt, thus, the private sector cannot contribute in infrastructure and public utilities agreements through PPPs. In the light of the Marxist ideology that was adopted by the 1971 constitution the private sector was not permitted to contribute in managing public utilities through PPP techniques. There were various amendments to the 1971 constitution in 2007 that relinquished the Marxist ideology to enable the private sector to participate in infrastructure projects and public utilities' construction and management through BOT/BOOT and PPP techniques. This constitutional trend was implemented before the promulgation of PPP legislation and after such promulgation. The constitutional declaration in Egypt 2011, the 2012 constitution and the 2014 constitution have not adopted a specific economic ideology but left the door open to private sector participation in all economic sectors and impliedly permitted private sector to participate in PPPs.

Gulf countries' constitutions left the door open to a wide role for the private sector participation in all economic activities and all economic sectors. This vision was adopted through decades by the Kuwait constitution of 1962, the

32 *Constitutional framework – state contracts*

UAE constitution of 1996, the Oman constitution of 1996 and the Kingdom of Bahrain constitution of 2002 as amended in 2012. The same vision exists in the Morocco constitution of 2011, the Tunisia constitution of 2014 and the Algeria constitution of 2016. MENA countries' constitutions adopted free market economy concepts that open doors to private sector participation in all economic sectors. Through decades, Gulf States' constitutions had not adopted socialist ideology but left the door open to a wide role for private sector participation in all economic activities and various economic sectors.

The constitutional framework of PPPs in the MENA region: natural resources and PPPs in the Egyptian constitution

Generally, there are no special provisions governing PPP transactions in the MENA countries' constitutions. It is important to note that there is no prohibition for PPP techniques in the MENA region current constitutions.

It is very important to differentiate between natural resources, particularly oil and gas concessions, and PPPs from the MENA region constitutional perspective.

The Egyptian constitution of 1971 stipulated that all-natural resources concessions must be granted by law in each concession (not pursuant to law).[5] Each concession of oil or gas or any concession concerning natural resources (such as mining concessions), must be granted by law (legislation) promulgated by the parliament in each case and not by any regulatory tool pursuant to law. The current constitution of 2014 stipulates the same.[6]

The constitution of Kuwait 1962 stipulates that any obligation to invest in natural resources or public utilities shall be granted by law and for a limited period of time.[7]

The Omani constitution 1996 provides that the income from natural resources is owned by the state, which maintains to keep it and offer the best exploitation for it taking into consideration state security constraints and the national economy interests. Granting any concession or investment to any of the country natural resources must be by law, for a certain period of time and consistent with national interests.[8]

The Bahraini constitution of 2002 as amended in 2012 stipulates that any concession to invest a natural resource or a public utility shall be granted by law and for a limited period of time. The preliminary procedures for granting such concession shall facilitate research, disclosure, publicity and competition.[9]

The Tunisian constitution of 2014 provides that 'natural wealth' (wealth from natural resources) belongs to the Tunisian people, and the state exercises

---

5 Article 123 of the Egyptian constitution of 1971.
6 See Article 32 of the 2014 constitution.
7 The Kuwaiti constitution, Article 152.
8 The Omani constitution, Article 11, 'Economic principles'.
9 The Kingdom of Bahrain constitution, Article 116.

sovereignty over it in its name. Related investment contracts are presented by the competent committee of the parliament. The agreements to be concluded shall be submitted to the parliament for approval.[10]

The Algerian constitution of 2016 pointed out that the state shall ensure the rational use and conservation of natural resources for the benefit of the coming generations. Legislation shall determine the modalities of application of this article.[11]

The developments of the legal framework of state contracts in MENA countries in legislation, regulation, polices and in contractual patterns (Egyptian case study)

Legislation

Egypt has been a leading jurisdiction in the MENA countries since the nineteenth century. The Egyptian legal system has greatly influenced MENA countries' legal systems and transferred French civil law legal culture to MENA countries as most of these legal systems were relying before only on Sharia'a law.

In the light of the current constitutional dynamics in MENA countries, particularly the amendments to the 1971 Egyptian constitution in 2007, there were rapid legislative and regulatory changes.

It can be said that the rigid patterns of administrative contracts as well as their substance and exorbitant features have significantly changed in the last decades in the civil legal culture, especially where infrastructure agreements with foreign private entities are concerned. These new legal patterns such as the introduction of the new International Public Works Agreements; Build, Operate, Transfer (BOT); Build, Own, Operate and Transfer (BOOT); and PPP transactions posed the start of a new era in Egyptian legal culture – one with unique, liberal mechanisms and stipulations. The Egyptian legal culture has great influence upon MENA countries' legal culture since the end of the nineteenth century and early twentieth century.

Legal cultural globalization has had its influence on legislation, litigation and the contractual regime of the administrative contract (in developed countries and in developing countries). For instance, in 2004, France issued Decree No. 559 of 2004, and in 2008 issued the PPP legislation[12] which has changed to a great extent the legal nature of the administrative contract (*Le Contrat Administratif*), and Brazil promulgated PPP legislation in 2004. The latter legislation was enacted mainly to increase the Inflow of Foreign Direct Investments (IFDI) in the infrastructure and public utilities' sector. The PPP legislation in Egypt, Kuwait, Dubai, Jordan and Morocco that is currently promulgated by MENA countries' parliaments is the direct result of legal globalization. Latin American states have

---

10 The Tunisian constitution, Article 13.
11 The Algerian constitution, Article 19.
12 Law No. 735 of 2008.

34 Constitutional framework – state contracts

remarkable legislative policies towards encouraging Foreign Direct Investment (FDI) in the infrastructure sector, particularly through PPP techniques.[13]

Despite the above-mentioned facts, states still maintain their roles as the employers, regulators and supervisors of these new types of contracts, although nowadays these roles are limited. This approach is consistent with Adam Smith's[14] and the Chicago School's[15] approaches as they are both leading economist schools. In the current decades, the role of the state in the MENA countries is confined to its basic functions in police, judiciary and defense. The state in PPPs and in most cases is a regulator and observer and there is a minimal intervention by the state in PPP contracts. In France as a leading civil law country, the state (*L'Administration*) still maintains its role to a great extent.[16] It supervises the PPP contract as an administrative contract and still has the authority to exercise its unilateral powers through penalties (e.g., penalty for delay and unilateral termination of the contract – *la résiliation administrative*).[17]

Despite some states' controversial attitudes towards the private sector and the trend towards the encouragement of FDI in the infrastructure sector, the latter trend is expected to open doors to the private sector to participate positively in economic life. The private sector must increase its role in building, financing systems and operating infrastructure projects relating to public utilities in developing states. This approach is particularly relevant to some Middle Eastern and North African states that have been the victims of Socialist ideologies and state interference in various economic activities in previous decades such as Egypt, Libya and Syria.

When the 1971 constitution was entered into force in Egypt, the expansion of the private sector's role in Egypt is codified by the constitutional amendments in 2007 that rejected socialism and Marxism. These ideologies were adopted by the 1971 constitution. The new constitutional modifications, nevertheless, adopted no specific ideology; they provided the opportunity for presidential and parliamentary elections to determine the necessary political and economic ideology to be followed during each presidential or parliamentary term. This flexible trend is a direct result of cultural globalization and the influence of free market economy policy on the national socio-economic culture. In conclusion, as the

---

13 FDI has significantly increased in Latin America, particularly before the economic crises of 2008, in Brazil and most Latin America developing states in infrastructure projects and after promulgation of the 2004 PPP Brazilian Act. For details, see: Cecilia Vidigal Monteira De Barros, PPPs in Brazil, *International Construction Law Review* 26, 2009, 2, 180–81.
14 Adam Smith, *The Wealth of Nations*, Wiley 2010.
15 Milton Freidman on Economics, selected papers, University of Chicago Press 2008.
16 Ragab Mahmoud, *Public-Private Partnership Contracts*, Dar Al Nahda Al Arabia 2007, in Arabic and for the same author see: *Partnership Contracts between Public and Private Sectors*, Dar Al Nahda Al Arabia 2010, in Arabic.
17 Ragab Mahmoud, *Public-Private Partnership Contracts*, Dar Al Nahda Al Arabia 2007, in Arabic and for the same author see: *Partnership Contracts Between Public and Private Sectors*, Dar Al Nahda Al Arabia 2010, in Arabic.

eminent economist Adam Smith[18] and Chicago School pointed out, the role of the state is confined to basic and fundamental functions and state intervention has to be limited to the minimum.

It is worth noting that the influence of the Anglo-American legal culture is clear upon MENA countries in the current constitutional trends, legislation, case law and new contractual patterns.[19]

Cultural globalization and the impact of New Public Economic Law upon legislation

Cultural globalization has influenced social life and economy and has considerably affected legal cultures of civil law countries. State international business transactions and the traditional Administrative Contract Theory were subject to the flow of liberal and global perspectives. The state in its transactions is not in an equal bargaining power with other private entities. Hence, administrative contracts include exorbitant clauses, such as the right of the administrative authority to amend or terminate a contract unilaterally. Further, the state may also unilaterally impose certain penalties upon the other contracting party. These may include a penalty for delay[20] and rescission of the contract (*la résiliation administrative*) as well as the forfeiture of deposits (performance bonds). The impact of legal cultural globalization is significant in the development of the domain of international state contracts, particularly PPPs. New substantive clauses have appeared in these contracts, including stabilization and arbitration clauses. The contractual regime has undergone various changes, especially with respect to the new types of PPPs concerning infrastructure projects. The main target of these new contractual mechanisms aims to finance, build and operate infrastructure projects (public utilities) in developing countries.

Legislation has significant developments in the area of PPPs and in the granting of concessions for infrastructure projects and public utilities. France issued Decree No. 559 (2004) for regulating PPPs in the French legal system, and afterwards Law No. 735 of 2008 was promulgated. The French *Conseil d'État* rejected cases to annul the PPP decree of 2004 as it is legal and not violating the *Principe de Légalité* and affirmed the legality of PPP transactions in the country.[21] In Latin American countries, there was a considerable trend to promote PPPs and grant concessions through legislation and to encourage IFDI, particularly in Brazil and

---

18 Adam Smith, *The Wealth of Nations*, Wiley 2010.
19 Mohamed A.M. Ismail, *Globalization and New International Public Works Agreements in Developing Countries, An Analytical Perspective*, Routledge 2011 and *Public Economic Law and the New Administrative Contract*, Al Halabi Publishing 2010, in Arabic.
20 Liquidated damages in common law jurisdictions are similar to penalty for delay in civil law jurisdictions but the latter has different legal nature as it is considered as penalty clause in the administrative contracts in the MENA countries legal systems.
21 Mohamed A.M. Ismail, *Globalization and New International Public Works Agreements in Developing Countries, An Analytical Perspective*, Routledge 2011.

36 Constitutional framework – state contracts

Argentina. The PPP legislation of Brazil of 2004 is the consequence of developments and enhancement of investment policies in the country.[22]

Egypt promulgated Laws Nos. 100 of 1996, 229 of 1996, 3 of 1997 and 22 of 1998 amending old existing legislation such as Law No. 129 of 1947 granting concessions for public utilities and Law No. 61 of 1958 granting concessions relating to the exploitation of natural resources and public utilities. Four new laws pertain to the electricity sector, the roads sector, specialized ports, civil aviation and airports. The latter laws are a real revolution in administrative contracts and state international administrative transactions. Further, Kuwait, Jordan, Morocco, Tunisia and Dubai have made significant progress in the growth of new PPP infrastructure transactions.[23]

There were various amendments to the previous state procurement law in Egypt No. 89 of 1998. Those amendments to the state procurement law are concerning contract price. New amendments grant the administration the authority to review contract prices every three months. The administration can exercise this power in cooperation with the contractor, pursuant to certain stipulations and parameters stated in Law No. 191 of 2008[24] amending State Procurement Law in Egypt. Currently Egypt has promulgated a new state contracting law.[25]

In conclusion, cultural and legal globalization have influenced civil law legal culture in Arab countries, especially concerning international administrative transactions and contracts entered by and between the state and foreign private entities. Public utility projects and PPP agreements (infrastructure projects) attract special emphasis. The entire legal regime of legislation, litigation and contractual regime was influenced by these transnational phenomena. Where state international transactions were concerned, a set of new rules and international customs have emerged from common law jurisdictions to the legal culture in developing states and created a new branch of public law in these countries. This branch of law is the Public Economic Law and is a result of the new changes in granting concessions, state procurement law amendments, and new arbitration legislation.

Regulation

The constitutional framework in the MENA region stipulates that the regulatory framework which is 'an administrative decree issued from the executive power' must be consistent with the constitution which is the constitutionality of

---

22 Cecilia Vidigal Monteira De Barros, PPPs in Brazil, *International Construction Law Review*, 26, Part 2, 2009, 180–81; Mohamed A.M. Ismail, *Globalization and New International Public Works Agreements in Developing Countries, An Analytical Perspective*, Routledge 2011.

23 Said Hanafi, and Khaled El Dardiry, 'PPPs in Egypt', *ICLR* 27, Part 4 (Oct. 2010), 432–447.

24 Mohamed A.M. Ismail, 'Globalization and Contract Price in the Egyptian State Procurement Law, New Trends', *The International Construction Law Review* 27, Part 1 (Jan. 2010).

25 Egyptian State Contracting Law No. 182 of 2018.

regulations' principle and consistent with legislation which is the principle of legality. Therefore, any regulation cannot impose or stipulate any provision or restriction that does not exist in legislation. The regulation has to set out the details pursuant to legislation, and the possible ways as well as the required procedures for its implementation. The MENA region constitutions have a complete judicial system for the review of constitutionality of regulations, which has to be in accordance with constitutions. This system exists, for instance, in the practice of the Egyptian Supreme Constitutional Court, Bahraini and Kuwaiti constitutional courts. Those constitutional courts exercise the judicial review upon the constitutionality of legislation and regulations. Meanwhile, Egypt has a *dual* judicial system and the Egyptian Conseil d'État exercises the judicial review upon the executive power's acts whether unilateral administrative decrees or bilateral acts which are the administrative contracts. As the Egyptian Conseil d'État maintains the application of the principle of legality, it is considered one of the main democracy guarantees in Egypt. MENA countries which do not have *Dual* judicial systems can assure the judicial review for the right application of the principle of legality through civil courts (administrative circuits).

The fundamental importance of the regulatory framework in administrative contracts is to regulate state procurement procedures to assure that the main themes and principles of the state procurement legislation are maintained. State procurement law in Egypt, Dubai and Kuwait is a fundamental procedural step to select any contractor with the state in state contracts. However, PPP legislation in Egypt, Kuwait and Dubai stipulates special procedural framework to select the contractor with the state as PPP contracts are not mere administrative contracts which normally contain excessive clauses. PPP contracts in the MENA countries, which have new and special nature different from traditional administrative contracts, require unique legislative and regulatory frameworks different from traditional concessions. It is worth noting that some MENA countries have promulgated new public procurement law for administrative contracts but not for PPPs. Egypt has promulgated a new public contracting Law No. 182 of 2018 and Kuwait also has promulgated new tender Law No. 49 of 2016.

Contractual patterns

As a result to the developments in constitution and legislation in the MENA countries, new contractual patterns, different from traditional concessions, began to appear such as BOT/BOOT, which have various contractual techniques and currently PPPs.

There are several reasons for the new contractual patterns to appear in state contracts such as legal globalization and the influence upon legislation, regulation, case law and contractual patterns.[26]

---

26 Mohamed A.M. Ismail, *Globalization and the New International Public Works Agreements in Developing Countries, An Analytical Perspective*, Routledge 2011.

There is an essential need to inject Foreign Direct Investments in the MENA region, the essential need for the MENA governments to finance infrastructure and public utilities' projects without extra burden upon the public budget, as there is budget deficit in most MENA countries, and after the current deterioration of the hydrocarbon prices in Gulf countries. It is important to note that BOT techniques appeared in practice in most MENA countries before promulgating BOT legislation until the present. PPP contracts also exist in practice before promulgating the PPP legislation, for instance in Egypt before the PPP law in 2010 and in Bahrain until present as a legal fact in practice without PPP law on the ground. As long as there is no constitutional ban for the state to enter into PPP contracts, there is a *'décalage'* between practice and legislation as practice recognizes PPP contracts as legal and economic facts before the PPP legislation is promulgated.

2 The substantive theory of states' contracts in MENA countries

Introduction

The administrative decision of the independent will of an authority is the most fundamental tool of public law vested by that authority to carry out its administrative duties.[1] However, authorities often enter into agreements with individuals or companies, as this is one of the most feasible means to achieve the administrations' objectives. Both parties, hence, come to conclude a 'contract' that outlines the undertakings of each party.

It is currently evident that administrations' contracts are not exclusively subject to a single body of law. They are rather categorized into:

I. Administrations' contracts under private law; and
II. Administrations' contracts under public law, termed as 'administrative contracts.'

The above-mentioned distinction has been primarily underscored by the Egyptian administrative judiciary, in litigation either before the Appeal Administrative Court or the Supreme Administrative Court. In one of the leading judgments, the Appeal Administrative Court on 9 December 1956[2] decided that

> It should be essentially noted that contracts concluded by a public authority are not exclusively of an administrative character. Often, an authority concludes agreements with another entity or with individuals, in accordance with

---

1 In analysing the distinction between state contracts and *Les actes unilatéral* in French doctrine, see: De Laubadere, *Traité des droit administratif*, LGDJ 1999, 3, 55 et seq., and in old French doctrine for this traditional Concept: L. Duguit, *Traite de droit constitutionnel*, I, 1921, 367; P. Ferrari, *Essai sur la notion de co-auteurs d'un acte unilatéral en droit administrative francais, Mél. Ch .Eisenmann*, 215 et seq.; for more elaboration; F. Moderne, *Autour de la nature juridique des accords conclus entre L'administration et les organisation professionnelles en matiére de prix*, Dr. Soc. 1975. 505 et seq. In Arab doctrine see El Tamawy, *The General Theory of Administrative Decrees, comparative study*, Dar El Fikr Al Araby 2017.
2 Case No. 870 of judicial year 5, filed by Mohamed Zidan vs. Ministry of Education, Ministry of Supply and Ministry of Finance.

40 *Substantive theory of states' contracts*

private-law provisions. Same shall accordingly fall within the jurisdiction of private law courts jurisdiction, as these contracts are not administrative contracts. Further, arguing that one party of a transaction is a public person is never a viable argument to assume that such contract is an administrative contract subject to the provisions of public law. The present court jurisdiction is confined to administrative contracts' related disputes, given the fact that a public person may conclude either civil contracts or administrative contracts.

Moreover, the Supreme Administrative Court constantly pursues the same argument in its rulings, among which the ruling issued on 24 March 1968 providing that:

> Contracts concluded between public juristic persons and individuals are not of the same nature as some bear an administrative character and other contracts are private law contracts whether civil or commercial. In some cases public juristic persons act in the capacity of individuals concluding civil contracts that fall under private-law provisions. For a contract to be recognized as an 'administrative' contract, one of the parties thereto must be a public authority, and the contracts relates to an activity of the public service. Further, such contract shall conform to Public law principles together with excessive conditions clauses.

Administrative law is concerned with administrative contracts[3] in its strict technical sense. Nevertheless, and as far as non-administrative contracts are concerned, this does not necessarily signify that both the authority and individuals thereto are of an equal status. Several administrative provisions apply to all administrations' contracts of all types, especially when selecting parties entering a contract with a public juristic person.

Moreover, administrative contracts differ substantially from private law contracts concluded by a public juristic person. The latter are governed by private-law principles. Such contracts shall be also subject to the rules and regulations applicable to contracts made by individuals as private law contracts. Administrative contracts, on the other hand, are patently featured with privileges vested upon the concerned public authority considering the nature of public service activity, which is not the case in respective relations binding individuals.

It is currently evident that administrative law, from a French perspective, is an independent law with its special norms, which are recognized by both French jurisprudence and judiciary along with Egyptian legislature. The Supreme Administrative Court on 2 June 1956 decided that:

---

3 For more analysis and elaboration on '*Le Contrat Administratif*' concept in civil law legal systems, see: De Laubadere, Modern, and Delvolvé, *Traité des Contrats Administratif*, Vol. I, 210 et seq. and Richer, *Droit des Contrats Administratifs*, 11th edn, LGDJ 2019, 85 et seq. In Arab doctrine, see the leading authority: El Tamawy, *The General Theory of Administrative Decrees, Comparative Study*, Dar El Fikr Al Araby 2017, and Badawy, *General Theory of Administrative Contracts*, Dar Al Nahda Al Arabia 1994, 5–109.

The nature of relations set by private law differs from that of public law. Civil Code rules govern relations under private law, and such rules may not apply to relations under public law, unless otherwise stipulated. Otherwise, administrative judiciary would not be obliged to apply respective Civil Code provisions, and shall have the discretion, within the realm of public law, to create necessary frameworks governing legal relations between an authority holding public services and individuals. Further, administrative judiciary may apply Civil Code provisions that it deems appropriate; may also disregard same if it is incompatible with such legal relations; and may develop it to achieve intended harmony. Administrative Law differs from Civil Code in that the first is dynamic apart from being legally bound. Similarly, administrative judiciary is distinct from civil judiciary in that it is not a mere executive judiciary that is mainly concerned with enforcing pre-stipulated provisions. It is rather a constructive-creative judiciary that pursues devising proper solutions and has thus set grounds for a self-sustaining system that derives from and builds upon public-law relations, needs of public services and the nature of respective activities. Further, it seeks to create a balance between the above public interests and individual interests. Administrative judiciary has created its own pioneering theories that outweigh those of private law either in regulating government-employee relation, in issues pertaining to public services that need to be sustained and well-managed, in administrative contracts and lability, or in any other form under public law.[4]

The administrative law has judicial origins relating to the administrative judiciary judgments as the administrative law is not yet codified. The Conseil d'État jurisprudence, in particular the Supreme Administrative Court judgments, provided through decades the basics of 'Administrative Contract Theory,' in addition to all theories of administrative law. The flow of legal culture started from the French Conseil d'État to Egypt and from Egypt to all MENA countries. The French legislature adopts judicial decisions into administrative contract stipulations, as the general theory of administrative contracts is strictly judicial in sense, making its provisions further dynamic to conform to the emerging needs of public services. Accordingly, that no administrative law can be tackled in MENA countries without clear reference to the Egyptian Conseil d'État decisions whether courts' judgments or legal opinion by the General Assembly for Legal Opinion and Legislation.

Administrative law theories have some similarities with private law, e.g., administrative decree theory, administrative seizure, etc. Administrative contracts' stipulations have similarity and overlapping with contract law in private-law theories, in particular the civil code principles of contract as one of the main sources of

---

4 A set of judgments issued by the Supreme Administrative Court, judicial year 1, p. 807, similarly its judgment dated 8 December 1956, judicial year 2, p. 129. Regarding the application of private-law provisions to relations under public law, a judgment delivered on 31 March 1962, judicial year 7, p. 527.

42 *Substantive theory of states' contracts*

obligation. In cases where administrative contract provisions include a great deal of rules that deviate from private law, it is essential to bear in mind that many of the Civil Code provisions regulating private contracts apply to administrative contracts. In his pleading addressing councilors of the French Conseil d'État in the leading case '*Olive*,'[5] the State Commissioner Mr. Rivet contends that: 'You are free in your jurisprudence. You craft and enforce rules. From the Civil Code, you invoke and enforce those rules that best conform to the needs of community life.'

Therefore, judicial precedents of the French Conseil d'État in relation to administrative contracts would note that the Conseil d'État adopts one of the following techniques:

- In some relatively minor cases, the Conseil d'État applies respective articles provided under the civil Code, with explicit reference to said article as stated in the Code[6];
- In other instances, the Conseil d'État applies principles and notions under Civil Code with no reference to same[7]; or
- In majority of cases, the Conseil d'État applies unmatched administrative provisions that distinguish administrative contracts from private law contracts concluded by a public juristic person.

Both the Supreme Administrative Court and the Appeal Administrative Court in Egypt had the chance to apply similar principles. In one of the leading cases The Supreme Administrative Court[8] sets the general framework that governs the relation between both private and public law, contending that: 'The Administrative Law has evolved, developing independent principles, however, the link still exists between Administrative Law and the Civil Code.' The court has provided in its judgment issued on 12 December 1959 that regarding rules set under the Civil Code on *force majeure* and fortuitous events:

---

5 Judgment of the French Conseil d'État dated 25 November 1921, case *Savonnerie H. Olive, Revue de Droit Public, Public Law Journal*, 1921, 107 and Mr. Rivet's pleading saying: 'You are free in your jurisprudence. You craft and enforce rules. From the Civil Code, you invoke and enforce those rules that best conform to the needs of community life.'

6 Judgment issued by the Conseil d'État on 17 December 1932, case *Crands Moulins de Corbeil*, p. 822, in which an explicit reference is made of Article No. (1116) on Fraudulence (*Dolus*); its judgment dated 9 February 1951, case *Ste Bornhauser*, p. 81, in which reference is made of Article No. (1917).

7 Refer to the notion of cause in administrative contracts, as stated in the report of Commissioner Mr. Theis, responding to the Council's judgment dated 29 January 1947 in case 'Michaux,' *Revue de Droit Public (R.D.P)*, 1948, p. 28 arguing that: 'According to Article No. (1131) of the Civil Code, a contract without a cause cannot come into force. The rule applies to administrative matters, which must be applied in view of the principles governing the organization and operation of the public services.'

8 The Egyptian Conseil d'État, The Supreme Administrative Court, 31 March 1962, judicial year 7, p. 527.

Substantive theory of states' contracts   43

Where these [rules] are applied within the context of relations under private law, the administrative judiciary has consistently taken them into consideration as a general principle to be applied while determining the administrative relations under public law, as long as they are in conformity with the functioning of respective public service, and ensure reconcilement of this latter with the individual interests.[9]

In its judgment dated 5 May 1962 the court further contends that Article No. (123) of the Civil Code that permits correcting typo faults in contracts applies to contractual relations, given the fact that it 'sets a general principle dictated by the *status-quo*, justice requirements and good faith.'[10] In its judgment dated 23 June 1962, the court also argues that:

Being guided by the nature of a contract together with mutual trust and confidence in accordance with commercial norms in transactions (Article 150, Civil) as a base to identify common intention of parties thereto would not be an obligatory rule to the court. Same might be an argument; however, the court shall have the discretion to consider or disregard same, if it deems that it is futile in recognizing the intention of parties thereto.[11]

Similarly, the appeal administrative court has applied the above principles. In its judgment issued on 19 January 1958, the court argues that Article No. (346) of

9 The Supreme Administrative Court, judgment dated 12 December 1959, judicial year 5, 106.
10 The Supreme Administrative Court, judgment dated 5 May 1962, judicial year 7, 779.
11 The Supreme Administrative Court, judgment dated 23 June 1962, judicial year 7, p. 1110. Judgments issued by the Supreme Administrative Court in this respect:

- Judgment dated 27 November 1965, judicial year 11, 52 (contract termination and damages) and 10 December 1966, judicial year 12, 260.
- Judgment dated 11 December 1965, judicial year 11, 128 (application of Article No. 704, Civil, POA) and 23 November 1968, judicial year 14, 56.
- Judgment dated 27 May 1967, judicial year 12, 110 (application of Article No. 249, civil, sale by sample).
- Judgment dated 18 November 1967, judicial year 13, 94 (application of Article No. 229, Civil, solidarity between creditors/debtors).
- Judgment issued on December 1967, judicial year 13, 166 (application of civil code principles pertaining to contracts interpretation).
- Judgment dated 10 February 1968, judicial year 13, 464 (Articles Nos. 549 and 552, reconciliation contracts and components).
- Judgment dated 2 March 1968, judicial year 13, 625 (Article Nos. 120 and 121, fault in contracts).
- Judgment dated 29 June 1968, judicial year 13, 1113 (Article No. 226, default interests) and 4 April 1970 (judicial year 45), 257.

44 *Substantive theory of states' contracts*

the Civil Code gives courts the power to grant the debtor a grace period(s), where necessary and without prejudice to respective creditor. It further contends that

> nothing prevents taking this principle into consideration in terms of transactions between individuals and the government, since this provision gives courts a right with empathy towards the debtor at the very essence, without prejudice to the creditor's entitlements. Thus, the court sets that it would be feasible to allow both the defendants to honor their obligations, and the Ministry to receive its entitlements, through instalment payments of the due amount in conformity with the defendants' resources, so that they would not suffer any further default upon demanding a full single payment.[12]

The court has further crafted such regulation in its judgment dated 22 March 1959 as follows:

> Article No. (187) of the Civil Code on prescription is meant to govern relations under private law which differ from those of public law. However, it is jurisprudentially and judicially acknowledged that administrative judiciary may invoke Civil rules compatible with the nature of relations under public law. Further, it may harmonize and develop same in conformity with the needs necessary for the functioning of public service, and ensure reconcilement of the rights of both public juristic person and individuals. Therefore, the court believes there is no restrictions over applying said Civil Code Article on prescription to relations relating to public law as well.[13]

Notwithstanding the special characteristics of administrative contracts, it is worth noting that there is an overlapping and similarities with other private law contracts whether civil or commercial, i.e., general stipulations regulating all contracts.

---

12 The Supreme Administrative Court, judgment dated 19 January 1958, judicial years 12 and 13, 43.
13 The Supreme Administrative Court, judgment dated 22 March 1959, judicial years 12 and 13, 179, Ruling dated 11 April 1970, judicial year 15, 64 (Article No. 148 on contracts execution).

- Judgment dated 20 March 1971, judicial year 16, 1975 (Article No. 447 on Latent defect).
- Judgment dated 25 December 1971, judicial year 17, 121 (Article No. 651, Civil, Prescription).
- Judgment dated 26 February 1972, judicial year 17, p. 263 (Article 599 on extension of contract period), which is to be tackled afterwards.

The evolution of administrative contracts in France

The administrative contract theory has spread from France to the Egyptian Conseil d'État and from the Egyptian Conseil d'État to MENA countries. Administrative contract theory has not been introduced into French administrative law until the early twentieth century. The criterion followed in distributing jurisdictions among ordinary courts and administrative courts mainly revolved around the notion of sovereignty or state power. Disputes arising in relation to the acts of authority or power exclusively fall within the jurisdiction of administrative courts. Such acts of authority often entail powers conferred upon authorities, which is not the case in private law.

French Conseil d'Etat had exerted considerable efforts to expand its jurisdiction. It has approached contracts that are for which no stipulations are set by analogy to those that are already provided in. Therefore, the Conseil d'État managed to expand its exercised jurisdiction through approaching public works contracts by means of an analogy with assistance contracts, contracts for lighting, water and household gas supplies in cities; among others, given the fact that such contracts feature public works at the very essence.[14]

With the early twentieth century, the Conseil d'État had dismissed the criterion derived from the concept of public authority. Instead, it opted for the concept of public utility. This is evidently patent in the court judgment dated 6 February 1903 in the leading case 'Terrier.' In his report Commissioner Romeo highlighted that administrative judiciary's jurisdiction covers all aspects related to regulating and the functioning of public services, whether national or local, and whether management of same falls under acts of authority or power. Contracts concluded by an authority in this respective are strictly administrative in sense, and thus all related disputes are adjudicated by administrative judiciary.

Such arguments underscore that there is an organic deterministic bond that connects both administrative law and public services. In the above report, however, Commissioner Romeo stressed that in terms of public utilities – although being a precondition for administrative judiciary to determine disputes related to the acts of an authority – the latter shall have the discretion to approach whatever means necessary under private law that it deems most feasible in the functioning of such public services.

The administration's contracts would thus acquire an administrative nature based on its substance rather than legislature's will. Furthermore, stipulations set by legislature providing that disputes triggered by a certain type of contracts fall within the jurisdiction of administrative courts would never be a viable argument to assume that same is governed by public-law rules.

---

14 Dr. Sarwat Badawy, PhD Thesis, *Le Fait du Prince dans Les Contrats Adminnistratives*, Paris 1955, p. 17.

The evolution of administrative contracts in Egypt

Egypt was not familiar with administrative judiciary until 1946, and it would be common sense to assume that administrative contract theory was only introduced to the Egyptian administrative judiciary after the above date. Approaching this fact requires analyzing the legal conditions in Egypt prior and after establishing the Conseil d'État. Further, it is important to highlight the concept of administrative contracts in the Egyptian Conseil d'État as well.

The concept of administrative contracts as considered by ordinary courts

It worth noting that Egyptian courts were not familiar with administrative provisions originally set by the French Conseil d'État. These provisions would pose the framework governing administrative contracts. They would opt for applying rules under the Civil Code, being convinced that a judge's duty is to enforce law rather than to create legal rules.This meaning is evidently clear in the decisions of both ordinary and administrative judiciary to dismiss the theory of unexpected circumstances *'L'imprivision'* that was even set by the French Conseil d'État in an earlier date.

The Mixed Court of Appeal provided in its judgment dated 31 March 1924 to dismiss the request of Alexandria Water Company to increase charges of services provided to households due to the extravagant high cost. It further obligated the company to approach an amicable agreement with the administration, contending that any exercise of authority over an administration's rights in this respect is out of the court's powers. Judiciary is only entrusted with interpreting inked agreements, to honor respective contractual stipulations without any unilateral changes thereto.[15] The same argument is pursued in the judgment delivered by Alexandria Mixed Court on 6 May 1926, arguing that the Egyptian Judiciary is not familiar with the theory of unexpected circumstances *'L'imprivision.'* It further contended that the main task of courts of law is to interpret contracts and to ensure honoring stipulations therein provided under the party autonomy of both parties. Such principles apply as well to concession agreements concluded by an authority[16].

Moreover, the same way both national and mixed courts, pursuant to Civil Code provisions, precluded parties to an agreement with the administration from approaching the theory of unexpected circumstances *'L'imprivision,'* it imposed restrictions over the administration concerning amending stipulations thereto under its unilateral will. This attitude builds upon the binding force of contracts in conformity with the principle *pacta sunt servanda*.

---

15 Mixed Judiciary and Legislation, judicial year 36, 281.
16 Gazette, judicial year 16, 255.

Substantive theory of states' contracts   47

In its judgment dated 13 June 1984, the Mixed Court of Appeal stressed the above principle responding to the authorities' attempt to relocate a slaughterhouse against the concessionaire's will. The court stated that: 'Agreements are made through party autonomy, and thus can be only amended within the set terms upon the will of parties thereto. Therefore, the preliminary judgment was legally proper dismissing the authority's request.'[17]

The court's decisions went to restrain the authority from increasing charges paid by beneficiaries to concession companies in consideration of services rendered.[18]

Although administrative contracts are generally governed by Civil Code principles, some of the judicial judgments have highlighted the special nature of administrative contracts and relation with public service. In its judgment dated 10 January 1933, the Mixed Court of Appeal stipulated that in case there are no applicable legislation regulating administrative contracts, courts should, upon adjudicating related disputes, consider principles specific to administrative contracts that can be derived from general principles of administrative law. Such law necessarily exists in every civilized state.[19]

Nevertheless, this approach remained theoretically bound, setting grounds for no clearly shaped legal framework for administrative contracts that would distinguish it from private-law contracts. However, the legislature had to intervene in several instances, mostly important among which is, the promulgation of Law No. (129) of 1947 on Public Utilities' concessions.

The concept of administrative contracts in the Egyptian Conseil d'État jurisprudence

Historical background

The Egyptian Conseil d'État played a significant role in the transfer and flow of administrative law rules particularly administrative contracts rules from Egypt to all MENA countries. The differentiation between administrative contracts' substantive rules and private law contracts whether civil or commercial substantive rules is of fundamental importance in practice as this differentiation is the determining factor between ordinary courts whether civil or commercial jurisdiction

---

17 Mixed Judiciary and Legislation, judicial year 6, 345. However, the Court authorized the administration to relocate the slaughterhouse to the new location, acting in the capacity of the police authorities, rather than a party thereto.

18 Judgment of Cairo Mixed Court issued on 2 March 1896, upheld by the Mixed Court of Appeal in its judgment dated 3 June 1896, Mixed Judiciary and Legislation, judicial year 8, 313, together with the judgment of Alexandria Mixed Court delivered on 6 May 1926, Gazette, judicial year 16, 255.

19 Mixed Judiciary and Legislations, judicial year 45, 114:

> ... special rules applied to administrative contracts, derived from general principles of law ... the administrative law that necessarily exists in every civilized state.

48 *Substantive theory of states' contracts*

and the Conseil d'État courts' jurisdiction. The Egyptian Conseil d'État practice through decades is of special significance in this context.

When the Egyptian Appeal Administrative Court was established in 1946, and areas of its jurisdiction were listed in full as adopted by the legislature until the Conseil d'État Law No. 47 of 1972 was promulgated and adopted new approach. The said law contained no provision on administrative contracts; accordingly, both ordinary courts (civil and commercial) and the Conseil d'État courts, maintained full jurisdiction over administrative contracts, although the Legal Opinion *Fatwa* Department in the Conseil d'État reserved its right in providing legal opinions on the issues including disputes or legal opinion arising out of administrative contracts. The case remained as is until the issuance of Law No. 9 of 1949, replacing Law No. 12 of 1946. The law has set new provisions including Article (5), stipulating that the Appeal Administrative Court shall have jurisdiction over disputes arising out of concession contracts, public works contracts and administrative supply contracts entered between the government and other contracting parties. The said new jurisdiction is characterized by the three following aspects:

First: It has not extended the Jurisdiction of the Appeal Administrative Court over all types of administrative contracts, however; it is only limited to the three major types of contracts: concession contracts, public works contracts and administrative supply contracts. Further, The Parliament's Legislative Affairs Committee justified such limitation contending that:

> ... not every contract of which the authority is a party shall be featured as an administrative contract, as the authority, like any other individual, may be a party to regular contracts. Since characterizing a contract as an administrative contract has been and still extremely controversial, and since jurists have not consented a standard that thoroughly defines the purpose of administrative contracts, being limited to these specific contracts in this regard is therefore enough to settle this long-standing controversy.

The above three administrative contracts are the most significant, though not the only administrative ones. Therefore, it was too extreme to base the justification of limiting jurisdiction to these contracts, as the standard of distinguishing administrative contracts has become evident enough as will be highlighted below.

The Egyptian Appeal Administrative Court has circumvented the Law No. 9 of 1949, following the steps of the French Conseil d'État, to extend its jurisdiction over administrative contracts. Thus, it began to adjudicate upon contracts not specified in the law provision, given that they are connected to one of the three said contracts. An example is the Appeal Administrative Court's ruling judgment on 26 December 1951 reading:

> As per Article (5) of Conseil d'État Law No. 9 of 1949, the present court shall have absolute and comprehensive jurisdiction over the settlement of

Substantive theory of states' contracts 49

disputes related to concession contracts, public works contracts and administrative supply contracts regarding all disputes and otherwise stemming therefrom. In light of the foregoing, it is clear that the disputes, i.e. the subject matter of the claim, whether an annulment or a compensation, have resulted out of the administrative contract, pursuant to which claimants have pledged to contribute to the expenses of a public works project. For example, constructing the courthouse building by granting the land on which the building is to be constructed in addition to an amount of money. This dispute is closely related to the public service contract, i.e. construction of a building and so is deemed related thereto and lies within the court's jurisdiction according to said Article. The plea as to lack of jurisdiction is out of place and shall be dismissed.[20]

Second: The jurisdiction vested upon the administrative judiciary pursuant to Law No. 9 of 1949 does not include all disputes related to the aforementioned three types of administrative contracts and is only confined to the disputes arising between the government and the other contracting party. The disputes arising between the concessionaire or the contractor and the third party in relation to any damages that they may incur due to the contractor or concessionaire's default, shall be deemed out of jurisdictions conferred upon the Appeal Administrative Court. However, such disputes fall within the jurisdiction of ordinary (civil and commercial) courts.

When Law No. 165 of 1955 was enacted, the legislature observed the defects of the previous situation[21] and Article 10 thereof stipulates that: 'the Conseil d'État shall solely adjudicate, as an administrative judiciary entity, upon disputes related to concession contracts, public works contracts and administrative supply contracts or any other administrative contracts.'

The Explanatory Note of said law justifies the new jurisdiction stating that:

> litigation upon compensation claims arising out of respective administrative decisions as well as litigation upon disputes arising out of concession contracts, public works contracts and administrative supply contracts or any other administrative contracts, fall within the joint jurisdiction of both the administrative and the ordinary judiciary. The flaws of such joint jurisdiction are well known, the least of which are the discrepancies between the foundational legal principles regulating legal relations. Consequently, it was considered that the litigation thereupon shall be referred to the administrative judiciary exclusively, being the naturally competent entity, whether these relations fall under the domains of administrative law or public law.

---

20 The Conseil d'État, judicial year 6, 2014.
21 Parties contracting with an authority had the choice to resort to administrative or Civil Code rules governing the dispute according to their interest, through choosing whether to appeal to courts of law or to the Administrative Judiciary Court.

50 *Substantive theory of states' contracts*

The considerations specified in the Explanatory Note are certainly valid.

The Conseil d'État Law (No. 47 of 1972) which is valid until present, the jurisdiction of administrative judiciary over disputes arising out of administrative contracts is provided in Paragraph 11 of Article 10, stating that: 'Courts of the Conseil d'État have the exclusive jurisdiction with the following matters' '... Eleventh: Disputes arising out of concession contracts, public works contracts and administrative supply contracts or any other administrative contracts.'

It is further noted that the provisions of said three laws does not restrain administrative judiciary's jurisdiction over disputes related to administrative contracts, so that such jurisdiction is no longer confined to a certain type of administrative contracts, but it covers all types of administrative contracts and it is extended to all disputes resulting out of such contracts.

The differentiation between administrative contracts' substantive rules and private law contracts (civil or commercial) substantive rules is of fundamental importance in practice as this differentiation is the determining factor between ordinary courts (civil and commercial) or the Conseil d'État courts' jurisdiction. The Legal Opinion *Fatwa* Department in the Conseil d'État was affected by this approach as evident in its opinions, most notably:

First: The penalty for delay fines, providing that:

> The nature of administrative contracts differs from that of civil contracts, because the first establishes a contractual relation between a public law person and a private law person, with a purpose to achieve public interest. However, the status of the contracting parties is not of an equal nature as they are not in an equal bargaining power, and public interest overweighs private interests of individuals. This objective shall also prevail over the terms of the contract and the contractual relationship when applied and interpreted. Moreover, the administration shall ensure that the penalty terms specified in a contract are suitable for the nature and value of the contract as well as the cases where urgent application is required in a certain time and manner to ensure smooth operation of the public service. If the performance of the administrative contracts is delayed, the damage incurred is assumed and pre-existent once the delay occurs, because the default in performing this contract entails – regardless of the inevitable other damages – a violation to the regulations and arrangements set and observed by the administration to avoid minor obstacles that might disrupt progress and coherence of the governmental activities. Thus, this violation harms the public interest, which shall always be considered in the administrative contracts.[22]

Second: even if it was related to the traditional concession contract, has ratified the remaining contracts in general. It states that:

---

22 Legal Opinion No. 637 of the General Assembly for Legal Opinion and Legislation, the Egyptian Conseil d'État, session 22 October 1956.

it is jurisprudentially and judicially acknowledged that the administration may, at sole discretion, amend the regulatory terms of the concession contract at any time according to the requirements posed by public interest without any need for the consent of the concessionaire. Such right is derived from the nature of the contract subject matter, namely public service. The basic rule dictates that an authority has the upper hand in the functioning and management of respective public services due to its relation to the public interest. Should be there any change in circumstances, and the system of the service decided upon contracting does not conform to the new circumstances and does not achieve the interest it has been originally established for, the general authority setting obligations shall change this system and commit the concessionaire, under its authority, to accept the system most likely to achieve public interest.[23]

Moreover, the Egyptian legislature has accepted what the administrative doctrine and jurisprudence have settled upon in this regard. In this sense, Article No. 5 of Law No. 129 of 1947 provided in the matter of public service concession that 'the concessioner shall, at all times and whenever necessary by public interest, have the right to amend, at sole discretion, the terms regulating the public service subject of obligations or its rules of utilization.'

The General Assembly for Legal Opinion and Legislation of the *Fatwa* Department is thought to have considered the previous provision as a mere application of the general theory of administrative contracts.

The criterion for distinguishing administrative contracts

Not all state contracts are administrative contracts under the public law. If they are administrative contracts, the Administrative Judiciary shall have the jurisdiction to decide upon the disputes arising from it. However, the concept of administrative contracts is exclusive to a certain category of the administration's contracts termed as 'administrative contracts.' Accordingly, how to distinguish administrative contracts from private law contracts whether civil or commercial as they are state contracts which are subject to private law? If the criterion approached to distinguish administrative contracts from other types of contracts is sometimes accurate, administrative doctrine and jurisprudence have reached a high level of clarity in the present time. However, since the Egyptian Conseil d'État is following the French Conseil d'État, it is enough to demonstrate the criterion currently being used by the French Conseil d'État whilst referring to respective norms applied in the Egyptian Conseil d'État in this regard. This part is to further highlight the features of our legal status in those cases where the situation in Egypt is different from that in France.

---

23 Legal Opinion No. 133 of the General Assembly for the Legal Opinion and Legislation, the Egyptian Conseil d'État, session 4 February 1956.

52 *Substantive theory of states' contracts*

The situation in France

The administrative contracts in France can be further categorized into two types:

First: Law-determined administrative contracts.
Second: Administrative contracts by Nature.

The above types will each be elaborated upon respectively:

Law-determined administrative contracts

The jurisdiction of administrative contracts tackled certain types of the administration's contracts introduced by the legislature into the jurisdiction of French administrative judiciary, whether in the *Les Conseils Préfecture*, which are currently known as the *Préfecture* Administrative Courts, or in the jurisdiction of the Conseil d'État. Since the Conseil d'État applies public-law rules, the result was that those contracts were deemed law-determined administrative contracts.

The Conseil d'État referred to these provisions to include in its jurisdiction those disputes related to many administration's contracts, which have not been expressly provided for, if there were a relation between them and the specified contracts.

This approach proved useful in the past when the administrative law was based on the public authority criterion; the idea that excludes administrative contracts – considering them as administering acts basically lacking the element of state power – from the perspective of the administrative law. However, after abandoning the previous criterion, the category of law-determined administrative contracts gained more momentum. Tackling law-determined administrative contracts provided in the French administrative law, it is concluded that these contracts fall under one of the following three categories:

First: Some law-determined administrative contracts are, continuously and due to their nature, regarded as strictly administrative contracts. Most notable examples are public services contracts, which were among the first administrative contracts to be defined by law. At the same time in the view of the French legal system, they are considered administrative contracts by nature. Hence, the basis upon which the French and Egyptian Administrative Judiciaries have depended on to broaden their jurisdiction to fit for many administrative contracts by nature was whether these contracts contained an element of the public services or not.[24] Accordingly, determining that the contract falls within the jurisdiction of the

---

24 For example, refer to the judgment of the Egyptian Conseil d'État issued on 26 December 1951, judicial year 6, 214 stating that: 'As per Article No. 5 of the Conseil d'État Law No. 9 of 1949, the present Court is competent to decide into the disputes arising out from obligation contracts, public work contracts and administrative supply contacts. In witness

Substantive theory of states' contracts 53

administrative judiciary is self-evident and then a contract is regarded as an administrative contract by nature not as defined by law.

Second: Sometimes, or even often, the contract providing that it is within the administrative judiciary's jurisdiction to decide into in the disputes arising from it is not considered an administrative contract by nature in all cases as this contract may – according to the features of the self-administrative contracts – be an administrative or a private law contract as the case may be. Thus, the idea of the law-determined administrative contracts arises if the contract is to be considered in all cases as an administrative contract just because the legislature decided that it is within the jurisdiction of the administrative judiciary to decide into in those disputes arising from it. However, the French Conseil d'Etat does not tend to use the previous approach in all cases, as it adopted an explanation providing that it shall not have the jurisdiction in this case unless the contract was administrative by nature as the case in supply contracts.

Third: finally, the contract providing that it is within the administrative judiciary's jurisdiction to decide into in disputes arising from it may be a private-law contract in all cases, which leads to the concept of the law-determined administrative contracts. The most prominent example for such a case is disputes arising from public property sale agreements. Moreover, it is believed that adding these disputes to the jurisdiction of administrative judiciary has been criticized due to historical reasons related to the French social and political circumstances. Hence, French Conseil d'Etat denies its jurisdiction to decide into in those disputes as much as possible[25].

Is the concept of 'the law-determined administrative contracts' valid in Egypt?

As noted above, the previous idea revolves around adding a contract-related disputes to the jurisdiction of administrative judiciary, referring to respective laws regulating jurisdictions of the Egyptian Administrative Judiciary. However, such reference was included in subsequent laws as follows:

First: Article No. 5 of Law No. 9 of 1946, which provides that: 'The Administrative Judiciary Court shall have the jurisdiction to hear disputes pertaining

---

hereof, it is evident that the disputes subject of claim arose from the administrative contract whereby the plaintiffs undertook to contribute in the expenses of the public service project, which is the construction of a courthouse by granting the land on which the project will be constructed plus a sum on money. Thus, this dispute is closely related to a public service contract, which is the construction of this building hence; the Court is competent to decide into this dispute in accordance with the provisions of the said article. In this sense, the Conseil d'État has extended its jurisdiction to the assistance contract by including such contract within the scope of the public services.'

25 André De Laubadère, *Traité Droit Administratif*, LGDJ 1999, 37.

54 *Substantive theory of states' contracts*

to the concession contracts, public works contracts and administrative supply contracts.'

Second: Article No. 10 of Law No. 165 of 1955 and Law No. 55 of 1959 provides that 'the Conseil d'État shall, through an administrative Judicial Association, have the exclusive jurisdiction to decide into disputes relating to concession contracts, public works contract, supply contracts or any other administrative contracts.'

Third: Paragraph No. 11 of Article No. 10 of the Conseil d'État Law No. 47 of 1972 which is valid until present, provides that only the Conseil d'État courts have the jurisdiction to 'decide into disputes relating to concession contracts, public works contracts, supply contracts and any other administrative contracts.'

After reviewing different stages the Egyptian Conseil d'État decided through the Appeal Administrative Court in its judgment issued on 9 December 1956 in which it states

> ... this jurisdiction is no longer exclusive to a specific number of administration's contracts; however, it includes all administrative contracts and is even extended to various disputes related to those contracts ... the administrative contracts in Egypt have become administrative contracts by nature based on their special characteristics rather than definition of law or the public opinion.[26]

Judicial criterion for distinguishing administrative contracts

An administrative contract can be defined – as prevailed in the French Conseil d'État Judiciary – as 'that contract concluded by a public juristic person for the sake of functioning or regulating a public service. It also shows an authority's intention to apply public-law provisions. More important, such contract must include excessive clauses unfamiliar in the private law or authorize the party entering an agreement with the authority to directly participate in the functioning of public service.'

This criterion – as shown from the above definition – is based on three principles:

1. A public juristic person must be a party to the contract;
2. The relation between the contract and the public service; and
3. The contract must contain excessive clauses.

Furthermore, this view was taken by the Appeal Administrative Court and the Legal Opinion (*Fatwa*) Department, adopted by the Supreme Administrative

---

26 Case No. 870 of judicial year 5, Mohammed Zidan vs. the Ministries of Agriculture, Education, Supply and Finance, Year 11, 76.

Substantive theory of states' contracts 55

Court and approved by the Supreme Constitutional Court acting in the capacity of a dispute-settlement court as follows:

- The Egyptian Appeal Administrative Court; however, expresses in its decision issued on 24 February 1957 that 'the Court has concluded that the contract entered into between a public juristic person and an individual does not require being regarded as an administrative contract. However, the criterion distinguishing these contracts from other private law contracts is not the capacity of the contracting party. It is the contract subject-matter whenever it is related to the regulation, operation, utilization, assistance or contribution of a public service along with an equal appearance of the public juristic person's intention to deal with the contract pursuant to the provisions of the public law. Thus, the Contract will ensure the provision of excessive clauses unfamiliar in the private law.'[27]
- The General Assembly for Legal Opinion *Fatwa* and Legislation adopted the same definition. For example, the Assembly has concluded in its legal opinion No. 637 dated 23 October 1956[28] 'The nature of administrative contracts differs from that of civil contracts, because the first establishes a contractual relation between a public law person and a private law person, with a purpose to achieve public interest. However, the status of the contracting parties is not of an equal bargaining power, since public interest overweighs private interests of individuals. This objective shall also prevail over the terms of the contract and the contractual relationship when applied and interpreted. Moreover, the authority shall ensure that the penalty terms specified in a contract are suitable for the nature and value of the contract as well as the cases where urgent application is required in a certain time and manner to ensure smooth operation of the public service.'
- The Supreme Administrative Court has also settled on the previous criterion. For example, it has concluded that 'a contract is deemed administrative if one of its parties is a public juristic person related to a public service along with excessive clauses in the context of private law ... .'[29] Furthermore, the court also applied this principle in its decision issued on 19 May 1962[30] in a certain case stating that: 'The lease contract of Port Fouad Fishery concluded between an administrative entity; the Ministry of Defense and the plaintiff is related to

---

27 Case No. 779 of judicial year 10. In the same meaning of its decision issued on 16 December 1956, case No. 223 of judicial year 10, it stated that: 'An administrative contract is a contract concluded by a legal person from the public law individuals for the purpose of managing or operating a public service whilst showing his/her intention to observe the style and provisions of the public law by including extraordinary clauses unfamiliar in the private law.' Judgments issued on 10 March 1957, judicial year 11, 254, and 12 May 1957 No. 1472 of judicial year 10.
28 Legal opinion No. 637, the combined principles adopted by the said Assembly. Mr. Ahmed Samir Abu Shadi, 1964 Edition, 751, No. 437.
29 Judgment dated 31 March 1962, judicial year 7, 527.
30 Judicial year 7, 890.

56 *Substantive theory of states' contracts*

a public service activity managed by the highest official of the governing authority. It is based on empowering someone to solely use and invest in public funds in a way affecting that service, which in this case is fishing that aims to achieve financial interests for the state's treasury. At the same time, it satisfies a shared public need by providing important food to the public to achieve common benefit. The contract terms contain excessive clauses unfamiliar in private law along with other clauses collectively stating that the authority is no longer determined on following the public law style, provisions, or means. However, these clauses use their privileges and rights as a public authority whilst establishing their contraction on the notion of authority and possession of a portion of the state's sovereignty and power. As a result, this group where the characteristics and features of the administrative contract is present is then subjected to the provisions of administrative law and falls accordingly within the jurisdiction of administrative judiciary.[31]

- Finally, the Supreme Constitutional Court – as a conflict-settlement court[32]– has been given the chance to tackle the administrative contract criterion in many judgments, where it emphasizes that 'for a contract to be recognized as an administrative contract, one of its parties must be a public juristic person contracting in its capacity as a public authority. It also must be related to the operation or management of a public service and having the characteristics distinguishing the administrative contracts, which is adopting the public law techniques in excessive clauses contained in these contracts compared to private-law relations.'[33]

This criterion of the administrative contract is the criterion that was adopted by the Egyptian Conseil d'État courts following the French Conseil d'État courts. This criterion is the same in all MENA countries as the administrative contracts' law and practice have flown from Egypt to all MENA countries.

---

31 The court still depends, excessively, on this triple criterion in its decisions to determine whether a contract is qualified as an administrative contract or not. Examples from its decision can be seen in many judgments for instance see judgments issued on 2 January 1965, judicial year 10, 386; 20 May 1967 judicial year 12, 1094; 1 July 1967, judicial year 12, 1217; 30 December 1967, judicial year 13, 359; 24 February 1968, judicial year 13, 557; and 11 May 1968, judicial year 13, 874, in which the Supreme Administrative Court has concluded that the contract does not qualify as an administrative contract. It further explained elements of the three criteria in details. In addition, the judgment issued on 18 May 1968, judicial year 13, 953 is another example for the detailed Judgment issued in this regard.

32 The Supreme Constitutional Court in Egypt has the judicial power as a court for conflict for the settlement of jurisdictional disputes between the ordinary courts whether civil or commercial on one hand and the Conseil d'État courts on the other hand.

33 For instance, judgment dated 19 January 1980 case No. 7 of judicial year 1, 244. The same provision repeated by the court in its ruling dated 29 July 1974, case No.10 of judicial year 4.

3 The principles of *Le Contrat Administratif* theory in MENA countries

Introduction

The most significant element in the administrative contracts' defining criterion is the excessive clauses' element.[1] It is a fundamental element whilst defining administrative contracts and distinguishing this contract from private law contracts whether civil or commercial. The crucial question is: to what extent do the excessive clauses exist in the traditional concessions? And how far do those excessive clauses affect party autonomy principle? As the administrative law principles in the MENA region were established by the French and Egyptian Conseil d'État, it is important to note that the following legal and judicial principles have spread from the French Conseil D'État and the Egyptian Conseil D'État to all MENA countries.

The choice of contracting parties to adopt the public law techniques

A contract entered into by the administration concerning a public utility is deemed to have met a necessary condition of administrative contracts. But that is not, by itself, enough for the contract to be identified as administrative. Decisions of the Egyptian Conseil D'État repeatedly highlight this key fact regarding the subject matter of administrative contracts. For instance, the Appeal Administrative Court, in its judgment dated 16 December 1956, states that:

> the relationship between the contract and the public service, despite being sufficient to identify the contract as administrative, is not sufficient by itself for that purpose. The rules of the public law are not inextricably tied to public services. The authority, for example, may not conclude the contract

---

1 The '*Le Contrat Administratif*' concept has unique characteristics in civil law legal systems, see: De Laubadere, Modern, and Delvolvé, *Traite des contrats adinistratifs*, LGDJ, Vol. I, 210 et seq. and Richer, *Droit des contrats adminiatratifs*, 85 et seq. In Egypt: El Tamawy, *The General Principles of Administrative Contracts*, Dar Al Fikr Al Araby 1991, 53, and Sarwat Badawi, *General Theory of Administrative Contracts*, Dar Al Nahda Al Arabia 1994, 5–109.

58 Le Contrat Administratif *theory*

in the manner stipulated in the public law, believing the private law to be more favorable because in that case the authority is treated as a private individual. Therefore, the criterion that distinguishes administrative contracts from private law contracts is not the nature of the contracting party, but rather the subject matter of the contract itself whenever it is related to the public service in any shape or form whatsoever. 'The exorbitant and uncommon clauses in the contract are also a distinguishing condition thereof, on equal footing with the subject matter of the contract.'

Similarly, the Egyptian Supreme Administrative Court, in all its judgment where discussions were raised on whether a contract is administrative or not, restates that having exorbitant or excessive clauses is among the defining features of administrative contracts. For instance, one of its judgment first establishes that the contract is related to a public service, then adds that

> the clauses of the contract include exorbitant clauses that are uncommon in the private law. There are other clauses that indicate that the intention of the Authority was to follow the manner stipulated in the public law, to adopt the provisions and methods of said law, and to benefit from its own privileges and rights as a public authority. It concluded the contract on the basis that it is entitled, as a public authority, to a part of the State's sovereignty and power. Therefore, this relationship, which bears the features and characteristics of administrative contracts, is subject to the provisions of administrative law.[2]

In this regard, it is noteworthy that the administrative law has evolved; at the beginning, it was completely based on the concept of public services, and the rules of said law were inextricably related to that concept. At that time, public services were exclusively of an administrative nature. Accordingly, a contract related to a public service was sufficiently identifiable as an administrative contract, since all administrative services are subject to the provisions of the public law.

Then, as mentioned earlier, the law evolved, and new sorts of public services emerged. It was no longer possible or feasible to make the new services fully subject to the rules of public law. The Supreme Administrative Court was given considerable freedom in choosing the method by which it can serve the public

---

2 Its judgment dated 19 May 1962, judicial year 7, 890. In its judgment, dated 21 March 1962, judicial year 7, 527, it states that 'if a contract is concluded for a private interest, and if none of the clauses thereof is uncommon in the private law, then such contract is subject to the private law. Disputes over said contract fall outside the jurisdiction of administrative justice.' And in its judgment, dated 24 February 1968, judicial year 13, 552 and concerning gravel sale contract, it decided that the contract, whose clauses include clauses such as 'paying the full price in advance before delivering the vended object' and 'paying the rent of the store in which the gravel is located after the end of 1955 (delivery date)' are common clauses in private law contracts.

interest. As a result, it was decided that contracts related to public services no longer had sufficient conditions to be considered administrative contracts, as the Authority may have decided to conclude them under the private law. That was the rationale behind the third and final distinguishing criteria of administrative contracts. In fact, as shall be demonstrated below, there is an opinion that considers this condition sufficient to distinguish administrative contracts, regardless of the relation between the contract and the public service.

The principal method adopted by the administrative judiciary in Egypt and France in order to detect bad faith by an authority in choosing the methods of the public law is to see, as per most of the rulings of the Egyptian administrative judiciary (both old and recent), if the contract contains any 'excessive or exorbitant clauses that are uncommon in the private law.'

The Supreme Administrative Court in this regard issued many leading decisions illustrating this judicial principle and the Court used several legal phrases to express its vision such as: 'adopting the method of the public law in certain clauses uncommon in the private law.'[3] Or 'its intention to adopt the method of the public law in a certain contract may be demonstrated by including a clause or several clauses uncommon in private law contracts.'[4] Or '[the Authority] followed the methods of the public law when concluding the contract by including exorbitant clauses uncommon within the scope of the private law.'[5] And 'the contract, issued by an authority representing the state and related to the operation of a public service, includes clauses that are uncommon within the scope of the private law.' Accordingly, the Supreme Administrative Court ruled that the permit issued to Maamoura Company for Housing and Development to operate a public service, namely a casino on the beach of Al Maamoura district, is deemed an administrative contract, given that the permit included exorbitant clauses as detailed by the Court.[6]

The Supreme Constitutional Court uses the same definition in its judgment. Therefore, the condition of 'having excessive and exorbitant clauses uncommon in the private law' is the current cornerstone of identifying administrative contracts.[7]

Although doctrine and jurisprudence in France and Egypt contend that administrative contracts must include exorbitant and uncommon clauses, it is extremely difficult to determine which clauses are uncommon in the private law. The reason for this difficulty is that the French Conseil d'État is too succinct in drafting its rulings. In most cases, it merely declares that the contract under

---

3 Judgment dated 2 January 1965, judicial year 10, 316.
4 Judgment dated 30 December 1967, judicial year 1, 359.
5 Judgment dated 11 May 1965, judicial year 13, 874.
6 Judgment dated 21 June 1980, judicial year 20.
7 For a longer explanation, see ibid., 85, 'The notion of exorbitant clauses or derogation of public right is undeniably the core component of the theory of administrative contracts. Indeed, it is the presence of such clauses in a contract that is par excellence the criterion that grants it an administrative nature.'

60 Le Contrat Administratif *theory*

question includes uncommon clauses, without explaining what those clauses are, then concludes that said contract is of an administrative nature. Such conventional wording can be noted in its ruling in the 'Peuaraya' case,[8] dated 21 January 1948, where it states that there is: 'a clause attributing to the public authority exorbitant prerogatives from the common law.'

The Conseil d'État sometimes attempts to define such clauses, as in its ruling in the 'Stien' case, dated 20 October 1950, in which it defined such clauses 'those that confer rights or places obligations upon a contracting party, where such rights and obligations are of a different nature from what may be freely agreed upon by parties within the scope of civil or trade law.'[9]

The administrative judiciary elaborates the clauses based on which it identified a contract as administrative. One of the clearest cases is the dispute ruling in the 'Paulabeuf' case, dated 27 July 1950, held that

> The agreement concluded between the State and Mr. Paulabeuf includes clauses uncommon in the private law. For instance, article (5) makes the Authority entitled to supervise and instruct the contractor with regards to the implementation of the works assigned thereto and the utilization of the quarry. Moreover, article (6) entitles the State, in case of default, to undertake the implementation by itself and to be reimbursed, as per payment orders, the amounts incurred in this regard without taking any measures except warning the contractor. Finally, article (10) confers upon the project [i.e. the management] the right one of the State prerogatives, namely to temporarily seize the necessary materials for the project if an agreement could not be reached with relevant parties.

This detailed rationale is the one adopted by the Egyptian Conseil D'État in most cases. For example, the Appeal Administrative Court[10] held that

> the contract concluded between the Cairo Court of First Instance and the defendant includes clauses whereby the defendant shall serve food and drinks at fixed prices annexed thereto. The contract also stipulates that the managing authority may increase or decrease said prices, and the Court's staff and users may get drinks at discounted prices. Additionally, the defendant shall comply with any orders by the contracting public authority to terminate a staff member for uncleanliness, misconduct, or any reason whatsoever. The contract also stipulates that the aforementioned Court may inspect cafeterias and staff members at any time and may order the defendant to clean the place or replace objectionable equipment at the defendant's expense. The Court is entitled to terminate the contract and vacate the

---

8 Siret, Rev., 1949. Part 3, 6.
9 Ibid., 505.
10 Ibid., 668.

Le Contrat Administratif *theory*   61

premises without alert or warning. All the clauses above are uncommon in similar private law contracts. Based on the foregoing, the contract under question bears the distinguishing features of administrative contracts, as it is related to a public service and includes excessive and exorbitant clauses that follow the methods of the public law.[11]

The Supreme Administrative Court adopts the same approach. It held that

> it is unquestionable that administrative contracts include clauses that are uncommon in civil contracts, with the purpose of guaranteeing the adequate functioning of relevant public services. Hence, the clause that entitles the authority to enforce penalties in case of violations is lawful. However, this does not give the authority free rein to impose fines without limitation as to the amount, as such fines are subject to supervision by the administrative judiciary to ensure that they are not arbitrary.[12]

The Court highlights that the contract is related to the public service by stating that 'accordingly, the contract was concluded based on the needs and functioning of the public service.' Further, it listed the excessive and exorbitant clauses therein, including the provisions that:

(a) Entitle the Permanent Authority for Land Reclamation to impose a fine of one (1) Egyptian pound upon breach of any clause;
(b) Grant said authority the absolute right to terminate the contract upon breach of any clause by the contractor; and
(c) Entitle the contracting authority to solely determine the contract clauses.[13]

Excessive or exorbitant clauses can be classified under major categories and can be spotted through certain presumptions, and those categories can be summed as follows:

---

11 Judgment dated 16 December 1956, case No. 223 of judicial year 10.
12 Judgment dated 13 May 1961, judicial year 6, 1012.
13 Judgment dated 31 March 1962, judicial year 7, 527.
   There are many examples of exorbitant clauses that the Supreme Administrative Court has been keen on highlighting, including its judgment dated 20 May 1967, judicial year 12, 1094, the right of the public authority to perform the contract at the expense of the defaulting contracting party and impose penalties on the same without recourse to court; its judgment dated 30 December 1967, judicial year 13, 359 on the clauses stipulating that services provided under education contracts shall be delivered, and that any party violating said clauses shall be liable to pay full expenses; its judgment dated 11 May 1968, judicial year 13, 874 on the right of the public authority to 'impose fines for not operating the facilities and to modify routes (i.e., river transportation routes), tolls, traffic system, schedules, etc.' and its judgment dated 18 May 1968, judicial year 14, 953 on the right of the Ministry of Education to completely negate the author's copyrights in favor of MoE, which shall henceforth be entitled to modify and edit the work under question as it deems fit.

62   Le Contrat Administratif *theory*

First: clauses granting privileges solely to the authority[14]

These privileges, included within the scope of the contract clauses, are considered the most distinguishing feature of administrative contracts; under such privileges, the authority may unilaterally compel the contracting party to bear responsibilities and the contracting parties are not in an equal power in the contractual relationship. Since the beginning of concluding administrative contracts, it has become evident that they violate the principle of equality of contracting parties. Individuals who intend to enter into a bid or a tender contract are obligated by the contract clauses once they apply, whereas the administration is only obligated later and may not be obligated at all. Individuals are contractually obligated once the contract is concluded, whilst the authority may bear no obligations whatsoever. It may even maintain the right to free itself from the contract.

Such clauses are particularly evident during the execution of the contract. The Authority often adds certain clauses in their administrative contracts, by which it may (a) modify, by addition or omissions, the obligations of the contracting party, (b) maintain the authority to monitor the execution of the contract, (c) change the method of execution, (d) temporarily halt execution, (e) unilaterally rescind and terminate the contract and finally (f) impose penalties in case of breach of obligations by the contracting party (even if there were no damages) without need to recourse to court and obtain judicial resolution.

These clauses are constantly underscored by the Egyptian administrative judiciary, whether in the judgment of the Supreme Administrative Court or the Appeal Administrative Court.

Second: excessive or exorbitant clauses granting the contracting party exceptional prerogatives in dealing with third parties[15]

Excessive clauses entitle the contracting party to practice certain prerogatives to the extent required for the performance of the contract, particularly when such prerogatives are usually practiced by the administration. Clearly, such clauses have no equivalent in contracts concluded between individuals whether civil or commercial within the scope of private law. Public service concession contracts often include clauses that entitle concessionaires to practice some excessive authorities of the police and the right of expropriation. Moreover, the amount

---

14 Andre De Laubadere, Franck Moderne and Pierre Delvolve, *Traite des Contrats Administratifs*, volume I, 2nd edn, LGDJ 1983, 150; 211 et seq.; Laurent Richer, *Droit Des Contrats Administratifs*, LGDJ 2008, 80; in Egypt and MENA countries: Soliman El Tamawy, *General Principles of Administrative Contracts*, 5th edn, 1991, 88; S. Badawi, *The General Theory of Administrative Contracts*, 1, 1994, 54; S. El Sharkawy, *The Administrative Contracts*, Dar Al Nahda Al Arabia 2003, 14; Supreme Administrative Court, case No. 559, session, 24 February 1968; case No. 2184, session 21 February 1987 and case No. 3128, session 24 January 1995; The General Assembly for Legal Opinion and Legislation, Legal Opinion No. 403, session 21 March 1990, dated 11 April 1990.
15 Judgment of the Conseil d'État dated 21 April 1950 in the *'Nuncie'* case, p. 231.

paid by end users (the public) to concessionaires is considered a fee, subject to the provisions of the public law, not a charge in exchange for services as in private law contracts. Some clauses in concession contracts do not grant an explicit mandate to practice the aspects of public authority. However, those clauses may have features that render them uncommon to private contracts. A concessionaire, for instance, may be granted the right to use and benefit from the public domain, thus becoming the holder of a *de facto* monopoly. As a result, such clauses limit the freedom of competitor projects. Additionally, public works contracts often include clauses that grant the contractor a temporary right of occupancy of private properties without the need for the prior consent of the owners. This is one of the prerogatives of public power often practiced by public authorities. Other contracts entitle parties contracting with the administration to seize movable properties by force.

Third: reference to standard conditions prepared by the administration[16]

Upon examining the method adopted by the administration in concluding contracts, we shall see that the administration often drafts standard conditions for a wide array of administrative contracts. These standard conditions are prepared and printed in advance prior to concluding the contract, and they are considered part of the concluded contract in addition to any other clauses agreed upon by the administration and the contracting party. But what if the contract does not include any excessive or exorbitant clauses and at the same time contains a reference to the standard conditions? Does this reference constitute an exorbitant clause that confers an administrative nature upon the contract? The answer depends on the nature of the standard conditions themselves. If they are excessive, exorbitant and uncommon in civil or commercial contracts, then the contract becomes of administrative nature, as reference to any document relevant to the public procurement process as an integral part of the contract as if they were explicitly stipulated in the contract itself.

Fourth: clauses that place the contract under the jurisdiction of the administrative judiciary[17]

The administration often adds clauses that place disputes arising from the contract under the jurisdiction of administrative judiciary. Are such clauses enough to identify a contract as administrative? The concept of 'administrative contract' is grounded on a similar basis according to the law, as such contracts are deemed administrative since the legislature has placed the settlement of disputes arising from them under the jurisdiction of administrative judiciary. The Conseil

---

16 *La reference à un cahier des charges de l'administration.* [The reference to standard conditions prepared or stipulated by the administration.]

17 '*Les stipulations attributives de competence.*'

64   Le Contrat Administratif *theory*

d'État does not recognize agreed-upon clauses related to jurisdiction in all cases, but rather endeavors to balance two principles, namely:

(a) The freedom of contracting parties to select between administrative contracts and private law contracts.
(b) That the administration cannot, in its agreements with individuals, modify or amend the legislative rules of jurisdiction because these rules are related to public policy.

Based on these two principles, it has been decided that jurisdiction clauses cannot solely affect the nature of a contract, but those clauses can reveal whether a contract is administrative or not[18] Therefore, the role of jurisdiction clauses can be viewed from two angles: firstly, they are of no use if the nature of the contract is clear. If the contract is administrative because it contains excessive, exorbitant and uncommon clauses, the jurisdiction clause is merely confirming an established fact. And if the contract is a private contract, the administrative judiciary will negate the jurisdiction clause because it violates the public policy legislative rules relating to jurisdiction.[19] Second, the jurisdiction clause can prove useful if the nature of the contract is unclear, i.e. the contract may be administrative or private based on the intention of the contracting parties. In such cases, if clauses are inconclusive on whether a contract is administrative because they are merely presumptions leading to probability rather than certainty, the jurisdiction clause, in addition to other presumptions, can be an important factor to identify the contract as administrative. The French Conseil d'État adopts this approach in early judgments such as the leading case of '*Ste. Des voiliers francais,*'[20] when the court held that 'traditions of the Ministry of the Navy'[21] were indicative presumptions. The ruling stated that: 'although the clause stipulating that disputes shall be settled by the administrative judiciary could not in itself confer jurisdiction, it nevertheless had the effect of indicating the parties' common intention as to the nature of the agreement concluded between them.'

Fifth: direct joint management of the public service by the contracting party and the administration[22]

A contract that does not include any excessive clauses or any of the presumptions is considered by the French administrative judiciary as an administrative

---

18 For a lengthy discussion, see De Laubadere, ibid., 81, 'it follows that the jurisdiction only has effect if it corresponds to the nature of the contract in which it was stipulated.'
19 Judgment of the French Conseil d'État, dated 28 July 1916 in the '*Sté. gén. de gaz du Midi*' case, the Collection, 330, and its judgment of 19 February 1926 in the '*Dep. De l'ain,*' the Collection, 191.
20 The Collection, 597. Judgment dated 19 June 1918.
21 *'La reference aux usages du département de la marines.'*
22 *'La participation directe du cocontractant à la gestion même du service.'*

Le Contrat Administratif *theory* 65

contract if it provides for direct joint management of the public service by the contracting parties.

Based on that understanding, the administrative judiciary settled on the view that a public service concession contract is an administrative contract at all times, because it obligates the concessionaire to personally participate in the management of the public service.

Nevertheless, some of the judgment of the French Conseil d'État indicate that participation in the management of the public service, as in the aforementioned cases, cannot by itself confer an administrative nature upon the contract. The public service also must be managed by virtue of the rules of public law, because it is these rules that require excessive clauses which are not recognized in private transactions between individuals.[23]

Traditional public utilities concession contract

The Public Utilities' Concession Contract is the most known administrative contract and probably the most significant one in practice. It can be defined as an administrative contract by which, the concessionaire – whether an individual or a company – shall be liable for the management and exploitation of an economic public utility against certain fees to be paid by end-users (the public), subject to the fundamental rules regulating public utility along with the Concession Contract terms and conditions.

In its judgment passed on 25 March 1956, The Egyptian Appeal Administrative Court defined the Concession Contract, as

> ... Concession of public utilities is simply an administrative contract by virtue of which, an individual or a company is mandated by the State or by any of its administrative bodies to undertake, at its own expenses and under its financial liability, to provide a public service as per legislation and regulations, in return for being authorized to exploit the project for a specified period of time and receive the tariffs gained. Concession is an administrative contract of a specific nature. Its subject-matter is to manage a public utility for a specific period of time. Concessionaires shall incur all the project

---

23 Judgment of the French Conseil d'État, dated 11 July 1948 in the '*jouvet*' case, Dalloz, 1948, section 3, p. 537, with a comment by Blaevoet, as well as its ruling of 14 May 1948 in the Jacquin case, *Journal of International Law*, 1949, 600. The latter judgment's subject-matter is that a municipality concluded a contract with an individual to launch fireworks on 14 July. The Conseil d'État decided that the contract is a civil contract and justified it by stating that 'considering that the public service in which the fireworks expert participated did not, as far as the fireworks are concerned, have any other *modus operandi* that would have given this operation a different character had it been performed on behalf of an individual.'

66   Le Contrat Administratif *theory*

expenses and financial risks and shall be entitled to a tariff to be collected from end-users (the public)....[24]

The traditional concession contracts' substantive clauses[25]

Public utilities' concession contract jurisprudentially and judicially contain two types of clauses:

A) **Contractual clauses**, which are subject to the *pacta sunt servanda* rule. These clauses do not cover how services are to be provided to the end-users. They can be revoked if the administration has exploited the service itself.

B) **Regulatory clauses:** These clauses can be amended by the administration at any time as required for the exploitation of public utility, and they stipulate the means to provide the service for end-users. The Appeal Administrative Court at the Egyptian Conseil D'État held that 'In case the State, being originally mandated for managing the public utilities, entrusts a third party to manage public utilities, the latter shall cooperate with the State and act as its deputy in one of its major responsibilities. This kind of deputation – or in other words, this indirect manner of management to the public utility – shall not be deemed a waiver or abandonment of the public utility by the State; however, it shall remain a guarantor and accountable before the public for the administration and exploitation of that service. To perform such duty, the State shall interfere in the public utility affairs as required for the public interest.'[26] Accordingly, the concession contract establishes in its key two subjects, a regulatory position that vests the concessionaire with rights derived from the public power and based on the public utility

---

24 Judicial year 10, p. 259. The Legal Opinion Department defined the Concession Contract in its legal opinion No. 369 issued on 16 December 1949 as 'A contract by virtue of which, an individual undertakes, at its own expense and under its responsibility, to administer a public service, taking its risks and the public works related to such administration, as appropriate. For this purpose, it shall be temporarily granted some public powers in return for a part of the revenues collected from the Public in return for such public service.'

25 The Appeal Administrative Court 27 January 1957 Case Nos. 485 and 1367 of judicial year 7. In Egyptian doctrine, see: El Tamawy, *The General Principles of Administrative Contracts*, Dar Al Fikr Al Araby, 5th edn, 1991, 108–124; S. Badawi, *The General Theory of Administrative Contracts*, 1994, 115–129. In French doctrine, see: De Laubadere, *Les Concessions et Contrats Voisins*, 283–299; Richer, *Droits des Contrats Administratifs*, LGDJ, 2008, 354 et seq. In Egyptian Conseil D'État, see the Supreme Administrative Court, session 17 January 1970, case No. 440, judicial year 11 and session 30 December 1977, case No. 110 of judicial year 23. In French jurisprudence, the distinction between concession public utilities and concession public works is clear, C.E. 10 April 1970, Beau and Lagarde, Rec. 243; C.E. 6 May 1991, *Syndicat intercommunal du Bocage*, A.J.D.A. 1991, 717; C.E. 26 September 1994, *Commune de Labenne*, D.A. 1994, No. 588. For more elaboration, see: Richer, *Droits des Contrats Administratifs*, 2008, 360.

26 Judgment issued on 27 January 1957, case No. 485 and 1367, judicial year 7.

Le Contrat Administratif *theory* 67

existence and exploitation. This regulatory position established by the concession and related to the public utility constraints.

The contractual liability, however, depends on the regulatory position and shall not preclude the issuance of new regulatory provisions related to the concession. The regulatory clauses are determined by an agreement entered between the administration granting the concession and the concessionaire. Yet, this agreement sets a rule establishing a legal or regulatory position, the State right to amend such position under its sole discretion, shall be undisputable.[27]

The Supreme Administrative Court confirms the same principles in its judgments. The judgment stated that:

It is jurisprudentially and judicially acknowledged that the clauses of the public utilities concession contract are divided into two types: regulatory clauses and contractual clauses. The regulatory clauses may only be amended by the concession's grantor under its sole discretion at any time, as required for the public interest, regardless of the concessionaire's acceptance. It is also evident that the tariffs or toll stations/roads and related regulatory terms that can be amended upon the sole discretion of the concession's grantor ... .[28]

Since the concession contract is closely related to the public utilities, it is consistently deemed an administrative contract. Therefore, it has been identified by the legislature as the first type of contracts to be referred to the jurisdiction of the Supreme Administrative Court to consider the disputes related thereto.

27 The Legal Opinion Department take the same characterization into account. For example, the opinion of the General Assembly No. 92, issued on 4 February 1956, Mr. Samir Abu Shady Collection, 53 reads: 'it is jurisprudentially and judicially acknowledged that the concession grantor may solely amend the regulatory clauses of the concession contract at any time according to the needs of the public service without depending on the concessionaire's consent. The right to amend the regulatory clauses is derived from the nature of the contract subject matter, i.e. the public service, as the fundamental rule states that the Public Authority has the upper hand in regulating and administering the public services, being related to the public interest. Should the conditions change, and the public service regulations, established at the time of contracting, are no longer consistent with the new conditions and do not achieve the public interest for which they have been established, the Public Authority granting the concession may change these regulations and impose on the concessionaire, at its free discretion, the regulations it deems likely to achieve the public interest. It is also recognized that the tariff and the related regulatory clauses which are subject to amendment by the sole discretion of the Authority and remain a one-sided work even if the amendment thereof is upon the request of the concessionaire or arising out of an agreement or negotiation therewith ...' See the Department Opinion No. 414, issued on 4 November 1954, Mr. Samir Abu Shady Collection, 54.
28 Judgment issued on 30 December 1977, case No. 110, judicial year 13, The Technical Bureau, Principle No. 23, 27.

68   Le Contrat Administratif *theory*

The legal nature of the concession of public utilities contract was controversial whether it is civil/commercial contract or an administrative contract. This contract was one of the most disputable contracts between the administration and individuals. In respect thereof, courts, especially mixed courts, announced that the administrative contracts are distinct from private law contracts for their close relevance to public services. One of the clearest examples for this is the Mixed Court of Cairo ruling issued on 2 April 1917, which held that 'Concession Contract shall constitute a public law contract.'[29] However, despite this fact, its provisions are predominated by the civil nature. Therefore, the legislature, as previously stated, had to regulate the administrative contract with specific provisions pursuant to Law No. 129 of 1947 on public utilities' concession, which considered the core principles regulating the administrative contracts.[30]

The significance of the concession contract, as mentioned before, is that it enables individuals or companies to substitute the Public Authority in the administration and exploitation of a public utility. This usually occurs by way of legal or actual monopoly, which requires the concessionaire to comply to all the rules regulating the public utilities upon managing and exploiting a project. On the other hand, this consideration led to the fact that some sort of control has been imposed on the administration itself upon granting concession contracts for management and exploiting public services, as some strong concession companies, especially those with foreign partners, represent a real threat to the State's interests and sovereignty. Article (137) of 1923 Constitution which was valid during the promulgation of the concession of public utilities' law, contains an explicit provision, stipulating that:

> Each concession contract and monopoly whose subject matter is utilizing resources from the resources of natural wealth in the State or interest of the interests of the general public, shall only be granted pursuant to law and only for a limited period of time.

It has been decided, according to the interpretation of this Article that a specific law shall be issued for each concession to be granted.

The Egyptian Appeal Administrative Court approved this opinion in its judgment issued on 24 June 1956, upon the settlement of the controversial views on the aforementioned Article (137) interpretation, which states that:

---

29 Gazette. VII, 105–307.

30 The explanatory note of the said law acknowledged these considerations, as its reads: 'Public service concession contracts, despite being an administrative contract, has been previously considered a civil or commercial contract and the contractual nature predominated all its clauses, and in that sense it is considered a *pacta sunt servanda principle* ... Accordingly, this contract, as per the provisions of the French Conseil D'État and French jurists' opinions, is considered among the administrative law affairs, and the public service has become a top priority; and the concessionaire began to cooperate with the Authority in performing works closely related to the public interest.'

Le Contrat Administratif *theory* 69

Accordingly, a concession shall not be granted in the cases specified in Article (137) hereinabove, unless pursuant to a law. The administration shall have no right or power to enter into a contract that falls within the jurisdiction of the parliament and has to be promulgated by a legislation. In case such contract is made, it shall be null and void for contravening the constitution and for being issued by an incompetent authority and shall have no effect or grant any rights.[31]

The General Assembly of the Legal Opinion (*Fatwa*) Department stated that:

There is a stable constitutional customary providing for a sort of parliamentary control over the executive authority regarding the concession of utilizing natural resources and public utilities. This control is not absolute and only restrictive to the main national utilities and natural public resources.[32]

The Egyptian Permeant Constitution of 1971, in Article 123 pointed out that:

The law defines rules and regulations on granting concessions of exploiting natural treasure resources and public services. In addition, it defines cases of

---

31 Judicial year 10, p. 365. On the merits of the case, the Court decided that the Decree-Law issued on 21 April 1926, on sponge fishing in Egyptian waters, providing for a concession on the right to sponge fishing in the Egyptian waters upon Cabinet Decision is in no violation of the constitution, even if it is subject to public bidding by virtue of Minister of Finance decision based on the ground that the legislator ' ... when issued the aforementioned Decree-law, ... was considering the idea that exploiting sponge hotbeds in the Egyptian waters has not levelled up to the significance and risk of being a natural resource of national wealth. It seems that the facts and circumstances at that time justified such opinion. It is clear from the Government Note on sponge fisheries that exploiting sponge hotbeds, 12 years after the issuance of the aforementioned decree-law, has been an individual, relatively small scale, and short-term activity exemplified in a limited number of licenses, not exceeding 15 licenses per year with an approximate annual revenue of EGP 3,000; thus, it was not appropriate to deem sponge a national treasure. In addition, not every natural resource in the State should be necessarily deemed a national treasure resource, so an exploitation concession could only be granted by virtue of a law. Given the foregoing, under the provisions of the Decree-law, enacted on 31 April 1926 and according to Article (137) of the Constitution of 1923, sponge exploitation concession shall be granted by the executive authority, in accordance with the conditions specified in the said Decree-law and in a manner by which such service shall not be deemed a State's natural resource. In cases where such description is met in terms of reality or otherwise predicted, such as organized large-scale and quite long-term exploitation, or by virtue of the terms and conditions usually contained in the concession contracts, exploitation concession shall only be granted by virtue of law.'

It is clear how the new constitution addresses the difficulty of granting a concession by law in such cases. This kind of difficulty has prompted the government to uphold this interpretation, which may not be consistent with the verbatim of Article 137 of the Constitution of 1923.

32 The Egyptian Conseil D'État, The General Assembly for Legal Opinion and Legislation, Opinion No. 944, Mr. Abu Shady Collection, p. 46.

70   Le Contrat Administratif *theory*

gratis disposition of state-owned real estates and alienation of movable properties and the relevant regulating rules and procedures.

Accordingly, granting concessions of public utilities and exploitation of the natural resources, under the constitution of 1971, was subject to Article 123 thereof and to Law No. 61 of 1958. Law No. 129 of 1947 is referred to for the Concession substantive provisions.[33]

The duration of traditional concession contract

One of the most important aspects that was regulated by Law No. 129 of 1947, is specifying the duration of the concession contract. Article (1) thereof stipulates a maximum of 30 years as the concession contracts' duration, thus, the legislature eliminated the old tradition under which, concessions were granted for 99 years.[34] The Law's Explanatory memorandum stated that:

> ... it is no longer acceptable, with the accelerated economic and social developments we witness today to grant concessions for a span of almost a century. The fact is that granting concessionaires a 30 year concession guarantees them to benefit for a period enough to compensate the construction expenses they incurred.

The new duration of the concession shall not apply on the preceding concessions only, but on the rest of the old concession durations as well, thus it should not last for more than 30 years.

The duration clause is one of the points distinguishing a concession contract from other similar contracts, and the Supreme Administrative Court distinguished

---

33 The Conseil D'État Legal Opinions, years 4 and 5, p. 96. In the same meaning, Opinion No. 1045 issued on 26 June 1952, Legal Opinions collection, years 6 and 7, p. 6. Earlier, on 1 December 1948, Third Year, 106, the Appeal Administrative Court issued a judgment on the Parliament work reading: 'Parliamentary works are divided into 4 sections: the first section includes pure legislative works related to the adoption of laws; the second section includes some acts to be submitted to the Parliament, by virtue of the Constitution, for approval whether due to its specific significance, its effect on the State's money or its effect on the public interest; the third section includes work related to the internal system of each council and the rights, duties, incentives and dismissal of members as well as maintaining the system inside each council, and the fourth section includes the behaviour of each council in its control over the executive authority.' By excluding the first section, which covers the actual legislation according to their specific nature, the Council further added: 'and all the decisions specified within these three sections are issued by the parliament in the form of laws different from the legislative laws in nature and purpose, namely applying all existing common legislative laws. As a result, the parliament may not violate another existing law when issuing such laws, contrary to the legislative laws, in which, the parliament may violate the provisions of a preceding law when approving the same.'
34 It is worth noting that the Suez Canal concession was granted for 99 years.

Le Contrat Administratif *theory* 71

between concession contracts and licensing the exploitation of a public utilities, and illustrated that the concession provisions specified in Law No. 129 of 1947 are not applicable on licenses of some public utility exploitation

> ... because they are temporary in nature, granted for a short period of time, non-renewable and may be revoked by the issuing authority at any time as per its explicit provisions. Hence, they shall not be governed by the provisions of Law No. 129 of 1947 as they are only exclusive to public utility concession contracts.[35]

Law No. 129 of 1947 has set a ceiling for profits that may be collected by the concessionaire, i.e. 10% of the capital employed or authorized by the concessioner, after deducting capital depreciation rate, whilst authorizing the concessionaire to set up a reserve within a specified number of years, where the profit does not reach the aforementioned ceiling. The explanatory note justified that vision: 'this amount (10%) shall be the normal ceiling for the concessionaire's remuneration as it may not covet – as the case may be – in industrial and commercial projects for unlimited profits. Exploitation of a public service is not speculative in nature as such projects. The significant risks inherent in them should be up to par with the hopes to achieve significant profits. In fact, the concessionaire is in a perfect position, having *de jure* or *de facto* monopoly which protects the latter from competition.... On the other hand, the theory of the unexpected circumstances detailed in Article (5) of the draft-law saves the concessionaire from major risks resulting from unexpected incidents and which cause potential loss in case of exploiting the public utility concession.'[36]

The Supreme Administrative Court, upon the aforementioned distinction between a public utility contract and a license for a public utility exploitation, has concluded that the administration shall have no right to require the exploiter of the public utility in the second case to return the profits amounts exceeding the 10%, because Law No. 129 of 1947 contains the following provision

> ... A concession is supposed to be granted for only relatively long periods counted by years, because Paragraph (1) (of Article (3) of the Law) stipulates that the profit percentage shall not be calculated except after deducting

---

35 Judgment issued on 17 January 1970, year 15, 140.
36 In this regard, the explanatory note further added: ' ... Finally, it has been concluded, particularly in the recent years in the French doctrine, that the public interest nature characterizing a public service concession and the fact that they are closely related, do not allow the concessionaire to gain from its exploitation significant profits that would inflict harms upon the beneficiaries. The draft law draws on the British legislation in specifying the concessionaires' original share by 10%. In Britain, old laws on concession of water distribution and gas lightening stipulate that the concessionaire's profits shall not exceed the percentage specified in the concession document, usually amounting to 10% of the capital. In case of not specifying such a percentage, the 10% shall be applied.'

72   Le Contrat Administratif *theory*

the corresponding capital depreciation rate, while Paragraph (2) stipulates that the profits exceeding such percentage shall be used in setting up a reserve for the years with profits less than the specified 10%. Such provisions are inapplicable to the licenses that may be granted for the exploitation of some public utilities because they are temporary in nature and are granted for short periods of time.

It is finally noted that some of the concession contract provisions are stipulated in Articles from 668 to 672 of the Egyptian Civil Law. This is one of the evidences illustrating the civil law predominance over some administrative articles. Despite the fact that the *travaux préparatoires* of the Egyptian Civil Law have decided that '...regulating the public services related contracting is connected to administrative legislation, in addition to civil legislation.'

> The draft-law evidently tackles the civil aspect of this contracting, and the principles adopted in this regard are only a confirmation of the tendencies manifested by the Egyptian Judiciary, which tried whenever possible by returning to the general rules, to fill the loophole in the existing legislation (precedent to the issuance of the new civil law). The draft law is also keen to decide only the provisions that may come in line with the Egyptian administrative legislation... .[37]

Egypt's administrative judiciary is the only jurisdiction in settling the disputes related to traditional concession contract or any other administrative contracts. It is recognized, according to the French vision, that the administrative judiciary is not obligated to respect the general rules contained in the civil law unless only to the extent to which such rules are deemed as merely an application to the general principles that do not conflict with the basics of the administrative law detailed hereinabove.

The traditional concession in MENA countries' civil codes

The articles contained in the civil law are not new. Article (668) defines the concession contract. Article (669) stipulates that the service shall be performed according to the terms of the concession contract, which is not new. Such clauses, according to the *travaux préparatoires* statement, are 'binding to the person or the company assigned to exploiting the public service, and binding to customers as well ... the due observation toward such clauses is attributed to its administrative regulations character.' Article (670) is an application of the rule of equal treatment of beneficiaries by public services, which is one of the rules regulating public utility. The same applies to Article (672) on improper implementation of pricing tariffs. Article (671) is deemed an application of the

37 Civil Law *Travaux Préparatoires* Group, Part 5, 68 et seq.

principle of the public utility change or adjustment capability as it entitles the Authority to reconsider the pricing lists. Finally, Article (673), whilst obligating the concessionaire to be liable for any failure or malfunction in the service tools save as cases of *force majeure*, it is deemed an application of the first batch of principles regulating public utility, i.e. the conduct of public utilities' regularity and continuity.

Accordingly, the civil law has not been restricted to a civil aspect in nature, as indicated in the *travaux préparatoires*; however, it has addressed administrative provisions. This is evidenced by the fact that the principles of the civil law are applied by the administrative judiciary without a need to a legal provision, and this proves its administrative nature.

End-users frequently receive the service pursuant to a private contract concluded between them and the concessionaire. Such contracts are civil contracts according to the French and MENA countries' legal systems. However, such civil contract is closely related to the concession contract as the clauses contained therein shall be within the scope of agreements and terms stipulated in the concession contract and both the concessionaire and the end-users shall not agree on otherwise.

These are the provisions characterizing a traditional concession contract, as we refer to the provisions of the general theory on administrative contracts, which are common in the concession contracts and other administrative agreements.

The legislative reforms in Egypt

Legislation has significantly developed with regard to granting concessions to infrastructure projects and public utilities. Law Nos. 100 of 1996, 229 of 1996, 3 of 1997 and 22 of 1998 amended long-standing legislation such as Law No. 129 of 1947 in respect to granting concessions relating to exploitation of natural resources and public utilities.

The four new laws cover the electricity sector, road sectors, specialized ports and civil aviation and airports, virtually marking a new advanced trend as far as administrative contracts and state international administrative transactions are concerned.

At this stage, it is appropriate to refer briefly to the legal regime governing BOOT transactions as part of the Egyptian legal system, in view of its critical importance in understanding the current situation of PPPs and the proposed modifications and enhancements to related legal regime. As pointed out previously, the legal regime controlling the concession-granting process for public utilities is governed by Law Nos. 129 of 1947 and 61 of 1958. The latter is concerned with granting concessions in the area of exploiting and exploring oil, gas and natural resources pursuant to Article (123) of the Egyptian Constitution. Both laws were promulgated more than a half century ago. In fact, dynamic contractual relationships needed rapid changes and modifications rather than static ones. Accordingly, the Egyptian Legislature realized that such outdated legislation was not applicable to BOOT transactions. The latter transactions are neither compatible with

74 Le Contrat Administratif *theory*

administrative contracts nor with their traditional nature. Therefore, the Egyptian Parliament promulgated the above-mentioned four new laws in the late 1990s for granting public utility concessions by virtue of BOOT agreements. These four are Law Nos. 100 of 1996, 229 of 1996, 3 of 1997 and 22 of 1998, granting BOOT concessions for the sectors of electricity, public roads and highways, airports and civil aviation and specialized ports, respectively.

The new legislation include various modifications and enhancements to the previous legal regime governing concession-granting in the field of public utilities. The concession-granting period has been extended from 30 years under the previous two laws to 99 years (as a cap) under the four new laws. In addition, the state now plays a limited role in the contractual process; it is merely the technical and financial supervisor of the entire process. It cannot unilaterally amend service prices offered by the concessionaire as was the case in the traditional concession legislation. Service pricing for end-users is subject to contractual clauses as well as to the consent of the foreign contractor rather than to a regulatory clause that could be amended unilaterally by the state.[38] State intervention in the contractual process in terms of BOOT agreements is very limited compared to the old regime in the traditional concession agreements concluded by and between the state and domestic contractors. The aim of current legislation is to meet economic expectations of foreign contractors at the time of tendering and also in the course of preparing technical and financial feasibility studies, especially given the fact that this is a long-term agreement that renders necessary, from the contractor's perspective, that a financial equilibrium be maintained during the span of the contract, which may last for decades.[39] Some of the fundamental legislative policies behind the promulgation of the current four laws aim to encourage private foreign entities to enter into international infrastructure project tenders announced by the Egyptian government. Moreover, these policies further aim to encourage major foreign entities in the sector to generate more FDI, as Egypt is a developing country that had intensively embarked on infrastructure developments a few decades ago. There is an essential need to promulgate new legislation for good transactions for all sectors in the country as well as detailed executive regulations that are compatible with each sector's needs.[40]

Conclusions

The excessive clauses in administrative contracts are directly relating to the powers that the state may exercise before the private contracting entity, whether juristic entity or an individual. Unlike private contracts, the administration has

---

38 For the regulatory clauses that can unilaterally be amended by the state, see in the Arab doctrine: Soad El Sharkawy, *The Administrative Contracts*, Dar El Nahda El Arabia 2003, 65.
39 Mohamed A.M. Ismail, *Globalization and New International Public Works Agreements in Developing Countries, An Analytical Perspective*, Routledge 2011, 62.
40 Ismail, ibid., 64.

Le Contrat Administratif *theory*   75

excessive powers in administrative contracts as those contracts are directly relating to the running of public utilities and the target to achieve public interests. The main four features of the administration's power are:

1. The right to observe the contracting entity's performance during the contract performance.
2. The right to alter the contracting entity obligations, whether to increase it, or to reduce it.
3. The right to impose certain penalties upon the contracting entity in case of default.
4. The right to terminate the contract without default from the contracting entity.

The Appeal Administrative Court of the Egyptian Conseil d'État pointed out that:

> the administration has to observe the contract performance, to impose penalties upon the contracting entity in case of default, to unilaterally alter the contract, and to unilaterally terminate the contract for public interests purposes if the contract performance is not necessary. The administration may exercise those rights and duties even if they are not stipulated in the contract as they are relating to public policy, without any justification relating to contract law stipulations which impose the power of the contractual clauses upon contracting parties in civil law, or the privity of contract. Unlike civil and commercial contracts, the contracting parties in administrative contracts are not in an equal bargaining power.[41]

The Supreme Administrative Court pointed out that:

> Administrative contracts directly relate to the public utilities and as a result to this fact, the administration has the power to observe and direct the administrative contract performance, and it can amend the contractual provisions from time to time to be more useful for the public utilities without any reliance on the contractual provisions power that is in favor of the private person. The administration may unilaterally terminate the contract and the private person may claim compensation if he has the right. This is different from the civil and commercial law contracts.[42]

Administrative contracts often contain excessive clauses that the administration can use with the private persons, in addition to legislation such as the state

---

41 Case No. 982 of the judicial year No. 7, session of 30 June 1957.
42 Judicial year 13, session 2 March, 1968, mentioned in Soliman Al Tamawy, *The General Principles of Administrative Contracts*, Dar Al Fikr Al Araby 2008.

76 Le Contrat Administratif *theory*

procurement laws in Arab countries and the regulatory framework. The nature of the administrative contract, as it is directly connected with the public utilities and public interests, is always the source to the powers which the contracting state can exercise in this contract and at the same time this nature imposes certain duties upon the contracting entity with the state. The results to this legal fact in MENA countries are:

1. If the contractual provisions of the administrative contract did not stipulate that the administration can exercise its powers in the contract, the administration still have the right to use its excessive powers if this is required to achieve the pubic interests. The source of those powers does not exist in the administrative contract itself, but it exists in the principles of the administrative law as stipulated in the Egyptian Conseil D'État case law, thus a contract that contains exorbitant clauses and extraordinary excessive powers in favor of the state has the administrative contracts nature.
2. For the above-mentioned legal justifications, if the contract contains some excessive clauses that enable the state to exercise unilaterally some powers, the contracting state can use other powers that are not stipulated in the contract, as the state relies whilst using the latter powers on the general principles of the administrative law and, in particular, the administrative contract principles which aim at achieving public interests.
3. The contracting state cannot by its consent in the administrative contract waive the right of the administration whether totally or partially, to exercise the excessive powers granted to the administration. It cannot even restrict those excessive powers, as those powers are the state powers which cannot subject to consent or agreement to waive it by the contracting state. Further, the waiver from exercising those powers is not subject to conciliation. In administrative law principles, any agreement to the contrary is void.

4 The trajectory of the legislative and regulatory intervention from MENA countries to permit PPP techniques

Introduction

The leading schools in economics such as Chicago school minimize state intervention in economic activities to the minimum; however, state intervention to permit PPP techniques through legislation and regulatory frameworks is necessary in MENA countries as the permissibility of PPP contracts was controversial in some MENA countries.

PPP techniques have been exercised in practice as there were many PPP projects in reality before promulgating PPP legislation in many MENA countries. This situation happened in Egypt and many other MENA countries.

PPP legislation in MENA countries is a codification of PPP techniques. Further, it creates a new procedural framework to select the private entity in PPP transactions different from the traditional Public Procurement law, which is convenient for traditional concessions but not for PPPs.[1]

MENA governments' intervention to create legislative and regulatory frameworks to govern procedural and substantive issues was necessary for PPP contracts providing that the party autonomy concept is the base for contractual transactions in PPP techniques. The source for obligations in PPP techniques and projects is the contract between the contracting parties. The necessity for MENA governments' intervention has legal and factual justifications, as the main concept for state transactions is to enter into administrative contracts, which in traditional concessions and other administrative contracts contain excessive clauses.[2] The trajectory of the legislative and regulatory intervention

---

1 It worth noting that there is no significant progress in PPP legislation model law to create a globally agreed standard model law. There are several international instruments such as the UNCITRAL Legislative Guide on Privately Financed Infrastructure Projects (2000), European Union concession-related materials including the Concession Directive of 2014, the UNECE Guidebook on promoting good governance in Public Private Partnership (2008) and various World Bank and PPIAF initiatives dealing with PPP, including the latest World Bank Benchmarking PPP Procurement 2017. See: Bruno De Cazalet, The expected benefit of CIS PPP model law, *International Business Law Journal*, 2017, 2, 97–114.

2 Ragab Mahmoud, *Public-Private Partnership Contracts*, Dar Al Nahda Al Arabia 2007, in Arabic and for the same author see: *Partnership Contracts Between Public and Private Sectors*,

78 *Intervention to permit PPP techniques*

from the MENA countries to permit new PPP patterns has historical developments particularly in Egypt, Kuwait and some other MENA countries. For instance, in Egypt the General Assembly for Legal Opinion and Legislation in the Egyptian Conseil d'État issued a legal opinion to decide that BOOT agreements are subject to the previous state procurement law, which was promulgated by Law No. 89 of 1989 as a result of the absence of a specialized legislation regulating procedural matters for BOT or PPP techniques.[3] State intervention was necessary, particularly as there is no constitutional ban in Arab constitutions.

Morocco and Tunisia as of 1 October 2014 indicated that many changes and transitions are taking place as governments improve the institutional framework for PPPs.

The main findings for some MENA countries include:

- **Egypt:** Has enacted specific PPP legislation No. 67 of 2010 as the first PPP legislation in the MENA region and has created an active PPP central unit. However, there remains scope for concessions under several sector-specific laws.
- **Jordan:** Has a good track record of successful infrastructure projects that have largely been procured under the existing privatization law. A PPP law that will become the exclusive legal regime for PPPs is working its way through the ratification process and will bring greater clarity to the legal framework.
- **Morocco:** Has a tradition of public involvement in infrastructure through concession arrangements. A PPP central unit was created in 2011. The central unit was also largely responsible for a new PPP law that was adopted by the House of Representatives in February 2014.

Egypt: before promulgating PPP legislation in 2010

Egypt has a long-standing tradition of concessions, starting with the Suez Canal in the nineteenth century, which was further developed through the country's concession legislation of 1947 (Law No. 129 of 1947) that still exists today. By derogation to the 1947 concession law, sector specific laws were enacted in the late 1990s for electricity, airports, specialized ports, and the railway and roads sectors, allowing more flexibility in the drafting of related concession agreements.[4]

Dar Al Nahda Al Arabia 2010, in Arabic; Sarwat Badawi, *General Theory of Administrative Contracts*, Dar Al Nahda Al Arabia 1994, in Arabic; Soad Al Sharkawi, *Administrative Contracts*, Dar Al Nahda Al Arabia 1998, in Arabic; Gaber Gad Nassar, *Administrative Contracts*, Dar Al Nahda Al Arabia 2005, in Arabic.

3 The General Assembly for Legal Opinion and Legislation, legal opinion No. 602, 4 June 2003, file No. 100/2/14.

4 OECD, *Public-Private Partnerships in the Middle East and North Africa, A Handbook for Policy Makers*, OECD Publications 39, available on: www.oecd.org/mena/competitiveness/PPP%20Handbook_EN_with_covers.pdf, Last accessed on 15 July 2019.

The legal regime governing the grant of concessions in public utilities is governed by the Concession Law for Public Utility No. 129 of 1947 and Concession Law for the Exploitation for Natural Resources No. 61 of 1958. The latter law is concerned with granting concessions in the exploitation and exploration of oil, gas and natural resources pursuant to the Egyptian constitution. Both laws were promulgated more than half a century ago. In fact, dynamic, contractual relationships need rapid changes and modifications rather than static contracts. However, in recent decades and particularly in the 1990s the Egyptian legislature has realized that this old legislation is not applicable to BOOT transactions and that they are in contradiction with the character of BOOT. Further, BOOT transactions are not compatible with the administrative contract (*Le Contrat Administratif*).[5]

New techniques have appeared in MENA countries in the past decades. BOT and BOOT and other similar techniques are new enhanced types of traditional concession agreements in developing countries, and have wide currency in Arab countries.

More than a decade ago, the Egyptian government promulgated partial legislative amendments to the traditional concession laws, which were themselves adopted more than half a century ago (Law No. 129 of 1947). These partial legislative amendments – laws No. 100 of 1996, No. 229 of 1996, No. 3 of 1997 and No. 22 of 1998 – granted BOOT concessions in four sectors: electricity, public roads and highways, airports and civil aviation, and specialized ports, respectively.[6] Many MENA countries had not codified BOT/ BOOT transactions in a unified legislation at the moment when PPPs rapidly began to appear in the region.[7]

Accordingly, the Egyptian Parliament promulgated four new laws in the field of granting public utility concessions through BOOT agreements. These are Laws No. 100 of 1996, No. 229 of 1996, No. 3 of 1997 and No. 22 of 1998,

---

5 Some authorities in Arab doctrine consider new types of state transactions such as BOT and PPP contracts as commercial contracts, see: Hani Sarie El Din, *Legal and Contractual Arrangements for Infrastructure Projects Financed by Private Sector*, Dar El Nahda El Arabia 2001, in Arabic, *Legal and Contractual Regime for BOT No 177*, El Ahram El Eqtisadi Book 2002, in Arabic; Mohamed A.M. Ismail, *Globalization and New International Public Works Agreements in Developing Countries, An Analytical Perspective*, Routledge 2011, and for the same author see: *International Infrastructure Agreements and PPPs in Developing Countries: Substantive Principles, with special reference to Arab and Latin American Countries, EPPPL*, Lexxion 2011.

6 Hani Sarie El Din, *Legal and Contractual Arrangements for Infrastructure Projects Financed by Private Sector*, Dar El Nahda El Arabia 2001, in Arabic, *Legal and Contractual Regime for BOT No. 177*, El Ahram El Eqtisadi Book 2002, in Arabic; Mohamed A.M. Ismail, *Globalization and New International Public Works Agreements in Developing Countries, An Analytical Perspective*, Routledge 2011, and for the same author see: *International Infrastructure Agreements and PPPs in Developing Countries: Substantive Principles, with special reference to Arab and Latin American Countries, EPPPL*, Lexxion 2011.

7 OECD, Public-Private Partnerships in the Middle East and North Africa, A Handbook for Policy Makers, 39, available on: www.oecd.org/mena/competitiveness/PPP%20Handbook_EN_with_covers.pdf, Last accessed on 15 July, 2019.

80 *Intervention to permit PPP techniques*

concerning the granting of BOOT concessions in electricity, public roads and highways, airports and civil aviation and specialized ports.

The abovementioned legislation included various modifications and enhancements to the existing legal regime, governing the grant of concessions in public utilities. The concession period has increased from 30 years in the previous two laws to 99 years (as a cap) in the four laws. The state plays a limited role in the contractual process; it is the technical and financial supervisors who have control over the entire process. It cannot unilaterally amend service prices offered by the concessionaire as is the case in traditional concessional legislation. Service prices to end-users are subject to contractual clauses as is the consent of the foreign contractor rather than regulatory clauses that can be amended unilaterally by the state.[8] State intervention in the contractual process in BOOT agreements is very limited compared with the old legal regime of traditional concession agreements if it is concluded by and between the state and domestic contractors. The aim of current legislation is to satisfy the economic expectations of foreign contractors at the time of tendering and preparing technical and financial feasibility studies, especially as this is a long-term agreement that, from the contractor's perspective, necessitates the maintenance of financial equilibrium during the span of the contract, which may last for many decades. Some of the fundamental legislative policies, behind the promulgation of the current four laws, aim at encouraging private foreign entities to enter into international infrastructure project tenders announced by the Egyptian government. Moreover, policies aim at encouraging major foreign entities in the sector to generate further FDI as Egypt is a developing country that intensively started infrastructure developments more than three decades ago.

Finally, Law No. 22 of 1998 concerning specialized ports included both procedural and substantive rules. Procedural rules concerning contractor selection are both competitive and transparent. The most substantive adjustment, as stated above, is the increase or ceiling of the BOOT concession duration not to exceed 99 years. These developments were important in the Egyptian legal system as the old Concession Law (which is applicable to other infrastructure sectors) stipulates a cap for concessions not to exceed 30 years (Law No. 129 of 1947).

Despite partial developments in the Egyptian legislation in BOOT transactions, a complete set of legislative and regulatory rules was still needed by that time. Partial legislation concerns some sectors, as stated above; meanwhile, other sectors require a new legislative policy which needs to be adopted.

Egypt: after promulgating PPP legislation in 2010

Egypt has established a PPP Central Unit (PPPCU) at the Ministry of Finance in 2006. The PPPCU role is preparing a portfolio of new projects, and conducting pre-feasibility studies for projects. A national PPP program was initiated in

---

8 For the regulatory clauses that can be unilaterally amended by the state in the Arab doctrine, see: El Soad Sharkawy, *The Administrative Contracts*, Dar El Nahda El Arabia 1998, 65.

Intervention to permit PPP techniques 81

2006, and called for comprehensive legislation to govern and regulate different PPP schemes.

In 2010, Egypt enacted specific PPP legislation, which was promulgated by Law No. 67 of 2010. The Egyptian PPP legislation provides clear and significant legal investment protection, in line with internationally recognized standards. The Egyptian PPP legislation adopts the international standards and concepts recognized by international organizations such as the World Bank, OECD and UN organs. In the light of a growing government interest in pursuing infrastructure PPPs, the traditional concessions model was abandoned in recent years in favor of a PPP techniques.

The 2010 PPP law has significantly increased PPP investments and the inward of FDI in infrastructure and public utilities projects. Instability since 2011 has delayed some projects, but there is currently a renewed emphasis on the role of PPPs, confirmed by the Egyptian government practice in new PPP projects since 2014.

PPP legal framework in Egypt

PPP legislation promulgated by Law No. 67 of 2010 and its executive regulations regulate partnership with the private sector in infrastructure projects, services and public utilities, which are the basis of the PPP legal framework. This PPP law is a comprehensive and reasonably workable legal framework for PPPs, but the same cannot be said for the granting of concessions in general; these can still be undertaken under numerous pieces of older legislation. The PPP law only applies to projects procured on a PPP basis with a minimum investment value of EGP 100 million (about £4,788 million). There are no legal restrictions on the sectors eligible for PPP. Projects can be concluded in commercial sectors, such as energy, transport, water, and oil and gas. Projects can be also concluded in noncommercial government services such as schools, hospitals and housing. If any of the criteria for dealing with a project under the PPP law are not met, the relevant sectors specific law applies. The Egyptian Electricity Law No. 87 for year 2015 plays a significant role as the legislation regulating electricity sector in Egypt.[9]

PPP institutional framework in Egypt

A PPP Central Unit was established by the Ministry of Finance in 2006 as the main entity responsible for the initiation and implementation of PPP projects in Egypt. The PPP Central Unit was established by the 2010 PPP law. It provides that the Minister of Finance stipulates the structure of the unit, while the executive regulations of the law determine the administrative and financial framework for operations. This includes the Unit's relationship with other public organizations, its

9 The African Legal Support Facility ALSF, PPP country Profile, Egypt, available at: https://www.aflsf.org/sites/default/files/PPP%20Country%20Profile%20-%20Tunisie.pdf, last accessed on 20 July 2019.

82 *Intervention to permit PPP techniques*

operational system and employee remuneration. In practice, the Unit is increasingly involved in the negotiation and execution levels of PPP bids and contracts. The law also provides that PPP 'satellite units' are to be established, whenever necessary, within the different administrative authorities.[10]

The law provides that a Supreme Committee for Public Private Partnership Affairs shall be formed and chaired by the prime minister. The PPP Supreme Committee is notably responsible for setting an integrated national PPP policy, endorsing use of the PPP structure for administrative authority projects, monitoring the financial resources allocation to meet obligations resulting from PPP contracts, issuing rules and general criteria for PPPs and endorsing standard PPP contracts for use in different sectors.

The PPP Central Unit provides technical, financial and legal expertise to the PPP Supreme Committee as well as to the PPP satellite units. It is responsible for setting and following up on procedures for the tendering and conclusion of PPP contracts, as well as their execution. The consent of the PPP Unit is necessary for the development and granting of PPP projects in Egypt, and the Supreme Committee for PPP Affairs must approve PPP tenders.

Kuwait before 2014: the situation before promulgating PPP legislation

Law No. 7/2008: regulating public private partnership (the 'PPP law')

The PPP law established a legislative framework, built upon the principles of transparency and competitiveness, to promote and facilitate PPPs in public infrastructure and land-based development projects in the State of Kuwait. PPPs can be undertaken by any public entity (Government Ministry or Department, or entity with an independent or supplementary budget) that enters into a contract with an investor (a private-sector company established under Kuwaiti laws) to implement a project, through the execution by an investor on land owned by the State, for a certain period. The focal point for the implementation of the provisions of the PPP law is the Partnerships Technical Bureau (PTB), Ministry of Finance.

The salient features of the law include:

- No public body may enter into a PPP contract without first obtaining the approval of the higher committee for PPPs. PTB provided technical support to the higher committee in its decision-making;
- The law limited the term of the PPP projects to 30 years. In certain cases (where proved necessary in the feasibility study), the committee may

---

10 OECD, Public-Private Partnerships in the Middle East and North Africa, A Handbook for Policy Makers, 39, available on: www.oecd.org/mena/competitiveness/PPP%20Handbook_EN_with_covers.pdf, Last accessed on 16 July, 2019.

Intervention to permit PPP techniques 83

approve a lifespan of 40 years. If the project's bid documents do not contain a term, its lifespan will be deemed to be 25 years;

- The PPP law also restricted the disposal or grant of any lien, mortgage, or other real rights to the subject PPP Pprojects;
- PPP Pprojects awarded prior to the PPP law's enactment cannot be amended, extended, or renewed. Any agreement stipulating otherwise will be considered void;
- A PPP project was subject to prior and subsequent review by the Audit Bureau of Kuwait;
- The state had to collect a fee from the project for use of state land;
- Two approved (by the PTB) appraisers evaluated the land's market value and usufruct rights (rent) value and used the lower value for assessing the value of the PPP project;
- A project exceeding KD 60 million had to be carried out by a PPP project company that will be a special-purpose vehicle formed as a Kuwaiti joint stock company, in which up to 40% shares would be offered to an investor. The majority of the remainder of the shares were offered to Kuwaiti citizens;
- The law allowed Unsolicited Proposals. The Proposal had to be a comprehensive feasibility study based on an unprecedented, innovative idea. If accepted by the higher committee, the project will still follow the regular procurement procedures; however, the Unsolicited Proposer will be given up to 5% advantage in the evaluation scores, at the discretion of the higher committee, should it choose to participate in the bidding;
- All companies listed on the Kuwait Stock Exchange were considered pre-qualified to bid for PPP projects. Unlisted local and foreign entities needed to apply for pre-Qqualification as and when projects were tendered, and had to be approved by the higher committee;
- The executive regulations the PPP law provisions have been issued under Decree No. 256/2008.

Institutional structure for PPPs

The institutional structure for the implementation of PPP projects, as presented in the PPP law and its regulations, consisted of the following four levels:

The council of ministers

The Council of Ministers had to:

- Allocate state-owned real estate, by means of a decree, to Arab or foreign diplomatic missions on a reciprocal basis, and to international and regional organizations in Kuwait upon a presentation by the Finance Minister pursuant to Article 1 of the law;
- Be responsible for selling and/or renting State-owned movable assets by means of a decree on the recommendation of the competent line

84 *Intervention to permit PPP techniques*

Minister, provided that its value is not greater than KD 50,000. State-owned movable assets may be disposed free of charge by a decision of the Council of Ministers if their value is not greater than KD 50,000, as per Article 1of the law;

- On recommendation of the higher committee, designate a project valued between KD 60–250 million as a project of 'special nature'. Special nature projects do not require the formation of a joint stock company or shortlisting of bidders; instead, companies listed on the Kuwait stock market;
- Exchange and other companies approved by the higher committee can compete for a PPP project, as per Article 6 of the law;
- Appoint civil servant specialists to the higher committee pursuant to Article 11 of the law.

The higher committee (HC) – set up under the provisions of Article 11 of the PPP law and Decree No. 145 of 2008

The HC was chaired by the Minister of Finance and consisted of the Minister of Municipality, Minister of Public Works, Minister of Trade and Industry, Under-secretary of Electricity and Water, Head of the Public Authority of the Environment, Head of the PTB and two experienced specialists to be named by the Council of Ministers from among civil servants, as per Article 11 of the law and Article 3 of Decree No. 145 of 2008. A representative of the public entity responsible for the project used to be invited to the meetings.

The HC and its PTB had special financial allocations as part of the Finance Ministry's budget, and its decisions took effect only after approval by the Finance Minister. The HC and PTB had to be charged with the following:

- Providing final approval (based on a report by the PTB) to the public entities before they can enter into a PPP contract, as per Article 4 of the law and Article 5 of Decree No. 145 of 2008;
- Developing general policies and approving detailed documents for the projects and Unsolicited Proposals of strategic and developmental importance to the national economy, as per Article 11 of the law and Article 5 of Decree No. 145 of 2008;
- Referring projects and Unsolicited Proposals to the PTB for study and preparing a report for the higher committee; approving projects (based on a report by the TB) before they are advertised, as per Article 11 of the law and Article 5 of Decree No. 145 of 2008;
- Determining which relevant public entity will take part in tendering the project and signing the PPP contract and monitoring the project's implementation and operation under the public entity's supervision and control, as per Article 11 of the law and Article 5 of Decree No. 145 of 2008;
- Giving the public entity the final approval for terminating the contract for public interest, as per Article 11 of the law and Article 5 of Decree No. 145 of 2008;

- Assigning a public entity to establish a public stock company for projects whose value is greater than KD 60 million, as per Article 5 of the law;
- Seeking approval of the Council of Ministers for exemption from flotation of a public stock company, instead resorting to competitive procurement for development projects of special nature, as per Article 6 of the law;
- Approving the reimbursement cost of the feasibility study conducted by an Unsolicited Proposer, as per Article 8 of the law;
- Approving the assignment of a contract to others, in full or part, and/or any change in the investor's legal form (only after the designing and implementation phase, and after an appropriate operation period of no less than three years), as per Article 13 of the law;
- Authorize the public entity to tender the management of projects through public auction, one year before they are accrued to the state, pursuant to the provisions of this law, as per Article 16 of the law.

The partnerships technical bureau (PTB) – set up under Article 11 of the PPP law and Decree No. 145 of 2008

The PTB was the focal point agency for Kuwait's PPP program. It was involved in all phases of the project from inception to financial close. It acted as the technical secretariat to the higher committee and support it in all its functions and decision making. The head of the PTB was a member of the HC *pursuant to Article 11 of the law.*

The PTB's role was:

- To draft and/or approve the terms of reference of the transaction advisor;
- To appoint a transaction advisor responsible for conducting the feasibility study and undertaking project procurement;
- To provide quality professional technical assistance to public entities undertaking PPP projects throughout the PPP project cycle in order to help them achieve a quality PPP outcome and comply with PPP law and its regulations;
- To recommend to the higher committee the granting or declining of approvals, in terms of PPP law and its regulations;
- To develop and disseminate PPP policy, guidebooks, standardization, and toolkits;
- To disseminate accurate and up-to-date PPP project information;
- To build PPP capacity;
- To build confidence and integrity in Kuwait's PPP market;
- To assign for every PPP project registered with the PTB a technical specialist, whose role was to:

  - Support the public entity through every step of the PPP life cycle, drawing on best practice from other projects, and provide guidance on how the public entity can optimally meet the requirements of PPP law and its regulations;

86 *Intervention to permit PPP techniques*

- Present a report to the head of the PTB, at various stages of approval, for onward recommendations to the higher committee for approving or disapproving a public entity's application;
- Facilitate efficient processing for approval of higher committee applications;
- Ensure that communication among the higher committee, the PTB, and the public entity is always managed professionally.

The public entities

The public entities had to:

- Enter into PPP contracts with local and/or foreign investors for projects on State-owned land after approval of the higher committee pursuant to Article 4 of the law;
- Act as *ex officio* member of the higher committee when its projects are involved, pursuant to Article 11 of the law;
- Collect a fee (rent for the use of land) from the investors if possible under the contract pursuant to Article 14 of the law;
- Monitor the performance of the investor and settle disputes as per the provisions of the PPP contract, or agree to settle disputes via arbitration pursuant to Article 15 of the law;
- Tender management of projects one year before they are accrued to the State, pursuant to the provisions of this law, through public auction pursuant to Article 16 of the law.

2014 and after: the situation in Kuwait after promulgating the PPP legislation

The Kuwait PPP Law No. 116 of 2014 establishes a legislative framework to promote PPPs in public infrastructure and services in Kuwait, based on the principles of transparency and competitiveness. A PPP is defined in the PPP law as:

> a project to implement an activity through which the State targets to provide a public service of economic, social or service importance, or to improve an existing public service or to develop, reduce the costs or increase the efficiency of any such service, procured by the Authority in cooperation with the public entity and in accordance with the PPP Model after the approval of the higher committee, provided it does not contradict with the provisions of Articles 152 and 153 of the Constitution.[11]

11 Article 1 of the Kuwaiti PPP legislation. It is worth noting that Articles 152 and 153 of the Kuwaiti constitution deal with granting natural resources and public utilities' concessions or any monopoly which has to be by law in each case and for a certain

The main features of the Kuwaiti PPP Law No. 116 of 2014 may be underscored in some major points. PPPs must follow the 'PPP Model' which, in Article (1) of the PPP law, is defined as:

> a model whereby a private investor invests in state-owned real property – if required – in one of the projects procured by the Authority in collaboration with one of the public entities after signing an agreement with the investor to implement or build or develop or operate or rehabilitate a service or an infrastructure project, and to provide financing thereto and operate or manage and develop the project, for a specified term, after which the project shall be transferred to the State; the foregoing shall be carried out in one of two forms: 1) the implementation of the project in consideration for fees – for services or works performed – to be paid to the investor by the end-users or by the public entities who have entered into an agreement with the investor, and whose objectives are in compliance with the project or by both the beneficiaries and the public entities; and 2) the purpose of the project is for the investor to implement a project with strategic importance to the national economy and to exploit it for a specified term. In both cases, the investor shall pay a fee for the use of any State-owned real property allocated for the project.

In accordance with this definition, the PPP model in Kuwait therefore requires the following criteria to be met:

- A private investor to invest in a project on state-owned property (if required);
- Procurement of the project by KAPP[12], in collaboration with a public entity;
- The signing of an agreement with the investor to implement or build or develop or operate or rehabilitate a service or an infrastructure project, to provide financing to this end and to operate or manage and develop the project, for a specific period; and
- Following the end of the agreement, the transfer of the infrastructure facilities to the State.

The salient features of the PPP law include:[13]

---

period of time, PPP Guidebook, Kuwait Authority for Partnership Projects, pp. 11–13, in Arabic, available at: http://www.kapp.gov.kw/Library/Files/Uploaded%20Files/arabic/2018-الشراكة%20عام%20مشاري20%ةيهلة20%الإرشادي20%الدليل.pdf, last accessed on 19 October 2019.

12 The PPP law of 2014 creates a new PPP governing authority, the Kuwait Authority for Partnership Projects (KAPP).

13 PPP Guidebook, Kuwaiti Authority for Partnership Projects, pp. 11–13, in Arabic, available at: http://www.kapp.gov.kw/Library/Files/Uploaded%20Files/arabic/2018-الشراكة%20عام%20مشاري20%ةيهلة20%الإرشادي20%الدليل.pdf, last accessed on 19 October 2019.

88 *Intervention to permit PPP techniques*

- In general, no public body may enter into a PPP contract without first obtaining the approval of the higher committee for PPPs;[14]
- KAPP provides advisory support to the higher committee in its decision-making;
- A time limit for PPP projects of 50 years[15] (if a project's bid documents do not contain a certain term, its lifespan will be deemed to be 25 years);
- Restrictions on the sale or mortgage of State land/public property in PPP projects, although security over the 'private assets' are permitted, which includes revenues of the project and shares in the project company;
- Provisions allowing the State to collect a fee from the project for use of State land;
- Projects exceeding KWD 60 million in value must be carried out by a PPP project company, which will be a Special Purpose Vehicle formed as a Kuwaiti joint stock company, in which no less than 26% and up to 44% shares would be offered to an investor, with the majority of the remainder of the shares being offered to the Kuwaiti citizens and public entities allowed to invest in the project (subject to these shares being held temporarily by KAPP until full operation of the project);
- Provisions allowing for Unsolicited Proposals of two types: (i) Initiative Projects and (ii) Distinguished Projects;
- Possibility of settlement of disputes through arbitration; and
- Grievance mechanism for violations of the PPP law and the executive regulations.

The Kuwaiti PPP law of 2014 provides for transition arrangements. Projects existing before the entry into force of the PPP law shall continue until the expiry of the term in the agreement or until termination. Upon the entry of the PPP law into force, no amendments, renewals or extensions may be given on such projects, and such projects shall be handed back to the State for re-tendering or for operating and managing the project itself (in accordance with Article 30 of the PPP law). Further transitional arrangements are in place for projects whose term has expired at the time the PPP law came into force. These may be granted a one-time extension for a maximum period of one year pursuant to their respective contractual provisions and subject to the approval of the higher committee.[16]

---

14 There are a few exceptions to this general rule, such as is the case with the Public Authority for Housing Welfare established under Law No. (47) of 1993, which may tender PPPs within its scope of work.
15 Under the IWPPP law and the IWPP regulations the time limit for PPP projects is capped at 40 years.
16 Article 7 of the Kuwaiti PPP law. PPP Guidebook, Kuwaiti Authority for Partnership Projects, 13, in Arabic, available at: http://www.kapp.gov.kw/Library/Files/Uploaded%20Files/arabic/2018-الشراكة20%مشاريع20%هيئة20%الإرشادي20%الدليل.pdf, last accessed on 19 October 2019.

Intervention to permit PPP techniques 89

It is worth noting that PPP executive regulations[17] were issued to set out further details on the project flow process, procurement, and implementation of PPPs in Kuwait.

Differentiation between the 2008 and 2014 legislation[18]

The PPP law replaces the previous Law No. 7 of 2008 regarding the Regulation of Build, Operate and Transfer (BOT) Operations, and the new PPP law was designed to support the Government of Kuwait's program to promote collaboration between the public and private sectors to develop infrastructure and to provide services to Kuwaiti citizens and local residents. More specifically, the legal framework under the new PPP law is aimed at enhancing the procurement process for PPP projects in Kuwait, clarifying the provisions for their implementation, and bringing it better into line with international standards to attract more private sector investments into Kuwait. The following points underscore the key differences between the two laws:[19]

- It is important to refer to the project company and shareholding structure as there are some differences between both previous and current legislation. The PPP law clarifies that, for projects that are estimated to be worth less than KWD 60 million in total cost, the successful investor shall establish a project company. For projects with total costs deemed to be above KWD 60 million, KAPP will establish a joint stock company with an exception for 'projects of a special nature' as detailed in Article 16 of the law. The method of calculating the value of the project is changed in the PPP law, such that only capital expenditure is considered in the calculation, which,

---

17 Decree No. 78 of 2015.
18 It is important to refer to the interface of PPP law in Kuwait with other legislation as the PPP law must be considered alongside the entire legal framework in Kuwait. These laws include, but are not limited to, land laws, companies' law, investment laws, environmental and social regulations. Before embarking on any PPP project in Kuwait, local legal counsel should be sought to understand how these laws might impact the project. One law has a particularly important role to play in PPPs, which is Law No. 39 of 2010 on the Incorporation of Kuwaiti Joint Stock Companies to Undertake the Building and Execution of Electricity Power and Water Desalination Stations in Kuwait (the IWPP law), and the associated IWPP executive regulations. Essentially, the IWPP Law outlines specific requirements concerning the construction and implementation of electric power and water desalination plant projects in Kuwait as part of a PPP arrangement. The IWPP Law governs those projects which fall under its mandate, including projects which are purely power projects without any water desalination component. In case of conflicts between the IWPP Law and the PPP law, the former will prevail. However, where the IWPP Law is silent on matters that, in turn, are covered in the PPP law, the provisions of the latter apply to such projects.
19 PPP Guidebook, Kuwaiti Authority for Partnership Projects, pp. 13–15, in Arabic, available at: http://www.kapp.gov.kw/Library/Files/Uploaded%20Files/arabic/الدليل%20الارشادي%20لهيئة%20مشاريع%20الشراكة-2018.pdf, last accessed on 19 October 2019.

90   *Intervention to permit PPP techniques*

Table 4.1

	Share allocation under the old law (%)	Share allocation under the PPP law (%)
Project sponsors (i.e. the successful bidders)	10% [Art. 5(b)]	26%–44% [Art. 13(2)]
Kuwaiti citizens, acquiring shares through a transfer offered to them	50% [Art. 5(c)]	50% [Art. 13(3)]
Joint stock companies listed on the Kuwait stock market	40% [Art. 5(a)]	–
Kuwaiti public entities (i.e. government entities)	May be allocated up to 20%, equally deducted from Kuwaitis and joint stock companies listed on the Kuwait Stock Market [Art. 5]	6%–24% [Art. 13(1)]

in theory, should reduce the cost for most projects, allowing more to fall under the KWD 60 million threshold. If a joint stock company must be established, specific share allocations are specified under both laws, though the percentages and entities are different as shown in Table 4.1.[20]

Also, any shares that are not subscribed after the transfer of shares can then be offered to the public entities or to the private consortium, rather than being auctioned, as was the case previously, which introduced uncertainty into the shareholding structure.[21]

- The previous law prohibited amendments to contracts or authorizations, even in the event of change in law. The PPP law now permits negotiations of contracts as far as the project's technical and financial aspects are

20 PPP Guidebook, Kuwaiti Authority for Partnership Projects, p. 14, in Arabic, available at: http://www.kapp.gov.kw/Library/Files/Uploaded%20Files/arabic/الدليل20%الإرشادي20%لهيئة20%مشاريع20%الشراكة-2018.pdf, last accessed on 19 October 2019.
21 Article 15 of the PPP law.

Intervention to permit PPP techniques 91

concerned during the tendering and bid evaluation stage[22] as well as amendments to contracts after signature.[23]

- The term of PPP contract has been extended to a maximum of 50 years, from 30 years under the previous law (and 40 years with Cabinet approval), with a default of 25 years if no term is specified in the bid documents, allowing more flexibility for structuring PPPs.[24]
- Leases on state-owned land under the PPP law will be back-to back with the PPP contract, that is, the term of the lease will be set forth in the tendering documents and will be the same length as the term of the PPP.[25] The PPP law specifically annuls a provision in the State Property law that limited the length of leases on State-owned land. Aside from that, in case of termination of a PPP Agreement, the land lease is automatically terminated.
- Assets ownership and security over project assets have some developments in the PPP legislation. Pursuant to the previous law, security over project assets and land was not permitted. Under the PPP law, permitted security now includes:

security over project assets owned by the private party;
a pledge over accounts (revenues in the project); and
shares in both the project company and the consortium company, even during the initial lock-in period.[26]

- The PPP law states that the split of public/private ownership of assets will be set out in the PPP contract.[27] Pursuant to the previous law, all project assets were to be considered as 'state property,' that is, they could not be secured, and had to be transferred back to the state at the end of the term without compensation. Pursuant to the new PPP law, certain project assets are now categorized as 'private assets,' that is, they are allowed to be mortgaged and, to the extent any of these assets are transferred to the Government of Kuwait, compensation is payable. Also, the new PPP law does not stipulate

---

22 Except for those aspects that are deemed non-negotiable, Article 17 of the PPP law.
23 PPP law, Article 36.
24 PPP law, Article 18, PPP Guidebook, Kuwaiti Authority for Partnership Projects, 16, in Arabic, available at: http://www.kapp.gov.kw/Library/Files/Uploaded%20Files/arabic/ الدليل20%الارشادي20%لهيىة20%مشاريع20%الشراكة-2018.pdf, last accessed on 19 October 2019.
25 PPP law, Article 18, PPP Guidebook, Kuwaiti Authority for Partnership Projects, 16, in Arabic, available at: http://www.kapp.gov.kw/Library/Files/Uploaded%20Files/arabic/ الدليل20%الارشادي20%لهيىة20%مشاريع20%الشراكة-2018.pdf, last accessed on 19 October 2019.
26 PPP Guidebook, Kuwaiti Authority for Partnership Projects, 15, in Arabic, available at: http://www.kapp.gov.kw/Library/Files/Uploaded%20Files/ arabic/الدليل20%الارشادي20%لهيىة20%مشاريع20%الشراكة-2018.pdf, last accessed on 19 October 2019.
27 Article 18.

92 *Intervention to permit PPP techniques*

any additional criteria for foreign companies to observe other than those applicable to all proponents participating in a tender process.

- It is worth noting that the PPP law has adopted significant developed steps that are consistent with international standards in PPPs public procurement.[28] The PPP law articulates some basic principles on the procurement process for PPPs, including the principle that the selection of investors should be transparent, open, competitive, and equal, in conformity with international best practice.[29] Unsolicited Proposals, or proposals originating from the private sector, require special consideration. The executive regulations provide that all projects that are initiated by Unsolicited Proposals must be competitively tendered, but different rules apply for the two different types of Unsolicited Proposals.[30]

Institutional structure for PPPs

The institutional structure for the implementation of PPP projects, as presented in the PPP law and the executive regulations, consists of the following institutions:

The higher committee (HC)[31]

The higher committee has the powers and authorities of acting as KAPP's board of directors. It is chaired by the Minister of Finance and consists of:

- The Minister of Municipalities;
- The Minister of Public Works;
- The Minister of Trade and Industry;
- The Minister of Electricity and Water;
- The Director General of the Kuwait Environment Public Authority;
- The Director General of KAPP;
- Three experienced specialists to be named by the Council of Ministers from civil servants; and

---

28 OECD MAPS 2018 available at: http://www.mapsinitiative.org/methodology/MAPS-meth odology-for-assessing-procurement-systems.pdf; The World Bank Benchmarking PPP Procurement 2017, available at: https://ppp.worldbank.org/public-private partnership/sites/ ppp.worldbank.org/files/documents/Benchmarking_PPPs_2017_ENpdf.pdf and Procuring Infrastructure The World Bank, Public-Private Partnerships, 2018, available at: Procuring Infrastructure Public-Private Partnerships.

29 Article 8 of the PPP law.

30 PPP Guidebook, Kuwaiti Authority for Partnership Projects, 15, in Arabic, available at: http://www.kapp.gov.kw/Library/Files/Uploaded%20Files/ arabic/2018-الشراكة20%مشاري20%عهيئة20%لهيئة20%الإرشادي20%الدليل.pdf, last accessed on 19 October 2019.

31 PPP Guidebook, Kuwaiti Authority for Partnership Projects, 17, in Arabic, available at: http://www.kapp.gov.kw/Library/Files/Uploaded%20Files/ arabic/2018-الشراكة20%عمشاري20%لهيئة20%الإرشادي20%الدليل.pdf, last accessed on 19 October 2019.

Intervention to permit PPP techniques 93

- A representative of the public entity responsible for the project under consideration, who shall be invited to the concerned meeting but will not have a right to vote.

The responsibilities of the higher committee include:

- Setting the general policies for projects and initiatives of strategic importance to the national economy, identifying priorities and approving detailed documentation related thereto;
- Approving the requests of the public entities for the procurement of PPP projects;
- Proposing PPP projects to public entities;
- Approving KAPP's proposed budget and final accounts;
- Approving the financial and administrative statutes as well as KAPP's employees' regulations and its organization structure;
- Identifying the relevant public entity that will participate in the procurement of a project with KAPP and that will countersign the PPP agreement and be responsible for its implementation and monitoring;
- Approving requests for allocation of land necessary for the implementation of PPP projects, in coordination with the competent authorities;
- Approving the studies and concepts of PPP projects and approving the procurement thereof;
- Approving the successful investor for a project, on the recommendation of KAPP;
- Approving PPP contracts to be executed by public entities;
- Deciding upon the requests of public entities for contract cancellation/termination (including for public interest); and
- Examining the semi-annual report of PPP projects.

The PPP law stipulates that the decisions of the higher committee will only have an effect after they have been approved by the Minister of Finance.[32]

The Kuwait Authority for Partnership Projects (KAPP)[33]

The PPP law has created a new PPP governing authority, the Kuwait Authority for Partnership Projects (KAPP), which replaced its predecessor, the Partnerships

---

32 Article 2 of the PPP law. PPP Guidebook, Kuwaiti Authority for Partnership Projects, p. 18, in Arabic, available at: http://www.kapp.gov.kw/Library/Files/Uploaded%20Files/arabic/الدليل%20الإرشادي%20لهيئة%20مشاريع%20الشراكة-2018.pdf, last accessed on 19 October 2019.

33 PPP Guidebook, Kuwaiti Authority for Partnership Projects, pp. 18–19, in Arabic, available at: http://www.kapp.gov.kw/Library/Files/Uploaded%20Files/arabic/الدليل%20الإرشادي%20لهيئة%20مشاريع%20الشراكة-2018.pdf, last accessed on 19 October 2019.

94 *Intervention to permit PPP techniques*

Technical Bureau (PTB). KAPP is overseen by a governing board (i.e. the higher committee) and will be staffed by a Director General appointed by the Council of Ministers.[34] KAPP has a budget provided directly from the state budget rather than from the Ministry of Finance.[35] It is primarily responsible for preparing PPPs, as well as advising the higher committee. It also ensures standardization and consistency in PPP projects in Kuwait through its responsibilities of setting out procedures and creating templates.

Specifically, KAPP is responsible for:[36]

- Conducting surveys and preliminary studies to identify projects and referring them to the higher committee;
- Reviewing and studying projects and initiatives prepared by the public entities or a concept proposer and submitting appropriate recommendations regarding the same to the higher committee;
- Assessing feasibility studies, preparing and completing the studies as needed, and submitting recommendations on projects to the higher committee;
- Preparing a guidebook for PPP projects;
- Setting a mechanism for submission of initiatives, as well as their methods of evaluation and procurement;
- Setting out approaches to evaluating the performance of approved PPP projects over the entire contract period;
- Developing contract templates;
- Preparing drafts of PPP contracts and terms of reference;
- Submitting recommendations to the higher committee for approval of the selection of a successful investor;
- Incorporating public joint stock companies for PPP implementation, and determining the capital of such companies;
- Developing PPP project programs and following up on their completion, and issuing necessary decisions in relation thereto;
- Compiling and submitting a semi-annual report on PPP projects to the higher committee for approval, prior to the Ministry of Finance presenting the same to the Council of Ministers;
- Following-up on PPP project implementation and addressing any associated obstacles in collaboration with the contracting public entity; and
- Proposing the exemption of projects from taxes and custom duties and raising such recommendations with the higher committee.

---

34 Upon nomination from the Minister of Finance.
35 Though KAPP's budget is supplemented by the budget of the Ministry of Finance, KAPP's resources are generated from funds allocated to it from the state budget as well as from fees offered for the services it renders.
36 PPP law, Article 6.

Public Entities[37]

public entities include any government, Ministry or Department, or any public entity with an independent budget that enters into a PPP contract to implement a PPP project. Their responsibilities include:

- Proposing projects to KAP for their review and recommendation to the higher committee;
- Participating in project procurement with KAPP;
- Executing, implementing and monitoring PPP contracts after approval by the higher committee;
- Recommending, where appropriate, contract cancellation/termination for the public interest;
- Collaborating with KAPP on project and contract management issues; and
- Providing all necessary means and support towards the project, including but not limited to land allocation, required budget for payments under PPP arrangements, required infrastructure, data and information, preparation of terms and conditions as well as technical advice.

Given that public entities have critical responsibilities in the procurement and management of PPP projects, it is important for the relevant public entity to be actively engaged from the beginning of the project initiation, through tendering and contract negotiation.

Pursuant to the executive regulations, for every project that is approved after the initial screening, KAPP is to set up a Competition Committee to represent the public entity and other relevant entities where needed, which will be responsible for reviewing or developing the project's studies, documents, tender and approval documents.[38] The Competition Committee will also participate in the procurement, review the technical and financial proposals, and supervise the public session scheduled for opening the financial tenders.

The legal opinion and legislation department[39]

The Legal Opinion and Legislation Department is crucial to the preparation of PPP contracts in Kuwait. While the Legal Opinion and Legislation department

---

37 PPP Guidebook, Kuwaiti Authority for Partnership Projects, p. 19, in Arabic, available at: http://www.kapp.gov.kw/Library/Files/Uploaded%20Files/arabic/الدليل%20الإرشادي%20لهيئة%20مشاريع%20الشراكة-2018.pdf, last accessed on 19 October 2019.
38 Article 3 of the executive regulations.
39 PPP Guidebook, Kuwaiti Authority for Partnership Projects, p. 20, in Arabic, available at: http://www.kapp.gov.kw/Library/Files/Uploaded%20Files/arabic/الدليل%20الإرشادي%20لهيئة%20مشاريع%20الشراكة-2018.pdf, last accessed on 19 October 2019.

96 *Intervention to permit PPP techniques*

does not have a formal role under the PPP law, it must provide legal advice on all government contracts and it is responsible for interpreting the laws and defending the State's interest. Therefore, the Legal Opinion and Legislation Department will be consulted during the process of developing the documentation related to PPP projects, i.e. the RFP, PPP contracts and negotiation of the same with the preferred bidder.

The state audit bureau

The PPP law stipulates that all PPP contracts (including related consultancy agreements) are subject to the ex-ante and ex-post auditing by the State Audit Bureau.[40] The State Audit Bureau plays an essential role in completing the procurement process for a PPP project. Pursuant to the executive regulations, its approval is required before a project can ultimately be awarded to the preferred bidder.[41] Accordingly, all relevant documentation (i.e. the RFP, the preferred bidder's proposal, minutes of the negotiations as well as the PPP contract that has been agreed between the parties) needs to be submitted to it for its review.[42]

PPP legal framework in Jordan

Jordan has a good track record of successful projects in key infrastructure sectors. A number of large PPPs were successfully signed over the past years. Examples include Attarat Oil-Share Fired Power Plant, Zarqa CCGT Power Plant, Daehan Wind Power Plant, Queen Alia International Airport Expansion Project8, Assamra Water Treatment Plant, Amman East Power Plant and the Medical and Industrial Hazardous Waste Treatment Plant. However, Jordan initiated a number of PPPs that were later withdrawn mainly due to limited project preparation. In light of significant infrastructure needs and the move towards enhanced private sector participation in long-term partnerships, Jordan officially launched its PPP programme on 23 June 2008. The Executive Privatization Commission (EPC), a governmental authority established under the privatization law, was tasked with drafting a new PPP law and the development and implementation of a PPP program as a continuation of its Privatization program. In 2014, a new PPP law was promulgated by Law No. 31 of 2014. Article 3 of the PPP law stipulates that: public private partnership projects shall have the following goals:

---

40 PPP law, Article 31.
41 The executive regulations, Article 44.
42 PPP Guidebook, Kuwaiti Authority for Partnership Projects, p. 20, in Arabic, available at: http://www.kapp.gov.kw/Library/Files/Uploaded%20Files/arabic/الدليل%20الإرشادي%20لهيئة%20مشاريع%20الشراكة-2018.pdf, last accessed on 19 October 2019.

- Constructing, rehabilitating, operating, and maintaining the public infrastructure;
- Encouraging the private sector to enter into investment partnership projects with the government body;
- Finding the necessary funding to support feasible projects presented by the government body;
- Benefiting from modern technologies, knowledge and expertise in project development and management.

The 2014 PPP law is the exclusive legal regime for the procurement of PPPs in Jordan covering all economic infrastructure sectors such as water, energy, transport, information technology, lease and management contracts.

PPP institutional framework in Jordan

Article 5 of the 2014 PPP law in Jordan pointed out that:

a. A Council, called (Public Private Partnership Council), shall be established under the chairmanship of the Prime Minister and membership of: 1. The Minister of Finance, 2. The Minister of Industry, Trade and Supplies, 3. The Minister of Planning and International Cooperation, 4. A minister nominated by the Prime Minister, 5. The Governor of the Central Bank of Jordan, and 6. The Unit Director
b. 1. The Council chairman shall name one of the Council members as his deputy. 2. The Council shall convene upon invitation from the chairman or his deputy whenever necessary. The quorum of the Council meetings shall be constituted by attendance of the majority of its members, and its decisions shall be taken by majority of its attending members at least.
c. The rules and procedures pertaining to regulating the works and meetings of the Council are determined pursuant to instructions issued by the Council for that purpose.

Article 7 of the PPP law in Jordan establishes a Unit called (Public Private Partnership Unit) in the Ministry of Finance, linked directly to the Minister. The Unit shall undertake the following tasks:

1. Identify the technical requirements that must be presented by the government body for any partnership project. These requirements shall include the financial feasibility of the project, the updated Sustainability Report, and the cost-benefit analysis.
2. Draft application forms for partnership projects.
3. Receive and register partnership project application forms Government Bodies.

98 *Intervention to permit PPP techniques*

4. Study partnership project applications submitted according to the application forms prepared by the Unit.
5. Review the project's feasibility study.
6. Review the negotiated contracts.
7. Approve the terms of reference governing the work of advisors engaged by the contracting bodies of the partnership project, and assist the said bodies in this procedure.
8. Provide technical support to the contracting bodies during the project implementation phases.
9. Participate in the committees formed by the contracting bodies for every project.
10. Document the feasibility studies, technical reports, and the evaluation reports of bidders, and keep a copy of the contract.
11. Assist the contracting bodies in obtaining the required licenses and approvals in coordination with the Investment Commission.
12. Conduct a general consultation regarding a proposed partnership project.
13. Participate in building capacities of the government body employees.
14. Draft guidelines and standard contractual provisions with terms of reference of partnership contracts, and improve the general principles and best practices to encourage development of partnership projects.
15. Identify the standard phases for partnership projects.
16. Assist the contracting bodies in setting up a periodic performance evaluation after awarding of the partnership project bid.
17. Prepare draft regulations and instructions required to implement provisions of this law and submit them to the Council.
18. Determine the requirements needed to prepare periodic reports for the contracting bodies regarding the concluded partnership projects for the purpose of obtaining the Council's approval of them.
19. Receive periodic reports from the contracting bodies pertaining to implementation of partnership projects and brief the Council on its work progress.
20. Assemble and study annual reports submitted by the contracting bodies and submit them to the Council.
21. Establish a database for partnership projects.
22. Follow up on the implementation of the Council's decisions and coordinate with the contracting bodies.
23. Adhere to disclosure standards according to the best international practices.
24. Carry out any other tasks assigned to it by the Council or Council of Ministers.

PPP legal framework in Morocco

In Morocco, PPPs were ruled by laws governing specific sectors. In the motorway sector, Decree N. 2-89-189 dated 2 February 1993 applying Law No. 4–89 pertaining to motorways authorized the State to grant motorway concessions with the right for the concessionaire to collect fees from the motorway users. More than ten motorway concessions have been granted to the Société Nationale des Autoroutes du Maroc for the design, financing, building, operation and maintenance of the motorway links between Rabat and Tangier, Tetouan and Fnideq, Casablanca and El Jadida or Rabat and Fes.[43]

In the port sector, the Decree Law No. 2-02-644 dated 10 September 2002 created the Tanger-Med special area and the Law No. 15–02 pertaining to ports respectively entitled TMSA and ANP to launch bidding processes, within which there were in some instances competing dialogue with the public body, for the concessions of container terminals, RoRo terminals, tug and rescue services and oil terminals. The concessionaire brought the financing and know-how, designed and built the terminals, operated them and collected fees in consideration for the services provided.[44]

In energy, a bidding process has been launched for the financing, design, construction, operation and maintenance of electricity production capacities against energy fees payable by the public.

The public work concession is also possible under Moroccan law even if this formula has not been used very often. This concept consists for the public body in granting the right for a private partner to occupy the public domain, to build a public construction work, to operate it and to collect fees from the users. There is no legal framework for such a concept, which is only mentioned briefly in the code of public procurement (to exclude it from the public procurement regime).[45]

To promote the increase of the participation of private sector in infrastructure projects, the Kingdom of Morocco created in 2014 new types of state contracts[46] implemented through the enactment of the PPP Law No. 86–12.[47] The purpose of this law is to establish a coherent legislative framework, which introduces innovation in award procedures for PPP projects, as these procedures must be consistent with sustainable development goals. Further, the PPP law creates substantive incentives to private sector to participate in the development of infrastructures in Morocco. For the purposes of the implementation of the PPP law, the PPP Decree No. 2-15-45 of 13 May 2015 was issued.[48] In the law preamble, the lawmaker indicates that the law and, also, the PPP contract targets to meet at best the citizen's expectations for infrastructure and public

---

43 Philippe De Richoufftz, The Moroccan PPP contract, *International Business Law Journal*, I. B.L.J. 2015, 5, 390.

44 Philippe De Richoufftz, The Moroccan PPP contract, *International Business Law Journal*, I. B.L.J. 2015, 5, 390.

45 Philippe De Richoufftz, The Moroccan PPP contract, *International Business Law Journal*, 2015, 5, 390.

46 Philippe De Richoufftz, The Moroccan PPP contract, *International Business Law Journal*, 2015, 5, 389–398.

47 Published on the Official Gazette No. 6332 of 5 February 2015.

48 Published on the Official Gazette nNo. 6365 of 1 October 2015.

100 *Intervention to permit PPP techniques*

services of good quality and the services rendered must comply with the equality and continuity principles.[49]

An interministerial commission for PPP contracts has been established and mainly composed of representatives of various Moroccan ministries, under the auspices of the Ministry of Economy and Finance. The purpose of this commission is to issue opinions on PPP contracts entered into with the state, preliminary assessments, and the award of the contract.

Articles 1 and 3 of the PPP law define PPPs and ensure that principles of equal access and treatment, objectiveness, competitiveness, transparency, and respecting best practices shall be upheld in the PPP procurement process. Nonetheless, a delegated management of public services (the 'DM') in accordance with the provisions of Law No. 54–05 of 14 February 2006[50] and Decree No. 2-06-362 of 9 August 2006[51] preceded the 2015 regulatory framework on PPPs. Furthermore, there are specific sectoral laws on concessions, which include: i) Law No. 4–89 relating to motorways promulgated in August 1992; ii) Law No. 15–02 relating to ports and creating the Ports National Agency and the Ports Operating Company promulgated on November 2005; iii) Law No. 52–02 relating to the organization and the operation of the national railway network promulgated in January 2005; and iv) Law No. 25–79 creating the Airports National Office as amended by Law No. 14–89 and Law No. 1-93-140. The previous legislative and regulatory instruments form the legal framework on PPPs in Morocco for the purposes of PPP procurement.

The PPP procuring authorities in Morocco include: public law entities or public juristic entities (*Etablissements publics de l'Etat*) excluding local authorities; and public law companies (*entreprises publiques*): pursuant to the provisions of Law No. 69–00 relating to State Financial Control of the Public Companies and other Entities. The public law companies who may enter into a PPP contract are (i) state companies whose share capital is wholly owned by public entities; (ii) public subsidiaries whose share capital is held more than half by public bodies and (iii) a mixed company whose share capital is owned up to 50% by public entities.

The approval of the Minister in Charge of Finances with regards to the feasibility of conducting the contracts under a PPP structure pursuant to Article 4 of the PPP Decree. In addition, the approval of the The Interministerial Commission on PPPs is necessary. Pursuant to Article (5/1) of the PPP Decree, the latter commission provides its opinion on the pre-feasibility evaluation report prepared by the procuring authority, to assure the opportunity to realize the project under the PPP contract.

---

49 Philippe De Richoufftz, The Moroccan PPP contract, *International Business Law Journal*, 2015, 5, 395.
50 The Official Gazette no. 5404 of 16 March 2006.
51 The Official Gazette no. 5454 of 7 September 2006.

The PPP law provides that PPP contracts can be subject to three different tender procedures: competitive dialogue, call for tenders and a negotiated procedure. The PPP law requires that the public authority carry out a preliminary assessment which must include a comparative analysis with the other frameworks of implementation of the project. In addition, the preliminary assessment considers the complexity of the project, the financial arrangement and the means of financing. However, contrary to what was implemented in France, the entering into of this contract is not strictly delimited. Indeed, the PPP law does not solely apply to contracts characterized by a trait of urgency or complexity, thus diminishing the risk of litigation. The PPP law also provides, following the example of the relevant French framework, that candidates can present a spontaneous offer to the public authorities considered under the PPP law. Consequently, the public authority can be presented with an innovative project by an operator, and, if the project addresses the public authority's needs and presents technical and financial innovations, it can decide to proceed to the necessary preliminary assessment of the project and initiate a competitive dialogue.[52]

The PPP law also provides that the public authority can conduct a negotiated procedure, without advertising or call for competition, with the operator when the spontaneous offer addresses an innovative and urgent need, whilst at the same time being financially competitive.

The PPP law in Morocco introduces a significant step in MENA countries to avoid the pitfalls in other countries' PPP legislation, not only the MENA countries but also in France.

The award of the PPP contracts aims to achieve a criteria of national preference that could be taken into account in order to support the local economy.

Legislative progress in PPP law in Morocco

The PPP law provides for a list of mandatory clauses which must be included in the PPP contract. These mandatory clauses concern some substantive issues such as the financial conditions of the PPP contract, as well as to the contract performance. The financial clauses pursuant to PPP law, the remuneration of the private partner will be paid, in its entirety or partially, by the public authority. In the event where the public authority does not pay the entirety of the remuneration of the private partner, it may be remunerated by the end users (the Public) through the cash flow generated by the project. This remuneration is linked to performance objectives, thus guaranteeing the compliant carrying out of the PPP contract. The corollary of these objectives is the possibility for

---

52 White & Case, Client Alert Energy, Infrastructure, Project and Asset Finance, https://www. whitecase.com/sites/whitecase/files/files/download/publications/alert-new-moroccan-ppp-law.pdf. Last accessed on 17 July 2019.

102 *Intervention to permit PPP techniques*

the public authority to impose penalties on the private partner, in the event where the latter does not fulfil its contractual obligations.[53]

The PPP law provides that the private partner may, for the benefit of the lending institutions, create security interests over its assets acquired or carried out under the performance of the PPP contract.[54] The type of security interests that can be granted is quite large since the PPP law considers 'all security interests'. Furthermore, the assignment of receivables by way of security does not appear confined in the sense that the amount of claims that can receive an act of acceptance from the public party, as assigned debtor, is not limited to 80% of the investment and financing costs. The maximum contract duration that is permitted pursuant to the PPP law is up to a maximum of 50 years. It also imposes the inclusion of a clause in the PPP contract pertaining to the allocation of risks between the parties, which is subject to the contractual practice of optimal risk sharing. Furthermore, the PPP law establishes a substitution right, whereby the public authority can replace the private partner with a substituted entity, notably in the event of a serious breach of its obligations. It should be noted that the PPP law also enables the lending institutions to ask the public authority to substitute the private partner with a new entity, in the case of a serious breach of its obligations.

In conclusion, the PPP law takes into consideration standard market practices, which are implemented in international project finance and should permit to avoid the main pitfalls observed in countries with similar frameworks.[55]

The PPP law in Morocco draws heavily on French law. It allows the use of PPPs in sectors where it is not appropriate to allocate operating risks to the private party including non-commercial sectors of a social infrastructure nature such as hospitals.[56]

PPP institutional framework in Morocco

The PPP Unit or the *Commission de Partenariat Public-Privé* has been established at The Ministry of Economy and Finance within the Directorate for State Enterprises and Privatization (DEPP). The PPP Unit is a cell dedicated to PPPs,

---

53 White & Case, Client Alert Energy, Infrastructure, Project and Asset Finance, https://www.whitecase.com/sites/whitecase/files/files/download/publications/alert-new-moroccan-ppp-law.pdf. Last accessed on 17 July 2019.

54 White & Case, Client Alert Energy, Infrastructure, Project and Asset Finance, https://www.whitecase.com/sites/whitecase/files/files/download/publications/alert-new-moroccan-ppp-law.pdf. Last accessed on 17 July 2019.

55 White & Case, Client Alert Energy, Infrastructure, Project and Asset Finance, https://www.whitecase.com/sites/whitecase/files/files/download/publications/alert-new-moroccan-ppp-law.pdf. Last accessed on 17 July 2019.

56 OECD, Public-Private Partnerships in the Middle East and North Africa, A Handbook for Policy Makers, p. 37, available on: www.oecd.org/mena/competitiveness/PPP%20Handbook_EN_with_covers.pdf, last accessed on 17 July 2019.

in order to establish a structured framework for the development of PPPs and broaden their fields of action.

The PPP Central Unit was established in September 2011 and has cooperated closely with a number of international institutions such as the European Investment Bank and the International Finance Corporation. This unit was notably in charge of the drafting and scoping of the new PPP law. It may also play a significant role in the development of PPP pilot projects.

In Morocco, the decision-making process for major infrastructure projects involves many sectors of the government. Projects are likely to involve a wide range of stakeholders, including decision-making committees across ministries for centrally procured projects.

PPP legal framework in Tunisia[57]

Tunisia has currently promulgated a PPP law which is Law No. 45/2015. The PPP law in Tunisia was promulgated in November 2015. Decree No. 771/2016 issued in June 2016 to establish the Strategic Council for PPPs and Decree No. 772/2016 issued in June 2016 created the procedural framework for awarding PPP contracts. Further, Decree No. 782/2016 issued in June 2016, permits the registration of real rights over the buildings, enterprises, and fixed equipment under PPP contracts. The other applicable sectoral laws are Law No. 12 of 11 May 2015 on the production of electricity from renewable energies.[58]

PPP institutional framework in Tunisia

The Ministry of Economy and Finance also houses a body tasked with PPPs, the *Direction générale des partenariats public-privé* (DGPPP) whose main role is to monitor the fiscal and financial risks of public spending on PPP projects. The DGPPP has also contributed to developing the draft legislation on PPPs, and will remain involved in the preparation and negotiation of PPP projects once the new PPP regime is in place. The *Direction générale d'audit et de suivi des grands projets* (DGASGP), also within the Ministry of Economy and Finance, is responsible for the audit and the OECD, in co-operation with the USC and the African Development Bank, has been engaged with the Government of Tunisia as it reforms its institutional framework for PPPs. As part of the *Operationalising PPPs in Tunisia* project, funded by the Deauville Partnership Transition Fund,

---

57 The African Legal Support Facility ALSF, PPP country Profile, Tunisia, available at: https://www.aflsf.org/sites/default/files/PPP%20Country%20Profile%20-%20Tunisie.pdf, last accessed on 20 July 2019.

58 The African Legal Support Facility ALSF, PPP country profile, Tunisia, available at: https://www.aflsf.org/sites/default/files/PPP%20Country%20Profile%20-%20Tunisie.pdf, last accessed on 20 July 2019.

104 *Intervention to permit PPP techniques*

the OECD expects to publish reports in the second quarter of 2015 that examine the legal, institutional and budgetary frameworks for PPPs in the country.

It is important to note that the concessions and PPP regime in Tunisia are separate from the public procurement regime (*régime des marchés publics*), which is governed by the 2014 Decree on Public Procurement (No. 2014–1039 of 13 March 2014). Accordingly, public procurement that does not involve concessions or PPPs is managed by a separate set of institutions.[59]

PPP legal framework in Algeria[60]

The legal framework in Algeria consists of the Presidential Decree No. 15/247 of 2 Dhou El Hidja 1436, corresponding to 16 September 2015 on the regulation of public contracts and public service delegations. It also consists of:

- Law No. 99–09 of 28 July 1999 on the control of energy;
- Law No. 02–01 of 5 February 2002, on Electricity and Public Distribution of Gas by Pipeline;
- Law No. 04–09 of 14 August 2004 on the promotion of renewable energies in the context of sustainable development;
- Law No. 12–2005 of 4 August 2005 on water;
- Executive Decree No. 05–495 of 26 December 2005 concerning the energy audit of major energy-consuming establishments;
- Ministerial Decrees of 2 February 2014: fixing the guaranteed purchase rates for the production of electricity from installations using the photovoltaic industry and the conditions of their application;
- Ministerial Decrees of 2 February 2014: fixing the guaranteed purchase rates for the production of electricity from installations using the wind energy industry and the conditions of their application.

Conclusions

The trajectory of the states' intervention in PPP legislation and regulation shows an increasing trend by MENA countries in recent years to intervene towards the codification of PPP techniques in the MENA countries' legal systems. Even though this intervention contradicts the principles of the Chicago school in economics, which minimizes state intervention to the minimum, this intervention from MENA states through legislation and regulation is clear evidence that

---

59 The African Legal Support Facility ALSF, PPP country profile, Tunisia, available at: https://www.aflsf.org/sites/default/files/PPP%20Country%20Profile%20-%20Tunisie.pdf, last accessed on 20 July 2019.

60 The World Bank Group, PPP Legal Resource Centre (PPPLRC), available at: https://ppp.worldbank.org/public-private-partnership/ppp-legal-framework-snapshots-0#A, last accessed on 22 October 2019.

unlike traditional concessions MENA states relinquish the role of the employer in favor of being only a regulator. Many MENA countries have codified PPP legislation such as Egypt in 2010, Kuwait, Morocco and Jordan in 2014, Dubai in 2015 and Tunisia in 2015. This trajectory by legislative intervention is supported by a detailed regulatory framework and new modified polices in many MENA countries that reflect the profile of innovation in award procedures in PPPs on the procedural grounds and how far PPP techniques are consistent with the socio-economic targets and the Sustainable Development Goals in practice. Innovation in the award procedures shows how PPPs can improve life, infrastructure and public services in MENA countries. The new PPP legislation supports the innovation in substantive rules in the PPP contracts, which represent a considerable step towards the liberalization of the administrative contract, in particular traditional concessions from the rigid excessive clauses 'Les clauses exorbitantes'.

MENA states' intervention reflects the high degree of flexibility in the economic ideology and legislative policy behind promulgating economic legislation as PPP legislation is one of the most significant steps from the economic angle because it represents the increasing trend of MENA countries to permit private sector participation in public utilities and infrastructure projects. The economic ideology behind promulgating such liberal economic legislation is clear in the Arab constitutions and it has been implemented in the current Arab PPP legislation.

States' intervention through legislation and regulation to permit PPP techniques and to formulate new policies in public utilities, services and infrastructure projects plays a considerable role to enhance the MENA countries' ranking in the international financial institutions' reports. MENA countries are exercising new polices to create new environment that promotes high threshold of protection to foreign investments and maintain better investments' atmosphere which facilitates the increase of inflow of FDI to MENA countries.

MENA states' intervention through legislation and regulation to permit the participation of the private sector in public utilities, services and infrastructure projects through PPP techniques is a remarkable step towards the implementation of 2030 vision goals in MENA countries. Many countries in the MENA region have established legal and economic frameworks and a chronology to achieve the 2030 vision goals. The role of states' intervention in the economic life has been considerably reduced.

It is important to refer to the fact that many Arab countries are taking steps to promulgate new PPPs legislation. The Kingdom of Bahrain is in the process of promulgating new PPP legislation to encourage the inflow of Foreign Direct Investments (FDI) to various economic sectors, and to subject PPP techniques to achieve the Sustainable Developments Goals towards the implementation of the 2030 economic vision. PPP started in practice in the Kingdom of Bahrain many years ago and yet legislation has not been promulgated.

5 PPPs in MENA countries' public procurements

Introduction

All public procurement of goods and services, including works, must be based on *value for money*. *Value for money* is not about achieving the lowest initial price: it is defined as the optimum combination of whole life costs and quality. This policy is set out in guidance issued by the UK Office of Government Commerce (OGC) to departments and is reproduced in Chapter 22 of Government Accounting.[1] Public procurement is an instrument of modernization of public administration, the ability to have efficient delivery of public services, because procurement is used as a procedure to enable a contractual relationship to deliver a public service. The smoother, the faster and the more efficient that procedure is, the better quality outputs for public services will be.

Goods and services should be acquired by competition unless there are convincing reasons to the contrary. The form of competition should be appropriate to the value and complexity of the procurement and barriers to the participation of suppliers should be removed.[2]

There are a number of ways of achieving *value for money* in procurement, such as by:

- Reducing the cost of purchasing and the time it takes – the processing overheads;
- Getting better *value for money* for goods and services purchased and improved quality of services;
- Improving project, contract and asset management;
- Making procurement decisions on the basis of a long-term view of *value for money* so that the focus is not on the lowest price;

---

1 Available at: www.gov.uk/government/collections/whole-of-government-accounts. And webarchive.nationalarchives.gov.uk/20130105135133/www.hm-treasury.gov.uk/d/Reg_Prop_and_VfM-November04.pdf Last accessed on 9 July 2019.
2 Available at: webarchive.nationalarchives.gov.uk/20130105135133/www.hm-treasury.gov.uk/d/Reg_Prop_and_VfM-November04.pdf, last accessed on 9 July 2019.

- Combining competition with innovative ways of procurement whilst managing the risks effectively;
- Drawing on latest advances in electronic commerce and good procurement practice; and
- Using a range of tools available that promote and can measure *value for money* gains.[3]

International public procurement procedures and PPPs are two major contemporary legal and policy instruments of public sector management, which link the public and private sectors and provide for the procedural and substantive interactions necessary for the effective and efficient delivery of public services. PPP techniques have been exercised in practice and there are many PPP projects in reality before promulgating PPP legislation in many MENA countries. The situation happened in Egypt and many other countries before promulgating PPP legislation. There is always a 'décalage' or gap between practice and the legislature. PPP legislation in MENA countries is a codification to the profile of innovation in PPP public procurements and the advanced and liberalized PPP techniques that represent a modernized approach different from the traditional concessions that contain excessive clauses, '*clauses exorbitantes.*' Further, PPP legislation creates a new procedural framework to select the private entity in PPP transactions different from the traditional public procurement legislation, which is convenient for traditional concessions but not for PPPs.

Statistics show that about 9 trillion USD is the global annual spending by governments for public contracts. This expenditure amounted to 12–20% of the total world GDP.[4]

A transparent and non-discriminatory government procurement becomes the best tool to achieve *value for money*[5] when the main subject of the procedural rules of legislation is to implement the principles of government procurement. In addition to transparency and non-discriminatory principles, there are other principles that are maintained in PPP legislation in Egypt, Kuwait and Dubai

---

3 Available at: webarchive.nationalarchives.gov.uk/20130105135133/www.hm-treasury.gov.uk/d/Reg_Prop_and_VfM-November04.pdf, last accessed on 9 July 2019.
4 OECD, Arabic translation of *Methodology for Assessing of National Procurement System (MAPS)*, 2016 version, Draft for Public Consultations, July 2016, 1.
5 Transparency in PPP procurement means ensuring that information about the PPP procurement and contractual administration regime and individual PPP opportunities is made available to all interested parties (and particularly to potential suppliers and service providers). It also entails the right of access to that information. At the same time, transparency calls for procurement policies and practices that are seen to be fair in all respects, with full information openly provided. Transparency encourages open and competitive procurement regimes thereby helping the government agency and the private sector entity achieve economic benefits. Supplier evaluation and contract award criteria should be made known to all interested competitors in advance for each individual project. Any changes relating to individual PPP opportunities should be made known to all participants. See: United Nations Economic Commission for Europe, *Guidebook On Promoting Good Governance in Public-Private Partnerships*, 2008, 46.

108 *PPPs in public procurements*

such as integrity, objectivity, accountability, fair competition, equal treatment, equality, objective evaluation for bids and balance. These principles when implemented reflect the efficiency of PPP legislation.

The transparency, objectivity, fairness of the process, and evaluation criteria for bids, are major themes in this chapter.[6] The chapter focuses on *de jure* data, which captures the characteristics of laws and regulations encompassing PPPs procurement rules and other relevant legal texts. This chapter is an attempt to reach an answer to the crucial question of whether MENA countries adhere closely to international good practices and principles as measured, for instance, by the Benchmarking PPPs Procurement Report issued by the World Bank in 2017, and the methodology of procurement assessment stated at the OECD MAPS or not.

The causality between a proper public procurement system of PPPs and the significant improvement of public services is established to show how to achieve public interests through adopting higher profile innovation for PPP procurement. This chapter aims to explore the profile of innovation in award procedures in PPPs in MENA countries and how it affects the socio-economic impact of a PPP project and how it can achieve Sustainable Development Goals for the real implementation of the 2030 vision in MENA countries.

The profile of innovation in the award procedures in PPP law in Egypt

Egypt's economy has continued to expand, with the IMF forecasting GDP growth with significant improvement in various economic sectors. For the past century and a half, the Suez Canal (i.e., one of the oldest concessions worldwide) has been a major conduit for international trade, including oil. For many centuries, Egypt has taken the lead in Arab MENA countries, and is still carrying out major governmental transformation in the aftermath of the 2011 revolution. Egypt has the third-largest GDP in the Arab world, after the oil-rich Saudi Arabia and the United Arab Emirates and it aims at increasing the inward of Foreign Direct Investments (FDI) in various economic sectors.[7] It is considerably more diversified than many economies in the region, with industry and agriculture as key contributors, making up 14.5% and 15.7% of GDP, respectively, according to the Central Bank of Egypt, as well as oil and gas extraction.[8]

---

6 The selection of the bidder should be undertaken following a transparent, neutral and non-discriminatory selection process that promotes competition and strikes a balance between the need to reduce the length of time and cost of the bid process and acquiring the best proposal. Along these lines, corruption should be penalized as well. See: United Nations Economic Commission for Europe, *Guidebook On Promoting Good Governance In Public-Private Partnerships*, 2008, 46.

7 The Egyptian Ministry of Finance, Targets for developments in Egypt through PPPs structures was shown in 2009, *Update on the National Program for Public Private Partnership, The Ministry of Finance Publications*, June, 2009, 6.

8 *The Central Bank of Egypt*, available at: www.cbe.org.eg/ar/EconomicResearch/Publications/Pages/AnnualReport.aspx, last accessed on 11 March 2018.

In the Egyptian legal system, administrative contracts are generally subject to the state procurement law No. 182 of 2018 and its executive regulations,[9] which stipulate that the only way to select any contracting entity with the state is mainly through a public tender under the state procurement law. Selecting the private partner in PPP projects through the previous state procurement law was a very complicated process before promulgating the Egyptian PPP law. After promulgating the PPP law in 2010, PPP agreements and selecting the private partner is no longer subject to the provisions of the state procurement law in Egypt (Article 1 from the Promulgation Articles, PPP law).

PPP legislation in Egypt strengthens the selection of private partners using the most efficient and innovative techniques for award procedures in public procurement, an approach that is clearly emphasized in the Egyptian PPP legislation. There are many strategic points that are considered creative and innovative steps towards achieving the international good practices and adopting international principles in public procurement for PPP. The administrative authority aims to achieve a *win-win* situation for the administration and the private partner together whilst maintaining a high threshold of the recognized international standards and principles during the selection process.

Article 19 of the Egyptian PPP Egyptian law stipulates that investor selection is subject to the principles of publicity, transparency, free competition, equal opportunity and equality pursuant to the rules and procedures of this law and its executive regulations. Publication, advertising and preparation for the participation competition are in accordance with the PPP Central Unit (PPPCU) in the manner described at the executive regulations of the PPP legislation.Generally, there is no special administrative organ in Egypt concerned with state procurement;[10] however, the PPP legislation in Egypt stipulates that a special pre-qualification committee (hereinafter referred to as 'the Committee') shall be established by an administrative decree from the concerned authority (the representative of the public juristic entity on the PPP contract). The Committee shall contain legal, technical and financial experts. Amongst its members there is one representative or more from the partnership unit at the administrative body if there is such a unit.[11] The executive regulations determine the competencies of this committee and its disciplines.

Investors whose names are not listed among qualified investors may question the Committee's decision in disqualifying them. Any objection to the Committee's decision must be forwarded to the PPPCU for evaluation and a decision. The executive regulations provide the time-bar and the procedures for filing an

---

9 Previously the Egyptian Public Procurement Law No. 89 of 1989 and its executive regulations.
10 It is important to refer to the fact that some Arab countries, such as the Kingdom of Bahrain, have an independent administrative organ concerned with bidding processes for all public juristic entities at the Kingdom.
11 The Egyptian PPP legislation, Article 20.

110 *PPPs in public procurements*

objection, including the procedures for decision-making. The mechanism for filing an objection or an appeal at this stage is one of the guarantees to ensure that there is objectivity, integrity, equal opportunity and equality in the preliminary stages for procurement.[12]

The administrative body may coordinate with the PPPCU in inviting qualified investors for introductory meetings to discuss issues relating to the project specifications and its preliminary conditions. Answers to all queries should be accessible to all qualified investors. Any qualified investor may request before the concerned authority of the administrative body to maintain confidentiality on his/her offer or his/her financial or economic expectations. This does not contradict the principle of transparency as it merely protects the economic and financial interests of the private investor.

Qualified investors are subject to equal opportunity and equality before law principles. To achieve the best quality for infrastructure and services that maintain regularity for public utilities, the concerned authority of the administrative body may decide to re-study specifications of the project and its preliminary conditions in the light of the abovementioned meetings and without violation to the qualification criteria. This must be done before issuing tenders' invitations.[13]

Egyptian PPP legislation allows the concerned authority at the administrative body to use a two-phase tendering process in the submission of the financial and technical tenders subject to prior consent from the PPPCU.[14] Phase one refers to the submission of a non-binding offer containing the main features of the financial and technical offer, followed by competitive dialogue,[15] whereas, phase two is the submission of the final offers for final evaluation. The executive regulations of the PPP legislation provide the rules and stipulations of tendering in these two phases.

Pursuant to Article 23 of the Egyptian legislation, the use of a dialogue process is maintained as it promotes fair competition and equality on the one hand, and enables the administrative authority to select the best technical and financial private partner without compromising the principles of integrity and objectivity on the other.[16] The public juristic entity shall maintain competition among qualified investors who submitted their non-binding offers through competitive dialogue and with each investor separately.[17] The aim of this dialogue is to obtain information regarding financial and technical offers. Dialogues must be confidential and must promote equality among qualified investors. It is worth noting that confidentiality provision in the Egyptian PPP legislation does not

---

12 The Egyptian PPP legislation, Article 20.
13 The Egyptian PPP legislation, Article 21
14 The Egyptian PPP legislation, Article 22.
15 The Egyptian PPP legislation, Article 23.
16 The Egyptian PPP legislation, Article 23.
17 The Egyptian PPP legislation, Article 23. In competitive dialogue see: S. Arrowsmith, *The Law of Public and Utilities Procurement*, Sweet & Maxwell 2018.

PPPs in public procurements 111

violate the principle of fair competition as confidentiality in this context aims, among other goals, at avoiding cartels or secret dealings against the administrative body that may result in any harm to public interest and the national economy. Confidentiality, in this context, also raises the threshold of protection to foreign investors as it protects their financial offers (contracts' prices and price formula offered by them) and keeps them confidential from competing private entities in the international markets. The executive regulations set the rules and disciplines in the conduct of these dialogues.

The administrative body, in coordination with the PPPCU, drafts the stipulations and specifications for the project. The stipulations and specifications shall define the conditions that are not negotiable with the investor.[18] The abovementioned conditions shall determine the mechanisms and basis for evaluation between offers, and, in case there is an evaluation with points, the evaluation criterion should be clarified, and the bases for comparison of the financial and technical offers must be highlighted with a score to each offer and with a mechanism for applying evaluation criterion to those offers. The legislative stipulations are provided to ensure objectivity, equality, fair competition, and to protect public interests.

For more liberalization in the process and without violating the principles of integrity and transparency, the administrative body shall invite qualified investors (and with no advertisements in newspapers as stipulated in previous procurement in Law No. 89 of 1989)[19] to discuss the stipulations pursuant to the rules and bases in implementing rules (i.e., the executive regulations for Egyptian PPP legislation).

PPP legislation in Egypt highlights the guarantees for public interest and regularity for public utilities by stipulating that the technical offer must contain the detailed specifications of the project to achieve the required standards for services in the project, in accordance with the conditions and specifications pointed out by the administrative body.[20]

As a matter of fact, the legislative policy behind the award procedures' provisions in the Egyptian PPP legislation is to achieve public interests; to maintain the best selection for the investor; to ensure that good standards for services and products are available through PPP patterns; to achieve the principles of the new PPP award procedures as it is set out in the PPP legislation;[21] to maintain regularity, continuity and good disciplines of public utilities; and to provide incentives to attract Foreign Direct Investments (FDI) to Egypt. The award procedures in PPP legislation in Egypt aim to create balance between achieving public interests and maintaining the fundamental principles for PPP award procurement on the one hand and creating through legislation and regulatory

---

18 The Egyptian PPP legislation, Article 24/d.
19 The Egyptian PPP legislation, Article 26.
20 The Egyptian PPP legislation, Article 27.
21 The Egyptian PPP legislation, Article 19.

112 *PPPs in public procurements*

framework the best environment to attract Foreign Direct Investments (FDI) on the other. The principle of equality principles in the Egyptian PPP legislation[22] is an assurance to the wider scope of application to the fundamental principle in Arab administrative law and practice of 'equality before public utilities.' However, the principle of equality in the PPP award procedures' context has a broad concept as it aims to strengthen the traditional equality principle in practice to achieve equality for investors before the administrative authority, equal opportunity among investors before administrative authority (the awarding authority), as well as equality among end-users before public utilities. Equality among end-users before public entities is one of the fundamental principles of administrative law in the Egyptian and Arab legal systems.[23]

As transparency, objectivity and equal opportunity are listed among the fundamental principles that govern the award procedures of PPP contracts in Egypt, the Egyptian PPP legislation permits offers to be submitted through a consortium consisting of more than one qualified investor, unless the administrative body stipulates that qualified investors must submit their offers individually. If a consortium has submitted an offer, any member of this consortium is prohibited from submitting any other offer, either directly or indirectly, and either as an individual or through another consortium, or through any other company that this investor owns the majority of its capital, or has a monopoly over its management, unless the administrative body stipulates otherwise.[24] Any offer that is submitted in violation of this paragraph is null and void. This legislative stipulation is a new provision in award procedures in the Egyptian legal system as it aims to ensure transparency, integrity, objectivity in public procurement, whilst maintaining fair competition and equal opportunity among investors.

Award evaluation process in the Egyptian PPP legislation

The Egyptian PPP legislation stipulates that the competent authority at the administrative body shall issue an administrative decree to form a Committee to receive offers and study each financial and technical offer. The Committee is composed of technical, financial and legal experts. The executive regulations shall provide for the competence and disciplines required from the Committee, as well as the bases for ranking offers of the technically accepted offers, and the grounds for disqualification of any offer. To ensure the right selection of the private partner, the Committee must have members from the legal opinion department at the Conseil d'État, Ministry of Finance, and PPPCU.

The Committee may form a sub-committee consisting of its members to study the offers from technical, financial and legal perspectives or may appoint

---

22 The Egyptian PPP legislation, Articles 19, 21 and 23.
23 Sarwat Badawi, *Administrative Law*, Dar Al Nahda Al Arabia 1985, in Arabic.
24 The Egyptian PPP legislation, Article 28/2.

other experts to exercise the same functions. The sub-committee has to submit a report on the result of its evaluation with recommendations to the Committee. The Committee will evaluate compatible offers according to the evaluation criteria provided by the administration, and, thereafter, decide for the best economically feasible offer for the state. Each offer is given an evaluation grade according to the bases and the mechanism in evaluation of offers that are provided in the final offer submission request. The individual grades are used in ranking the technically accepted offers. The principle of *value for money* is highly considered by the Egyptian legislature.Offers that are not compatible with stipulations and specifications have to be rejected. The offerors with accepted technical offers are invited to attend the financial offers' selection session. The project has to be awarded to the offeror who is financially feasible among technically accepted offerors after applying the 'relative weight' as a selection criterion, of the technical and financial criteria in the specifications. The executive regulations shall clarify the rules for the evaluation of technical and financial offers. As a tool to assure the selection for the best offer, the Egyptian PPP legislation stipulates that negotiations may be exercised with the winning offeror to clarify some issues and details of the financial and technical conditions. Negotiations should not deal with any contractual clauses that are considered non-negotiable clauses in the invitation to the offer. Any amendments to the technical or financial conditions that reduce the standards that the offer contains are prohibited.[25]

The profile of innovation in the award procedures in PPP law in Kuwait

In the Kuwaiti PPP Legislation 2014 and its Executive Regulations, the selection of the investor in PPP legislation is subject to the principles of transparency, openness, freedom of competition, equal opportunity and equality.[26]

PPP legislation in Kuwait considers PPP techniques as an exception from the public procurement law in Kuwait. PPP procurement and all rules for submitting offers and their financial and technical assessment, the competent entity, documentation, pre-qualification and post-qualification, objections from the competent entity decisions, its procedures, time-bar, its rules and procedures, and competitive dialogue are organized by the executive regulations if not organized by PPP legislation.[27] In addition to PPP legislation, the executive regulations shall regulate the general bases for projects tendering, and the advertising for these projects in the media.[28]

---

25 The Egyptian PPP legislation, Article 31.
26 The PPP legislation in Kuwait, Article 8.
27 The PPP legislation in Kuwait, Article 9.
28 The PPP legislation in Kuwait, Article 27.

114 *PPPs in public procurements*

The executive regulations point out the methods for proposing PPP projects and the approval mechanism.[29] The proposal for the procurement and implementation of a PPP project may be submitted by public entities if a public entity wishes to propose a project that falls within its competences in accordance with the PPP law. The public entity shall submit a request to the public authority along with the comprehensive feasibility studies of the project. The higher committee approves the request of the relevant public entity for the procurement of a PPP project in accordance with a PPP model, and it may propose PPP projects to public entities. The private sector may submit before the authority a draft concept along with preliminary feasibility studies, for the implementation of a project.

The authority, in coordination with the public entity, shall review the feasibility studies presented by the aforementioned entities and finalize the same, as needed, in order to submit an appropriate recommendation thereon to the higher committee. The authority may prepare the project's comprehensive feasibility studies and procurement documents, and, it may, in all cases, seek support from advisory firms and specialized offices whether local or foreign as it deems suitable for this purpose in accordance with the provisions of the laws and regulations.

The executive regulations of the Kuwaiti PPP legislation point out that a competition committee shall be established. The authority shall establish, following the approval of the higher committee and in accordance with the requirements of the business, a committee for each PPP project named 'Competition Committee,' in which the public entity(ies) whose competences and responsibilities correspond to the nature of the project shall be represented, by at least one member being no less than an assistant undersecretary, and provided that technical, financial and legal expertise are also represented therein. The Committee shall review, complete and prepare the project-related studies, instruments and procurement documents, and shall approve the same. The Committee shall also evaluate the technical and financial offers and shall supervise the public session set for opening the financial envelopes of the technically accepted offers.[30]

The method for the approval of concepts proposed by the private sector is evaluated as the authority shall, in coordination with the proposed public entity, present the results of the initial feasibility studies of the concepts proposed[31] by the private sector to the higher committee along with the authority's recommendation for the preliminary approval of the project as an initiative or

---

29 The Executive Regulations of the PPP legislation in Kuwait, Article 2.

30 The Executive Regulation of the PPP legislation in Kuwait, Article 3.

31 Article 1 of the Executive Regulations defines the Concept Proposer as any natural person or legal entity, Kuwaiti or non-Kuwaiti, presenting a concept for the implementation of a project in accordance with the PPP model before the authority through a preliminary feasibility study of the project in compliance with the state's strategy and development plan for the approval and the procurement thereof in accordance with the provisions of the law.

PPPs in public procurements 115

a distinguished project or the rejection thereof. In case of approval of a project concept, the concept proposer shall be granted a period of six months to prepare the comprehensive feasibility studies unless the authority decides, based on the nature of the project, to grant him an additional period for this purpose in accordance with the terms and proceedings set by the authority and approved by the higher committee.[32]

The authority shall present to the higher committee the results of the comprehensive feasibility study, whether prepared by the competition committee, the private sector or the public entity, along with the authority's recommendations for the approval of the project and its procurement in accordance with the PPP model, or the rejection thereof. If the approval of the project in accordance with the PPP model is recommended, the recommendation shall include a proposed method of competition for the procurement of the project either through a competitive bidding process or a competitive tender process; type of proposed PPP model to be adopted; identification of the public entity(ies) which has/have competences and responsibilities for a project of this nature, in order for them to participate in the preparation of the procurement documents, approve the technical specifications, participate in the evaluation of offers in preparation for the award of the project, sign the PPP agreement and follow-up on the implementation and operation until the transfer to the State; the proposed timetable for the project's procurement stages and proceedings; the proposed investment term; the proposed exemptions and privileges as well as any specific advantage to be granted if the project was submitted through a concept for approval; the proposed service to be provided, its economic, social and/or service importance, or whether it is a development or improvement of an existing service or reduction of the cost thereof or improvement of its efficiency.[33] This is the method for approval of proposed projects.

The higher committee shall issue its decision regarding the submitted projects in light of the recommendations presented by the authority.[34]

The expression of interest can be implemented as the authority may announce the request for expression of interest for PPP projects, as a procedure preceding the qualification proceedings, in order to assess the interest and willingness of the private sector to participate in the implementation of the project prior to undertaking the procurement proceedings, in the Official Gazette and other local or international media that are suitable with the nature of the project, and through the publication of the same on the website of the authority.[35]

The announcement shall include necessary details about the project. The duration for receipt of a request for expression of interest shall be no less than two

---

32 The Executive Regulation of the PPP legislation in Kuwait, Article 4.
33 The Executive Regulation of the PPP legislation in Kuwait, Article 5.
34 The Executive Regulation of the PPP legislation in Kuwait, Article 6.
35 The Executive Regulation of the PPP legislation in Kuwait, Article 13.

116   *PPPs in public procurements*

weeks from the date of publication of the announcement. The requests for expression of interest may be accepted through electronic mail.

The authority shall review and study the requests for expression of interest submitted by the investors. The authority shall, upon that study, decide on the feasibility for undertaking the proceedings set by the law and invite interested parties for pre-qualification to participate in the competition for the implementation of the project or to refrain from undertaking such proceeding, in preparation to present a recommendation in this respect to the higher committee.

The invitation for qualification is also regulated. The authority shall, following the approval of the higher committee on the PPP project and the determination of the PPP model and the method of procurement in accordance with the provisions of Article (8) of the executive regulations, in collaboration with the public entity appointed by the higher committee, announce the invitation for qualification for the project in the Official Gazette and at least two Kuwaiti dailies in both Arabic and English, and in local or international media as may be deemed necessary in accordance with the nature of the project, as well as publishing it on the website of the authority. The duration for submission of the qualification requests shall be no less than 15 days from the date of publication in the Official Gazette unless it was decided to undertake a post-qualification in which case the duration shall be included in the duration for submission of proposals.[36]

The terms for qualifications stipulate that each investor wishing to participate in a project being tendered in accordance with the provisions of the law shall prove its capacity to implement the project and fulfill its obligations. The determination of the investor's capacity is undertaken through qualification proceedings. The higher committee may either undertake a pre-qualification or a post-qualification process based on the recommendation of the authority and in accordance with the nature of the project, in order to ensure the proper selection of investors capable of implementing each project separately.[37]

Pre-qualification and/or post-qualification proceedings

After the approval of the higher committee of the feasibility studies and qualification documents, the authority shall announce the acceptance of requests for qualification from investors wishing to invest in a PPP project through the pre-qualification proceedings, in order to ensure the ability of the applicant for a request for qualification to implement the project, based on the terms and conditions specified in the qualification documents.[38] The higher committee may decide to merge the qualification phase with the request of proposals phase; in this case the qualification of investors wishing to invest in the project

36 The Executive Regulations of the PPP legislation in Kuwait, Article 14.
37 The Executive Regulations, Chapter Five, Article 15, et seq.
38 The Executive Regulations of the PPP legislation in Kuwait, Article 16.

PPPs in public procurements 117

shall be considered a post-qualification. The terms of post-qualification shall be similar to that of the pre-qualification. The investor wishing to invest shall present the qualification documents in an envelope that is separate from the other envelopes containing the technical and financial proposals. The envelopes of post-qualification shall be opened prior to the opening of the technical and financial envelopes and a list of the qualified applicants shall be prepared and submitted to the higher committee for approval prior to reviewing and evaluating the technical and financial proposals. The investors who do not meet the post-qualification criteria may request the reimbursement of their bid bonds.[39]

Qualification decision process

The qualification decision process has to be exercised by the competition committee, which shall review and study the requests for qualification submitted by the investors, and it shall prepare a report addressing all of its review and the results of the evaluation of the qualification requests, as well as the investors that are approved to participate in the second phase of the procurement, the investors who are proposed to be excluded and the justifications of any such exclusions. A report regarding the same shall be presented to the authority. After reviewing the aforementioned report, the authority shall present its recommendations with regards to the requests for qualification to the higher committee so that it may issue an appropriate decision in this matter. The authority shall notify the investors of the final decision regarding their requests for qualification at the addresses stated in their requests.[40]

The invitation for submission of proposals is highlighted in the executive regulations. The authority in collaboration with the public entity shall invite the qualified investors to collect the project's procurement documents and to submit their proposals. The invitation shall be made through publication in the Official Gazette and at least two Kuwaiti dailies in both Arabic and English and other local or international media as may be deemed necessary as per the nature

---

39 The Executive Regulations of the PPP legislation in Kuwait, Article 17. Article (18) details the Qualification Documents as follows: 'Taking into consideration the special nature of each PPP project, the qualification documents shall comprise the following: 1. Information for the parties wishing to apply for qualification indicating the means for preparation and submission of the request of qualification; 2. A description of the PPP project procured for investment including its location, nature and main features as well as the surface of the proposed land for project implementation, if any; 3. A statement of specific expertise that the investor is required to meet in order to be qualified in the qualification phase; 4. Qualification standards; 5. The deadline for collection of qualification documents, indicating the date and hour thereof; 6. The place and the method of submission of qualification documents; the higher committee may decide to accept them through means of electronic communication; and 7. The deadline for submission of qualification documents which shall be no less than 15 days as of the date of the publication of the announcement for qualification in the Official Gazette.'
40 The Executive Regulations of the PPP legislation in Kuwait, Article 21.

118 *PPPs in public procurements*

of the project, as well as through publication on the website of the authority, as the authority deems appropriate in this regard.[41]

The investors may submit inquiries with regards to the terms of qualifications and competition in accordance with the conditions and limitations set in the qualification documents and project procurement documents.[42]

The procurement of the project is in two stages. The higher committee may, based on the recommendation of the authority, decide to procure the project in two stages in accordance with the nature and requirements thereof, and conduct a competitive dialogue[43] at the intermediary bid-submission of the process in order to obtain clarifications in relation to the elements of the technical and financial offers presented during this stage.

In the second stage, final proposals shall be submitted.If the project is to be procured in two stages, the authority in coordination with the relevant public entity must, during the first stage, prepare the procurement documents provided they include the general information regarding the project, its specifications, standards and performance indicators or requirements for financing or its specific basic contractual arrangements and any other information as the authority deems necessary; the obligation for the investor to submit its suggestions with regards to its annotations or observations made on the project's documents, to be reviewed by the competition committee and taken as guidance during the stage of preparation of the final project procurement documents; the initial offers shall not include any information or financial data regarding competitive prices to be offered by the investor.

The offers submitted at this stage shall be limited to the technical, legal, environmental and general financing issues as well as topics permitted under the terms of reference. Upon receipt of the initial offers and the review and study thereof, the authority may invite the investors that have presented their offers to undertake a competitive dialogue with them with regards to their proposed

---

41 Pursuant to Article 31 of the Executive Regulations, et seq., the invitation for submission of proposals shall include the following: 1. The deadline for the collection of the project's procurement documents; 2. The relevant public entity(ies) that will enter into the PPP agreement and the appendices thereto; 3. The investment term; 4. The location of the project stating whether it is being implemented on state-owned land; 5. The fees due and the method of collection of the project's procurement documents, after signing the confidentiality agreement; 6. The deadline for submission of proposals indicating the date and hour which shall be no less than 90 days after the date of publication of the invitation in the Official Gazette, as well as the method and place for submission; 7. The incentives and tax and custom exemptions granted for the project. The proposals may be submitted by electronic means of communication which support the necessary confidentiality provided the prior approval of the higher committee thereon.

42 The Executive Regulations of the PPP legislation in Kuwait, Article 32.

43 The Competitive Dialogue is defined in Article (1) of the Executive Regulations, et seq., as: the terms and proceedings adopted by the authority when having an intermediary bid submission in order to receive the suggestions of the private sector with regards to the project's components and procurement terms.

PPPs in public procurements 119

comments made to the project's elements and the initial terms for its procurement. If the aforementioned invitation to the investors is made, the investors must all be granted an equal opportunity or duration for discussion.

The authority must review and study any amendments and prepare appropriate recommendations thereon to be presented to the higher committee to consider approval thereof as the project's procurement documents.[44]

As the Kuwaiti legal system aims to achieve a high standard of objectivity, equality and to maintain free competition, the evaluation of offers procedures are of great significance as the competition committee shall undertake the evaluation of the technical proposals based on the standards and weights stated in the project's procurement documents, prior to reviewing the financial offer. A proposal that does not include a bid bond as stated in the procurement documents shall be rejected. The evaluation of the technical offer must consider provisions for technical safety included in the offer, including the technology to be used and techniques complying with the terms specified in the project's procurement document, the environmental standards specified under the procurement documents, an evidence of the quality of the services and facilities to be implemented and provided through the project and their conformity with standards and performance indicators specified under the terms of reference, the extent to which suitability between the main components of the project have taken into consideration the provisions of the technical offer and the financial offer.[45]

The competition committee shall submit a report with respect to the evaluation of the technical offers along with its recommendations to the authority for approval thereof. The authority shall notify the investors whose technical offers were approved and those who were rejected.

The competition committee shall arrange a public session to open the financial envelopes for the offers submitted by the investors. The qualified investors who have submitted their offers in connection with the project being tendered shall be invited. A representative of the relevant public entity(ies) shall also be invited to attend the session. The financial envelopes shall be opened in alphabetic order of the bidders' names. The value of each proposal shall be read out and shall be recorded in a schedule made for this purpose. In the case of inclusion of several values within the same proposal, the highest value shall be retained, without prejudice to the authority's right to exclude or reject such proposal in accordance with the terms of the project's procurement documents.[46]

The competition committee must prepare a report in connection with the evaluation of the technical and financial offers. The report must consider the conclusions made during the public session in preparation for the submission thereof to the authority, including its recommendation for the appointment of

44 The Executive Regulations of the PPP legislation in Kuwait, Article 34.
45 The Executive Regulations of the PPP legislation in Kuwait, Article 37.
46 The Executive Regulations of the PPP legislation in Kuwait, Article 38.

120 *PPPs in public procurements*

the preferred investor and the subsequent investor in terms of preference among the submitted proposals.[47]

Submission of one proposal

In the case of submission of only one proposal or if the other proposals are invalid because they are in breach or they do not comply with the terms for participation in the competition, the competition committee must prepare a report in this respect and submit it to the general director of the authority in preparation for the presentation of the same before the higher committee along with the recommendation he deems appropriate.

The higher committee may decide to approve the sole offer or to re-procure the project or to undertake amendments it deems appropriate in the project's procurement documents or it may cancel the investment opportunity without any liability whatsoever.

The authority shall invite the preferred investor to negotiate the offer it has submitted along with the details and clarifications thereon and its reservations to the project's procurement documents.In all cases, the negotiations shall not address any contractual terms deemed in the invitation for submission of proposals as being non-negotiable or as material deviations according to the project's procurement documents. No amendments may be undertaken with respect to the technical and financial terms and conditions upon which the proposals have been evaluated. The negotiations may not lead to an amendment in the competition terms presented to the preferred investor or relieve it from its liabilities in accordance with the provisions of the terms of reference under the risk allocation schedule specified in the project's procurement documents.[48]

The authority shall in collaboration with the public entity(ies) stated in the decision of the higher committee prepare the project procurement documents in accordance with the provisions of the law, ensuring the non-disclosure of confidential technical, economic and financial information of the project submitted by the concept proposer and specifically the technical designs of the project and

47 The authority shall specify in light of the recommendation presented by the Competition Committee the preferred investor as being the provider of the best proposal in accordance with the Terms of Reference based on which the project is being procured. The authority must notify the concerned investor and the public entity of the investor that was determined as being the preferred investor in order to proceed with the negotiations with it. The authority must also notify the other investors who passed the financial proposals phase of their ranking. The authority shall keep the bid bond of the preferred investor and the subsequent investor in the ranking and it may release the bid bonds of the other investors unless it decides to keep them until the appointment of the successful investor or the expiry of the duration of the submitted bonds or their refusal to renew their bonds or the extension thereof as per the terms provided for under the project procurement documents. *See* The Executive Regulations of the PPP legislation in Kuwait, Article 39.
48 This whole framework was detailed in Article 42 of the Executive Regulations of the PPP legislation in Kuwait.

any technique proposed for the implementation thereof as well as any other confidential information.[49]

The grievance mechanism

A Grievance Committee[50] shall review all complaints and grievances submitted by concerned persons with regards to any proceeding or decision issued in violation of the provisions of the PPP law and/or its executive regulations.

The complaint shall be submitted to the Committee within 15 days after the notification to the concerned person or after the concerned person became aware of such decision. The Committee shall have a secretary in charge of receiving complaints submitted to the Committee and of preparing registers to record all such complaints and grievances along with associated memoranda, documents and files.[51] The Committee represents a higher threshold of protection to investors in PPP projects to achieve the right application of international standards adopted by PPP law and its executive regulations. The Committee is a pivotal tool that guarantees the implementation of PPP law and regulations' basic principles of objectivity, transparency, equality, equal opportunity and fair competition.

The profile of innovation in the award procedures in PPP law in Dubai

PPP in the UAE or the wider Gulf states has been well known for many years.[52] Dubai has partially embraced PPP in the form of operation and maintenance contracts such as the Dubai Metro (rather than full PPP). Gulf states' governments also have successful history of quasi-PPP in the electricity and water sectors such as the ADWEA IWPP program.[53]

There are several new procedures especially drafted in the PPP law in Dubai for better selection for the private partner. This new procedural framework reflects the profile of innovation in award procedures in Dubai.[54]

---

49 The Executive Regulations of the PPP legislation in Kuwait, Article 56.
50 The Grievance Committee is the Committee established in accordance with Article (32) of the law for the review of complaints and grievances submitted by concerned persons against decisions or proceedings undertaken by the higher committee or the authority.
51 The Executive Regulations of the PPP legislation in Kuwait, Article 70.
52 It is worth noting that in 2017, the UAE Cabinet issued resolution (1/1) on the procedures manual for partnership between federal entities and private sector. The manual intends to diversify the mechanisms for developing the strategic infrastructure projects and improve the quality of services. It also provides a general framework for project lifecycle of partnerships with private sectors.
53 Allen & Overy, Dubai Embraces PPP again, available at: https://www.jdsupra.com/legal news/dubai-embraces-ppp-again-13626/ last accessed on 4 February 2020.
54 It is important to note that the Guide to Public Private Partnership in Dubai is of fundamental importance. It is published by the Department of Finance, Government of Dubai. Available at: www.dof.gov.ae/en-us/publications/Lists/ContentListing/Attachments/377/Guid%20to%20PPP%20.pdf.

122   *PPPs in public procurements*

PPP legislation in Dubai stipulates in Article 14 that a special Committee for PPP shall be formed, and it shall carry out and exercise all duties mentioned in Dubai PPP law. The investor selection shall be subject to the principles of publicity, transparency, fair competition, equal opportunity, equality, advertising for the competition and public interest considerations.[55]

Projects are to be approved by (a) the director general of the relevant government department, if the total costs to the government are less than AED200m, (b) the Department of Finance (DoF), if total costs are between AED200m and AED500m and (c) the Committee, if the costs are higher (Article 8), although any financing obtained by the project company is to be approved by the government department (in coordination with DoF) (Article 36). It is not clear whether the Article 8 approval is to be calculated on the basis of capital costs or (noting the maximum 30-year tenure) whole-life project costs. In any case, given the thresholds, it is likely that the majority of projects will require Committee approval. In addition, Article 5(C) makes it clear that no PPP contract may be made if the government entity does not have a budget allocation for the whole of the project. Given Dubai's budget is allocated on an annual basis, this adds to the expectation that the majority of projects will require Committee approval, notwithstanding Article 8. Increased Committee approval could be viewed positively, as it should help to bring consistency to large-scale projects.

However, the principal benefit of the Dubai PPP law is that it codifies the pre-procurement process, as well as the procurement process, that government departments must follow in order to procure a PPP project. Article 24 includes the process to be followed in cancelling any tender. In-line with global market practice, no compensation is permitted to be paid to any bidder on cancellation of any project.

Articles 26, 32 and 34 contain minimum content requirements in relation to any PPP contract. More details are to be clarified in the regulations and guidebook to be issued by Department of Finance under Article 9, which again is consistent with other PPP legislation across the world.[56]

Article 36 provides that only the project company shall be liable for any third-party financing of any project. Article 39 revokes any other laws to the extent of any conflict, which presumably would include Dubai's public debt law (Dubai Decree No. 24 of 2007 and Committee Decision No. 1 of 2008) given Articles 8 and 36.

However, most of the above is subject to exemption should the Committee so approve (Article 7(5), 15(2), 26(18), 27(B), 31 and 38) or DoF (Articles 7(5), 9, 21(B), 26(18) and 29(B)).

---

55 The PPP legislation in Dubai, Article 14/A.
56 Guide to Public Private Partnership in Dubai published by the Department of Finance, Government of Dubai. Available at: www.dof.gov.ae/en-us/publications/Lists/ContentListing/Attachments/377/Guid%20to%20PPP%20.pdf.

PPP legislation in Dubai confirms that it will not apply the Procurement Law No. 6 of 1997 other than where the PPP contract contains no clear provision on a matter. Implementing PPP schemes in Dubai assumes that there is a new procurement system in Dubai for PPP as the application of the Procurement Law No. 6 of 1997 would create unpredictabilities. The traditional procurement law in Dubai contains several requirements concerning tender conditions, timescales and contract terms, which do not sit easily with either PPP procurement process or PPP contract. PPP legislation in Dubai contains provisions relating to the pre-qualification, tender and selection processes and PPP contract terms including bidding terms and conditions and financial security; conditions of the PPP contract, bid bond value, performance bond value calculations and means of comparing bids; and tender scoring and evaluation procedures.[57] These provisions provide the public juristic entity with a high degree of flexibility to specify the tender and contract conditions on a case by case basis. The overriding award criteria is the 'most financially and technically advantageous bid,' but the government entity has a discretion to specify the detail of this, including the balance between technical and financial criteria, in the tender documents. PPP legislation allows private entities to make Unsolicited Proposals for PPP projects and allow the public juristic entity to contract directly with the entity that makes such a proposal. There is no requirement for such proposals to be put to tender.[58]

The PPP legislation does not apply to electricity and water projects that are governed by the Electricity and Water Sector Law No. 6 of 2011 or simple works contracts or supply contracts that are governed by the Procurement Law No. 6 of 1997.[59]

Direct contracting in Dubai PPP legislation

Dubai PPP legislation points out that irrespective of sub-clause of Article 14/A, the public juristic entity may enter into direct contracting (without tendering) with the project company if there is a new and creative project offered by this company.[60] The criterion for selecting the private investor through direct contracting is to offer a new and creative project by this investor. The direct contracting mechanism undermines, to some extent, objectivity, equality and fair competition principles in selecting a private partner. It may be argued that direct contracting remains a rapid and liberal mechanism for selection of the

---

57 The PPP legislation in Dubai, Articles 14 to 24.
58 The PPP legislation in Dubai, Articles 12 and 14. *See* also: DLA Piper, *Infrastructure Update, Dubai's New PPP Law*, available at: www.dlapiper.com/~/media/Files/Insights/Publica tions/2015/10/Dubais%20New%20PPP%20Law.pdf, last accessed on 1 November 2019.
59 *Infrastructure Update, Dubai's New PPP Law*, ibid.
60 The PPP legislation in Dubai, Article 14/c.

124 *PPPs in public procurements*

private partner since it avoids bureaucracy. It is, to some extent, against equal opportunity, equality and fair competition principles.

To assure transparency, equal opportunity and free competition, the Dubai PPP legislation illustrates that administrative bodies must start the procedures by undertaking the necessary process for the qualifications of companies that may enter with the government in partnership and ensuring that the project and its details are advertised in the media before starting award procedures. The administrative body may start preliminary meetings with the qualified partners to discuss the specifications of the project and the preliminary conditions.[61] This mechanism is intended to ensure the best specifications for the project, to continue running public utilities in a regular manner, and to apply the *value for money* principle in public utilities' projects.

The qualified partner may stipulate confidentiality upon the administrative body and request nondisclosure of any information regarding its economic or financial expectations relating to the project subject to partnership. It is argued that confidentiality in this context is to protect investors from unauthorized disclosure of their financial secrets to their competitors. A counter argument, however, suggests that confidentiality provision violates the principle of transparency.

Further, dealing with a qualified partner should be in the light of the principles mentioned in Article 14, that is, to procure equal opportunity and absolute equality among them. If the administrative body amends specifications of the project, with no violation to qualifications criteria, it has to expressly advertise in the media, with enough time before starting receiving offers.[62] This legislative stipulation does not only ensure the application of fair competition principle, but it is also in accordance with the good international practices that are mentioned by the OECD MAPS, OECD Recommendations and the World Bank Benchmarking Report on PPPs Procurement 2017.[63]

The profile of innovation in the award procedures in PPP law in Morocco

The profile of innovation in the award procedures is clear in the PPP law and PPP decree in Morocco as the socio-economic impact of any PPP project has to be assessed during the award process. Pursuant to Articles 2(3) and 8 of the PPP law, and 4(2) of the PPP decree, assessments when procuring PPP projects would include 'requisites of sustainable development' and the project's 'social impact.' Pursuant to Articles 2(3) and 8 of the PPP law, and 4(2) of the

---

61 The PPP legislation in Dubai, Article 15.
62 The PPP legislation in Dubai, Article 16.
63 The World Bank, Benchmarking Public-Private Partnerships Procurement Benchmarking PPP Procurement: Assessing Government Capability to Prepare, Procure and Manage PPPs 2017, available at: https://ppp.worldbank.org/public-private-partnership/sites/ppp.world bank.org/files/documents/Benchmarking_PPPs_2017_ENpdf.pdf.

PPP decree, assessments when procuring PPP projects would include 'risk allocation of the project, with identification of the risks that face the relevant competent authority, the private partner, and others, and the means of its allocation.'

Pursuant to Articles 2(2) and 8 of the PPP law, and 4(2) of the PPP decree, assessments when procuring PPP projects would include a pre-assessment of 'a comparative analysis with other structures for implementing the projects that justifies the resort to PPP contracts.'

Pursuant to Articles 2(3) and 8 of the PPP law, and 4(2) of the PPP decree, assessments when procuring PPP projects would include 'the total cost of the project' and pre-assessments include 'the financial components of the project and means of financing.'

A draft PPP contract has to be included in the request for proposal pursuant to Article 13.3 of the decree. This draft PPP contract outlines the rights and obligations of the Private Partner and the competent authority.

Pursuant to Article 10 of the PPP decree, three representatives of the bid evaluation committee would be from the relevant procuring authority, two members from the ministry competent with finance, in addition to other optional members being experts in the field.

The procuring authority has to publish a public procurement notice of the PPP. Therefore, the procuring authority must publish an '*avis de publicité*' of the procurement process of the PPP contract pursuant to Article 3 paragraph 2 of the PPP law and Articles 11 and 12 of the PPP decree. The means of publication are as follows: (i) the procuring authority's website; (ii) the procurement contract's website and (iii) at least two local journals chosen by the procuring authority, one in Arabic and one in a foreign language.

Article 12(4) of the PPP decree provides that the periods in the published invitation should be a minimum of 30 days with regards to competitive dialogues and the call for tenders with pre-selection of bidders should be a minimum of 40 days in open tenders.

Article 13 of the PPP decree stipulates that the tender documents should provide information regarding the stages of the procurement process that includes the requisites to submit bids, the criteria for choosing them, their duration, the type of procedures and the period for which inquiries are permitted.

According to Articles 2 and 5 of the PPP law and 32 of the PPP decree, the project must go through a pre-qualification process, and within the competitive discussion, the public entity can reduce the number of bidders using successive stages in order to obtain a restrictive list. Moreover, Article 17 of the PPP decree provides that when the procuring authority chooses specific criteria to be applied to tenders generally, it must communicate such choice with all bidders at the same time and under the same circumstances.

Currently, most of the projects include pre-qualifications criteria in the tender documents.

Article 20(3) of the PPP decree permits any candidate to submit inquires to the relevant procuring authority about information concerning the announced tender or consultancy folder.

126 *PPPs in public procurements*

Article 20(3) of the PPP decree obliges the procuring authority to disclose questions and clarifications within the specified time periods to all candidates.

Article 5 paragraph 5 of the PPP law and 30(2) of the PPP decree permit competitive dialogues to take place, in which the procuring authority may ask contributors to clarify, complete, or improve their tenders.

The procuring authority would be permitted to disclose this type of information resulting from competitive dialogues but requires the written prior approval of the concerned candidate in which precise information was provided.

Article 8 of the PPP law provides that the contract would be awarded to the candidate who presented the most economically advantageous tender in accordance with the preset criteria in the law. However, in accordance with Article 17(1) of the PPP decree, other criteria may be taken into consideration by the procuring authority insofar as they are objective, non-discriminatory, and relate to the PPP contract.

An abstract of the PPP contract together with the award notice are published in the Official Bulletin and in any other publicity means, including online, according to Article 11 of the PPP law and 42 of the PPP decree.

According to Article 8 of PPP law, 'the public entity shall inform the other candidates about the rejection of their bids in a period not exceeding 60 days.' And according to Article 20 of the PPP decree, the competent authority informs the candidates that have not been selected by any means of communication.

According to Article 7 of the PPP law, the PPP contract can be concluded in the form of a negotiated procedure in cases where: there is a lack of capability for conducting the service for technical and legal reasons except by one private sector actor; there are urgent matters resulting from legal/regulatory provisions (from unanticipated events by the public entity); and public and national defense issues. Articles 33 and 40 of the PPP decree reiterate this.

Article 9 of the PPP law provides that the public entity may be approached by a private actor with an innovative project idea at the technical, economic and financial level, in order to conclude a PPP contract.

According to Article 9 of the PPP law and 37–39 of the PPP decree, the procuring authority would ensure the innovative nature of the proposal and conduct a prequalification assessment on that basis, where Article 37 of the Decree specifies certain criteria.

According to Article 9(4) of the PPP law and 40(3) of the PPP decree, the procuring entity may resort in competitive dialogue, open tenders, or restricted procedures methods, after conducting the pre-assessment and negotiated procedure to accept the innovative idea.

The procuring authority grants a minimum period of time to additional prospective bidders (besides the proponent) to prepare their proposals. The general rules in Article 12(4) of the PPP decree would apply, which specify a 40 day minimum period with regards to open tenders.

According to Article 9(6) of the PPP law and 34 and 41 of the PPP decree, the unsolicited offeror may receive 'arbitrary' lump-sum compensation when the bid is unsuccessful.

According to Article 18 of the PPP law, the public entity controls the implementation of the contract and the way the private partner respects the purposes and quality of the service. Details of the means to conduct such management would be included in the PPP contract.

The procuring or contract management authority has to establish a monitoring and evaluation system of the PPP contract. According to Article 18 of the PPP law, the public entity controls the implementation of the contract and the way the private partner respects the purposes and quality of the service. Details of the means to conduct such management would be included in the PPP contract.

Article 18(4) of the PP Law provides that the private partner submits any documents or information to the public entity in the aim to control the implementation of the contract.

Article 18(5) of the PPP law provides that the contractor shall provide the public authority an annual progress report on the implementation of PPP contract work.

In accordance with the article 12 of the PPP law, the substitution, the transfer and the conditions of change to the shareholding structure of the private partner are mandatory provisions of the PPP contract and if such mandatory provision is not adhered to, the public entity may substitute the private partner to ensure the continuity of the public service pursuant to article 21 of the PPP law.

The regulatory framework expressly regulate the modification or renegotiation of the PPP contract, after the contract is signed by the contracting parties. Article 23 of the PPP law specifically addresses these circumstances, which may be initiated by any party to the contract but with the ultimate consent of the public entity and provided it does not change the nature of the contract or affect its balance. It is suggested that the balance in this regard is the financial equilibrium of the contract in favor of the contracting parties the private partner and the public entity.

Article 23 of the PPP law refers to modifications to the PPP contract provided they do not change the nature of the contract or 'affect its balance,' in which the latter term addresses safeguards to any changes to risk allocation of the contract. The balance in this regard is not confined to risk allocation but it is suggested that it extends to include the financial balance or financial equilibrium of the contract as the risk allocation has many angels and economic dimension.

In accordance with Article 12 of the PPP law, the contract balance in the case of hardship or force majeure are mandatory provisions of the PPP contract (paragraph 9). In accordance with the Article 26 of the PPP law, the PPP contract may be terminated by mutual agreement in case of force majeure.

The PPP contract may provide for the settlement of disputes to resort to conciliation, conventional mediation, arbitration or judicial proceedings (Article 27 of the PPP law).

Article 26 provides for grounds for termination of PPP contracts which include:

128 *PPPs in public procurements*

- Force majeure;
- Disruption of the PPP contract's economic equilibrium;
- Termination on public interest grounds;
- Amicable termination;
- Private partner's serious breach of contract.

According to Article 26(4) of the PPP law, the contract determines solely the indemnities in cases of force majeure, the disturbance of the equilibrium of the contract, or the termination by agreement.

The profile of innovation in the award procedures in PPP law in Jordan

According to Articles 6(a)(3) and 17 of the PPP law, the PPP Council must attain the Council of Ministers' approval of PPP projects. Article 6 of the PPP regulation provides that the Council's approval is to be procured before launching the procurement process. Article (5) of the Law provides that the Council shall comprise six members, two of which shall be the Minister of Finance and the Governor of the Central Bank.

Pursuant to Articles 6(a)(4) and 17 of the PPP law and Article 32/f of the PPP regulation, the Council must approve the PPP contract in its final version. Articles 5 and 32 of the PPP regulation stipulates that the Council has to approve the final awarding of the partnership project bid and the winning proposal; in addition to that, the Council has to approve the final draft of the partnership contract.

Crucial assessments have to be conducted when identifying and preparing a PPP in order to inform the decision to proceed, such as socio-economic analysis (cost-benefit analysis of the socio-economic impact of the PPP project). Pursuant to Articles 10(A) of the PPP law and 2 and 5(a)(1)(F) of the PPP regulation, a feasibility study shall be prepared. This study is defined as an analytical study that covers different aspects such as legal, technical, social, economic, environmental, financial and financing aspects of the project. The PPP unit shall evaluate this study in accordance with Article 3(d)(2)(b) of the PPP regulation based on the previously mentioned criteria.

Comparative assessment has to be exercised to evaluate whether a PPP is the best option when compared to other procurement alternatives. The evaluation focuses on *value for money* analysis and a public sector comparator. Pursuant to Articles 10(a) of the PPP law and 5(b)(2) of the PPP regulation, the contracting authority shall prepare a cost-benefit analysis and feasibility study to be submitted to the PPP unit, in which contributors provided includes a *value for money* analysis to conclude whether PPPs are the best option for the project.Environmental impact assessment is of fundamental importance to

PPPs in public procurements 129

the PPP procurement process in Jordan. Articles 10(a) of the PPP law and 5 (b)(2) of the PPP regulation identify that the contracting authority shall prepare a cost-benefit analysis and feasibility study to be submitted to the PPP unit.

Article 2 of the PPP regulation as previously displayed, defines the feasibility study as:

> The analytical study prepared by the contracting authority addressing the institutional, legal, technical, environmental, social, economic, financial, and other aspects of the proposed partnership project during the project's standardized cycle. The study should also identify the need for government support to guarantee the sustainability and continuity of the project and clarify the realization of *value for money*, the ability to bear costs, risk analysis and diversification, and any other requirements based on the nature of the project.[64]

Pursuant to Article 19(b) of the PPP regulation, the PPP draft-contract and the request for proposal are part of the tender documents. Article 7/B/11 of the PPP law provides that the PPP unit shall assist the contracting parties in obtaining the required licenses and approvals in coordination with the Jordan Investment Commission. The PPP contract and the request for proposal are part of the tender documents according to Article 19(b) of the PPP regulations. In coordination with Jordan Investment Commission, the PPP unit has to assist the contracting parties in obtaining required licenses pursuant to Article 7/B/11 of the PPP law.

To achieve the best required standards for the contracting state, and to be compatible with the international standards, there are two committees of bid evaluation that may be formed pursuant to the PPP law, more specifically, a steering committee and a technical committee. The technical committee evaluates the bids and provides the steering committee with its findings/report. Article 4/b of the PPP regulation indicates that the steering committee includes representatives of the relevant government entities who have the legal, financial, technical and other expertise necessary for the project in addition to a representative of the PPP unit and the person in charge of the project as appointed as such by the contracting entity. The steering committee has a chairman. The chairman of the steering committee is appointed by the contracting entity. On the other hand, there is nothing in the PPP law and the PPP

---

64 Geoffrey Hamilton, *FDI – the Global Crisis and Sustainable Recovery*, Working Paper for Public Private Partnerships, and *FDI as a Means of Securing a Sustainable Recovery*, paper submitted to the Fourth Columbia International Investment Conference, Vale Columbia Centre, Columbia Law School, Columbia University, 5–6 November 2009.

130 *PPPs in public procurements*

regulation relating to specific qualifications of the technical committee. The PPP regulation under Article 4/c merely sets out that the chairman of the technical committee is the person in charge of the project as appointed as such by the contracting entity.[65]

According to Articles 8 and 10(a) of the PPP regulation, publication is made by the contracting entity in Arabic and English in two local daily newspapers, on the websites of both the contracting entity and the PPP unit, and, if necessary, in a foreign newspaper published abroad. Publication in such means covers:

1. The request for expression of interest prior to the initiation of the PPP tender process and in the event the PPP unit determines that such publication is needed.
2. The request for pre-qualification once the PPP tender process has been initiated.[66]

    The timeline granted by the procuring authority to potential bidders to submit their bids is highlighted in Articles 19 and 22(H) of the PPP regulation.

Article 5 (c) (2) of the PPP regulation stipulates explaining the tender's invitation stage, '2- The contracting party shall comply with the invitation to tender procedures in accordance with the provisions of this Regulations.' Article 6 provides that 'The contracting party shall initiate, upon obtaining the approval of the Council, procedures of placing the Tender's invitations in coordination with the Unit.' Article 9 stipulates that the default nature of the restricted tendering where,

> The prequalification process will be open to all those interested, provided that it is not confined to those who replied in response to an "Expression of Interest Invitation" pursuant to paragraphs (c), (D), and (E) of Article (8) of this Regulation.

Article 16 of this Regulation provides the technical committee shall prepare a prequalification assessment report and submit it to the steering committee, provided that the report includes the committee recommendations, and a brief list of prequalified bidders. The steering committee shall review the report and submit it to the contracting party along with the necessary recommendation to

---

65 The World Bank Group, Procuring Infrastructure Public Private Partnership, 2018, available at: https://bpp.worldbank.org/en/data/exploreeconomies/jordan/2018, last accessed on 1 November 2019.
66 The World Bank Group, Procuring Infrastructure Public Private Partnership, 2018, available at: https://bpp.worldbank.org/en/data/exploreeconomies/jordan/2018, last accessed on 1 November 2019.

obtain approval. A- The steering committee shall review the report and submit it to the contracting party along with the necessary recommendation to obtain approval. B- The contracting party shall review the report and define the list of prequalified bidders who will be notified by official registered mail or official electronic mail in reply to the invitation to prequalification. C- The contracting party shall post the list of the prequalified bidders on its website and on the website of the unit. D- The contracting party shall notify the bidders who did not qualify (or were precluded) by official registered mail or official electronic mail in response to the prequalification invitation. E- The decision of the contracting party to exclude the bidders or disqualify them shall be written and justified.

The tender documents detail the procedures for the procurement process providing to all bidders. This is to maintain equality and equal opportunity between bidders.

Article 11 stipulates: A- In the prequalification invitation, the contracting party shall determine the standards of the qualification of the bidders and is entitled to request that they attach other data or illustrative documents to prove compliance with those standards. B- The prequalification standards include the following: 1- The technical capability to implement the partnership project, including any necessary qualifications or experiences related to the implementation of similar partnership projects, depending on the case. 2- Financial solvency, including the ability to provide financing and capital if required by the partnership project, in addition to average annual revenues. 3- Evidence that the company is a member of a consortium, in case the interested party is in the form of a consortium, and the suggested role of each consortium member in the partnership project. 4- Any other standards demanded by the nature of the partnership project as per what the unit deems suitable. C- The contracting party shall submit the prequalification invitation advertisement to the Unit for review prior to announcing it. D- Subject to the provisions of Article (10) of this Regulation, the invitation to partake in the procedures of prequalification, in addition to the standards of prequalification stated in Paragraph (b) of this Article, include the following: 1- A brief description of the partnership project and the nature of the role required to be performed by the private sector. 2- Procedures for receiving responses to the prequalification invitation and the deadline for receiving them at the specified location.

Article 19: The documents relating to placement of tender of the partnership project and its award include the following: A- Invitation to tender, including 1- Integrated information relating to the partnership project. 2- Conditions and procedures for preparing and receiving bids (proposals), the number of copies to be submitted, and the deadline for submission of bids, as well as the location for delivery.

Article (11) of the PPP regulation provides that the initial-qualification criteria is defined in the initial qualification invitation. The specified criteria is respected in practice, in the light of Article 25 (c) of the PPP regulation, which stipulates that 'The technical committee shall evaluate the technical proposals that are consonant with this Regulation and the requirements of the invitation to tender in accordance with the evaluation standards shown in the invitation to tender.'

132 *PPPs in public procurements*

Interested parties and/or potential bidders may submit questions to clarify the public procurement notice and/or the request for proposals.

Article 13 of the PPP regulation stipulates that the technical committee has the following duties and responsibilities: A- Determine the suggested qualification standards for the prequalification process. This will be reviewed by the steering committee and submitted along with necessary recommendations to the contracting party for approval. B- Prepare the invitation to prequalification and the list of documents to be reviewed by the steering committee and submit them along with necessary recommendations to the contracting party for approval. C- Respond to inquiries of interested parties concerning prequalification.

Pursuant to Article 20: A- The contracting party, in coordination with the unit, may call the prequalified bidders to a preliminary meeting, preceding the submission of proposals, to discuss matters relating to the project specifications and preliminary conditions, provided that the inquiries and replies are provided to the prequalified bidders who have attended the preliminary meeting or those absent. In the light of Article 20 (A) of the PPP regulation, confidential information pertaining to the bidders and questions and clarifications, may be disclosed by the procuring authority to all potential bidders.

To achieve a high standard of transparency, and notwithstanding confidential information pertaining to the bidders, the procuring authority discloses the content and the results of the pre-bid conference to all bidders. Article 20 (c) stipulates that:

> The contracting authority may, with the approval of the Unit, decide to reconsider the tender documents and to amend them, or to extend the term of the tender, based on the preliminary meeting referred to in Paragraph (A) of this Article, without impinging on the prequalification standards, provided that the contracting party distributes the amendment or change to the prequalified bidders within the time period stated in the tender documents.

Article 11 (B) of the PPP regulation provides that financial documents have to be presented with the bid. Pursuant to this sub-clause, technical and financial documents have to be presented. Sub-clause (B) provides: B- The prequalification standards include the following: 1- The technical capability to implement the partnership project, including any necessary qualifications or experiences related to the implementation of similar partnership projects, depending on the case. 2- Financial solvency, including the ability to provide financing and capital if required by the partnership project, in addition to average annual revenues. 3- Evidence that the company is a member of a consortium, in case the interested party is in the form of a consortium, and the suggested role of each consortium member in the partnership project. 4- Any other standards demanded by the nature of the partnership project as per what the Unit deems suitable.

Article 22 (D) of the PPP regulation provides that 'D- The financial envelope includes all the financial documents specified in the request for proposals, namely: 1- Financial proposal for the partnership project 2- Any other information stated in the invitation to tender (RFP).' Further, Article 27 of the PPP regulation stipulates that:

A- The steering committee shall announce the date, time and venue of opening the financial envelopes for the proposals that are technically qualified. B- The technical committee is responsible for opening the financial envelopes and ascertaining that its contents meet the requirements of this Regulation and the invitation to tender, subject to disqualifying the non-conforming proposals, and not listing them within the evaluation process. C- The financial proposals conforming to the provisions of this Regulation and the request for proposals from the technical committee in accordance with the evaluation standards contained in the request for proposals.

Articles 25 and 27 of the PPP regulation provide that proposals have to be assessed technically and financially according to the assessment criteria mentioned at the request for proposals. This process outlines the significance of this process as a tool to achieve *value for money* concept.

The procuring authority may cancel the partnership project tender pursuant to Article 31 of the PPP regulation. Article 31(A) (3) provides that

A- It is permissible to cancel the partnership project tender by virtue of a decision issued by the contracting party based on the recommendation of the Unit grounded in the recommendation of the steering committee and with the approval of the Council, at any time, in the following cases: 3- In case there is only one bidder in the prequalification stage.

Sub-clause (B) of this Article confirms that the: 'B- The bidders in the partnership project tender are not entitled to claim any compensation based on the consequence of the cancellation decision, unless the invitation to tenders states otherwise.'

The contracting entity is obliged to inform the pre-qualified applicant whether they have been selected as pre-qualified bidders or their application has been rejected.

To achieve objectivity, transparency, equality principles, if the technical proposal does not meet the minimum extent of the technical standards, the bidder shall be notified with the justified written decision. As a matter of legal logic that is supported by practice, this applies to all winning bidders and rejected bidders as both have to be notified with the justified written decision for acceptance or refusal. Article 26 of the PPP regulation provides that:

A- The technical proposals that do not meet the minimum extent of the technical standards stated in the invitation to tender and the tender documents shall be rejected by virtue of a justified written decision issued by the contracting party on the recommendation of the technical

134   *PPPs in public procurements*

committee based on the recommendation of the steering committee. B-The contracting party shall send the rejection decision to the submitters of the rejected bids by registered mail or official electronic mail in responding to the prequalification invitation. C- The financial proposal envelopes particular to the bidders that were rejected shall not be opened. They are entitled to recover them after rejection of grievance or the expiry of the period referred to in Paragraph (A) of Article (30) of this Regulation.

Article 29 stipulates that:

A- The contracting party shall notify the best bidder for the tender via registered mail or the official electronic mail for response to the prequalification invitation. B- The contracting party shall return the bid bond guarantee to the non-winning bidders upon expiry of the validity period of the bond, in accordance with what is stated in the tenders invitations or during nineteen (19) work days following the signing of the contract, whichever comes first, and the contracting party may request extending the period of the validity of the bond.

Further, Article 30 outlines the grievance process as follows:

A- Those bidders for the partnership project tender wishing to express grievance regarding the decisions pertaining to prequalification, and the technical and financial qualification for the submitted bids, shall submit grievance to the Council seven (7) work days from the day after his notification of the decisions referred to in this Paragraph. B- The Unit is responsible for receiving grievances submitted to the Council by the bidders for the partnership project concerning the decisions referred to in Paragraph (A) of this Article, as per the hereunder: 1- Non-acceptance of the grievance and dismissing it in form in case it is submitted after the passage of the period referred to in Paragraph (A) of this Article provided that the Unit submits its opinion in this regard to the Council. 2- Acceptance of the grievance in form in case it is submitted within the legal period and expresses its opinion thereon and submitting it to the Council. 3- The Council may, prior to deciding on the grievance, request any clarifications it deems necessary from the petitioner of grievance. The Council may form a special committee to look into any of the grievances submitted to it. 4- The Council shall issue its decision regarding the grievance submitted by virtue of a majority of the attending members within fifteen (15) days from date of submission thereto. The decision of the Council in this regard is final. 5- The Council Secretary is responsible for notifying the submitter of grievance of the decision via the email shown in the grievance.

PPPs in public procurements 135

PPP final contract

Article 32 stipulates some guarantees in favor of the winning bidders upon drafting the final draft of the PPP contract, such as for the purposes of preparing the final version of the contract it is permissible to hold negotiations between the steering committee and the best bidder. Second, it is possible for the technical committee, the project consultant and the Unit to participate in the negotiations as the situation may require. Third, it is inadmissible for the negotiations to impinge on the conditions stated in the contract which are regarded as non-negotiable in accordance with what is stated in the tender documents. Fourth, it is impermissible at the negotiations stage to undertake any alterations to the technical and financial conditions based on which the best bidder was chosen.

The contracting state have also some guarantees for the public interests considerations. For instance, it is impermissible during the negotiations stage to undertake any amendment on the basis of risks apportionment stated in the sustainability report. Second, in case negotiations with the best bidder fail, the steering committee may end negotiations and notify the bidder in writing of the reasons for ending them. In this case, the steering committee shall initiate negotiations with the second best bidder in accordance with the evaluation report. Conversely, if negotiations with the best bidder succeed, the Unit shall do the following:

1. Review the contracts concerning which there was negotiation.
2. Obtain the approval of the Council of the final award of the partnership project tender and to recognize the winning bid.
3. Recommend in conjunction with the contracting party to obtain the approval of the Council of the draft contract in its final form, provided that the Council decision includes authorizing the contracting party to sign the contract in its approved form.
4. Notify the best bidder of the award decision via registered mail or electronic mail at the address officially stated in the response to the prequalification invitation.

It is clear that the PPP law, regulation and polices in Jordan are compatible with the international standards as they are trying to achieve equality before the law, equal opportunity, fairness, objectivity, principles and, in addition, *value for money* as this economic perspective is one of the most significant principles governing PPP transactions for the contracting state. The PPP law and regulation in Jordan are subjected to achieve the PPP principles as they are recognized by the eminent international organizations in the international arena.

How can innovation in PPP public procurement support sustainable production and consumption and the shift to a circular economy?

A circular economy is one that designs most pollution and waste out of the system, extracts the maximum value from resources and allows natural capital to regenerate.

136 *PPPs in public procurements*

This would not only protect the environment, but also contribute to economic growth, increasing GDP by up to 7% in the EU by 2030. But how can countries transition from a linear, resource-intensive system to a fully circular economy?[67]

Innovation in PPP public procurement is instrumental in making consumption and production more sustainable. There are numerous examples of new technologies, processes, services and business models that are re-shaping product life cycles from design through production and usage to disposal and recycling. Businesses across the world have invested extensively in this direction.

UNECE advocates for People First Public Private Partnerships, exploring new ideas and arrangements to increase access to essential services, lessen social inequalities and preserve the environment whilst transforming the economy.

There is a range of experiences for the UNECE region to draw upon. The 2015 EU Circular Economy Package includes around 50 measures from production and consumption to waste management and markets for secondary raw material. Finland, for example, is one of the pioneers of innovative partnerships for a circular economy and has adopted an ambitious national roadmap.

Cities and regions can provide venues for experimenting with different partnerships and solutions and have the flexibility and scope for policy experimentation. Their high business and consumer density, their universities and research institutes and connectivity, make them ideal locations for innovation hubs, incubator spaces and urban farming.

Initiatives in Astana, Birmingham, Nokia, and Lyon demonstrated how city-level innovative partnerships can drive the transition towards sustainable production and consumption. Birmingham's industrial symbiosis approach, part of its overall sustainable economic development strategy, promotes the use of waste materials and by-products as inputs in production in other parts of the economy. Lyon's 'Chemistry Valley' has emerged around diversified and integrated multi-site activity in chemistry, energy and the environment.

It is suggested that in PPPs, Arab legislation award procedures should insist on using technologies that are friendly to the environment. The transfer of technology during recent decades is playing a significant role in facilitating the cultural and legal globalization process. It allows the application of new techniques in public procurements in PPPs. Furthermore, international public works agreements, nowadays, play an important role in spreading environmentally friendly technologies from developed states to developing nations.[68] Environmental

---

67 The UNECE Committee on Innovation, Competitiveness and Public-Private Partnerships met in Geneva on 26–28 March 2018 to discuss ways to make production and consumption more sustainable, as outlined in Sustainable Development Goal 12.

68 Methane is of special concern since it generates a global warming effect 23 times that of CO_2. For details on the role of PPPs in mitigating climate change and increasing FDI, *see* G. Hamilton, *FDI – the Global Crisis and Sustainable Recovery,* Working Paper for Public Private Partnerships, and *FDI as a Means of Securing a Sustainable Recovery,* paper submitted to the Fourth Columbia International Investment Conference, Vale Columbia Centre, Columbia Law School, Columbia University, 5–6 November 2009. For more information, *see* also

PPPs in public procurements 137

legislation stipulations currently tend to be an integral and compulsory part of tender documents. Hamilton pointed out an example in Canada (Vancouver city's efforts to reduce emissions in 2001) where there was a private partner who financed, designed, built, owned and operated a landfill and a 2.9 kilometers pipeline to take gas from the landfill to a nearby agricultural complex, where they built a common power-generating plant. The latter plant was built by the private partner to generate electricity to supply 5000 homes and to reduce carbon dioxide emission by approximately 200,000 tons per year (emission of about 40,000 cars).

UNECE supports economies in transition in their efforts to design and implement such policy through policy analysis, recommendations, regional policy dialogue and capacity building.[69]

New standard on zero tolerance to corruption will help to unlock potential of public private partnerships for achieving the sustainable development goals

A new standard on zero tolerance to corruption in PPPs developed by UNECE will help to catalyze countries' efforts to strengthen transparency, accountability and effective governance of investment in public infrastructure and service delivery, which will be key to achieving the Sustainable Development Goals (SDGs).

Corruption constitutes a major barrier to economic development and significantly undermines the implementation of the UN 2030 Agenda for Sustainable Development. It presents a challenge to investment in infrastructure, for which the SDGs identify financing in the form of PPPs as essential in order to fill the estimated USD 3.3 trillion per year investment gap worldwide.

OECD estimates that bribery consumes 10.9% of the total transaction value in public procurement globally, whilst Transparency International has estimated that corruption in construction could add as much as 50% to a project's cost. It further estimated that 10 to 30% of investment in a publicly funded construction project might be lost through mismanagement or corruption.[70]

J.D. Sachs, *Common Wealth 'Economics for a Crowded Planet,'* Penguin Books, 2008, Chapter 4, Global solutions to climate change, 84–114. *See* also: C. BOVIS, 'Editorial', in *EPPPL, 1/2010*; and for the same author: *EC Public Procurement: Case Law and Regulation, OUP, 2006*; Mohammed A.M. Ismail, Legal globalisation and PPPs in Egypt, *EPPL*, 1/2010; Ismail, *Globalization and New International Public Works Agreements in Developing Countries*, Routledge, 2011, Chapter 4. For more elaboration see: Ayşem Mert and Philipp Pattberg, How Do Climate Change and Energy-Related Partnerships Impact Innovation and Technology Transfer?: Some Lessons for the Implementation of the UN Sustainable Development Goals, *The Cambridge Handbook of Public-Private Partnerships, Intellectual Property Governence, and Sustainble Development*, Margaret Chon, Pedro Roffe, Ahmed Abdel-Latif (eds.) Cambridge University Press 2018, 289–305.

69 The UNECE Committee on Innovation, Competitiveness and Public-Private Partnerships met in Geneva on 26–28 March 2018.

70 OECD MAPS, 2018, available at: www.mapsinitiative.org/methodology/MAPS-methodology-for-assessing-procurement-systems.pdf, last accessed on 1 November 2019.

138 *PPPs in public procurements*

The new international standard on zero tolerance to corruption in PPPs adopted at the intergovernmental session of UNECE's Working Party on PPPs on 22 November 2017 aims to improve governance, reduce risks – and therefore costs – and strengthen trust and accountability in PPP procurement. The standard will not only help to save money but will also foster sustainable partnerships between governments and the private sector.

> Scaling up investment in key infrastructure will be essential to meet the ambitious objectives of the 2030 Agenda for Sustainable Development. Countries' adoption of the standard on Zero Tolerance to Corruption in PPPs serves as a powerful symbol of their commitment to building sustainable partnerships underpinned by accountability and good governance in the financing of vital public development projects.[71]

The standard includes principles and recommendations on PPP procurement that can be incorporated within national legal and administrative systems. To facilitate compliance with the standard, governments may consider making its conditions binding and subject to judicial or administrative review for all public and private actors involved, imposing penalties in the case of infringement.

A concrete roadmap is needed for implementation providing guidance on tackling corruption and improving effective coordination at all stages of PPP procurement. From the conceptual phases through to bidding, contract finalization and performance monitoring.

The standard's recommendations have been developed in response to key challenges facing governments in navigating successful PPP procurement, which include among others avoiding conflicts of interest, protecting whistle-blowers, and ensuring compliance with laws and codes of ethics.

Innovation in PPP award procedures to encourage Foreign Direct Investments (FDI) in Arab countries[72]

G20 Guiding Principles for Global Investment Policymaking points out the objective for investment policy, that is, 'With the "objectives of (i) fostering an open, transparent and conducive global policy environment for investment, (ii) promoting coherence in national and international investment policymaking, and (iii) promoting inclusive economic growth and sustainable development.'

The non-binding principles to provide general guidance for investment policymaking are proposed by the G20 members as follows:

---

71 UNECE Executive Secretary Olga Algayerova.

72 *G20 Trade Ministers Meeting Statement: Annex III*, 9–10 July 2016, Shanghai, available at www.wto.org/english/news_e/news16_e/dgra_09jul16_e.pdf, last accessed on 15 February 2017.

PPPs in public procurements 139

1. Recognizing the critical role of investment as an engine of economic growth in the global economy, governments should avoid protectionism in relation to cross-border investment.
2. Investment policies should establish open, non-discriminatory, transparent and predictable conditions for investment.
3. Investment policies should provide legal certainty and strong protection to investors and investments, tangible and intangible, including access to effective mechanisms for the prevention and settlement of disputes, as well as to enforcement procedures. Dispute settlement procedures should be fair, open and transparent, with appropriate safeguards to prevent abuse.
4. Regulation relating to investment should be developed in a transparent manner with the opportunity for all stakeholders to participate, and embedded in an institutional framework based on the rule of law.
5. Investment policies and other policies that impact on investment should be coherent at both the national and international levels and aimed at fostering investment, consistent with the objectives of sustainable development and inclusive growth.
6. Governments reaffirm the right to regulate investment for legitimate public policy purposes.
7. Policies for investment promotion should to maximize economic benefit, be effective and efficient, aimed at attracting and retaining investment, and matched by facilitation efforts that promote transparency and are conducive for investors to establish, conduct and expand their businesses.
8. Investment policies should promote and facilitate the observance by investors of international best practices and applicable instruments of responsible business conduct and corporate governance.
9. The international community should continue to cooperate and engage in dialogue with a view to maintaining an open and conducive policy environment for investment, and to address shared investment policy challenges.

These principles can serve as a reference for national and international investment policymaking, in accordance with respective international commitments, and taking into account national, and broader, sustainable development objectives and priorities.

How innovation in award procedures in PPP in Arab countries can improve socio-economic developments

As PPP legislation in Arab countries aims at achieving and implementing fundamental principles in award procedures stipulated in the international practice on the one hand, PPP award procedures in Arab legislation aims to create clean environment which increases the threshold of protection to foreign investors through fighting corruption and aims consequently to increase incentives for foreign investments which raise the inward of FDI to Arab countries. Principles of achieving public interests, integrity, objectivity,

140 *PPPs in public procurements*

equality, equal opportunity, free competition, fair competition, publicity, and transparency are pivotal mechanisms to fight corruption and they are the same principles which procure better environment to increase the inward of FDI to Arab countries. In the Egyptian PPP legislation,[73] Kuwaiti PPP legislation[74] and Dubai PPP legislation,[75] the Arab legislature assures the fundamental importance of the abovementioned principles. It is true that there is an overlapping between the principles that govern award procedures in PPP legislation in Arab countries and principles that attract FDI to Arab countries as they are similar principles that are required to maintain better environment to various economic sectors. Principles for both targets may cooperate to encourage PPPs, socio-economic developments, increasing productivity and developing infrastructure, enhancing services in Arab countries.

As award procedures aim to achieve objectivity, integrity, equal opportunity, fair competition and many other principles, it likewise aims to enhance the life of ordinary citizens in Arab countries whether these countries have special PPP legislation or not. Award procedures aims to attain properly structured PPP projects that are more likely to provide *value for money* to the government and be commercially viable for the private partner.The innovation in award procedures is a pivotal tool to enhance the life of Arab ordinary citizens as follows:

1. Awarding PPP projects aims to the increase the inward of FDI to Arab countries. Increasing the inward of FDI to various economic sectors in Arab countries is a fundamental factor to fight unemployment and decrease the unemployment rate. The increase of unemployment rate in Arab countries is a fundamental factor behind the increase of crime and terrorism in the Middle East region. PPP projects create thousands of job opportunities in Arab countries in various economic sectors.
2. The increase of PPP projects in Arab countries enhances the quality of products and services in those countries as in most cases the private partner is a huge multinational company which has unique profile and distinguished experience in the PPP projects' fields. The private partner injects its technological input and modern techniques to achieve the best standards for the running and management of public utilities as these inputs and techniques have direct positive impact to the end-users' life.
3. The increase of PPP projects in Arab countries maintains sustainable developments in Arab countries, which has direct impact on ordinary citizens' lives and the standard of living, education, health and other crucial services offered by Arab states.
4. The increase of PPP project transfers modern and advanced technologies to Arab countries through awarding many PPP projects in these countries.

---

73 The Egyptian PPP legislation, Articles 19–33.
74 The Executive Regulations of the PPP legislation in Kuwait, Articles 8, 9 and 27.
75 PPP legislation in Dubai, Articles 3, 14–25.

PPPs in public procurements 141

5. Transfer of technology is a pivotal factor to create highly qualified trained expertise and labor in Arab countries as citizens of Arab countries shall have more job opportunities in PPP advanced technology projects.
6. Arab countries shall have the opportunity to export qualified and trained labor and expertise to the surrounding countries and to other regions of the world as a result of awarding PPP projects in Arab countries and its leading role in the Arab region to create highly qualified expertise.
7. Awarding PPP projects would inject billions of hard currency to Arab countries, which maintains the stability of the currency exchange rate in the Arab region as it increases the supply of hard currency in Arab markets against the demand.

6 The international dynamics of PPPs

Introduction

Factual economic statistics

The World Investment Report[1] highlights that the global Foreign Direct Investment (FDI) flows dropped by 13% in 2018, to US$1.3 trillion – the third consecutive annual decline. Developing country flows managed to hold steady (rising by 2%), which helped push flows to the developing world to more than half (54%) of global flows, from 46% in 2017. In 2019, FDI is expected to recover by around 10%, but the level of flows remains below the average of the past ten years. New national investment policy measures show a more critical stand towards foreign investment, while international investment policymaking is in a dynamic phase.

The 2030 Agenda to achieve the Sustainable Development Goals (SDGs) provides an opportunity for the development of traditional patterns of administrative contracts to attract investment in PPPs-relevant activities, adopt the highest levels of PPP standards and compliance. The achievement of shifting from the total reliance on oil and gas economy to a digital economy is one of the main goals in the Gulf countries.

The UN increasing role

The other United Nations organs' affiliates are exercising remarkable efforts towards subjecting PPPs to achieve Sustainable Developments Goals. In May 2019, the five United Nations Regional Commissions were working together to make PPP 'fit for purpose' for the 2030 Agenda for Sustainable Development.[2]

---

1 The UNCTAD, The World Investment Report 2019, available at: www. https://unctad.org/en/pages/PublicationWebflyer.aspx?publicationid=2460, UNCTAD, last accessed 22 October 2019.
2 Available at: www.unece.org/info/media/presscurrent-press-h/ecid/2019/the-five-united-nations-regional-commissions-to-work-together-to-make-ppp-fit-for-purpose-for-the-2030-agenda-for-sustainable-development/doc.html. Last accessed on 18 June 2019.

The increased cooperation between the public and private sectors to achieve the SDGs were given a boost as such models would make PPP a stronger tool to close the huge infrastructure gap that exists, especially amongst the low- and middle-income countries. The model being promoted is called 'People-first' and advocates a broader concept of PPP – not just *value for money* but also 'value for people' – with five key outcomes: increased access and equity, replicability, sustainability and resilience, economic effectiveness and stakeholder engagement.

The coming together of the Executive Secretaries of the UN Regional Commissions took place during the 4th International PPP Forum 'The Last Mile: Promoting People-first PPPs for the UN 2030 Agenda for Sustainable Development' hosted by the UNECE at the Palais des Nations in Geneva, in cooperation with the United Nations Economic Commission for Africa (ECA).

Speaking at the occasion, UNECE Executive Secretary Olga Algayerova strongly supported this new initiative of Regional Commission cooperation in the area of PPPs. She declared that People-first PPPs underline the basic premise that the private sector has to be mobilized behind the SDGs in innovative ways. While UNECE is proud to have taken a lead in this area, she said, it was fully aware that Europe had much to learn from the other regions and the new models emerging elsewhere. She concluded by arguing that corruption has been one of the chief reasons for PPPs having a bad name in Europe and hence that was the reason why UNECE had given priority to this problem in its Standard on a Zero Tolerance Approach to Corruption in PPP Procurement.

It is argued that there is a need to give more caution with respect to grants and fiscal suitability but scope in several sectors offer real hope for the future in renewable energy and also in broadband and IT. The ECA was supporting the other Regional Commissions to promote the PPP model and make it 'fit for purpose' for the 2030 Agenda for Sustainable Development.[3]

UNCITRAL's PPP legislative guide[4]

In January 2020, the United Nations Commission on International Trade Law (UNCITRAL) adopted an updated Legislative Guide on Public Private Partnerships (PPPs) in addition to the UNCITRAL Model Legislative Provisions on Public Private Partnerships.

---

3 Ms. Vera Songwe, The Executive Secretary of United Nations Economic Commission for Africa (ECA).

4 Available at: https://uncitral.un.org/en/working_groups/1/pfip?utm_source=CCSI+Mail ing+List&utm_campaign=d3e76b1335April_newsletter_2019&utm_medium=email&utm_ter m=0_a61bf1d34a-d3e76b1335-57387505, last accessed on 23 October 2019.

144 *The international dynamics of PPPs*

There is an essential need worldwide for a tested recipe book on infrastructure investment. In many cases, governments look to long-term PPPs with private companies to help to achieve their infrastructure objectives. Risk management and benefits in these relationships is challenging and the proper balance often elusive, even in developed countries that are well equipped to structure and oversee them. Ideally, an infrastructure recipe would call for a number of recognizable ingredients to attract private capital, and straightforward methods to process it.

Achievement of the SDGs requires quality infrastructure, not just quantity addressed specifically by SDG No. 9, which aims at building a resilient infrastructure, promoting inclusive and sustainable industrialization and fostering innovation.

Countries need an infrastructure that promotes economic development, jobs, and widespread public benefit. The finance ministers of Francophone low-income countries, for example, have articulated their needs in infrastructure PPPs, and they make it clear that they will not accept just any PPP – they want public investment projects that target universal access to services in sectors such as education, health, water and energy, with reduced costs and risks of PPPs. While '*value for money*' and management of fiscal and financial risks are essential, so is management of the nonfinancial risks of PPPs, such as environmental, social and governance risks.

This means that countries cannot focus solely on facilitating and strengthening processes and legal frameworks around procurement, and contract negotiation, implementation and termination. They must also select and advance infrastructure projects in a way that minimizes all material risks, including sustainability risks, and maximizes economic, environmental and social sustainable development objectives, all of which must be supported and advanced by the PPP regulatory framework.[5]

PPP contractual relationships often last for decades so it is incumbent on governments to foresee these risks and benefits, to anticipate them, and to integrate them early on in any project. Any regulatory framework for PPPs must equip countries to do this.

Today's PPPs are amazingly complex and command a multidisciplinary approach to succeed. Considering the appetite for PPPs, a legislative guide to PPPs intended for use by governments must take a more holistic approach to better describe and help address the recurrent sustainability challenges that PPPs face. Any UN instrument that helps to enable PPPs must explicitly place PPPs in today's world and not the world of 20 years ago. It must do its part to help countries manage the environmental and social risks and realize the sustainable

---

5 Motoko Aizawa and Brooke Guven, *UNCITRAL's PPP Legislative Guide Must be Fit for Today's PPPs*, http://ccsi.columbia.edu/2019/03/29/uncitrals-ppp-legislative-guide-must-be-fit-for-todays-, last accessed on 23 June 2019.

The international dynamics of PPPs 145

development benefits of PPPs. UNCITRAL owes it to its member states to modernize the Legislative Guide to make it fit for today's PPPs.[6]

An enabling provision for the conclusion of PPPs projects requires a definition of the projects covered.[7] These projects are always developed in accordance with a contract setting out the mutual obligations of the parties and providing for related contractual arrangements, for instance, financing, building or rehabilitating the infrastructure, operating the service, supplying, off taking, etc. PPPs can be described as mutually beneficial contractual arrangements, trying to achieve *win-win* situations as a contractual target for both parties. The *win-win* situation is not recognized in administrative contracts in civil law countries, such as France and MENA countries, where states do not have equal bargaining power with the private investor. In PPP contracts, resources are contributed by both the public and private partners (including provision of private finance, professional and other knowledge, expertise, and skills on the one hand, and granting of rights, such as rights over land and to exclusive operation of infrastructure on the other).[8]

Transforming our world: the 2030 Agenda for sustainable development[9]

This Agenda is a plan of action for people, the planet and prosperity. It also seeks to strengthen universal peace and develop larger freedom. It is recognized that eradicating poverty in all its forms and dimensions, including extreme poverty, is the greatest global challenge and an indispensable requirement for sustainable development.[10] The 17 SDGs and 169 targets demonstrate the scale and ambition of this new universal Agenda. They seek to build on the Millennium Development Goals and complete what these did not achieve. They seek to realize the human rights of all and to achieve gender equality and the empowerment of all women and girls. They are integrated and indivisible and balance the three dimensions of sustainable development: the economic, social and environmental.

The goals and targets will stimulate action over the next 15 years in areas of critical importance for humanity and the plane. The SDGs are determined to

---

6 Motoko Aizawa and Brooke Guven, *UNCITRAL's PPP Legislative Guide Must be Fit for Today's PPPs*, http://ccsi.columbia.edu/2019/03/29/uncitrals-ppp-legislative-guide-must-be-fit-for-todays-, last accessed on 23 June 2019.

7 Available at: https://uncitral.un.org/en/working_groups/1/pfip?utm_source=CCSI+Mailing+List&utm_campaign=d3e76b1335April_newsletter_2019&utm_medium=email&utm_term=0_a61bf1d34a-d3e76b1335-57387505, last accessed on 23 October 2019.

8 Available at: https://uncitral.un.org/en/working_groups/1/pfip?utm_source=CCSI+Mailing+List&utm_campaign=d3e76b1335April_newsletter_2019&utm_medium=email&utm_term=0_a61bf1d34a-d3e76b1335-57387505, last accessed on 23 October 2019.

9 Available at: https://sustainabledevelopment.un.org/post2015/transformingourworld. Last accessed on 22 October 2019.

10 The UN Sustainable Development Agenda is available at: www.un.org/sustainabledevelopment/development-agenda/, last accessed on 22 October 2019.

146 The international dynamics of PPPs

protect the planet from degradation, including through sustainable consumption and production, sustainably managing its natural resources and taking urgent action on climate change, so that it can support the needs of the present and future generations.

The SDGs are intended to ensure that all human beings can enjoy prosperous and fulfilling lives and that economic, social and technological progress occurs in harmony with nature.

The interlinkages and integrated nature of the SDGs are of crucial importance in ensuring that the purpose of the new Agenda is realized. If we realize our ambitions across the full extent of the Agenda, the lives of all will be profoundly improved and our world will be transformed for the better.[11]

The UN has adopted a historic decision on a comprehensive, far-reaching and people-centered set of universal and transformative goals and targets. The UN is committed to working tirelessly for the full implementation of this Agenda by 2030. The UN recognizes that eradicating poverty in all its forms and dimensions, including extreme poverty, is the greatest global challenge and an indispensable requirement for sustainable development. The UN is committed to achieving sustainable development in its three dimensions – economic, social and environmental – in a balanced and integrated manner.

It is a fundamental target to resolve between now and 2030, to end poverty and hunger everywhere; to combat inequalities within and among countries; to build peaceful, just and inclusive societies; to protect human rights and promote gender equality and the empowerment of women and girls; and to ensure the lasting protection of the planet and its natural resources. The UN resolves also to create conditions for sustainable, inclusive and sustained economic growth, shared prosperity and decent work for all, taking into account different levels of national development and capacities.

This is an Agenda of unprecedented scope and significance. It is accepted by all countries and is applicable to all, taking into account different national realities, capacities and levels of development and respecting national policies and priorities. These are universal goals and targets that involve the entire world, developed and developing countries alike. They are integrated and indivisible and balance the three dimensions of sustainable development.

The goals and targets are the result of over two years of intensive public consultation and engagement with civil society and other stakeholders around the world, which paid particular attention to the voices of the poorest and most vulnerable. This consultation included valuable work done by the General Assembly Open Working Group on Sustainable Development Goals and by the United Nations, whose Secretary-General provided a synthesis report in December 2014.

---

11 The High-level Political Forum on Sustainable Development is the central UN platform for the follow-up and review of the 2030 Agenda for Sustainable Development adopted at the United Nations Sustainable Development Summit on 25 September 2015.

In these goals and targets, the UN is setting out a supremely ambitious and transformational vision that envisages a world free of poverty, hunger, disease and want, where all life can thrive. The UN vision envisages a world free of fear and violence. A world with equitable and universal access to quality education at all levels, to health care and social protection, where physical, mental and social well-being are assured. A world where we reaffirm our commitments regarding the human right to safe drinking water and sanitation and where there is improved hygiene; and where food is sufficient, safe, affordable and nutritious. A world where human habitats are safe, resilient and sustainable and where there is universal access to affordable, reliable and sustainable energy.

The vision of a world of universal respect for human rights and human dignity, the rule of law, justice, equality and non-discrimination; of respect for race, ethnicity and cultural diversity; and of equal opportunity permitting the full realization of human potential and contributing to shared prosperity.

The vision of a world in which every country enjoys sustained, inclusive and sustainable economic growth and decent work for all. A world in which consumption and production patterns and use of all natural resources – from air to land, from rivers, lakes and aquifers to oceans and seas – are sustainable. One in which democracy, good governance and the rule of law as well as an enabling environment at national and international levels, are essential for sustainable development, including sustained and inclusive economic growth, social development, environmental protection and the eradication of poverty and hunger. One in which development and the application of technology are climate-sensitive, respect biodiversity and are resilient.

The new Agenda is guided by the purposes and principles of the Charter of the United Nations, including full respect for international law. It is grounded in the Universal Declaration of Human Rights, international human rights treaties, the Millennium Declaration and the 2005 World Summit Outcome Document. It is informed by other instruments such as the Declaration on the Right to Development.

The UN reaffirms the outcomes of all major UN conferences and summits that have laid a solid foundation for sustainable development and have helped to shape the new Agenda. These include the Rio Declaration on Environment and Development; the World Summit on Sustainable Development; the World Summit for Social Development; the Programme of Action of the International Conference on Population and Development; the Beijing Platform for Action; and the United Nations Conference on Sustainable Development ('Rio+ 20').

The UN reaffirm all the principles of the Rio Declaration on Environment and Development, including, *inter alia*, the principle of common but differentiated responsibilities, as set out in principle 7 thereof.

The challenges and commitments contained in these major conferences and summits are interrelated and call for integrated solutions. To address them effectively, a new approach is needed. Sustainable development recognizes that eradicating poverty in all its forms and dimensions, combatting inequality within

148 *The international dynamics of PPPs*

and among countries, preserving the planet, creating sustained, inclusive and sustainable economic growth and fostering social inclusion are linked to each other and are interdependent.

The world today is at a time of immense challenges to sustainable development. Billions of our citizens continue to live in poverty and are denied a life of dignity. There are rising inequalities within and among countries. There are enormous disparities of opportunity, wealth and power. Gender inequality remains a key challenge. Unemployment, particularly youth unemployment, is a major concern. Global health threats, more frequent and intense natural disasters, spiraling conflict, violent extremism, terrorism and related humanitarian crises and forced displacement of people threaten to reverse much of the development progress made in recent decades. Natural resource depletion and adverse impacts of environmental degradation, including desertification, drought, land degradation, freshwater scarcity and loss of biodiversity, add to and exacerbate the list of challenges that humanity faces. Climate change is one of the greatest challenges of our time and its adverse impacts undermine the ability of all countries to achieve sustainable development. Increases in global temperature, sea level rise, ocean acidification and other climate change impacts are seriously affecting coastal areas and low-lying coastal countries, including many least developed countries and small island developing states. The survival of many societies, and of the biological support systems of the planet, is at risk.

It is also, however, a time of immense opportunity. Significant progress has been made in meeting many development challenges. Within the past generation, hundreds of millions of people have emerged from extreme poverty. Access to education has greatly increased for both boys and girls. The spread of information and communications technology and global interconnectedness has great potential to accelerate human progress, to bridge the digital divide and to develop knowledge societies, as does scientific and technological innovation across areas as diverse as medicine and energy.

The UN announced 17 SDGs with 169 associated targets that are integrated and indivisible. Those targets are setting out on the path towards sustainable development, devoting ourselves collectively to the pursuit of global development and of '*win-win*' cooperation that can bring huge gains to all countries and all parts of the world.[12]

The SDGs reaffirm the importance of the Universal Declaration of Human Rights, as well as other international instruments relating to human rights and international law. Further, the goals emphasize the responsibilities of all states, in conformity with the Charter of the United Nations, to respect, protect and promote human rights and fundamental freedoms for all, without distinction of

---

12 The UN Sustainable Development Agenda is available at: www.un.org/sustainabledevelop ment/development-agenda/, last accessed on 22 October 2019 and available at: https://sus tainabledevelopment.un.org/post2015/transformingourworld. Last accessed on 22 October 2019.

The international dynamics of PPPs 149

any kind as to race, color, sex, language, religion, political or other opinion, national or social origin, property, birth, disability or other status.[13]

The new goals and targets came into effect on 1 January 2016 and will guide the decisions we take over the next 15 years. Those goals are committed to ending poverty in all its forms and dimensions, including by eradicating extreme poverty by 2030.[14]

States are strongly urged to refrain from promulgating and applying any unilateral economic, financial or trade measures not in accordance with international law and the Charter of the United Nations that impede the full achievement of economic and social development, particularly in developing countries.[15]

How can PPPs be subjected to serve SDGs in the light of the international organizations' practice?

Sustainable Development Goals[16]

- Goal 1. End poverty in all its forms everywhere. By 2030, eradicate extreme poverty for all people everywhere, currently measured as people living on less than $1.25 a day. Ensure significant mobilization of resources from a variety of sources, including through enhanced development cooperation, in order to provide adequate and predictable means for developing countries, in particular least developed countries, to implement programs and policies to end poverty in all its dimensions.
- Goal 2. End hunger, achieve food security and improved nutrition and promote sustainable agriculture.
- Goal 3. Ensure healthy lives and promote well-being for all at all ages.
- Goal 4. Ensure inclusive and equitable quality education and promote life-long learning opportunities for all.
- Goal 5. Achieve gender equality and empower all women and girls. End all forms of discrimination against all women and girls everywhere. Eliminate all forms of violence against all women and girls in the public and private spheres, including trafficking and sexual and other types of exploitation.

13 Available at: https://sustainabledevelopment.un.org/post2015/transformingourworld, Last accessed on 22 October 2019; and The UN Sustainable Development Agenda is available at: www.un.org/sustainabledevelopment/development-agenda/, last accessed on 22 October 2019.
14 Marco Ceruti, Sustainable development and smart technological innovation within PPPs: the strategic use of public procurement, *European Procurement & Public Private Partnership Law Review*, 2017, 12(2), 183–191.
15 Available at: https://sustainabledevelopment.un.org/post2015/transformingourworld. Last accessed on 22 October 2019 and The UN Sustainable Development Agenda is available at: www.un.org/sustainabledevelopment/development-agenda/, last accessed on 22 October 2019.
16 Available at: https://sustainabledevelopment.un.org/post2015/transformingourworld. Last accessed on 22 October 2019.

150 *The international dynamics of PPPs*

- Goal 6. Ensure availability and sustainable management of water and sanitation for all.
- Goal 7. Ensure access to affordable, reliable, sustainable and modern energy for all. By 2030, ensure universal access to affordable, reliable and modern energy services, increase substantially the share of renewable energy in the global energy, double the global rate of improvement in energy efficiency, enhance international cooperation to facilitate access to clean energy research and technology, including renewable energy, energy efficiency and advanced and cleaner fossil-fuel technology, and promote investment in energy infrastructure and clean energy technology, expand infrastructure and upgrade technology for supplying modern and sustainable energy services for all in developing countries, in particular least developed countries, small island developing states, and land-locked developing countries, in accordance with their respective programs of support.
- Goal 8. Promote sustained, inclusive and sustainable economic growth, full and productive employment and decent work for all.
- Goal 9. Build resilient infrastructure, promote inclusive and sustainable industrialization and foster innovation.
- Goal 10. Reduce inequality within and among countries.
- Goal 11. Make cities and human settlements inclusive, safe, resilient and sustainable.
- Goal 12. Ensure sustainable consumption and production patterns.
- Goal 13. Take urgent action to combat climate change and its impacts.
- Goal 14. Conserve and sustainably use the oceans, seas and marine resources for sustainable development.
- Goal 15. Protect, restore and promote sustainable use of terrestrial ecosystems, sustainably manage forests, combat desertification, and halt and reverse land degradation and halt biodiversity loss.
- Goal 16. Promote peaceful and inclusive societies for sustainable development, provide access to justice for all and build effective, accountable and inclusive institutions at all levels.
- Goal 17. Strengthen the means of implementation and revitalize the global partnership for sustainable development. Among those means are the enhancement of the global partnership for sustainable development, complemented by multi-stakeholder partnerships that mobilize and share knowledge, expertise, technology and financial resources, to support the achievement of the sustainable development goals in all countries, in particular developing countries, Encourage and promote effective public, public private and civil society partnerships, building on the experience and resourcing strategies of partnerships.

It is recognized that middle-income countries still face significant challenges to achieve sustainable development. In order to ensure that achievements made to date are sustained, efforts to address ongoing challenges should be strengthened through the exchange of experiences, improved coordination, and better and

The international dynamics of PPPs 151

focused support of the United Nations Development System, the international financial institutions, regional organizations and other stakeholders.[17]

The UN underscores that, for all countries, public policies and the mobilization and effective use of domestic resources, underscored by the principle of national ownership, are central to our common pursuit of sustainable development, including achieving the sustainable development goals. It recognizes that domestic resources are first and foremost generated by economic growth, supported by an enabling environment at all levels.[18]

Private business activity, investment and innovation are major drivers of productivity, inclusive economic growth and job creation. The diversity of the private sector, ranging from micro-enterprises to cooperatives to multinationals are of fundamental importance to achieve the economic structure of any developing economy.

International trade is an engine for inclusive economic growth and poverty reduction, and contributes to the promotion of sustainable development.

International organizations' standards

PPP award procedures in Egypt, Kuwait and Dubai are fundamental tools in implementing the basic principles adopted by OECD MAPS and OECD Recommendations on Public Procurement 2015.[19] For instance, the Egyptian legislation develops effective, accountable and transparent administrative organs such as the PPP Central Unit (PPPCU) at the Egyptian Ministry of Finance. PPP legislation aims at promoting public procurement practices that are sustainable, in accordance with national polices and priorities. The award process is a very crucial stage in the government procurement chain. Efforts in promoting competition, transparency, equal treatment, and objectivity, on the one hand, while preventing corruption, on the other hand, play a fundamental role in public procurement process.

In Egypt, Kuwait and Dubai, PPP legislation and its executive regulations require the procuring entity to have objective awarding criteria that aim to protect public interests and public funds.

There are various mechanisms and guarantees to prevent corruption and bureaucracy in PPP legislation in Egypt, Kuwait and Dubai. On-line bidding system exists (to some extent) in some Arab countries as one of the mechanisms to maintain objectivity, fight corruption and avoid bureaucracy. Arab countries have not yet implemented a full on-line bidding system.

---

17 The UN Sustainable Development Agenda is available at: www.un.org/sustainabledevelop ment/development-agenda/, last accessed on 22October2019.

18 Irina Zapatrina, Sustainable development goals for developing economies and public private partnership, *European Procurement & Public Private Partnership Law Review*, 2016, 11(1), 39–45.

19 OECD, *Methodology for Assessment Procurement Systems 2018*, available at: www.mapsinitiative. org/methodology/MAPS-methodology-for-assessing-procurement-systems.pdf, last accessed on 22 October 2019.

152 *The international dynamics of PPPs*

Generally, the type of legal system and whether it is a common law or civil law weighs heavily on the type of PPP legislative and regulatory frameworks that exists in a particular jurisdiction. Jurisdictions with 'common law' legal systems tend to rely on policy documents and administrative guidance materials, whereas jurisdictions with 'civil law' legal systems are more likely to set up a detailed PPP framework in a binding legal document or statute or legislation.[20] Egypt, Kuwait and Dubai have civil law legal systems.[21] The selection of the private partner is usually carried out through a public tendering process, applying either general public procurement legislative and regulatory rules, or procurement legislative and regulatory rules specially adopted for PPP.

It is of fundamental importance that award procedures in PPP legislation achieve the agreed standards recognized by the international organizations. The sub-indicator adopted by the OECD is significant in the PPP award procedures context in Egypt, Kuwait and Dubai. The purpose of the sub-indicator, as it is stipulated by the OECD, is to determine: a) the structure of the regulatory framework covering public procurement; b) the extent of its coverage; and c) the public access to the laws and regulations.[22]

It is important to underscore the following legal facts:

1. The profile of innovation in award procedures in Egypt, Kuwait and Dubai in PPP projects is significant in PPP legislation and regulation. A fair assessment of the quality and effectiveness of the PPP procurement system in Egypt, Dubai and Kuwait, the OECD MAPS is of special significance as in most cases, PPP Arab legislation has implemented OECD principles in award procedures. The review of the legislative and regulatory frameworks in Arab countries as well as World Bank Benchmarking Report on PPP Procurement 2017, shows that Arab legislation and regulations have implemented the internationally accepted good practices. Further, the developments of PPP award procedures in Arab countries have direct positive impact on the inward of foreign investments to Arab countries as well as the potential significant improvements on the socio-economic life of citizens.

---

20 Benchmarking Public Private Partnerships Procurement Benchmarking PPP Procurement: Assessing Government Capability to Prepare, Procure and Manage PPPs 2017, 22, available at: https://ppp.worldbank.org/public-private-partnership/sites/ppp.worldbank.org/files/documents/Benchmarking_PPPs_2017_ENpdf.pdf; The World Bank Group, Procuring Infrastructure PPPs 2018, available at: https://ppp.worldbank.org/public-private-partnership/library/procuring-infrastructure-ppps-2018.

21 The World Bank, Benchmarking Public Private Partnerships Procurement Benchmarking PPP Procurement: Assessing Government Capability to Prepare, Procure and Manage PPPs 2017, 22, available at: https://ppp.worldbank.org/public-private-partnership/sites/ppp.worldbank.org/files/documents/Benchmarking_PPPs_2017_ENpdf.pdf; The World Bank Group, Procuring Infrastructure PPPs 2018, available at: https://ppp.worldbank.org/public-private-partnership/library/procuring-infrastructure-ppps-2018.

22 OECD MAPS, 2016, sub-indicator 1 (a), the scope of application and coverage of the legislative and regulatory framework, 10–11.

The international dynamics of PPPs 153

2. OECD recommendation of the Council on Public Procurement, advices harmonizing public procurement principles across the spectrum of public services delivery, as appropriate, including for public works, public private partnerships and concessions. When delivering services under a wide array of arrangements with private-sector partners, adherents should ensure as much consistency as possible among the frameworks and institutions that govern public services delivery to foster efficiency for the government and predictability for private-sector partners. It is clear that Arab PPP legislation eliminates the application of the states' procurement legislation in Egypt, Kuwait and Dubai and applies the current promulgated PPP legislation.[23]
3. The World Bank Benchmarking Public Private Partnership Procurement Report 2017 pointed out that:

The PPP Procurement thematic area explores a range of elements that spread throughout the procurement process, such as bidders' access to procurement-related information, the clarity and comprehensiveness of the procurement documents, the qualification of bid evaluation committee members, the bid selection criteria used, the way governments deal with cases of sole proposals, and the restriction on negotiation during the award phase. The recognized good practices that could be drawn from the areas covered in the procurement of PPP projects are summarized below.

Good practices, which help to ensure fair competition and transparency during the PPP procurement process, are:

- The bid evaluation committee members meet minimum technical qualifications;
- The procuring authority publishes the public procurement notice online;
- The procuring authority grants at least 30 calendar days to potential bidders to submit their proposals;
- The tender documents detail all the stages of the procurement process; assessing government capability to prepare, procure and manage PPPs;
- Potential bidders can submit questions to clarify the public procurement notice and/or the request for proposals and the answers are disclosed to all potential bidders;
- Bidders prepare and present a financial model with their proposal;
- The procuring authority evaluates the proposals strictly and solely in accordance with the evaluation criteria stated in the tender documents;
- The procuring authority follows a specific procedure in the case that only one proposal is submitted to guarantee '*value for money*';
- The procuring authority publishes the award notice online;

23 OECD, *Recommendation of the Council on Public Procurement*, 13.

154 *The international dynamics of PPPs*

- The procuring authority provides all bidders with the results of the PPP procurement process including the grounds for the selection of the winning bid;
- Any negotiations between the selected bidder and the procuring authority after the award and before the signature of the PPPs contract are restricted and regulated to ensure transparency;
- The procuring authority publishes the signed PPPs contract online.[24]

It is clear that PPP legislation in Egypt, Kuwait and Dubai have implemented most of the above-mentioned procedures suggested by the World Bank PPPs Benchmarking Report in 2017. It is suggested that most of the Arab countries who are progressing with the promulgation of new PPP legislation have to adopt the above-mentioned procedures.

4. In some economies, procuring authorities can also use a 'competitive dialogue' procedure, which involves more extensive engagements with two or more bidders as they prepare their proposals. In this procedure, bidders submit technical proposals, which are then subject to feedback and discussion with the procuring authority. These discussions allow them to align their proposals with the authority's needs before they submit a final proposal. In 45% of the surveyed economies, competitive dialogue either is allowed by law or takes place in practice. The latter case can be seen in Bangladesh, Canada, Jamaica, Myanmar, and the United States. Even where competitive dialogue is possible, its content and results are not always disclosed to all potential bidders, as in Egypt, where there are no requirements for such disclosure of information.[25] The OECD Recommendation of the Council on Public Procurement, pointed out that the government should engage in transparent and regular dialogues with suppliers and business associations to present public procurement objectives and to assure a correct understanding of markets. Effective communication should be conducted to provide potential vendors with a better understanding of the country's needs, and government buyers with information to develop more realistic and effective tender specifications by better understanding market capabilities. Such interactions should be subject to due fairness, transparency and integrity safeguards, which vary depending on whether an active procurement process is ongoing. Such interactions should also be adapted

---

24 The World Bank, Benchmarking Public Private Partnership Procurement, 32: Assessing Government Capability to Prepare, Procure and Manage PPPs 2017, available at: https://ppp.worldbank.org/public-private-partnership/sites/ppp.worldbank.org/files/documents/Benchmarking_PPPs_2017_ENpdf.pdf.

25 The World Bank, Benchmarking Public Private Partnerships Procurement Benchmarking PPP Procurement: Assessing Government Capability to Prepare, Procure and Manage PPPs 2017, 37, available at: https://ppp.worldbank.org/public-private-partnership/sites/ppp.worldbank.org/files/documents/Benchmarking_PPPs_2017_ENpdf.pdf.

The international dynamics of PPPs 155

to ensure that foreign companies participating in tenders receive transparent and effective information.[26]

5. It is suggested that in PPP Arab legislation award procedures should insist upon using technologies that are friendly to the environment. The transfer of technology during recent decades plays a significant role in facilitating the cultural and legal globalization process. It allows the application of new techniques in public procurements in PPP. Furthermore, international public works agreements, nowadays, play an important role in spreading environmentally friendly technologies from developed states to developing nations.[27] Environmental legislation stipulations currently tend to be an integral and compulsory part of tender documents. Hamilton pointed out an example in Canada (Vancouver city efforts to reduce emissions in 2001) where there was a private partner who financed, designed, built, owned and operated a landfill and a 2.9 kilometer pipeline to take gas from the landfill to a nearby agricultural complex, where they built a common power generating plant. The latter plant was built by the private partner to generate electricity to supply 5000 homes and to reduce carbon dioxide emission by approximately 200,000 tonnes per year (emission of about 40,000 cars).

6. According to the OECD Recommendation of the Council on Public Procurement, Arab states should ensure that procurement officials meet high professional standards for knowledge, practical implementation and integrity by providing a dedicated and regularly updated set of tools, for example, sufficient staff in terms of numbers and skills, recognition of public procurement as a specific profession, certification and regular trainings, integrity standards for public procurement officials and the existence of a unit or team analyzing public procurement information and monitoring the performance of the public procurement system. It is suggested that Arab countries should provide attractive, competitive and merit-based career options for procurement officials as this is of fundamental importance, and as it promotes the national and international good practices in career development to enhance the performance of the procurement workforce.[28]

---

26 OECD, *Recommendation of the Council on Public Procurement*, 9.

27 Methane is of special concern since it generates a global warming effect 23 times that of CO2. For details on the role of PPPs in mitigating climate change and increasing FDI, *see* Geoffrey Hamilton, *FDI – the Global Crisis and Sustainable Recovery*, Working Paper for Public Private Partnerships, and *FDI as a Means of Securing a Sustainable Recovery*, paper submitted to the Fourth Columbia International Investment Conference, Vale Columbia Centre, Columbia Law School, Columbia University, 5–6 November 2009. For more information, *see* also J.D. Sachs, *Common Wealth 'Economics for a Crowded Planet,'* Penguin Books, 2008, Chapter 4, Global solutions to climate change, 84–114. *See* also: C. Bovis, 'Editorial', in *EPPPL*, 1/2010; and for the same author, *EC Public Procurement: Case Law and Regulation, OUP, 2006*; M. A.M. Ismail, *Legal Globalisation and PPPs in Egypt*, EPPPL, 1/2010; Ismail, *Globalization and New International Public Works Agreements in Developing Countries*, Routledge 2011, ch. 4.

28 OECD, *Recommendation of the Council on Public Procurement*, 11.

156 *The international dynamics of PPPs*

7. A fundamental question arises regarding Articles 8 and 9 of the Kuwaiti PPP legislation of 2014: Can executive regulations stipulate or impose new award procedures' rules that do not exist in the Kuwaiti PPP legislation of 2014? Is this a matter of unconstitutionality pursuant to the Kuwaiti constitution? Executive regulations may provide details, procedures only within the legislative framework stipulated in the Kuwaiti PPP legislation. For instance, can executive regulations stipulate award evaluation criteria that does not exist in legislation? Can executive regulations add to the award evaluation criteria that is stipulated in legislation?[29] The question of unconstitutionality remains unanswered!

8. On-line bidding system does not fully exist in Arab countries; however, using technology in award procedures is growing as it is one of the tools of the current legal globalization phenomenon in Arab countries. It is suggested that using fully automated system in on-line bidding is one of the guarantees to achieve best practices in award procedures particularly maintaining objectivity, integrity, and avoiding bureaucracy.

9. Only about 15% of the world economies have an issue of sole bidders being regulated with greater detail. In those economies, the law mandates a special procedure that needs to be followed before awarding PPP projects. This is the case, for example, in Egypt, where the regulatory framework specifies the conditions and process for accepting sole bids. A single bid may be accepted through a decision by the competent authority based on the recommendation of the bid evaluation committee, after the approval of the Supreme Committee for PPP affairs, if the public interest does not allow for retendering procedures, or if retendering would be futile, and if the sole bid is technically acceptable and meets the specifications of the tender.[30] As OECD recommendations states, governments should use competitive tendering and limit the use of exceptions and single-source procurement. Competitive procedures should be the standard method for conducting procurement as a means of driving efficiencies, fighting corruption, obtaining fair and reasonable pricing and ensuring competitive outcomes. If exceptional circumstances justify limitations to competitive tendering and the use of single-source procurement, such exceptions should be limited, pre-defined and should require appropriate justification

---

29 *See* M.A.E. Bana, *The Judicial Review Upon the Constitutionality of Regulations*, Dar El Nahdah El Arabia 1992, in Arabic.

30 The World Bank, Benchmarking Public Private Partnerships Procurement Benchmarking PPP Procurement: Assessing Government Capability to Prepare, Procure and Manage PPPs 2017, 35 and 36, available at: https://ppp.worldbank.org/public-private-partnership/sites/ppp.worldbank.org/files/documents/Benchmarking_PPPs_2017_ENpdf.pdf. The report refers to the situation in Nigeria: 'Similarly, in Nigeria, although the regulatory framework allows for direct negotiation with a sole bidder, it requires the procuring authority to ensure that the bid is technically and financially advantageous compared with market prices and to include, in the record of procurement proceedings, a statement of the grounds for its decision and the circumstances justifying the single-source procurement.'

The international dynamics of PPPs   157

when employed, subject to adequate oversight taking into account the increased risk of corruption, including by foreign suppliers.[31]

10. Direct contracting in Dubai PPP legislation is of a great concern, as it may violate equality, objectivity and fair competition principles.

Conclusions

Arab countries that have PPP legislation and regulation have developed public procurement legal instruments and practice comparing it with the traditional public procurement in administrative contracts. PPPs legislation and regulation in Arab countries have considerably influenced the international organizations' recommendations and methodologies in establishing a proper legal framework in PPP public procurement, which aims at maintaining transparency, accountability, objectivity, equality, fair competition and integrity. As a result, the profile of innovation in award procedures has significant developments.

Government procurement has considerable economic relevance for the high percentage of the Gross Domestic Product (GDP) in developed and developing countries in both domestic and international levels' statistics.[32] Government procurement provisions also play a central role in international trade agreements.[33] As efficiency is one of the main goals for government procurement, the Arab legislatures in Egypt, Kuwait and Dubai play a significant role in incorporating provisions that promote innovation in the award procedures in their respective PPP legislations. To achieve many targets for Arab governments, PPP legislation in Arab countries has created a new procedural framework for the award of PPP contracts to private sector entities. The new rules are clear in the Egyptian PPP legislation No. 67 of 2010 and its executive regulations, the Kuwaiti PPP Legislation No. 116 of 2014 and its executive regulations, and the Dubai PPP legislation No. 22 of 2015.

Innovation in public procurements in PPP legislation in Egypt, Kuwait and Dubai, shows how PPP can improve life, infrastructure and services in Arab countries. It is important to note that many Arab countries have already initiated the promulgation of their respective PPP legislation, which are similar to Egypt, Kuwait and Dubai. For instance, the Kingdom of Bahrain is about to enact its PPP legislation to encourage the inflow of Foreign Direct Investments (FDI) to various economic sectors as well as many other Arab countries.

It is important to note that the legislature in Arab countries upon drafting PPP legislation and regulation has realized that the legislative obstacles in the existing public procurement legislation are not suitable for PPP techniques.

---

31 *OECD Recommendation of the Council on Public Procurement*, Directorate for Public Governance and Territorial Development, 8.

32 G.M. Racca, R.C. Perin, and G.L. Albano, *Competition in the Execution Phase of Public Procurement, Public Contract Law Journal*, 2011, 41(1), 92.

33 G.M. Racca, ibid., 93, et seq.

7 The main substantive mechanisms of PPP contracts in MENA countries

Introduction

Public private partnerships (PPPs) are now being used in many countries to develop infrastructure projects. Typically, PPP transactions are based on a network of complex legal agreements; however, at the center of each transaction there is normally a PPP contract, in the form of a modernized concession agreement or similar document, between a government or other public entity (the contracting authority) and a private company or a consortium of companies (the private partner). The complexity and sophistication of PPP transactions, and the fact that they are often heavily negotiated to reflect the characteristics of a given infrastructure project, frequently means that considerable time and expenses are involved in preparing and finalizing PPP contracts. This has led many interested parties to ask if it is possible to reduce the costs, and speed the process, by standardizing the provisions found in such contracts. In some countries, efforts have been made to develop complete standardized PPP agreements for different types of infrastructure projects: road, railways, ports, power generation, etc. To date, however, there is no universally accepted language for substantive clauses for such agreements on an international basis. Given the variety of PPP transactions globally, the different legal systems that exist in various countries, and the need to have 'tailor-made' provisions to deal with the individual characteristics of specific projects, it follows that the development of comprehensive PPP agreements on an international basis is likely an unrealistic goal. However, there may be merit in focusing on certain contractual provisions dealing with particular substantive legal issues encountered in every PPP contract, such as the issues of contract price, financial equilibrium, risk assessment, termination rights, dispute resolution, etc.[1]

This chapter examines the pulse and dynamics of the new contractual mechanisms in PPPs in the MENA countries. It analyses legal developments in the fields of concession contracts and privately finance projects and institutional

---

1 The World Bank Report on the Recommended PPP Contractual Provisions, https://ppp.world bank.org/public-private-partnership/sites/ppp.worldbank.org/files/ppp_testdumb/documents/150808_wbg_report_on_recommended_ppp_contractual_provisions.pdf, last accessed on 19 August 2019.

Substantive mechanisms of PPP contracts 159

PPPs. In particular, it is important to cover new contractual concepts in public sector transactions. It reflects the nexus of the state with the private sector and the compensatory and remunerative approach by the state in the delivery of public services, which delineates the regulatory treatment of the contractual interfaces between public and private sectors. In this chapter '*Le Contrat Administratif*' substantive theory will be developed in the light of legal globalization relevant to MENA countries. The chapter sheds light on the innovation of the new PPP contracts' substantive clauses.[2]

There are many examples for the new substantive mechanisms in PPP contracts in the MENA region such as first, the contract price. In traditional concessions, the administration (public juristic entity) can unilaterally amend the contract price; meanwhile, in PPP contracts any amendments to the contract price must be through mutual consent of the contracting parties. Second, the theory of the change of circumstances '*l'imprevision*' in the MENA countries' legal systems stipulates that the court has to maintain, through judicial judgment, the financial equilibrium of the contract. The contracting parties cannot

---

2 Innovation in contract price is one of the main features of PPP legislation. The Egyptian PPP legislation in Article 8 permits the contracting parties to stipulate in the contract that they can amend this contract to maintain financial equilibrium (the law pointed out to the unforeseen circumstances and if there are any new legislation which may violate financial equilibrium). Article 31 of the PPP legislation of Dubai stipulates that in case of unforeseen circumstances, the contract can be amended to promote financial equilibrium. Article 36 of the PPP legislation of Kuwait pointed out that the amendment of the partnership agreement may be agreed upon in accordance with the principle and the rules provided for under the agreement, if unforeseen circumstances occurred after the conclusion of the partnership agreement, including amendments to the laws in force at the time of conclusion of this agreement and leading to a financial imbalance of the agreement. PPP legislation in Egypt, Dubai and Kuwait contains provisions to maintain financial equilibrium during performance and until the final completion of the contract through contractual mechanisms and without need to start litigation or arbitration. PPP legislation in Egypt and Kuwait contains provisions to maintain stabilization for the price against change of laws during contract performance and until final completion. It is appropriate to refer, briefly, to the profile of innovation in some substantive issues. This issue relates directly to contract price and the new mechanisms by which contractors can guarantee that the contract price shall not violate their economic expectations during performance and until the end of the project. PPP agreements are complex long-term agreements and price value must be stable during the contract duration and until the end of performance. Contract price, generally, has become nowadays a dynamic process rather than a static process as in the past and in the light of the traditional theory of *Le contrat administratif*. In public works agreements as it is in most traditional administrative contracts, it is suggested that review to contract price should be on a monthly basis in order to update the value of payments and to face the rapid change in raw materials prices in the Egyptian markets. For instance, in the first month of performance, the first certificate equals £E100,000, meanwhile, the true value of the 19th or the 20th certificate (assuming that each certificate equals £E100,000) is £E118,000. The current depreciation of the Egyptian pound caused fundamental unpredictability to contractors with the state. Following this concept, it is clear that there is an essential need to update the value not the price (i.e. the true value of the Egyptian pound in month zero equals £E1, whilst it equals £E0.78 in month 36). It is suggested that currency units at the time of contracting should equal the same units at the final completion date of the project.

160 *Substantive mechanisms of PPP contracts*

maintain the financial equilibrium of the contract through legal opinion from the Egyptian Conseil D'Etat or any judicial department of the legal opinion in Gulf countries or through negotiations with the contracting parties. Pursuant to PPPs legislation in Egypt, Kuwait and Dubai, Morocco and Tunisia the contracting public juristic entities can maintain the financial equilibrium automatically through direct negotiations with the contracting parties. This chapter represents a genuine innovation in the English legal text regarding the MENA countries from academic and analytical substantive perspectives. It represents the deterioration of the traditional theory of '*Le Contrat Administratif*' in PPP transactions as it shows the liberalization of PPP contracts' substantive clauses from the traditional exorbitant clauses that exist are traditional concessions as one of the main types of administrative contracts.[3]

PPP legislation in Arab countries has unique innovation in many substantive aspects that differ from the traditional concession exorbitant clauses. Contract price is one of the new main substantive aspects as contract price in PPP contracts is not subject to unilateral amendments by the contracting authority. Further, contract price can be amended by the contracting parties without reliance on financial equilibrium theories (such as *L'imprevision*) and without recourse to litigation or arbitration. The Egyptian PPP legislation in Article 8 permits the contracting parties to stipulate in the contract that they can amend this contract to maintain financial equilibrium (the law pointed out to *L'imprevision* or the unforeseen circumstances and if there is any new legislation that may violate financial equilibrium). Article 31 of the PPP legislation of Dubai stipulates that in the case of unforeseen circumstances, the contract can be amended to promote financial equilibrium. Article 36 of the PPP legislation of Kuwait points out that the amendment of the partnership agreement may be agreed upon in accordance with the principle and the rules provided for under the agreement, if unforeseen circumstances occurred after the conclusion of the partnership agreement, including amendments to the laws in force at the time of conclusion of this agreement and leading to a financial imbalance of the agreement. PPP legislation in Egypt, Dubai and Kuwait contains provisions to maintain financial equilibrium during performance and until the final completion of the contract through contractual mechanisms and without need to start litigation or arbitration. PPP legislation in Egypt and Kuwait contains provisions to maintain stabilization for the price against change of laws during contract performance and until final completion of the project. The profile of innovation is clear in substantive issues in PPP contracts. This issue relates directly to contract price and

---

3 Sharif Youssef, The new regulatory framework for PPPs in Egypt: a pro investment step?, *International Construction Law Review*, 2017, 34(4), 406–429. Shaaban Ahmed Ramadan, *Negotiations to Conclude Public-Private Partnership Contract and Responsibility Resulting from the Breach of it in the Egyptian Legal System*, Dar Al Nahda Al Arabia 2016 (in Arabic); Hani Arafat Subhi Hamdan, *Legal System for Public-Private Partnership Contracts, Comparative Study*, Dar Al Nahda Al Arabia 2016–2017, in Arabic.

the new mechanisms by which contractors can guarantee that the contract price shall not violate their economic expectations during performance and until the end of the project. PPP agreements are complex long-term agreements and price value must be stable during the contract duration and until the end of performance. Contract price, generally, has become nowadays a dynamic process rather than a static process as in the past and in the light of the traditional theory of *Le contrat administratif.*

Due to currency deprecation in some MENA countries, and in particular in public works agreements, as they are long-term agreements, and as it is the case in most traditional administrative contracts, it is suggested that a review of contract price should be on a monthly basis in order to update the value of payments and to face the rapid change in raw materials prices in the Egyptian markets, for instance. The depreciation of the Egyptian pound in the current years caused fundamental unpredictability to contractors with the state. Following this concept, there is an essential need to update the value not the price. (i.e. the true value of the Egyptian pound in month zero equals £E1, whilst it equals £E0.78 in month 36). It is suggested that currency units at the time of contracting should equal the same units at the final completion date of the project.

It is worth noting that Bahrain's PPP draft-law is expected to be one of the best PPP legislations in MENA countries following the Egyptian PPP legislation. Bahrain's PPP draft-law has developed the substantive clauses of states' traditional concessions and states' administrative contracts. It has new approach of liberalization of state contracts from the exorbitant clauses and opens the door for the contracting parties to exercise the party autonomy principle. It is expected to offer a better threshold of protection to foreign investors and to increase the inward of FDI to Bahrain.[4]

The main substantive provisions of the PPP contract

Administrative authorities may enter into PPP contracts pursuant to which a project company shall be entrusted with the financing, constructing, equipping and operating infrastructure projects and public utilities, and making their services available or financing and rehabilitating such utilities with an obligation to maintain what has been constructed or rehabilitated, and to provide services and facilities necessary for the project to be capable of production or service provision regularly and progressively throughout the PPP contract duration.

---

4 Bahrain's PPP draft-law, Article 29 refers to PPP contract substance or contract stipulations. Article 33 mentions securities over project assets not public juristic entity assets. Article 34 allows assignment, Article 37 points out 'Equality,' which is an administrative law principle. Privileges to some end users have special rules in MENA countries' administrative law. It is worth noting that this under the condition that the same end users must be in the same legal position as administrative law principles stipulate in Arab countries.

162 *Substantive mechanisms of PPP contracts*

The partnership contract shall include the basic provisions governing the partnership and the mutual commitments between the parties, in particular the following:[5]

1. The nature and scope of the works to be performed and/or the services to be provided by the project company as well as the stipulations for their implementation.
2. The conditions for the provision of such services and the extent to which the project company enjoys exclusive rights, if any, under the partnership contract.
3. Facilities that the contracting administrative authority is obliged to provide, including assistance that the contracting administrative authority may provide to the project company in obtaining the licenses and approvals necessary for the implementation of the partnership project.
4. Any requirements related to the establishment of the project company and the minimum capital.
5. Ownership of the assets of the project and the obligations of the parties as appropriate with respect to obtaining the project site and any necessary rights in kind in accordance with the laws and regulations of the hosting country.
6. The provisions for ownership transfer at the end of the project.
7. The responsibility of obtaining authorizations, permits and approvals.
8. Mutual financial obligations and their relation to the funding mechanism.
9. The product sale price or the service availability payment on which the project is based, and the rules for its determination and amendment, either by an increase or decrease, as well as the method of adjusting it for inflation indexes and changes in interest rates, if required.
10. Means of quality assurance and quality control, and supervision as well as administrative, financial and technical monitoring of the project operation, utilization and maintenance.
11. Regulating the right of the administrative authority to amend the conditions of the project's construction, equipment, maintenance, operation and utilization and other obligations of the project company, in addition to the basis and mechanisms of compensation for such amendments.
12. Types and amounts of insurance on the project, and the risks of its operation or utilization, and executive warranties issued in favor of the administrative authority, and provisions and procedures for their release.
13. Determination of the basis of risk allocation in respect of change in law, sudden accidents, *force majeure*, or discovery of antiquities, as the case may be, and the resultant compensation.
14. PPP contract duration, cases of early or partial termination, and the rights of the related parties.

---

5 The Egyptian PPP law, Article 34.

15. Cases where the administrative authority has the right to unilaterally terminate the PPP contract, as well as the financial obligations resulting from the use of such right.
16. Regulation of handing over the project at the expiry of the PPP contract duration, or in case of unilateral, early or partial termination of the PPP contract.
17. The fees of the project company, whether in the form of fees or charges, for the use of the facility or the provision of services, the regulatory tool for imposing or modifying any of these fees and payments, if any, that may be paid by the contracting administrative authority or any other public body.
18. Procedures for reviewing the approval of the contracting administrative authority for engineering designs, construction plans and specifications, and the procedures for selecting, final inspection, approval and acceptance of the PPP project facility.
19. The extent of the obligations of the project company, where necessary, to ensure that the service is adjusted to meet the actual demand for it, continuity and availability under the same conditions mainly for all users with respect to the equality before public utilities principle as a leading principle in administrative law in the MENA countries.
20. The right of the contracting administrative authority or any other public body to supervise the works to be carried out by the project company and the services to be provided, and the conditions under which the contracting authority may request amendments in respect of works and conditions of service, or take such reasonable measures as may be deemed appropriate to ensure operation of the PPP project facility and properly deliver business and services in accordance with the legal and contractual requirements to be applied.
21. The extent of the commitment of the project company to submit reports and information on its operations to the contracting administrative authority or any other public authority.
22. The rights of the contracting administrative authority to review and approve the contracts that the project company intends to conclude, especially the contracts with the shareholders of this partnership or other related entities;
23. Performance bonds and its main stipulations.
24. Ways of settling any dispute between the parties regarding the PPP contract.
25. The extent to which either party may be exempted from liability for default or delay in fulfilling any obligation under the PPP contract, due to circumstances beyond their reasonable control.
26. Duration of the PPP contract and the rights and obligations of the parties upon its expiry or termination.
27. How to calculate compensation in case of the financial equilibrium of the PPP contract was affected.

164   *Substantive mechanisms of PPP contracts*

28. The law governing the mechanisms for settling disputes that may arise between the contracting administrative authority and the winning investor in the PPP contract.
29. Rights and undertakings of the parties with respect to confidential information.
30. Measures to be taken to be consistent with the local the environment laws and regulations of the hosting country.

It is important to note that PPP contracts must deal with the following substantive legal and financial issues in details:

Ownership of PPP project assets

The PPP contract shall specify, as appropriate, assets owned by the contracting administrative authority or any other administrative body, and assets owned by the project company. The PPP contract also identifies assets belonging to the following categories:

1. Assets that the project company must return or transfer its ownership to the contracting administrative authority or to any other entity specified by the contracting administrative authority.
2. Assets that the contracting administrative authority may purchase, upon its selection, from the project company.
3. Assets that the project company may keep or dispose of when the PPP contract expires or terminates.

The project company shall be committed to preserving the assets related to the operation of the project and its rights and commit to maintain and care for and use such assets for their intended purposes. The PPP contract shall include provisions regulating the ownership of the project facilities and assets for the PPP contract duration and upon its expiry or early termination.

Possession of rights related to the project site

Unless otherwise provided in the PPP contract, the contracting administrative authority or any other public body shall transfer to the project company the rights relating to the project site, including the right of ownership, if necessary to carry out the project, or to provide assistance, as appropriate, in the transfer of those rights.

In case of expropriation to the project site from individuals for public interests' purposes, the procedures of expropriation or temporary seizure of real estate for the implementation of the PPP project shall be subject to the provisions stipulated in the Real Estate Expropriation Laws for the public interests in the hosting country.

No seizure or executive procedures shall be undertaken with regard to facilities, tools, machinery, or equipment allocated for the implementation of a PPP contract and for the operation or utilization of the project subject of the PPP contract. Moreover, according to the PPP contract the project company shall not sell or arrange any right over the project's monies, assets, and facilities that are being constructed or rehabilitated, except for the purpose of implementing the replacement and renewal program stipulated in the PPP contract, and only after obtaining the approval of the competent authority. However, as an exception to the previous paragraph, an arrangement for an accessory real right could be granted to the project company for the purposes of financing based on a prior written approval from the administrative authority in accordance with the terms mentioned in the PPP contract.

Primary bond

A primary guarantee shall be provided with each proposal submitted. The bond may not be returned in any of the following cases:

1. If the proposer withdraws or amends his proposal after the expiration of the deadline for the submission of proposals.
2. If the winning proposer fails to sign the PPP contract.
3. If the winning proposer fails to provide the performance bond.

The national manual of provisions and procedures of PPP contracts shall regulate the types, form and amount of primary bond and all rules, provisions and procedures relating to their submission.

Performance bond

The investor who submitted the winning proposal must offer performance bond after the award decision. Generally, in MENA countries, the rules and procedures of the PPP contracts regulations established by MENA governments shall govern the rules and provisions relating to the performance bond, its amount, the date of its submission, the procedures for its return and other matters.

Establishment of the project company

The PPP contract may allow for the project company to operate the project, provide the service or the product to the administrative authority, which will, in turn, provide the service or the product to the end-users. In the Egyptian PPP law, upon the approval of the Cabinet, based on a recommendation of the Supreme Committee for PPP Affairs and in light of the reports prepared by the PPP Central Unit, the project company may utilize the project and sell the product or provide the service to whoever is specified by the administrative authority. The PPP contract may include articles concerning its renewal.

The contracting administrative authority may require the winning proposer to establish a company in accordance with the national laws whose sole purpose is

166   *Substantive mechanisms of PPP contracts*

to execute the PPP project, provided that the condition of incorporation of the company is included in the request for proposals or in the invitation documents. The company shall take one of the forms determined by a decision of the Minister, in coordination with the Minister concerned with trade affairs.

The minimum contractual capital of the project company and the procedures for obtaining the approval of the contracting administrative authority for the Memorandum and Articles of Association shall be specified in the PPP contract.

The investor may participate in the establishment of the project company in accordance with the rules and provisions stipulated in the national guide of the provisions and procedures of PPP contracts.

The project company shall submit to the contracting administrative authority periodic reports on the construction, equipping, rehabilitation, maintenance, operation, and utilization works executed by the project company in accordance with the PPP contract.

Confidentiality

Documents and information contained in the proposals submitted by the investors who responded to the call for expressions of interest or request for proposals shall be kept confidential. Neither party may disclose any technical or price documents or other documents or information obtained in the course of discussions, meetings or negotiations without the consent of the other party, unless the disclosure of documents or information is in accordance with the provisions of the valid laws or pursuant to a court order.

Financial arrangements

The project company may impose, charge fees for the use of the partnership project facility, or services in accordance with the partnership contract. The partnership contract shall specify the mechanisms for setting or fixing fees or the remuneration.

The contracting administrative authority shall have the power to agree to make direct payments to the project company in addition to the right of the company to impose or charge fees or charges for the use of the facility or its services, or payments made by the contracting administrative authority instead of imposing or charging for the use of the facility or its services.

The Egyptian PPP law clarifies that the contracting administrative authority is entitled to enter into direct agreements with the project's financing institutions and the project company, to regulate the method of payment of the financial obligations of the administrative authority to the project company and the financing institutions. Such agreements may include a provision whereby the competent Ministry of Finance guarantees the administrative authority's payment of its contractual financial obligations. Such agreements shall include a provision regulating the right of the financing institution to step in and assume the role of the project company in executing the provisions of the PPP contract, or to appoint a new investor after the approval of the competent authority in case the project company defaults in either performing its material obligations, or meeting the quality levels established by law or in the PPP contract, in a manner that entitles the competent authority to terminate the PPP contract.[6]

Create security rights

The project company may create a security right on any of its funds and rights for the purpose of obtaining financing for the implementation of the PPP project, including funds and rights relating to the PPP project, unless otherwise specified in the PPP contract.

The right to guarantee may be restored to the following funds:

1. Movable or real property owned by the project company.
2. Revenues of the project company.
3. Shares of the project company.
4. Any other rights to be determined by a decision from the concerned public body.

A security right may not be established on the assets of the enterprise owned by the contracting administrative authority or any other administrative body, or the funds and rights allocated to the public interest.

Assignment of PPP contract

The rights and undertakings of the project company contained in the PPP contract may not be assigned to third parties without the prior written consent of the contracting administrative authority.

The PPP contract shall specify the conditions to be taken into consideration when agreeing to assign the rights and undertakings of the project company, including the acceptance by the assignee of all the obligations contained in the PPP contract and proof of its technical and financial capacity to implement the PPP project.

Transferring the majority of the shares of the project company

Unless the PPP contract provides otherwise, the majority of shares of the project company may not be transferred to third parties without the written consent of the contracting administrative authority. The PPP contract shall specify the conditions to be taken into account in approving the request for the transfer of the majority of the shares.

---

6 The Egyptian PPP law, Article 38.

168   *Substantive mechanisms of PPP contracts*

The term 'majority of the shares' is defined normally in practice if the project company is intended to transfer more than half of the capital of the project company or the ownership of rights or a certain number of shares so that the buyer of the shares can control its decisions.

Pursuant to the Egyptian PPP law, the project company shall not be dissolved, or its legal structure changed, or its capital reduced unless there is an approval from the competent authority of the contracting administrative authority. The articles of incorporation of the project company shall include a prohibition on the transfer of its shares prior to the date of completion of the construction, equipping, or rehabilitation works, and the transfer of shares owned by the majority of the equity holders of the project company after such date, unless a prior written approval is granted by the competent authority of the administrative authority. In all cases, pledging of the project company shares shall not take place except for the purposes of financing or refinancing the PPP project. Any procedure or action that is inconsistent with the provisions of this article shall be deemed to be null and void.

Measures to transfer PPP project assets

The PPP contract should clarify:

1. Mechanisms and procedures for transferring the assets of the PPP project to the contracting administrative authority.
2. Compensation to which the project company may be entitled in respect of assets transferred to the contracting administrative authority or to the project company or purchased by the contracting administrative authority.
3. Transferring the necessary technology to operate the facility.
4. Training the employees of the contracting administrative authority or the company that will replace the project company to operate and maintain the project.
5. The project company shall continuously provide support services and several resources, including the supply of spare parts, for a reasonable duration after the project has been transferred to the contracting authority or to the new company.

The commitment to provide service

The PPP contract shall specify, as appropriate, the limits of the undertakings of the project company to ensure:

1. Modifying the service in order to meet the actual demand for it.
2. Regularity of service.
3. Providing the service under the same conditions to all users respecting the principle of equality for users before public utilities.

The project company may, after obtaining the approval of the contracting administrative authority or the competent public authority, issue rules governing the use of the facility and the provision of the service.

Equality among end-users

The project company shall be committed to the equality of end-users of the services provided by the PPP project. This approach is consistent with the equality before public utilities principle as a fundamental principle in administrative law and the equality principle as a constitutional principle in the MENA countries' constitutions. It may, in exceptional circumstances, establish preferential conditions for a specific category of users in accordance with the rules agreed upon with the contracting administrative authority.

The project company entitled, pursuant to the PPP contract, to utilize the project shall be committed to guarantee that all beneficiaries of products or services provided by the project are treated equally, with regard to the provisions governing the sale of such products or provision of such services. Whenever the public interest so necessitates, and after the approval of the competent authority, the project company may decide to provide special treatment for specific categories of beneficiaries who enjoy equal legal rankings, provided that such treatment shall be executed in accordance with general rules determined in advance and provided that within each category all beneficiaries shall be treated equally. The project company shall be responsible for providing compensation against any damages resulting from the violation of the provisions set forth in this chapter.

Granting preference to local services, local goods and national labor

In most MENA countries, the project company is committed to granting preference to suppliers of services and goods necessary for the implementation of the PPP project among national companies or companies controlled by nationals, subject to the following conditions:

1. The ability of these companies to provide services or goods according to the necessary standards and on time.
2. The increase in the cost of providing services or goods by such companies shall not exceed 10% of the costs provided by other companies.
3. The terms and conditions applicable to the provision of services or goods shall be highly competitive with those of other companies.

The project company is committed to recruiting national employees and workers to carry out the PPP project provided that they have the necessary qualifications, in accordance with the conditions set out in the guide to the provisions and procedures of the PPP contracts.

Compensation against the risk of amendments to laws and/or regulations

The PPP contract shall specify the provisions relating to the right of the project company to receive compensation and the basis of its assessment as a result to any amendment in the national laws or regulations applicable to the infrastructure facility or the service it provides. The compensation is due if such an amendment increases the cost of implementing the PPP contract significantly or decreases the value of what the project company receives comparing with the performance and implementation costs and their expected value.[7]

Changing of circumstances and financial equilibrium: the right to modify the terms of the PPP contract

The administrative authority is entitled to amend the conditions of construction, equipment, rehabilitation and other works as well as the services availability payment agreed upon under the PPP contract. If the PPP contract includes the entitlement of the project company to operate or utilize the project, and if required for the public interest, the administrative authority has the right to amend the rules of operation or utilization including the sale prices of products or services. These modifications will only take place within the scope agreed upon in the PPP contract and after the approval of the Supreme Committee for PPP Affairs, and without prejudice to the right of the project company, or the administrative authority (as the case may be), for compensation in accordance with the conditions and rules stipulated in the PPP contract. If the sale price of the product or the services provision payment is amended, such an amendment shall not have a retroactive effect.

In the case of the occurrence of unforeseen circumstances after execution of the PPP contract, including amendments to laws or regulations that were enforceable at the time of execution of the PPP contract, it may be agreed to amend the PPP contract in accordance with the conditions and rules stipulated in the PPP contract.[8]

PPP contract shall determine the limits of the right of the project company to amend the PPP contract by adding provisions related to compensation in case the cost of performing the contract increases significantly or if the value of the company revenues from such performance is significantly reduced compared to the implementation costs, and its expected value, as a result of:

1. Changes in economic or financial conditions.
2. Amendments to laws and regulations that do not apply to the infrastructure or service facility provided by the project company.

---

7 Antoine Mazin, Dealing with political risk in PPP infrastructure projects: legal recommendations based on recent cases, *International Business Law Journal*, 2017, 3, 189–202.
8 The Egyptian PPP law, Article 8.

In the cases provided for in items (1) and (2) in the list above, the following conditions shall be met:

1. The changes in economic or financial conditions and/or the amendments to laws and regulations occurred after the conclusion of the contract.
2. The above-mentioned changes and amendments were beyond the control of the project company.

The above-mentioned changes and amendments are of a nature that the project company could not expect during the conclusion of the PPP contract.

The PPP contract shall establish the rules of procedure for the amendment of its provisions after the occurrence of any of the cases provided for.

Duration of the PPP contract

The PPP contract shall include a period of not more than the stipulated period in the national legislation starting from the date of its conclusion or the date specified by the contracting administrative authority in coordination with the Supreme Committees in the MENA countries.

The contracting administrative authority may, after obtaining the approval of the Supreme Committees in the MENA countries, approve the extension of the contract term due to any of the following circumstances:

1. Delays in the completion of the operation or disruption of operation due to circumstances beyond the reasonable control of either party to the contract.
2. Suspension of the project for reasons attributable to the contracting administrative authority or any public body without any intervention by the project company.
3. An increase in costs arising from requirements of the contracting administrative authority that was not originally envisaged in the PPP contract, and the project company could not recover those costs without such an extension.

The contracting administrative authority may, with the approval of the Supreme Committee, conclude the PPP contract for a period of more than the stipulated duration.

In Egyptian PPP law, the PPP contract duration shall not be less than five years and shall not exceed 30 years from the date of completion of the construction works and equipping works, or completion of the rehabilitation works, provided that the total value of the PPP contract is not less than one hundred million Egyptian pounds. However, the Cabinet, based on the recommendation of the Supreme Committee for PPP Affairs, may agree to conclude a PPP contract for more than 30 years, if it is required due to a material public interest. The project company shall not start to receive any payments in return for the sale of products or availability of services, in accordance with the performance levels indicated in the PPP contract, until the contracting administrative authority issues a certificate accepting the quality level of the works, or products or services available.

172 *Substantive mechanisms of PPP contracts*

Supervise the implementation of the project

The contracting administrative authority along with other concerned authorities regulating and monitoring the utilities and the services subject of the PPP contract, shall follow up on the project company during the construction and equipping of the project, and provision of the products and for services subject of the PPP contract, and shall ensure the fulfillment of quality levels determined by the law; and may, in this regard, designate representatives on its behalf to monitor execution in accordance with the terms and provisions stipulated in the PPP contract and without prejudice to the criteria and monitoring bases set out by law if the PPP contract includes the entitlement of the project company to operate or utilize the project, the administrative authority, in agreement with the project company, and under the supervision of the concerned authorities regulating and monitoring the utilities and services subject of the PPP contract, shall form a committee to ensure that the product or services rendered meet the required standards, as well as submitting periodic reports. In Egyptian PPP law, the Executive Regulations shall specify the committee's system of work and the reports to be submitted by it. In the case mentioned above, the project company must provide the committee with all required documents, information, or data necessary for the committee to undertake its role and to allow the committee to visit and inspect the sites at any time, in accordance with the provisions of the Executive Regulations of this law.

The contracting administrative authority shall be responsible for supervising the execution of the project, ensuring the achievement of the highest required performance levels, evaluating the performance of the project company and continuing the availability of the requirements, standards, arrangements and equipment stipulated in the PPP contract.

The contracting administrative authority shall submit a periodic report to the Supreme Committees in the MENA countries on the results of supervision and evaluation of the PPP project, containing its observations, recommendations and actions taken in accordance with the rules to be determined by a decision of the administrative authority and in most of the MENA countries after the approval of the cabinet in the concerned MANA country.

The contracting administrative authority, after coordination with the concerned department, may assign supervision and evaluation tasks to experts or entities having the necessary technical capabilities to carry out these tasks. This outsourcing is a new approach in the MENA countries to exercise a higher threshold of technical expertise upon supervision of the implementation of the project as this higher threshold of supervision has a positive impact to the public utility's management standards.

On the other hand, in Egyptian PPP law, the project company shall provide the administrative authority with its shareholders' agreements and draft contracts intended to be entered into by it with third parties for the purpose of executing the works and services subject of the PPP contract, in accordance with the procedures and timing specified in the Executive Regulations. The administrative authority shall have the right to object to the conclusion of such contracts within a period not exceeding 60 days from the date of their submission. An objection shall be made in case it is proven that the third party contract counterparties have been previously bankrupted or are subject to liquidation procedures, or have been previously convicted or, in case of a judicial person, whoever legally represents it has been subject to a final court judgment for an immoral crime, or have been struck off the vendor lists of the contracting administrative authority or if there are national security considerations that necessitate such objection.

Environment, health and safety

The PPP contract must stipulate that the project company must also warrant that environmental, health and safety conditions are met for the employees and the end-users of the project.

Breach of contractual undertakings

The contracting administrative authority, after coordination with the concerned department, may temporarily operate the facility on its own or with the assistance of another investor, in case the project company breaches substantially its contractual undertakings, or if there is a serious error or an inability to achieve the quality and performance levels prescribed in accordance with the PPP contract.

The contracting administrative authority shall, after coordination with the concerned department, notify the project company of the breach, error or failure to achieve the quality and performance levels and request its adjustment within the period specified in the notification.

The above-mentioned principles shall not prejudice any damages or penalties prescribed to the contracting administrative authority under the PPP contract.

The administrative authority has the right, either directly or through a selected third party, to manage the operation or utilization of the project if the project company materially breaches its obligations in operating the project or meeting the quality levels set by law or in the PPP contract, and does not remedy such breach, and the lenders do not step in to remedy such breach within the period provided for in the PPP contract from the date of their notification of such breach, without prejudice to the project company's obligation to compensate the administrative authority for the damages resulting from such breach.

PPP contract amendments and renewal

In the Egyptian legal system, articles of the PPP contract or its supplementary agreements shall not be amended unless approved by its parties. If the undertakings of the contracting administrative authority are related to financial obligations of any other administrative authority, such amendment shall not be effective unless there

174 *Substantive mechanisms of PPP contracts*

is a prior written consent from such authority. The project company shall not waiver the PPP contract or any of its rights or undertakings thereunder except for the purpose of financing and after a prior written consent from the competent authority of the contracting administrative authority. Any agreements inconsistent with the provisions of this article shall be deemed to be null and void. This means that this legislative provision is a mandatory rule in the Egyptian Legal system.

PPP contract may contain provisions dealing with its renewal.[9]

Termination of the PPP contract

The contracting authority may, after consultation with the Supreme Committees in the MENA counties, terminate the PPP contract in any of the following cases:

1. If the project company is unable to fulfill its obligations or is found to be unwilling to implement them due to insolvency, breach or other reasons.
2. For compelling reasons relating to public interest. In that case, the project company shall be compensated in accordance with the provisions of the PPP contract.

The PPP contract shall specify how the compensation due to either party to this contract shall be calculated, if necessary, in the event of termination of the contract. Compensation shall be for the fair value of the work performed under the contract, the costs to be incurred or the losses incurred by either party, including the expected profits.

Governing law and disputes resolution

In most MENA countries' legislation, the national laws and regulations of the hosting country shall be the law applicable to PPP contracts.

Egyptian PPP law provides that the PPP contract shall be subject to the provisions of the Egyptian law. Any contrary agreement shall be deemed to be null and void. This means that this legislative provision is a mandatory rule in the Egyptian legal system.

After the approval of the Supreme Committee for PPP Affairs, it may be agreed to resolve disputes resulting from the PPP contract through arbitration, or any other non-judicial means of dispute resolution according to what was stipulated in the PPP contract.[10]

The PPP Jordanian law[11] provides that partnership contracts shall be governed by Jordanian law. The parties to the partnership project contract may

---

9 The Egyptian PPP law, Article 37.
10 The Egyptian PPP law, Article 35.
11 The Jordanian PPP law, Article 16.

Substantive mechanisms of PPP contracts 175

agree to settle the disputes pertaining the partnership project contract through alternative disputes resolution methods.

The Morocco PPP law does not provide for specific provisions. The parties to the contract are free to decide the applicable law. Provision is left to the liberty of the parties who may foresee conciliation procedure, conventional mediation, arbitration or judicial means (Article 27).[12]

Settlement of project company disputes with third parties

If the project company is committed to providing services to the public or operates publicly available infrastructure facilities, the contracting administrative authority may require the company in the PPP contract to establish simple and effective mechanisms for settling claims submitted by users of the infrastructure facility or the services it provides.

The project company and its shareholders shall be free to choose appropriate mechanisms for the settlement of disputes arising between them.

The project company shall be free to agree on appropriate mechanisms for settling disputes between it and the suppliers, contractors or suppliers and others dealing with them.

Risk assessment

Risk assessment in public sector contracting is embedded by the choice of prescribed terms and conditions, which by design, are formalized within a contract to mitigate a menu of recurrent or common risks. Whilst the interpretation, incorporation and reasonableness of the contractual terms and conditions are readily acknowledged amongst legal practitioners as a fundamental pillar for risk assessment, the dynamic patterns associated with risk remains undervalued. To fully account for the dynamic nature of risk, a tool for mapping the migration of risk has been developed to provide a new method of ex ante risk assessment to the design and inception of public sector contracts.[13]

Identifiable risks in PPPs[14]

Some of these risks would arise under other procurement methods, for example, a design and build or design, build and operate contract, but they have

---

12 Morocco PPP law pointed out that: '*La loi ne prévoit pas de dispositions spécifiques. Les parties au contrat sont libres de décider du droit applicable. Disposition laissée à la liberté des parties qui peuvent prévoir une procédure de conciliation, de médiation conventionnelle, d'arbitrage ou judiciaire (L.art.27).*'

13 Katherine Bloomfield, Risk assessment in public contracts, *EPPPL*, 1/2019.

14 The Dispute Resolution Board Foundation, Fostering common sense dispute resolution worldwide, UNECE Publication, April 2017, Guidance on the Use of Dispute Boards in Public Private Partnership (PPP) Projects, https://www.unece.org/fileadmin/DAM/ceci/

176   *Substantive mechanisms of PPP contracts*

a greater impact under PPP because of the length of the project period and/or the fee basis. Other risks are unique to the PPP structure.

Key risks: up to and during construction phase[15]

- Allocation of pre-construction risk of permits; rights of way; expropriation.
- Changing user demands; changes in law; political risk.
- Interface between the design and build sub-contractor and the operation and maintenance sub-contractors, for example, where performance outputs do not meet the required standards.

Key risks: operation and maintenance phase[16]

- Interface between design and build or and operation/ maintenance sub-contractors (as above).
- Changing user demands; changes in law; political risk.
- Length of contract period.
- Hand back of asset.

Key risks: throughout the project[17]

- The approach of the public body/SPV/lenders to risk transfer, i.e. that all risk has been passed down to the sub-contractors.[18]
- Lack of experience of public authorities in preparation for and management of long-term contractual relationships.[19]

---

documents/2018/PPP/Forum/Documents/White_Paper_Guidance_on_the_Use_of_Dispute_Boards_in_PPP_Projects.pdf, last accessed on 5 October 2018.

15 The Dispute Resolution Board Foundation, Fostering common sense dispute resolution worldwide, UNECE Publication, April 2017, Guidance on the Use of Dispute Boards in Public Private Partnership (PPP) Projects, https://www.unece.org/fileadmin/DAM/ceci/documents/2018/PPP/Forum/Documents/White_Paper_Guidance_on_the_Use_of_Dispute_Boards_in_PPP_Projects.pdf, last accessed on 5 October 2018.

16 The Dispute Resolution Board Foundation, Fostering common sense dispute resolution worldwide, UNECE Publication, April 2017, Guidance on the Use of Dispute Boards in Public Private Partnership (PPP) Projects, https://www.unece.org/fileadmin/DAM/ceci/documents/2018/PPP/Forum/Documents/White_Paper_Guidance_on_the_Use_of_Dispute_Boards_in_PPP_Projects.pdf, last accessed on 5 October 2018.

17 The Dispute Resolution Board Foundation, Fostering common sense dispute resolution worldwide, UNECE Publication, April 2017, Guidance on the Use of Dispute Boards in Public Private Partnership (PPP) Projects, https://www.unece.org/fileadmin/DAM/ceci/documents/2018/PPP/Forum/Documents/White_Paper_Guidance_on_the_Use_of_Dispute_Boards_in_PPP_Projects.pdf, last accessed on 5 October 2018.

18 Antoine Mazin, Dealing with political risk in PPP infrastructure projects: legal recommendations based on recent cases, *International Business Law Journal*, 2017, 3, 189–202.

19 See UK National Audit Office report on High Speed Rail Link HS 2 of June 2016 [www.nao.org.uk/report/progress-with-preparations-for-high-speed-2].

Substantive mechanisms of PPP contracts 177

There are certain common themes relative to risk allocation and therefore potential areas of friction. We identify five central issues, namely (i) how to make PPPs resilient in times of change; (ii) the multi-party nature of an availability based PPP with its large number of interfaces to be managed; (iii) the public authority's often unrealistic expectations of such projects and, in concession arrangements, the public's demands and expectations; (iv) the measurement of the output and (v) the project's lifetime, which can be up to 50 years.

Adaptability and resilience in times of change[20]

A huge issue for PPPs is the ability within their structure to deal with major changes. Some changes can be dealt with within the project agreement. For example, changes in work scope can be instructed as variations and the project agreement will provide as to how these will impact on the availability fee and the prescribed outputs. Other changes which may be imposed upon the parties may not be able to be accommodated within the contractual structure. For example, changes in the economic environment when debt becomes more or less expensive may have an impact on services.

There may be changes in public demand and the political climate. The terms of a contract, no matter how detailed, cannot deal with such external pressures or influences.

Multiple interfaces[21]

One of the challenges with availability-based PPPs is the number of contracts and therefore interfaces among the parties. Wherever an interface exists there are issues of allocation of risk. None more so than in PPPs. As a result, some very complicated contract terms have been devised in the mature PPP market to deal with these interfaces. For example, the concept of complete 'pass through' of service fee reductions by the SPV to whatever sub-contractor is in place at that time regardless of where the ultimate liability lies. This is even the case where the deductions are not justified under the project agreement – it is 'pay now, argue later.' This has a real influence on parties' behaviors, not always for the better. When disputes arise in mature availability-based PPPs they tend to

20 The Dispute Resolution Board Foundation, Fostering common sense dispute resolution worldwide, UNECE Publication, April 2017, Guidance on the Use of Dispute Boards in Public Private Partnership (PPP) Projects, https://www.unece.org/fileadmin/DAM/ceci/documents/2018/PPP/Forum/Documents/White_Paper_Guidance_on_the_Use_of_Dispute_Boards_in_PPP_Projects.pdf, last accessed on 5 October 2018.
21 The Dispute Resolution Board Foundation, Fostering common sense dispute resolution worldwide, UNECE Publication, April 2017, Guidance on the Use of Dispute Boards in Public Private Partnership (PPP) Projects, https://www.unece.org/fileadmin/DAM/ceci/documents/2018/PPP/Forum/Documents/White_Paper_Guidance_on_the_Use_of_Dispute_Boards_in_PPP_Projects.pdf, last accessed on 5 October 2018.

178 *Substantive mechanisms of PPP contracts*

come 'bottom up' from the sub-contractors to the SPV, on the basis that the sub-contractor is at the end of the payment chain and deductions stop with them. Dispute resolution provisions in standardized project agreements and associated contracts tend not to have been drafted with that in mind, as explained more fully below.

Issues as to multiple interfaces do not arise in the same way with concession PPPs.

Public authority expectations[22]

In availability-based PPPs one of the biggest risks can be the belief of certain public authorities that, because it is not its own capital project, all risk lies with the SPV. This is then perpetuated by the SPV being obliged, because of how it is funded, to pass all such risks down to its sub-contractors. This is because of the insistence of lenders to the SPV that it, the SPV, is kept practically free from risk. This can compromise any collaborative culture in trying to resolve issues around service delivery, and user expectations. The SPV is usually not resourced itself to manage these projects, relying almost entirely on its sub-contractors project managing the delivery. Pushing down the risks through application of deductions to sub-contractors can result in the SPV and the funders believing that there are no live issues to address. This can mean that any dissatisfaction of the public authority/end user is not identified before it starts to have an effect on the sub-contractors' cash flow and therefore performance through service fee deductions.

To take an example, a design and build contractor delivers a waste water plant to the operator under a PPP. The operator, despite being involved in the performance tests at completion, complains several months later that the plant does not work as needed and it cannot achieve its performance standards without major additional work. The design and build contractor has been paid its sub-contract price in full. The SPV withholds part of the annual payment from the operator because of its failure to meet specified performance standards. The operator is left contractually to make a claim against the design and build contractor under an interface agreement, with no involvement from the SPV. Because the operator is left short of funds and having to pursue the design and build contractor, it is dis-incentivized from working with the SPV to maximize the value/ capacity of the plant. The relationship with the SPV and the most efficient effective means of operating the plant are both at risk.

---

22 The Dispute Resolution Board Foundation, Fostering common sense dispute resolution worldwide, UNECE Publication, April 2017, Guidance on the Use of Dispute Boards in Public Private Partnership (PPP) Projects, https://www.unece.org/fileadmin/DAM/ceci/documents/2018/PPP/Forum/Documents/White_Paper_Guidance_on_the_Use_of_Dispute_Boards_in_PPP_Projects.pdf, last accessed on 5 October 2018.

Substantive mechanisms of PPP contracts 179

In the situation outlined above, the lenders priority is to keep the SPV 'whole'. It is key to its funding agreement that the deductions made by the public body are passed down in full to one of the sub-contractors regardless of whether that sub-contractor is the party responsible for the problem. If the deductions reach a certain level, this will be an event of default under the lending agreement, which has significant consequences, leading to possible termination of the project agreement and potential SPV insolvency. In a concession PPP there is a complete transfer of risk from the public authority to the SPV as, in reality, the SPV steps into the place of the public body as service provider.

Measurement of the output[23]

One of the differentiating factors of an availability-based PPP is that its success is dictated by how and to what extent it achieves defined outputs. A key element of the PPP contract is the output specifications or standards and the matrices by which their success or failure is measured. They are linked to the payments made under the contract as deductions are applied for failures to meet the availability and performance-based outputs. Recurring deductions will constitute acts of default with associated termination risk. In countries with more developed PPPs, a significant number of disputes arise on the interpretation and application of these outputs and the methods of measurement. It is recognized that applying a 'legalistic approach' to the operation of the project agreement or sub-contracts when such issues arise is unlikely to achieve the best outcome for the project.

Length of project period[24]

There are risks arising from the length of project period particularly in concession PPPs.[25] Typical contract periods are upward of 20 years – sometimes 30 years and over. In concession agreements the level and expectations of the public service to be delivered by the concessionaire undoubtedly change over the contract period. The concession agreement often does not regulate how this is done or the implications for the concessionaire. In the availability-based PPP

---

23 The Dispute Resolution Board Foundation, Fostering common sense dispute resolution worldwide, UNECE Publication, April 2017, Guidance on the Use of Dispute Boards in Public Private Partnership (PPP) Projects, https://www.unece.org/fileadmin/DAM/ceci/documents/2018/PPP/Forum/Documents/White_Paper_Guidance_on_the_Use_of_Dispute_Boards_in_PPP_Projects.pdf, last accessed on 5 October 2018.
24 The Dispute Resolution Board Foundation, Fostering common sense dispute resolution worldwide, UNECE Publication, April 2017, Guidance on the Use of Dispute Boards in Public Private Partnership (PPP) Projects, https://www.unece.org/fileadmin/DAM/ceci/documents/2018/PPP/Forum/Documents/White_Paper_Guidance_on_the_Use_of_Dispute_Boards_in_PPP_Projects.pdf, last accessed on 5 October 2018.
25 Antoine Mazin, Dealing with political risk in PPP infrastructure projects: legal recommendations based on recent cases, *International Business Law Journal*, 2017, 3, 189–202.

180 *Substantive mechanisms of PPP contracts*

the challenges of a long contract period include the life cycle of the assets. Compensation for changes in the law will often be regulated by the project agreement. However, policy changes in the sector, which fall short of legislation, may also have significant financial implications on delivery of the services. These would include, for example, employment law changes. Often the project agreement is completely silent on this.

PPPs are output based and such outputs may require to be adjusted to reflect changing demands and trends as referred to above.

The contractual arrangements generally include, but not limited to, obligations on the private entity to design, finance, build or rehabilitate a public infrastructure, to maintain and operate the infrastructure concerned and to provide defined services for a specified period; obligations on the public authority to provide access to the land and to the rights and permits necessary for the construction of the infrastructure and delivery of the service by the private party; clear allocation of risk and reward between the parties based on a fair equilibrium commensurate with established best practices for the particular nature of the venture; and payment mechanism based on the performance of the infrastructure service, with remuneration being provided by the public authority or by the end users (or a combination of both). Where the obligation of the private party is to deliver a full public service on behalf of the public authority and to recover entirely or mainly from the end users, the PPP is a concession; in other cases, it is a publicly funded PPP. PPPs may be exclusively publicly funded, or by concessions alone, or include a combination of both payment mechanisms.

It is recommended that PPPs are permitted to be concluded in accordance with the provisions of the PPPs law, in the light of the legal fact that contract provisions supersede legislative provisions if the latter provisions are not mandatory rules. PPP contracts should include:

a) A planning and preparation process as set out in the PPPs law, and in other relevant laws, which includes assessments of the social, economic and other impact of the proposed project, and comparative assessments of the available project delivery mechanisms.

b) A contract planning process that addresses the contractual arrangements set out in the preceding paragraph and includes commercial terms that appropriately balance the interests of both parties, considering also the interest of the end users, the time necessary for the private entity to amortize all costs and make a reasonable profit. This time is the main criteria for assessing the length of the contract.

c) Provisions for termination of the contract at the expiry of the term or in various situations and related calculation of the financial and other consequences including provision providing for a transfer of the infrastructure in good operating condition to the public authority, generally without compensation (unless the contract provides otherwise).

PPPs are neither traditional procurement nor, on the other hand, a privatization mechanism.

Substantive mechanisms of PPP contracts 181

Conclusions, bespoke PPP contract

As there is no one agreed PPP contract for PPP projects, the parties have to bespoke the most convenient PPP contract which illustrates the risk factors and risk allocation for the contracting parties and assumes higher risks for the private sector. One of the main purposes behind PPP techniques and the liberalization of the tradition concessions and traditional administrative contracts is to create a new platform of contractual techniques that were not recognized in administrative contracts in the MENA countries. The new distribution of risks' allocation in the PPP contract is an impact to the legal globalization in administrative contracts in particular concession agreements.

Impediments to the performance of PPP contracts

A breach of mutual contractual obligations committed by any of the contracting parties may disrupt the functioning of the public utility. However, some impediments not in the form of contractual breach may result in the absolute impossibility of performing the contractual obligations; some others may lead to destabilizing the contract's financial equilibrium. It is important to explore the impediments to the performance of PPP contracts and the reasons behind the impossibility of executing the contractual obligations. Force majeure and its effect upon exemption from liability shall be examined. The foundations of the Prince Theory in terms of the contract's financial equilibrium, unforeseen circumstances and unforeseen physical difficulties are detailed. It is fundamental to examine the effect of the new conditions introduced to the PPP contracts and PPP legislation to maintain the contract's financial equilibrium.

The impossibility of executing the contractual obligations in PPP contracts

Force majeure and its effect upon exemption from liability

A fundamental concept of contract liability is the existence of a contractual breach and damage and the causality between them.

The impossible execution of an obligation can be factual or legal. An external cause is a hardship, force majeure, the debtor's breach or a third party's tort. The force majeure or the accidental event must be impossible to prevent, such as an earthquake, flood, volcanic eruption or an outbreak of war, all of which make the PPP project's execution impossible.

The force majeure must be warranted by two conditions: the first condition is that the event is accidental; the second condition is that the event cannot be prevented. The external cause eliminates the causality link (*lien de causalité*)

182 *Substantive mechanisms of PPP contracts*

between the breach and the damage and can be a force majeure, an accidental event, a breach by the debtor or an act by a third party.[26]

Force majeure is a purely legal concept forged by the lawmaker as a preventive measure against any matter that may cause a breach of contractual obligations where it becomes impossible to perform them.[27]

Article 165 of the Egyptian civil code stipulates that:

> If a person proves that the damage has occurred due to an external cause beyond his control, such as an accidental event, a force majeure, or a tort by a third party, he is not obligated to compensate for such damage unless otherwise specified in a text or an agreement.

In the light of the above Article (Article 165 of the Egyptian civil code), the external cause can be a force majeure or an accidental event. A force majeure or an accidental event must be unpreventable and unforeseeable.

The Egyptian Court of Cassation ruled that a force majeure must be unforeseeable and unpreventable. These two conditions are drawn from precedents exclusively examined by the courts; the cassation courts of all MENA countries concluded the same vision.[28]

The unforeseeable nature of the event is the first condition that must be established in this respect; a person is deemed negligent if he or she could foresee the event and did not take the necessary precautions to avoid the consequential effects. The criteria of unforeseeable must be an objective one,

---

26 See Abdel Wadood Yehia, *The Summary in the General Theory of Obligations, Sources of Obligations*, Part I, Dar Al Nahdah Al Arabia 1989, 256; G.H. Trietle, *Frustration and Force Majeure*, Sweet & Maxwell, Chapter 5, 191; Hugh Beale, *Chitty on Contracts, General Principles*, 30th edn, Vol. 1, Sweet & Maxwell 2008, 1479; Ewan McKendrick, *Force Majeure and Frustration of Contract*, 2nd edn, LLP, 1995, 3–19 and *Force Majeure in French Law*, 21–31; Wallace, I.N. Duncan, *Hudson's in Building and Engineering Contracts*, 11th edn, Vol. 1, Sweet & Maxwell, 1995, 655. In administrative contracts see: Laurent Richer, *Droits de Contrats Administratifs*, LGDG, 2008, 214; A. De Laubadere, F. Moderne and P. Delvolve, *Traite de Contrats Administratifs*, T-2, Paris, LGDJ T.2, 727. In building contracts in comparative jurisprudence and international customs, see: Christopher S. Thomas, *Aspects of Building Contracts: A Comparative View of English and French Law in the Light of Potential Harmonization*, PhD thesis, School of Law, Kings College, London, 1995; Phillipe Lane Bruner, Force majeure under international law and international construction contract model forms, *ICLR*, Part 2, April 1995, 274; Douglas Jones, Force majeure in Australian construction law, *ICLR*, Part 2, April 1995, 295; Stanley Jeremiah, Insurability of force majeure events in construction contracts, *ICLR*, Part 2, April 1995, 319; John C. Chen, Force majeure in construction contracts, Taiwan, *ICLR*, Part 2, April 1995, 328.
27 Pronchai Wiwatpattarakul, A critical examination of the concept of force majeure at Thai law and its impact in the context of construction contracts, *ICLR* 1, 174.
28 Egyptian Cassation Court, Civil Cuircuit, Session of 27/3/1980, case No. 979 of 47, *The Collection of the Technical Bureau*, judicial year 31, Rule 183, 930.

Substantive mechanisms of PPP contracts 183

where the event cannot be foreseen by even the most prudent person, which makes it absolutely – and therefore not relatively – impossible.[29]

The second condition to be established is related to the unpreventable nature of the event. *Impossible* means absolute impossibility, whereupon there is an absolute impossibility of performing the obligation.

If both conditions are established, the debtor is exempted from the contractual liability, and the causality link (*Lien de Causalité*) between the breach and damage is then ruled out; hence, there is no ground for compensation in either case.[30]

The concept of force majeure has great significance in all legal systems. In the English system, force majeure is dealt with by the 'frustration of contract.'[31] The Egyptian judiciary has an objective criterion whereupon it is absolutely impossible to perform the obligations, and the force majeure or the accidental event is unpreventable, which makes such performance absolutely impossible, not only to the debtor but also to any other person in the same position as the debtor.[32]

Force majeure in the comparative judiciary

The French Conseil D'Etat expanded the concept of administrative force majeure whereupon the contracting party might request to terminate the contract with appropriate compensation, if any. According to this theory, the contracting party is entitled to withdraw from the contract where it is impossible to perform the obligation placed upon it.[33]

Within the scope of administrative force majeure, the contract is terminated under the continuity of an accidental circumstance or difficulties faced by the contracting party where it is impossible to carry out execution, or when the contract's financial equilibrium is destabilized beyond the reasonable level estimated by both parties during the drafting of the contract. It is then an area between the force majeure and its conventional concept and the theory of unforeseen circumstances.[34]

---

29 Abdel Wadood Yehia, *The Summary in the General Theory of Obligations, Sources of Obligations,* Part I, 1989, 256, 258.
30 Egyptian Cassation Court, Civil Circuit, session of 29/1/1976, *The Collection of the Technical Bureau,* judicial year 46, Rule 243, 27.
31 Hugh Beale, *Chitty on Contracts, General Principles,* 30th edn, 2008, 1, 1479; Treitel, *Frustration and Force Majeure,* 2nd edn, 2004; McKendrick, *Force Majeure and Frustration of Contract,* 2nd edn, 1995.
32 The Supreme Administrative Court, Judgment No. 689–4, 12/12/1969, 5/15/106 – *Forty Years Collection of Court Judgments,* 473.
33 Laurent Richer, *Droits de Contrats administratifs,* LGDG 2008, 214–215.
34 M. Said Amin, *General Principles for the Performance of Administrative Contracts,* 1991, 295–6; Laurent Richer, *Droits de Contrats Administratifs,* LGDG 2008, 214–15.

184　*Substantive mechanisms of PPP contracts*

This was determined following the Conseil D'Etat recognition that a force majeure was not a reason to exempt the contractor from contractual obligations or from delaying performance, unless otherwise specified in the contract. The matter remained as such until 1858, where the jurisprudence construed that the opinion of the French Conseil D'Etat was under the influence of the principle of *Pacta sunt Servanda*.

Force majeure in the Egyptian Conseil D'Etat

The Egyptian judiciary confirmed the established approaches adopted by Egyptian jurisprudence with regard to force majeure. The Supreme Administrative Court decided that where the impossibility to perform an obligation was attributed to an external cause, 'the obligation to perform is then lifted, whether performance in kind or by way of compensation.' An external cause is an accidental event, force majeure, debtor's breach or a third party's tort. A force majeure or an accidental event must be unforeseeable and unpreventable; if these two provisions exist, such event is then unpredictable and beyond the control of not only the debtor but also the most prudent person. The criterion is objective and not subject to the ordinary individual; nevertheless, it requires absolute impossibility. The force majeure or accidental event must be unpreventable; thus, if it is preventable, though unforeseeable, it is not a force majeure or accidental event. It must also render the execution absolutely impossible, not only for the debtor but also for any person who is in the position of the debtor. This point makes the distinct difference between a force majeure and an accidental event and the accidental events that render the execution cumbersome but not impossible. The effect of a force majeure or an accidental event varies according to the circumstances; if it was the sole cause for the damage that occurred, the causal link is then ruled out, which, in turn, provides an exemption from responsibility. The consequence can be the suspension of the execution and not the exemption from performing the obligation, until such an event has ended. Both parties may modify their agreement in accordance with the effect of the force majeure or accidental event; for example, they may agree that the debtor shall not be exempted from the obligation and shall be responsible for the consequence of any external cause. Hence, although it is impossible to perform the obligation due to an external cause, such a performance is not lifted but is replaced by compensation, where the debtor is like an insurance entity, and the creditor is the insurer against any event attributed to a force majeure. The aforementioned principles were codified in the MENA countries' civil codes. Whilst these principles are applied within the context of relationships under private law, the administrative judiciary has consistently taken them into consideration as a general principle to be applied in determining the administrative relations under public law, as long as it is in conformity with the functioning of the public utility and ensures the reconcilement of this latter with the individual interests.[35]

---

35 The Supreme Administrative Court, Judgment No. 689–4 (12/12/1969, 5/15/106) – *Forty Years Collection of Court Judgments*, 473.

Substantive mechanisms of PPP contracts 185

The Supreme Administrative Court at the Egyptian Conseil D'Etat also held that where an event was foreseeable though unpreventable, or *vice versa*, it was not deemed a force majeure and did not give rise to an exemption from responsibility. The Supreme Administrative Court also mentioned in its judgment that the intervention made by the Supreme Council of Antiquities was foreseeable and cannot be deemed an external cause or a force majeure, since it was expected – when concluding a contract – to suspend the work when there were archaeological finds on site.[36]

The Supreme Administrative Court added that the contracting parties might not modify their agreement to change the effect of force majeure, for example, by agreeing that the debtor would bear the consequential effect.[37]

Force majeure and international arbitral awards

The concept of force majeure has been applied in several international arbitral awards.

A dispute was related to a contract concluded between a Turkish company (B) and the Libyan authorities for the construction of an airport in Tripoli, Libya (main contract).

On 8 March 1973, (B) subcontracted a Belgian company (A) based on the FIDIC contract form under Libyan law. An explosion in the airport during execution of the work gave rise to execution and payment problems of the subcontract. Both parties suspended the contract performance claiming that the other party had committed a breach of the contract (by virtue of a letter dated 11 April 1974 from (B), and a letter dated 21 May 1974 from (A)).

In March 1975, (A) initiated the arbitration procedures before the International Chamber of Commerce (ICC) in Paris, pursuant to the arbitration clause set forth in the contract, with a claim for payment of the work's value by virtue of the subcontract and compensation for a breach of contractual obligations committed by (B). Nevertheless, (B) commenced a counterclaim for a breach of contractual obligations committed by the subcontractor (A).

The tribunal ruled to have jurisdiction to settle the dispute arising from the subcontract and the individual contracts between (A) and (B) for the execution of the remaining works. The tribunal ruled that the subcontract breach committed by (B) was not a consequence of the breach committed by (A), which must be compensated, and that the counterclaim filed by (B) was not acceptable as it was based upon the same grounds and facts. In its justification of exempting (A) from any responsibility, the tribunal stated that the explosives were a force majeure, and (A) could not be held accountable for any serious breach in performing the contractual obligation. However, since the explosives were planted in airport

---

36 The Supreme Administrative Court, Judgments No. 1320 and 1340–12 (15/2/1969, 14/48/373 – *Forty Years Collection of Court Judgments*, 474.

37 Ibid.

186   *Substantive mechanisms of PPP contracts*

ground – a target of recurrent artillery shelling during the war – this was a predictable situation; nevertheless, the significance and quantity of the explosives were far beyond the parties' estimate. This was evidenced by the mutual correspondence between the parties: the owner (the Libyan government), their representatives and the consultant as they indicated on several occasions the force majeure aspect with regard to the existing explosives. On the other hand, in order to resolve the problem between the parties regarding the removal of the explosives, (A) confirmed that it had acted with due diligence and observed the instructions given by the consultant, which allowed for the timely removal of these explosives. On that basis, the tribunal concluded that no breach could be attributed to (A).[38] In another dispute,[39] the respondent was performing a turnkey contract for the construction of a factory when a war broke out in the region, and the relationship between the parties' countries was compromised. The claimant in the dispute was a government-run company, and the respondent was entrusted to supply and operate the industrial equipment.

The initial effect of the outbreak of war was to repatriate the respondent's personnel who were of the same nationality. The second effect was that the respondent's government stated that the credit facility previously provided had been withdrawn. By the end of the war, the claimant requested the respondent to complete the work to be executed under the contract; the latter refused such a request since it was impossible for the contract's personnel to return to work in that country, nor to be insured, in addition to the fact that the financial facility that had been provided by their government had been withdrawn.

In an interim award regarding whether there was a case of force majeure, the tribunal decided that such a force was existent until the ceasefire. The arbitration tribunal judged that the respondent had reasons not to perform the contractual obligation by virtue of the claimant's law and Article 6/2 of the contract.

In addition to the risks posed by the war, which had forced the respondent not to perform the obligation, the agency letter sent by the respondent's government had requested that person to continue providing the necessary services and production by virtue of the letter of credit, since it was impossible to secure visas for the personnel to return to the claimant's country.

The claimant's defense stated that had the respondent sent a notice to the claimant, pursuant to Article 6/2, explaining the complications caused by the government and those related to the visa acquisition, the claimant would have empowered the respondent to perform the contract, given the national importance of the project. Hence, the respondent's government and the political situation in the country did not ultimately represent a risk of any sort that could

---

38 Award of 25 June 1980, case No. 2763, Sigvard Jarvin, and Yves Derains, *Collection of ICC Arbitral Awards*, (1974), 157.

39 Award made in case No. 1703 in 1971, Sigvard Jarvin and Yves Derains, *Collection of ICC Arbitral Awards*, (1974), 6. See also: Philip Iane, Force majeure under international law and international construction contract model forms, *ICLR*, 1995, 12, 274.

have prevented the execution of the project. The tribunal did not find that the respondent had exerted any effort to obtain the entry visas. The respondent did not prove that he or she had notified the claimant, pursuant to Article 6/2 of the contract, of the intention to resume the performance of the contractual obligation, since the claimant had provided finance for the remaining works prescribed in the contract.

On that basis, the tribunal ruled out a case of force majeure.

This award shows that there was no event that the parties could not prevent; rather, there was an omission by the respondent for delaying the application for entry visas. The respondent was partly held accountable for the non-performance of the contractual obligation; therefore, the arbitral tribunal overruled the claim of a force majeure for the lack of its necessary conditions.

Difficulty of performing the obligation in PPP contracts

The concept of the contract's financial equilibrium[40] is one of the most important topics in contract frustration theory and practice. It is important to study the Prince Theory, Theory of Unforeseen Circumstances 'L'imprivision', and Theory of Unforeseen Physical Difficulties.

The Prince Theory ('Le Fait du Prince') in public works agreements

Whilst the administration in an administrative contract has the right to unilaterally modify the undertakings of the contracting party with direct decisions, such a right is met with a corresponding right: to ensure the contract's financial equilibrium.[41]

The jurisprudence and judiciary recognize the right of the administration to unilaterally modify the contracts, based on public interest constraints. To apply such a theory, several conditions must be fulfilled as follows:

Jurisprudence defines the Prince Theory's application as a special procedure whereby the contract's clauses can be directly modified, having an effect upon the contract performance and imposing upon the contracting party new unexpected burdens.

The French judiciary provided the example of police procedures that led to an increase of the contracting party's obligations, such as the decision issued by the administration – the police in this case – requesting the contracting party to

---

40 For elaboration on this concept, see, S. El Tamawy, *The General Principle of Administrative Contracts*, 5th edn, Ain Shams University Press 1991, 61.

41 Ibid., 631. In the French doctrin, see: De Laubadere, Moderne, and Delvolve, *Traité des contrats administratifs*, T-2, LGDJ, 515 et seq. S. Badawi, *Le fait du prince dans les contrats administratifs*, LGDJ, 1954. In the Arab doctrine, see: Dr. Abdel Azim Abdessalaam Abdel Hameed, *The Effect of the Prince Theory upon the Performance of Administrative Contracts*, 1989; Anas Ga'far, *Administrative Contracts*, Dar Al Nahda Al Arabia, 170.

188   *Substantive mechanisms of PPP contracts*

relocate the electric wires for public safety reasons,[42] as well as the decision issued by the administrative authority to the contracting party, upon which new burdens were imposed, by virtue of its power of supervision and direction. Another example was public works or physical works carried out by the administration causing injuries to the contracting party with regard to contract performance or increasing contractual obligations.

Jurisprudence also considers that the promulgation of laws or regulations would increase the contracting party's obligations towards the administration, as a general procedure, according to the Prince Theory in administrative contracts. The French Conseil D'Etat was of the opinion that the general procedure that was not directly addressed to the contracting party would not be compensated, except in two cases: first, where the contract explicitly stated such clause and second, where such procedure was unexpected; hence, the Prince Theory was not applied, but rather the theory of unforeseen circumstances.

Where the general procedure results in a direct modification of the contract terms, whether by stopping their implementation, or by modifying them or by prematurely terminating the contract, the contracting party must be compensated on the basis of the Prince Theory, regardless of the legitimacy of these laws.[43]

The general procedure must also modify the external conditions for the execution, which would be more difficult for the contracting party to carry out. According to the French Conseil D'Etat, the rule is that the contracting party may not be indemnified for the damage sustained in such circumstances, except for extremely particular cases; as such, it can be said that the rule is to rule out the compensation, and the exception is to rule for it.[44]

The Egyptian judiciary adopted the same approach. In its judgment issued on 16 June 1953, the Administrative Court ruled out the compensation of a company claiming for injuries sustained due to having been levied with a council tax for electricity although it was not a burden added to the company's obligations or destabilizing the contract's financial equilibrium. On 28 October 1964, the General Assembly of the Legal Opinion and Legislation ruled out the compensation of the Technical Company for Public Works for price differences for the supply of materials due to the 1956 war, a commission for Misr Company for Foreign Trade, an export bonus, a logistic duty and

---

42 S. Badawi, *Le fait du prince dans les contrats administratifs*, LGDJ, 1954, 104 et seq.

43 Judgment of the French Conseil d'État issued on 23 March 1994 in the case of *Ste Energie electrique de la Basse – Loire*. The Conseil d'État ruled out the compensation in certain cases for different reasons. See the thesis of Badawi, *Le fait du prince dans les contrats administratifs*, LGDJ, 1954, 167 et seq.

44 See the thesis of Badawi, ibid., 207 et seq. and the judgment of the French Conseil d'État issued in January 1945 in the case of *Ste anonyme motobloc*, where it ruled out the compensation on the basis of the Prince Theory in the area of taxes and duties that rendered the execution difficult. See also, The Administrative Court – 16/6/1953 – *Forty Years Collection of Court Judgments*, judicial year 7, 1578.

a maritime duty. The grounds for such ruling were that these sums of money were not in direct connection with the contracting administrative authority, where there must have been a special or general procedure issued by the administration to apply the Prince Theory, leading to a special injury incurred upon the contracting party, where he or she was the sole injured party by such general decision.[45]

The Conseil D'Etat in Egypt summarized the provisions for the application of the Prince Theory in administrative contracts as follows:[46]

1. That there is an administrative contract.
2. That the injury is committed by the contracting authority.
3. That the injury affects the contracting party regardless of how grave the injury is.
4. That it is assumed that the contracting authority was not wrongful when taking such a harmful decision since it has a contractual obligation without a breach.
5. That the procedure taken by the authority is not expected.
6. That the contracting party has sustained a personal injury where he or she is the sole injured party by such general decision.

The harmful act is committed by the contracting authority

The act must be committed by the contracting authority and not by any juristic entity other than the entity that concluded the contract; otherwise the condition of the Prince Theory is not fulfilled,[47] and we may apply the theory of unforeseen circumstances where appropriate.

The injury sustained by the contracting party is a personal unexpected injury

The General Assembly of the Legal Opinion and Legislation at the Egyptian Conseil D'Etat confirmed that it was necessary to have this condition, that the injury sustained by the contracting party was a personal injury where no third party was affected by the general decision. The claim of the contracting companies for price increases to the contracts concluded with the Ministry of Housing before applying Law No. 63 of 1964 of Social Security had no legal grounds. The said law obligated all companies and not only the contracting companies to increase their social security contributions for seasonal laborers; hence, the

---

45 Legal opinions issued by the General Assembly of the Counsel Department, judicial year 19, 51.
46 The Supreme Administrative Court – Judgment No. 56–12, 20/5/1961, 6/141/1133 – Damascus, *Forty Years Collection of Court Judgments*, 42.
47 The Supreme Administrative Court – Judgment No. 1562–10 and 67–11, 11/5/1968, 13/117/874 – *Forty Years Collection of Court Judgments*, 424.

190   *Substantive mechanisms of PPP contracts*

Prince Theory could not be applied as the promulgation of such law was an expected procedure. The lawmaker declared in Law No. 92 of 1959 that the plan was to extend the social insurance benefits to cover all laborers, which rebuts that such increases were not expected.[48]

The procedure is issued by the contracting administrative authority

The Supreme Administrative Court at the Egyptian Conseil D'Etat confirmed that the intervention of the Administrative Courts to realize the administrative contract's financial equilibrium, in application of the Prince Theory, would be possible when its conditions were fulfilled, including the condition that the harmful act was committed by the contracting administrative authority. In the case that such an act was taken by a juristic entity that did not conclude the contract, one of the Prince Theory's conditions was not then fulfilled and thus the theory could not be applied. However, this did not stop the application of the theory of unforeseen circumstances where appropriate.[49]

The General Assembly of the Legal Opinion and Legislation concluded that the contract between the Ministry of Irrigation and a number of contractors for the execution of certain works in the Ministry's departments and Inspection Offices during the financial year 1969/1970 did not grant those contractors any rights to address the Ministry with a claim for price differences, as a result of an increase of the price tariffs of steel and cement or due to receiving quantities of imported steel in lieu of local steel, whether such price increases took place subsequent to concluding the contract or during the contract performance. These procedures were taken by an authority other than the contracting authority (Ministry of Irrigation), which meant that a fundamental condition for the application of the Prince Theory was not fulfilled.[50]

The effect of fixing the tender prices upon the application of the prince theory

The administrative judiciary decided to fix the tender prices of the agreement concluded between the supplier and the administration as from the date of submitting the tender until the handover of the work, subject to the contract. These prices were not subject to any changes that might occur during the contract term, whether the reasons for such changes were related to foreign currency fluctuation, price increases or change in import, production or any other duties. The contracting party might not refer to the Prince Theory or the

---

48 Legal Opinion No. 297 on 11/3/1965, session 24/2/1965, 19/88/309 – *Forty Years Collection of Court Judgments*, 426.
49 CaseNo. 562 of Year 10Q – session 11/5/1968.
50 File No. 78/1/46 – session 11/7/1971, *Modern Administrative Encyclopedia*, 1st Edn, Vol. 18, 873.

Substantive mechanisms of PPP contracts 191

theory of unforeseen circumstances to rest the claim for damages for injuries sustained due to any of the aforementioned changes.[51]

The consequences of applying the prince theory

Upon the fulfillment of the theory's conditions and as a consequence of the act committed by the public authorities, the injured party was granted full compensation, in addition to possible exemption of delay fines, if it was established that such an act made it difficult for the party to execute the work on time; it might even exempt the contracting party from the execution of the contract if the Prince Theory resulted in the impossible execution.

The contracting party had the right to terminate the contract in case the Prince Theory resulted in an excessive increase of that person's obligations.[52]

Jurisprudence had divergent opinions in establishing a compensation for the contracting party in the case of fulfilling the Prince Theory's conditions.

The Egyptian Conseil D'Etat decided that the contract's financial equilibrium was the grounds for entitlement to compensation. The administration must restore such equilibrium every time it was destabilized, as a result of an act committed by the authority.[53]

Doctrine supports the notion of financial equilibrium as a general rule, which was to obligate the administration to ensure the contract's financial equilibrium every time it was destabilized, whether it was the result of an act committed by the contracting authority or caused by an external factor beyond its control.[54]

It has been suggested that the notion is as dangerous and inexact as it is generalized, giving rise to compensation to the contracting party even if the financial equilibrium is not caused by the administration.[55]

However, it is not a correct notion as the compensation ruled for the contracting party, due to a breach committed by the authority to the contract's economies, does not always correspond with the contract's financial equilibrium

---

51 The General Assembly of Legal Opinion and Legislation, File 78/1/29, session 28/10/ 1964, *Modern Administrative Encyclopedia*, 1st edn, Vol. 18, 882.

52 El Tamawy, *The General Principle of Administrative Contracts*, 5th Edn, 1991, 653. See the effect of the Prince Theory and the theory of unforeseen physical circumstances in restoring the administrative contract's financial equilibrium under unforeseen circumstances: Amin, *General Principles for the Performance of Administrative Contracts*, 302 et seq.; Jean-Quentin De Cayper, *Le fait du prince libere t'il une enterprise public, revue de droit des affaires internationals*, No. 8, 1993, 959.

53 The Supreme Administrative Court, case No. 1562 of year 10Q, 67 of year 11Q – session 11/5/1968.

54 See those who represent this approach, De Soto, a comment published in the *Laws Journal* in 1950, 455.
See also an explanation of this notion in the Egyptian judiciary, a judgment issued by the administrative court on 30 June 1957.

55 Mohamed A.M. Ismail, *International Public Works Agreements Arbitration*, Al Halabi, 2003; S. Badawi, *Le fait du prince dans les contrats administratifs*, LGDJ, 1954, 24.

192 *Substantive mechanisms of PPP contracts*

that was taken into consideration when the contract was concluded. MENA countries' doctrine provides two examples for such case: The contracting party may wrongly accept unfavorable prices when concluding the contract. If the authority intervenes in the contract performance afterwards, the court shall rule for full compensation, not based on the price accepted by the party at the time of concluding the contract but based on the real price at the time of the authority's intervention in the contract performance. This theory also applies in the case of price increases after concluding the contract, as the judge, when issuing a judgment, takes account of the new prices for compensation and not those specified at the time of concluding the contract.

The second example is the case of terminating the contract by the administration without any breach committed. The notion of financial equilibrium cannot warrant the compensation ruled by the Administrative Court, as the financial equilibrium cannot be hypothetically discussed for a non-existing contract.[56]

Another jurisprudential opinion was that the second rule for compensation was the authority's contractual responsibilities. Those who did not recognize the notion of the contract's financial equilibrium called for this rule. As such, the administration had a contractual responsibility without a breach as the Prince Theory assumed that the authority was not wrongful when committing such act; however, the responsibility had different grounds.

Contract's financial equilibrium complements the administration's contractual responsibility without a breach, but it is a responsibility to maintain the contract's financial equilibrium.

Professor *De Laubadere* was of the opinion that there was no difference between both notions, as according to the Prince Theory it was a contractual responsibility based upon the contract's financial equilibrium.[57]

This construes the condition currently imposed by the French Conseil D'Etat: that the Prince Theory is applied when the act is committed by the administration, and the compensation is denied where the act is performed by a public authority other than the contracting authority, which distinguishes between responsibility in the case of applying the Prince Theory to unforeseen circumstances and the unforeseen physical difficulties. This conciliatory approach is in line with sound legal logic as the contractual liability is due to the application of the Prince Theory that causes an injury to the contracting party and destabilizes the contract's financial equilibrium, although such injury is not grave. If during the contract performance, the authority commits an act that requires the application of the Prince Theory, it has a contractual liability based upon the need to restore the contract's financial equilibrium.

---

56 S. Badawi, *Le fait du prince dans les contrats administratifs*, LGDJ 1954, 25.
57 De Laubadere, Moderne, Delvolve, *Traité des contrats administratifs*, T-2, LGDJ.

Substantive mechanisms of PPP contracts 193

The prince theory ('Le Fait du Prince') in PPP contracts

The Prince Theory first requires the existence of an administrative contract. PPP contracts, although complex in its nature, still contain some of the characteristics of the administrative contract, including provisions and exceptional rules sometimes contravening the general rule.[58]

The General Assembly of the Legal Opinion and Legislation of the Egyptian Conseil D'Etat concluded that the agreement between the supplier and contracting authority to fix the prices included in the tender as from the date of submitting the tender and until the handover of the job, subject to the contract, implied that these prices were not subject to any changes that might occur during the contract term. This was concluded whether the reason for such changes were related to foreign currency fluctuation, price increases, change in import, production or any other duties.

The rationale behind this is that the contracting party may not hold the contracting authority responsible for any increase that may occur to these prices. This may not be claimed whether such increase was due to foreign currency fluctuation or to any other circumstances, or it was an increase in import, production or any other duties, unless otherwise explicitly specified, as is the case of the contracting authority's right to modify the work subject of the contract, with some auxiliary works, based upon the power granted to the authority in this regard.

In such a case, the contracting party undertakes to maintain the prices submitted. However, fixing the tender prices, as from the date of submitting the tender and until the handover of the work subject of the contract, implies a corresponding right to the contracting party. This right is that these prices are not subject to changes that may affect their stability, such as change in import, product or any other duties.

The facts in the present dispute are, however, contrary to the above case. The contracting company undertook not to claim for any price increases, whether it was due to foreign currency fluctuation, price increases or changes in import, production or any other duties, unless otherwise set forth in the contract, as was the case with the rights of the contracting authority to modify the work subject of the contract. The contract specified that the contracting authority was exempt from responsibility to restore the contract's financial equilibrium.

Theory of unforeseen circumstances 'L'imprivision'

The theory of unforeseen circumstances was established within the provisions of the MENA countries civil codes, considering that the change in circumstances – during the contract performance – is the most important cause for the contract's financial equilibrium, which requires restoring the contract's economies.

---

58 See Chapter 3 of this book.

194 *Substantive mechanisms of PPP contracts*

Since this theory is founded within the provisions of the civil codes, it is appropriate to refer to the general literature related to the Egyptian civil code construing this theory.[59]

The basis of this theory was founded in the administrative contracts in the French Conseil D'Etat where it was set forth to address the accidental economic circumstances during World War I and recognized the right of the contracting party to compensation in the case of those unforeseen circumstances. The purpose of this compensation was to sustain the functioning of the public utilities that provided citizens with services.[60]

The French Conseil D'Etat stipulated that in order to fulfill the condition of compensation entitlement, an unforeseen circumstance must be unexpected;[61] however, it ruled out the claim for compensation if the price increases were expected, which did not destabilize so much the contract's economics.[62]

The theory of unforeseen circumstances in MENA countries' jurisprudence

The Egyptian Conseil D'Etat established the foundations for the application of the theory of unforeseen circumstances in general, following the model of the French administrative judiciary, which was the founder of this theory.

The Supreme Administrative Court at the Egyptian Conseil D'Etat confirmed that the application of the theory of unforeseen circumstances in jurisprudence and administrative judiciary was subject to the occurrence of incidents or circumstances, which are natural or economic, during the contract performance or an act committed by a third party other than the contracting authority. The court stipulated that the contracting party could neither expect nor prevent these circumstances when concluding the contract and that they caused that individual serious injuries giving rise to grave destabilization of the contract's economics. The rationale behind the application of such theory, after fulfilling its conditions, was to obligate the authority to bear jointly the loss occurred during such unforeseen circumstances, so as to ensure the contract performance and the public utility's sustainability. The role of the administrative judge was

---

59 See the Arab jurisprudence: Ga'far, *Administrative Contracts*, Dar Al Nahda Al Arabia, 163; Abdessalaam Abdel Hameed, Abdel Azim, *The Unforeseen Circumstances and Physical Difficulties upon the Performance of Administrative Contracts*, 1990; Abdel Wadood Yehia, *Summary in the General Theory of Obligations, Sources of Obligations, Part I*, 1989. In the French jurisprudence, see: De Laubadere, Moderne, De Laubadere, Moderne et Delvolve, *Traite de Contrats Administratifs*, T-2, Paris, LGDJ, T.2, 559; Jacques Clement and Daniel Richer, *Les Marchés Publics de Travaux des Collectivités Territoriales*, Economica, 208 et seq.; Richer, Laurent Richer, *Droits de Contrats Administratifs*, LGDG, 2008, 210.
60 Jacques Clement and Daniel Richer, *Les Marchés Publics de Travaux des Collectivités Territoriales*, 208.
61 C.E., 30 May 1916, *Compagnie generale d'eclairage de Bordeaux*, Leb., 125.
62 C.E., 7 July 1976, *Societe demongeot, inedit*; C.E., 17 June 1981, *Commune de Papeete; see:* Jacques Clement and Daniel Richer, *Les Marchés Publics de Travaux des Collectivités Territoriales*, 208.

limited to rule for a suitable compensation without modifying the contractual obligations.[63]

The Supreme Court confirmed in another judgment that in order to apply the theory of unforeseen circumstances, the contract's economies must be gravely destabilized as this theory was based upon the concept of absolute justice – a mainstay of the administrative law. In addition, the purpose of this theory is to realize the public interest by ensuring the systematic and consistent functioning of the public utility and prompt services delivered to the public. The contracting party's intent was to help realize the public interest by fulfilling the obligation in an honest and adequate manner in consideration of a profit and fair return. This required understanding and collaboration to overcome the difficulties and impediments to perform the contract.

The court explained in this judgment the theory's purpose and essence and confirmed that the occurrence of unforeseen circumstances did not render the execution impossible, but cumbersome to carry out, destabilizing the contract's economies and causing losses to the contracting party exceeding the normal losses that any contracting party might have sustained.

In this regard, the court held that the purport of the theory of unforeseen circumstances is that, where circumstances or events take place during the administrative contract performance and are not expected when concluding the contract, by which the contract's economies are destabilized, and where such circumstances or events do not render the contract performance impossible but rather more cumbersome and more costly than reasonably estimated by both parties, and where the loss resulting therefrom is grave, exceptional and unexpected, exceeding the normal loss that any contracting party may sustain, the injured party has the right to request the other party to bear jointly the loss by partly compensating therein. As such, a new obligation is added to the contracting party's obligations that were not included in the contract, which means imposing an obligation upon the debtor in the administrative contract to pay the creditor a compensation to ensure the proper execution of the contract, so long as these unforeseen circumstances or events cause a loss to the debtor, which can be deemed as destabilizing the contract's economies.

It is evident that the Supreme Administrative Court imposed an obligation upon the administration to pay compensation to ensure the proper execution of the contract so long as these unforeseen circumstances or events caused a loss to the debtor, which could be deemed as destabilizing the contract's economies. Nevertheless, the court asserted that the compensation paid by the creditor must be a part of the compensation for the loss sustained by the debtor who was not entitled to claim for compensation based on loss of profits or unrealized gains.

---

63 The Supreme Administrative Court, Judgment No. 1562–10, 67–11, 11/5/1968, 13/117/ 874 – *Forty Years Collection of Court Judgments*, 440. This theory was established by virtue of a judgment issued by the French State Council on 30 March 1916 – C.E., 20 Mars 1916, *Compagnie generale d'eclairage de Bordeaux*, Leb, 125.

196 *Substantive mechanisms of PPP contracts*

The court added that to estimate the destabilization of the contract's economies, considering its occurrence, all losses affecting the contract's economies must be taken into account. The contract must be considered, not as individual elements as some elements could be compensated, thereby offsetting other elements that caused a loss. As such, the contract's economies' destabilization could not be noticed or ascertained unless all the work related to the contract was completed.[64]

The Supreme Court held that the application of the theory of unforeseen circumstances in administrative contracts, and other matters related to the public law, was subject to the occurrence of such unforeseen circumstances during the contract performance and not after the contract completion.[65]

The Supreme Court distinguished between the accidental event and force majeure, describing that the unexpected price increases during the execution of administrative contracts, which gave rise to an increase of the contracting party's burdens by the grave losses that individual would sustain to the extent of gravely destabilizing the contract's economies, was an accidental circumstance and not a force majeure.[66]

Two important points are worth mentioning to consider them unforeseen circumstances in PPP contracts, namely: the effect of successive legislation and foreign currency change upon the contract performance and the effect of the legislative stability clauses on resolving this problem.

The impact of successive legislation and the exchange rate of the foreign currency upon the contract performance

The General Assembly of the Legal Opinion and Legislation in the Egyptian Conseil D'Etat issued an opinion that the application of a new legislation, such as the Law of General Tax on Sale promulgated under Law No. 11 of 1991, affected the sales prices set forth in contracts concluded before the enforcement of the said law, as the contracting companies agreed in the contracts with the pharmaceutical company that the value of the contracting work was total and final. As such, pursuant to the civil code provisions, the company might not claim for price increases resulting from the application of the Law of General Tax on the basis that it would have rendered the contract performance difficult. It was not apparent from the documents that the application of the said law would affect only the contracting company by sustaining grave loss destabilizing

---

64 The Supreme Administrative Court, Judgment No. 46–14, 17/6/1972, 17/83/576 – *Forty Years Collection of Court Judgments*, 442; The Supreme Administrative Court, Judgment Nos. 1223 and 1224–27, 18/12/1984, 30/45/250 – *Forty Years Collection of Court Judgments*, 446.

65 The Supreme Administrative Court, Judgment Nos. 843 and 922–26, 20/11/1982, 28/18/86 – *Forty Years Collection of Court Judgments*, 458-9.

66 Administrative Court, Judgment No. 2150–6, 9/6/1962, 7/96/1024 – *Forty Years Collection of Court Judgments*, 458.

Substantive mechanisms of PPP contracts 197

the contract's economies; thus, one of the conditions of the theory of unforeseen circumstances was not fulfilled, and the General Assembly ruled against compensation on this basis.[67] In such a case, the General Assembly restricted the application of the theory and did not consider the successive tax legislation as causing financial burdens on the party or grounds for compensation on the basis of the theory of unforeseen circumstances since it did not give rise to grave losses.

In another opinion, the General Assembly concluded that the Prime Minister's decree to devalue the Egyptian pound against the U.S. dollar was a general exceptional event, pursuant to Article 147/2 of the civil code, where both parties could not expect it when concluding the contract. For the sake of argument, if the party should have expected that the government might seek to devalue the Egyptian currency, the contracting party could not predict how far this devaluation would be; thus, the results and effect of this procedure upon the contract's financial equilibrium must exceed what the party would have expected when concluding the contract. In both cases, if the loss sustained by the party with the obligation to perform the contract rendered the fulfillment of the obligation cumbersome and gave rise to serious loss, the other party should jointly bear such loss, to make it reasonably bearable for that party. This means that the expected loss should be borne by the party with the obligation to perform the contract, whereas the unexpected loss should be jointly borne by both parties, to mitigate its gravity.[68]

In another opinion, the General Assembly concluded that the tender's general conditions, according to Article 20, stipulated that the tenders must be submitted for the supply of goods based upon the tax rate, production duties and any other duties applicable at the time. In case the abovementioned rates and duties changed in the period between submitting the tender and the deadline for the supply of goods, and the supply took place within the specified period, the difference should be settled accordingly, on condition that the contractor had proofs of paying the duties on the supplied goods based upon the modified increased rates. If the modification required reducing the rates, the difference should be deducted from the contract's value unless the contractor had proofs that he or she paid the duties based on the original rates before the modification. Article 62 of the general conditions stated that 'the final statement shall apply the rates included in the price tables, regardless of any price changes or currencies fluctuation.' It also stated that 'the contractor shall bear all price increases

---

67 The General Assembly's legal opinion No. 328 on 24/4/1993, session, 28/3/1993, 47, Opinion No. 127 on 31/1/1993 – Session 31/1/1993, 47 – *Forty Years Collection of Court Judgments*, 461–462.

68 Legal Opinion No. 360 of 17/7/1954, *Modern Administrative Encyclopedia*, 1st edn, Vol. 18, 1986/1987, 796, Rule No. 568.

198 *Substantive mechanisms of PPP contracts*

for the materials, freight, shipping, all types of insurance, and labor costs during the work's period, and may not request any increase or change the prices he accepted.'

By specifying these provisions, the court judgment varies according to the accidental reason affecting the tender's value. If the reason is attributed to market volatility and currency fluctuation, the contractor must bear the consequences, whether it is an increase or decrease in prices; if the reason is attributed to modification in taxes and duties, the ministry must bear the consequences as provided in Article 20, whether the reason affecting the tender's value has taken place before or after the contract conclusion.[69]

This shows that the Egyptian Conseil D'Etat was hesitant to consider the market volatility and currency fluctuation as unforeseen circumstances, as the General Assembly had – in its opinion – considered it to be unforeseen circumstances on one occasion, and the Supreme Administrative Court denied such consideration on another.

The same applies to the tax and customs legislation. In a judgment issued by the Supreme Administrative Court in the 1960s,[70] the court considered the modification of taxes and customs duties as unforeseen circumstances, which would not be valid without legislation. In the 1990s,[71] the General Assembly refused to consider the Law of General Tax on Sale as unforeseen circumstances unless – as expressed by the court – it rendered the contract performance difficult. The above-mentioned principles were well established, decades ago, in the MENA countries' jurisprudence.

The theory of unforeseen physical difficulties in PPP contracts

Where there is a physical impediment to the performance of the contract, such as a rocky layer during the excavation process, rendering the fulfillment of the contractual obligations difficult and extremely cumbersome for the contracting party, this is considered a physical difficulty that was not taken into account when concluding the contract and setting up the prices.

In such a case, will the contracting party refuse to execute the obligations with the consequential damage that may occur to the public utility, subject of the administrative contract which was concluded for the developing, regulating or operating of such public utility?

---

69 The Supreme Administrative Court – case No. 1186 of year 10Q – session of 25/11/1967, *Modern Administrative Encyclopedia*, Vol. 18, 797–898, Rule No. 570.
70 Ibid.
71 The General Assembly's legal opinion No. 328 on 24/4/1993, session (28/3/1993)47, Opinion No. 127 on 31/1/1993 – Session (31/1/1993)47 – *Forty Years Collection of Court Judgments*, 461–462.

The establishment of the theory in the French and Egyptian Conseil D'Etats

This theory was established under the provisions of the French Conseil D'Etat, and the first judgment thereby issued was *Duche* on 24 June 1864. The Conseil D'Etat ruled in its judgment for compensation to the contracting party for any unforeseen physical difficulties that individual had encountered during the contract execution.[72]

The Conseil D'Etat granted the contractor the right to compensation for the unforeseen physical difficulties encountered during the contract execution, where they were not attributed to the contractor or to the administration.[73]

The theory was applied by the Egyptian Conseil D'Etat and consequently Arab doctrine, in the first judgment issued by the Administrative Court on 5 May 1953. However, the jurisprudence was of the opinion that the judgment had confused the theory of physical difficulties with that of unforeseen circumstances, as the former required full compensation whilst the latter required partial compensation to the extent that it would restore the contract's equilibrium and reinstitute its economies.

The administrative judiciary in Arab countries developed the theory of unforeseen physical difficulties based upon the judgments issued by the Supreme Administrative Court and the established opinion issued by the General Assembly of the Legal Opinion and Legislation in the Egyptian Conseil D'Etat Egypt. In its old opinion issued in 1964, the General Assembly defined the theory of unforeseen physical difficulties, whereby the company could claim more payments than what was agreed upon, as follows:

> If the contracting party encounters, during the performance of his obligations, purely unexceptional physical difficulties that cannot absolutely be foreseen at the time of concluding the contract, and that make the contract performance a cumbersome mission, he has the right to full compensation for the injuries caused by such difficulties.

---

72 Ga'far, Anas, *Administrative Contracts*, Dar Al Nahda Al Arabia, 2000, 183; Ga'far, *The Theory of Unforeseen Physical Difficulties in Civil Works Contracting, a Study of the Key Economic and Legal Aspects*, Shalakany Law Firm Publications, 1995, 186. See also the Arab doctrine regarding the same notion: Abdessalaam Abdel Hameed Abdel Azim, *The Unforeseen Circumstances and Physical Difficulties upon the Performance of Administrative Contracts*, 1990; Anwar Raslaan, The theory of unforeseen physical difficulties, a study published in the *Journal of Law and Economy*, 1984, Issues Nos. 3, 4 of 1980, 825 et seq. See also the French doctrine: Laurent Richer, *Droits de Contrats Administratifs*, LGDG, 2008, 208; David Chabanal and Pierre Jouguelet, *Marches Publics de Travaux*, 2nd edn, Le Monteur 1994, 159 et seq.; De Laubadere, Moderne et Delvolve, *Traite de Contrats Administratifs*, T-2, Paris, LGDJ T.2, 499 et seq.

73 Ga'far, *The Theory of Unforeseen Physical Difficulties in Civil Works Contracting, a Study of the Key Economic and Legal Aspects*, Cairo: Shalakany Law Firm Publications 1995, 187.

200 *Substantive mechanisms of PPP contracts*

The compensation must fully cover all injuries by paying an extra amount added to the agreed upon prices.

The General Assembly specified the conditions for compensation according to this theory, which are summarized as follows:

1. These difficulties are physical, extraordinary, and exceptional.
2. These difficulties are physical and unforeseen, or it was not possible to foresee them at the time of concluding the contract.
3. The execution requires costs exceeding the prices agreed upon in the contract, and increases the burdens borne by the contracting party.[74]

Within these boundaries and controls, the contractor has the right to claim compensation; however, if one of the above conditions is not fulfilled, the theory cannot be applied, and the contractor has no right to any compensation.[75,76]

These are the main principles for the theory of unforeseen physical difficulties as established by the Egyptian Conseil D'Etat, which is based upon the consideration of justice and the special nature of administrative contracts.[77]

The financial equilibrium of PPP contracts and the current PPP legislation in the MENA countries

MENA countries' legislation has adopted new ideologies in state contracts that were not known in traditional concessions and administrative contracts. Those ideologies represent an increasing approach towards the liberalization of the administrative contracts traditional theory and resent an attempt to maintain the financial equilibrium of the PPP contract through new mechanisms which allow the contracting authority to re-adjust contract price through direct negotiations and to avoid litigation or arbitration as a dispute settlement mechanism try to achieve financial equilibrium. Direct negotiations with the contracting authority are more rapid and flexible processes than litigation and arbitration. The negotiations process is less expensive. It is worth noting that a comparison between civil codes approach in the MENA countries and administrative judiciary approach on the one hand and the PPP legislation approach on the other hand shows the significant progress in the legislature approach in dealing with the unforeseen circumstances and the financial equilibrium. The contracting

---

74 Judgment No. 800 of 34, 19/5/1992, *Forty Years Collection of Court Judgments*, 464–76 – Rule No. 267.
75 Legal Opinion No. 95 of 4/2/1964, session 29/1/1964, 18-69-186 – *Forty Years Collection of Court Judgments*, 463–4.
76 The General Assembly's legal opinion No. 95 on 4/2/1964, session 2/1/1964, 18-69-186 – *Forty Years Collection of Court Judgments,* 466–8, rule No. 268.
77 Ga'far, *The Theory of Unforeseen Physical Difficulties in Civil Works Contracting, a Study of the Key Economic and Legal Aspects*, Shalakany Law Firm Publications, 1995, 209.

Substantive mechanisms of PPP contracts 201

authority maintains financial equilibrium without recourse to any disputes' settlement mechanism.

The Egyptian PPP law points out that in the case of the occurrence of unforeseen circumstances after execution of the PPP contract, including amendments to laws or regulations that were enforceable at the time of execution of the PPP contract, it may be agreed to amend the PPP contract in accordance with the conditions and rules stipulated in the PPP contract.[78]

PPP law in Dubai stipulates that a PPP contract may be amended according to the basis and rules of the unforeseen circumstances. Administrative Decrees issued to implement this law shall clarify the rules to apply the unforeseen circumstances theory, how to compensate the private partner and how to amend the PPP contract.[79]

Kuwaiti PPP law points out that the amendment of the partnership agreement may be agreed upon in accordance with the principle and the rules provided for under the agreement, if unforeseen circumstances occurred after the conclusion of the partnership agreement, including amendments to the laws in force at the time of conclusion of this agreement and leading to a financial imbalance of the agreement.[80]

Morocco PPP law provides that the contracting parties have the right to maintain the financial equilibrium of the contract in case of force majeure or unforeseen circumstances.[81]

The Tunisian PPP law stipulates that the partnership contract is concluded between the public person and the project company for a duration, taking into account in particular the depreciation period of the investments to be made and the financing methods selected. The contract partnership is not renewable. Exceptionally, the contract may be extended for a maximum of three years in cases of an emergency to ensure the continuity of the public service, in the case of force majeure or during the occurrence unpredictable events, after the notice conformity of the General Public Partnership Authority referred to in Article 38 of this Law.[82]

---

78 The Egyptian PPP law, Article 8.
79 Dubai PPP law, Article 31.
80 Kuwaiti PPP law, Article 36.
81 Morocco PPP law, Article 17. '*Droit au maintien de l'équilibre du contrat en cas d'évènements imprévus ou de force majeure.*'
82 Tunisian PPP law, Article 17 reads as follows '*Art. 17 – Le contrat de partenariat est conclu entre la personne publique et la société du projet pour une durée déterminée en tenant compte notamment de la durée d'amortissement des investissements à réaliser et des modalités de financement retenues. Le contrat de partenariat n'est pas renouvelable. Exceptionnellement, le contrat peut être prorogé pour une durée maximale de trois ans dans les cas d'urgence pour assurer la continuité du service public, dans le cas de force majeure ou lors de la survenance d'évènements imprévisibles, et ce, après l'avis conforme de l'instance générale de partenariat public privé mentionnée à l'article 38 de la présente loi.*' Journal Officiel de la République Tunisienne – 1 er décembre 2015, No. 96, p. 2857.*

202 *Substantive mechanisms of PPP contracts*

The legislative policy behind the above-mentioned provisions contained in PPP legislation in the MENA countries is to achieve the following:

- Maintain the financial equilibrium of the PPP contract regarding the fact that the implementation of the contractual undertakings is usually for a long duration.
- In such a long duration, many unpredictabilities many occur, in particular the local currency depreciation, raw material price change, in addition to many other economic and financial factors.
- The main outcome of this new legislative approach, which is different from the traditional approach of the unforeseen circumstances theory in the MENA countries civil codes, is how the administration can achieve the contractual equilibrium without recourse to litigation or arbitration. The contractual equilibrium may be achieved through direct negotiations between the contracting parties.
- The target of the direct negotiations between the contracting parties is to re-adjust the contract price to maintain the continuity of public utilities and to achieve the best practice of the principle of running the public utility with regularity and continuity.
- The encouragement of the flow of FDI into MENA countries is of a great significance in the views of PPP legislation as it is one of the main targets to adopt PPP techniques in legislation and to use them in practice many years even before the promulgation of the PPP legislation in MENA countries.
- It is important to note that a financial equilibrium must be maintained for both contracting parties: the contracting authority and the private partner. If the financial equilibrium is maintained for the private partner and not for contracting authority, this may be described as a positive discrimination in favor of the private partner. In a PPP contract that is a long-term agreement, the financial equilibrium has to be maintained in favor of both the private partner and the contracting authority in order not to violate the financial and economic expectations of the private entity and it has to be maintained for the contracting authority to achieve public interests.
- To maintain an easy, flexible and rapid process for the modifications to the PPP contracts, which aim at achieving financial equilibrium and the expectations of both contracting parties.[83]

---

83 In contract modifications in the UK see: Katie Smith, A risk worth taking? Practical application of the law on contract modifications in the context of PPP accommodation projects, *Public Procurement Law Review*, 2019, 1, 16–25; and S. Arrowsmith, *The Law of Public and Utilities Procurement*, 3rd Edn, Vol. 1, Sweet & Maxwell, 2014, pp. 597–604. In the EU context see: S. Arrowsmith, *The Law of Public and Utilities Procurement*, 3rd edn, Vol.1, Sweet & Maxwell, 2014, pp. 597–604; K. Hartley and M.W. Liljenbol, 'Changes to Existing Contracts under the EU Public Procurement Rules and the Drafting of Review Clauses to Avoid the Need for a New Tender' (2013) 22 *P.P.L.R.* 51–73 on review clauses; S.T. Poulsen, 'The possibilities of amending a public contract without a new competitive tendering procedure under EU law' (2012) 21 *P.P.L.R.* 167–187.

8 Arbitration as dispute resolution mechanism in PPPs in MENA countries

Introduction

PPP contracts' disputes assume that a dispute may arise between the project company on the one hand and the contracting state on the other. Therefore, private-public arbitration has special significance in this context. This chapter provides an in-depth and clear analysis of the subject matter. Using a chronological order, it answers the questions of: how does the Egyptian legal system look at private-public arbitration? How is public interest protected in private-public arbitration, particularly in PPP transactions.[1]

This chapter is an attempt to provide an analysis to private-public arbitration in the Egyptian legal system, before and after 1994. Before the promulgation of the Arbitration Act in Egypt in 1994, there was considerable debate concerning private-public arbitration following the legislative prohibition, as a general principle, in Article 2060 of the French civil code. However, the latter prohibition in the French civil code is not absolute. In 1997 there was a legislative amendment to Article/1 of the Egyptian Arbitration Act, which is significant to the theme of this monograph. This chapter, further, analyses the situation in Kuwaiti law and in the Saudi arbitration law of 2012, Qatar arbitration law of 2017 and the new UAE Arbitration Act 2018.

There are special difficulties relating to private-public arbitration such as: are there any restrictions imposed by legislation before recourse to arbitration in private-public arbitration, in particular in PPPs and BOT/BOOT agreements. In addition, can arbitrators in private-public arbitration act as an *amiable compositeur*? Or does the legal nature of PPP contracts in Arab countries assumes that the national law is the only applicable law to state contracts whether traditional concessions or otherwise?

This chapter is an attempt to answer many questions that remain unanswered in MENA academia and practice.

---

1 In the English Arbitration Act 1996 see: Stavros Brekoulakis and Margaret Devaney, Public-private arbitration and the public interest under English law, *Modern Law Review*, 2017, 80(1), 22–56.

204 *Arbitration – dispute resolution mechanism*

The substantive nature of administrative contracts, among other factors, was the main reason behind rejecting private-public arbitration in Egypt, before the promulgation of the Egyptian Arbitration Act in 1994 and again before its amendment in 1997. The Egyptian Arbitration Act No. 27/1994 was the first legislation in the MENA region to appear adopting the (United Nations Commission on the International Trade Law) UNCITRAL Model Law.[2] It is important to refer to the fact that Egypt has for a long time ratified the New York and ICSID conventions. In addition, the influence of the cultural and legal globalization phenomena on the Egyptian legal system was one of the main reasons behind the rise of private-public arbitration.[3]

2 Mahmoud Samir ElSharkawy, *International Commercial Arbitration*, Dar El Nahdah El Arabia 2011, in Arabic; Fathi Wali, *Arbitration Law in Theory and Practice*, Monsha'at Al Marref, Alexandria 2007, in Arabic. Following the Egyptian legislature, some Arab countries have codified new arbitration acts adopting directly the UNCITRAL Model Law such as: Oman (1997), Jordan (2001), Saudi Arabia (2012), Bahrain (2015), and Qatar (2017), UAE (2018). Arbitration legislation was firstly promulgated in Egypt in 1994 and it was directly influenced by the UNCITRAL Model Law. In 1997, Oman has followed the Egyptian Arbitration Act. Jordan, Saudi Arabia and Qatar were directly influenced by the Egyptian methodology and drafting in arbitration legislation. The Kingdom of Bahrain has published the UNCITRAL Model Law as amended in 2006 to its Official Gazette in addition to nine promulgation articles. The Egyptian Arbitration Act 1994 as amended in 1997, Article 1, stipulates the consent of the concerned minister to start private-public arbitration proceedings in administrative contracts as it concerns huge amount of public funds. The Saudi Arbitration Act 2012, Article 10/2, stipulates that any public juristic person cannot start private public arbitration without the Cabinet's consent unless there is a legislative provision permits arbitration. This applies to private public arbitration in administrative contracts' disputes or otherwise. The Qatar Arbitration Act 2017 stipulates in Article 2/2 that private public arbitration in administrative contracts is only permitted with the consent of the Prime Minister or the authority delegated by him. For more details see: Mohamed A.M. Ismail, *International Public Works Agreements' Arbitration in Gulf Countries*, a book published by The Arbitration Centre for the Gulf States 2018, in Arabic.

3 Cultural globalization is a cultural socioeconomic phenomenon. Culture is influenced to a great extent by globalization and it represents a set of practices, values, beliefs, and customs acquired by individuals as members of a distinctive society and resulting from interaction among people. With respect to the economic dimension of globalization, Stiglitz has highlighted the problems caused by globalization in some parts of the world, as it generates unbalanced outcomes, both between and within countries. See: Joseph Stiglitz, *Globalization and its Discontents*, W.W. Norton 2004; Joseph Stiglitz, *Making Globalization Work*, W.W. Norton 2007; Brian Snowdon, *Globalisation, Development and Transition*, Edward Elgar 2007. Nowadays, globalization plays a significant role in enhancing comprehension between legal cultures. The rise of private-public arbitration in Egypt and Arab countries, which were directly influenced by the UNCITRAL Model Law, is a direct result of the cultural and legal globalisation. Further, the influence of the Anglo-American legal culture is remarkable upon Arab Civil Law Legal Culture, particularly in legislation, case law, and the rise of new contractual patterns in state contracts such as Private Public Partnerships (PPP) and Built Own Operate (BOT) agreements. See: Mohamed A.M. Ismail, *Globalization and New International Public Works Agreements in Developing Countries, An Analytical Perspective*, Routlegde 2011, 1–8 with a foreword by H.H. Humphrey Lloyd QC.

Arbitration – dispute resolution mechanism 205

This chapter analyses the decisions of the Egyptian Conseil d'État regarding private-public arbitration before and after 1994 as the Conseil d'État in Egypt aims at creating a sensible balance between applying public law principles and protecting private liberties.

This chapter also deals with private-public arbitration in Egypt and provides an analysis of how public interests and public funds are safeguarded in private-public arbitration in the light of the controversial views that were elaborated regarding arbitration by state actors. This chapter raises fundamental questions such as: to what extent are public interests safeguarded in private-public arbitration in the light of the Egyptian constitutions and Egyptian legislation? Are the public interests compromised if the public actors recourse to private-public arbitration? What are the legislative tools in Egypt that regulate private-public arbitration and consider it as a safeguard to public interests? The answer to these questions is the theme of this chapter, which is divided into four sections. As the Egyptian case study is of fundamental importance to this chapter, the second section scrutinizes private-public arbitration and administrative contract constraints in Egypt from constitutional and legislative perspectives in addition to the analysis of the Egyptian Conseil d'État decisions; the third provides for the main features of PPP arbitration, and the fourth highlights special difficulties relating to private-public arbitration in Egypt and how public interests are safeguarded in the light of those difficulties.

Private-public arbitration in Egypt

In the Egyptian legal system, private-public arbitration has a broad meaning, as it contains all disputes that are arbitrable between states (public juristic persons) and private persons, whether contract-based arbitration or otherwise, and whether commercial arbitration or investment treaty arbitration. This section mainly focuses on the contract-based private-public arbitration in the MENA countries' legal systems. PPP arbitration is a very important type of private-public arbitration.

Pursuant to the dynamic constitutional ideology in economic matters,[4] which was adopted by Egyptian constitutions 1971, 2012 and 2014, there was no explicit constitutional prohibition to private-public arbitration. The question of private-public arbitration and whether it is permissible in the Egyptian legal system or not was initially raised when the state is in a dispute includes an administrative contract. The question also raises the competent judicial authority, given the fact that pursuant to the Conseil d'État law, administrative

---

4 The Egyptian constitutions in 1971 as amended in 2007, the 2012 constitution, and the 2014 constitution, have not adopted certain economic ideology such as the Marxist ideology that the Egyptian constitution of 1971 previously adopted upon its promulgation in 1971. Even during the period between 1971 and 2007 during the adoption of the Marxist ideology, there was no constitutional prohibition to private public arbitration in Egypt.

206 *Arbitration – dispute resolution mechanism*

contract disputes fall within the jurisdiction of the Conseil d'État courts,[5] not ordinary civil or commercial courts.

Historically, there were various angles of the rejection of private-public arbitration in Egypt. The most significant from the Conseil d'État departments' perspectives were: first, the public interests' constraints, which stipulate that administrative contracts' disputes are of significant importance in Egypt because they are considerably concerned with public juristic persons, mainly, state public utilities on the one hand, and public funds on the other. Second, the angle of the exclusive jurisdiction of the Egyptian Conseil d'État with administrative disputes and particularly administrative contracts' disputes. In the Egyptian legal system, administrative contracts' disputes fall within the jurisdiction of the Conseil d'État courts, therefore, they do not fall within the jurisdiction of the ordinary courts of the Egyptian judiciary whether civil or commercial.[6,7] The jurisdictional angle of the Egyptian Conseil d'État had various arguments to support the rejection of private-public arbitration such as the interpretations to Article 172 of the Egyptian constitution of 1971, and the Conseil d'État Law No. 47 of the 1972 law concerning the exclusive jurisdiction of the Egyptian

---

5 See: Case 5837 of 44, judgment dated 20 February 1990, Supreme Administrative Court. The General Assembly for Legal Opinion and Legislation confirmed that arbitration in administrative contracts is permissible in 1989 and 1993. In the session on 18 December 1996, the General Assembly denied permissibility of arbitration in administrative contracts whilst interpreting Article 1 of the Egyptian Arbitration Act 1994, and before the 1997 amendment.

6 For the aims of administrative contracts in France *(Le Contrat Administratif)* and in Egypt see: André de Laubadere, Frank Modern and Pierre Delvolvé, *Traité des contrats administratifs*, LGDJ 1983, vol. I, 210 et seq; see also ibid., vol. II; Laurent Richer, *Droits des Contrats Administratifs*, LGDJ 1995, 85 et seq; and for the same author see 6th edn, L.G.D.J, 2008, 90; In Arab doctrine, see Soliman El Tamawy, *General Principles of Administrative Contracts*, 5th edn, Dar El Fikr El Araby 1991, in Arabic.

7 In 1989, debate started regarding the permissibility of private public arbitration, and there was a legal opinion by the General Assembly for Legal Opinion and Legislation at the Egyptian Conseil d'État, permitting private public arbitration in administrative contracts. Article 1 of the Egyptian Arbitration Act 27/1994 (before amendment) provides that:

> ... the provisions of the present law shall apply to every arbitration between parties of the public law or private law notwithstanding the nature of the legal relations subject of dispute in cases where such arbitration is taking place in Egypt or if it is an international commercial arbitration taking place abroad, where the parties thereof agree on the present law as the governing law.

The legislative amendment 9/1997 to the provision of Article 1 states that a second clause should be added to Article 1 of the Arbitration Act 27/1994, which reads as follows:

> 'In all events it is permissible to agree on arbitration in disputes arising from administrative contracts upon the approval of the competent minister or his pro tempore involving public legal persons and no delegation is permissible in this regard'. The concerned minister's consent must be obtained before starting private-public arbitration only in administrative contracts' disputes.

Conseil d'État courts to settle administrative disputes. The Egyptian legal system was influenced by Article 2060 of the French civil code.[8] Notwithstanding the controversial angels that dealt with private public arbitration from the late eighties and until 1997, private public arbitration in Egypt, as a concept, can be in administrative contracts' disputes, or any other arbitrable dispute, whether contractual or otherwise, where any public juristic person is a party to the dispute.[9]

Before the promulgation of the Arbitration Act 1994; private-public arbitration in Egypt had critical situation relating to various and controversial approaches adopted by the Conseil d'État departments. Nevertheless, after the promulgation of the Arbitration Act 1994, the interpretation of Article 1, which permitted private-public arbitration, was controversial; therefore, there was an essential need to the legislative amendment to this Arbitration Act in 1997. The following parts of this section shall explain in chronological order the various approaches in the Egyptian legal system before and after the promulgation of the Arbitration Act 1994 towards private-public arbitration.

Private-public arbitration in the Egyptian legal system, before 1994

Before promulgating the Arbitration Act No. 27 of 1994, private-public arbitration was very controversial[10] and there were various judicial approaches to

---

8 In France, the prohibition of public entities to enter into arbitration agreements is set out under the first paragraph of Article 2060 of the French civil code as follows:

> One may not enter into arbitration agreements in matters of status and capacity of the persons, in those relating to divorce and judicial separation or on controversies concerning public bodies and institutions and more generally in all matters in which public policy is concerned.

This prohibition is considered to be a general principle of French public law. However, it is not absolute. Therefore, the prohibition can be modified through an express legislative provision or a valid treaty. Consequently, there are several exceptions to this principle by legislative or treaty means (i.e. disputes arising from PPPs can also be submitted to arbitration pursuant to PPPs law of 2008). The Egyptian legislature adopted the same vision and permitted private-public arbitration by Article 1 of the Egyptian Arbitration Act 1994 as amended in 1997.

9 It has been decided in the Egyptian legal system that the administration can enter into both administrative contracts and civil contracts; see Ismail, *Globalization and New International Public Works Agreements*, Routledge, 2011; and in Arab doctrine, Sarwat Badawi, *Administrative Contracts*, Dar Al Nahda Al Arabia, 1994, in Arabic. Private-public arbitration can be in any arbitrable dispute, where the state is a party to the dispute, and in all state contracts (whether administrative or civil).

10 The rejection of private-public arbitration in Egypt has started before the promulgation of the Arbitration Act 1994. However, in the light of Article 1 of the Arbitration Act 1994 (before its amendment in 1997) and despite Article 1 of 1994 Act stipulated that private-public arbitration is permissible, the General Assembly for Legal Opinion and Legislation of the Conseil d'État provided an interpretation to this Article as it has general phrases which do not confirm that private-public arbitration is permissible. (See the Legal Opinion of the

208 Arbitration – dispute resolution mechanism

whether private-public arbitration is permissible or not. There was no constitutional prohibition, in the 1971 constitution, to private-public arbitration in Egypt.[11] Pursuant to the 1971 constitution, which was valid until 2011, Article 167 stipulates[12] that determining and changing the jurisdiction of judicial power is only possible by legislation that is promulgated by parliament pursuant to procedural and substantive criteria in constitutional law. This law cannot be amended according to the principle of parallelism of legal rules (*Parallelism des forms*).[13] This is a fundamental rule to promulgate a legislation to permit private-public arbitration as the latter legislation will impliedly amend the Conseil d'État law regarding the administrative judiciary jurisdiction, which was exclusively restricted and confined to the Conseil d'État courts.

Legislation stipulates in Article 10 of the Conseil d'État Law No. 47 of 1972, which was promulgated directly after the 1971 constitution, that the Conseil d'État has the jurisdiction to settle administrative contracts' disputes and all other administrative disputes. The General Assembly of Le Conseil d'État in its legal opinion in 1993 found that the right interpretation to Article 10 is to draw the line between the jurisdiction of the ordinary courts whether civil or commercial courts on the one hand and the Conseil d'État administrative courts on the other hand.[14]

In Egypt, commentators pointed out[15] that the approach adopted by the Supreme Administrative Court was clear in its judgement issued in the session of 20 February 1990,[16] as it was denying administrative bodies access to private-public arbitration to settle disputes, because private-public arbitration is not explicitly permitted by a legislative provision. There was another decision of the Appeal Administrative Court issued in 9 December 1990[17] when the court stated in this judgement that Article 10 of the Conseil d'État Law No. 47 of

---

General Assembly, session of 18 December 1996.) Thus, the Egyptian parliament promulgated new legislation by Law No. 9/1997 amending Article 1 of the Arbitration Act 1994.

11 Article 172 of the 1971 constitution provides for the following: 'The Conseil d'État shall be an independent judiciary body and shall have the competence to decide in administrative disputes, and disciplinary actions. The law shall determine its other competencies.' The 2012 constitution (Article 174), and the 2014 constitution (Article 190), which is applicable now, contain the same provision.

12 Article 167 of the 1971 constitution of Egypt stipulates: 'The law shall determine judiciary authorities and their functions, organize the way of their formation, define conditions and procedures for the appointment and transfer of their members.'

13 A piece of legislation may only be amended by another piece of legislation of an equal degree and rank pursuant to procedural and substantive stipulations (criteria) for law promulgation. The 2012 constitution (Article 174) and the 2014 constitution (Article 190) stipulate the same principle in the Conseil d'État jurisdiction.

14 The General Assembly for Legal Opinion and Legislation 10 March 1993.

15 Mohamed Kamal Mounir, Arbitration in administrative contracts (1991) 337, 1 *Administrative Law Journal* 337 in Arabic; Mohammed Maged Mahmoud, Administrative contracts and the international arbitration clause (1993) 35, 1 *Administrative Sciences Journal*, in Arabic.

16 For an analytical study to this judgement see: Mohamed A.M. Ismail, *International Construction Contracts Arbitration*, Al Halabi Publishing 2003, in Arabic, 505.

17 Case 5837/44 judicial year.

Arbitration – dispute resolution mechanism 209

1972 provides that the Conseil d'État courts are exclusively competent to decide on the following matters:

> First [...] Eleventh: Disputes pertaining to concession contracts, or public works, or supply agreements, or any other administrative contract.

This is provided for in a legislative provision, and may not be amended to allow private-public arbitration by regulation, which is an administrative decree of lower rank on the hierarchy of legal rules. Thus, a legislative provision is needed to allow private-public arbitration in the Egyptian legal system.[18] The same situation exists in the French legal system as an exception to Article 2060 of the French civil code, which prohibits private-public arbitration as a general principle subject to exceptions only through a legislative provision.

The issue of the permissibility of private-public arbitration was initially raised when a contract was concluded between the Ministry of Construction and Urban Communities, and the Construction and Planning Group. The said contract provides in Article 10 that the parties have agreed that disputes arising from the execution of the contract or the interpretation of the provisions thereof shall be resolved by an arbitration tribunal. The Second Committee of the Opinion Department[19] thus decided to refer the subject to the General Assembly, to decide on the principle of permissibility of private-public arbitration in administrative contracts. In the views of the Second Committee, private-public arbitration in administrative contracts was a controversial issue.

The General Assembly[20] defined arbitration as an agreement to refer a dispute to one or more arbitrator(s) to decide thereupon, by an arbitral award, instead of the competent court. The Assembly added that the agreement may be mentioned in the contract establishing the legal relation, and it is thus considered an arbitration clause. The Assembly maintains that arbitration is based on two foundations, namely the will of litigants and a legislative provision that permits arbitration[21] as arbitration constitutes an exception to the general principle of

---

18 Pursuant to Egyptian constitution of 1971, Article 167 (and the following constitutions), determining and changing the jurisdiction of judicial power (authority) is only permitted by legislation that is promulgated pursuant to procedural and substantive criterions in constitutional law.

19 For the role and ranking of the Second Committee in the hierarchy of the Legal Opinion Section of at the Egyptian Conseil d'État see note No. 3.

20 Upon scrutinizing the subject, the Assembly reviewed the provisions of Articles 167 and 172 of the constitution of Egypt promulgated in 1971; Articles 501, 502, 506, 509 of the Code of Civil and Commercial Procedures 13/1968; and Articles 10 and 58 of the Conseil d'État Law No. 47/1972.

21 See an earlier opinion of the Assembly number 96 dated 15 January 1970 – Administrative Encyclopaedia, vol. 10, 152 and cassation 2, appeal 194/37j, the hearing of 15/2/1972, 168 – Golden Encyclopaedia, vol. 4, 565.

210 *Arbitration – dispute resolution mechanism*

the right of litigation, which is stipulated in the constitution and in legislation.[22] Moreover, party autonomy does not exclusively suffice to rule on their disputes by way of arbitration, as this should take place within the rules set by the legislature to regulate arbitration and its procedures. Any dispute cannot be settled by arbitration unless there is an explicit legislative provision. This is a constitutional stipulation by Articles 167 and 172 of the 1971 constitution, which was applicable by that time, and currently Article 190 of the 2014 constitution.

The General Assembly's opinion was relying on articles[23] of the Code of Civil and Commercial Procedures and Article 58 of the Conseil d'État law, which permit the administrative bodies to resort to arbitration in their contractual disputes (administrative or civil). Article 58/3 provides for the fact that any ministry or public juristic person or state authority is bound not to conclude or accept or permit any contract or reconciliation or arbitration or execute any arbitral award exceeding the value of 5000 Egyptian pounds without consulting the competent opinion Department at the Conseil d'État. If the public person was prohibited from agreeing on arbitration, the legislature would not have required it initially to submit this agreement or execute the arbitral award to the Conseil d'État for review.[24] However, given the absence of legislative provision regulating arbitration in contractual disputes where a public juristic person is a party, it is necessary to refer to the general conditions of arbitration and the procedures thereof, set out in the Code of Civil and Commercial Procedures, which do not contradict the nature of the administrative transactions, and the Conseil d'État law. Meanwhile, it does not make sense to say that the Conseil d'État courts are competent to decide exclusively on administrative contract disputes, pursuant to Article 10 of the Conseil d'État law. The purpose of Article 10 is to determine the demarcation line between the jurisdiction decided for the Conseil d'État administrative courts and that of the ordinary courts whether civil or commercial courts.[25]

The second legal opinion of the Assembly was issued upon seeking an opinion on the permissibility of agreement on arbitration in administrative contract disputes. The Second Committee for Opinion reviewed the contract concluded between the *Awqaf* Ministry and *Al-Ahram* Centre for Organization and Microfilming affiliated with the *Al-Ahram* Press Institution, as the contract contained a provision permitting the resort to arbitration for disputes' settlement arising

---

22 In the Egyptian constitutions, litigation is the general principle as the right to litigate is a constitutional right (i.e. see Article 68 of the 1971 constitution, and Article 97 of 2014 constitution).

23 Articles 501, 502, 506, and 509 of the Code of Civil and Commercial Procedures No. 13/1968.

24 In practical reality, public juristic persons send contracts and arbitration agreements for review to the legal opinion departments at the Conseil d'État, pursuant to the Conseil d'État Law No. 47/1972. They rarely send any arbitral award for revision. In cases of revision to an arbitral award, the Conseil d'État cannot amend or alter the arbitral award.

25 The General Assembly for Legal Opinion and Legislation Departments at the Conseil d'État, file No. 54/1/265, hearing of 17 May 1989.

from this contract. The issue was submitted to the General Assembly as it is controversial in practice.[26] The General Assembly reviewed the previous opinion referred to in the hearing of 17 May 1989 permitting the recourse to private-public arbitration in administrative disputes. The General Assembly concluded that the right approach is to permit agreement on resorting to private-public arbitration in administrative contracts, in this case based on the same reasoning set out in the legal opinion of 1989. Further, the General Assembly decided that administrative contracts' disputes in private-public arbitration are subject to the application of the substantive legal principles of the administrative contract which aims at achieving public interests.[27] This principle means that private-public arbitration shall be exercised in the light of public law and in particular administrative law principles.

The General Assembly interpreted in its two previous legal opinions the intent of the legislature of Article 10 of the Conseil d'État law and the fact that it has been enacted to differentiate between the competencies of the administrative and the ordinary civil judiciary, which maintains that this Article does not contradict the provisions of the 1971 constitution. The constitution and Article 10 of the Conseil d'État law were interpreted by the Assembly in the light of the practical considerations required by the nature of the new administrative contracts and the relevant state economic transactions that require private-public arbitration as a rapid mechanism for settling disputes. The General Assembly created a sensible balance between the permission of private-public arbitration on the one hand and safeguarding public interests through respecting administrative law, particularly substantive administrative contracts principles on the other.

Arab doctrine pointed out that the key characteristic of states *per se* is sovereignty,[28] which is the essence of the legal personality of the state.[29] The basic characteristic in the arbitration clause provided for in contracts is the element of acceptance. Some scholarly opinions clarify the essence of the problem, which lies in the meaning of sovereignty in this context. The question in this context is how it is permissible to treat the state as individuals when it simulates those

---

26 Clause 16 of the contract provides the following: 'The Parties agreed that any dispute or disagreement that arises during the execution of this contract shall be resolved amicably. In cases where it becomes impossible to settle amicably, the Parties shall resort to arbitration, where each Party appoints two arbitrators, and notifies the other Party of their names; provided the four arbitrators select a presiding arbitrator ... the arbitral award shall be binding and final for both Parties.' Legal opinion issued on the session of 10 March 1993. The arbitral tribunal consists of five arbitrators, which is rare in arbitral tribunals' composition in arbitration practice in Egypt.

27 Legal opinion issued on the session of 10 March 1993.

28 In this context, sovereignty means that state disputes must be heard and settled before state courts and not arbitration. This is one of the main features of state power.

29 W. Laurence Craig, William W. Park, and Jan Paulsson, *International Chamber of Commerce Arbitration*, 3rd edn, Oceana Publications Inc, 2000, 661.

212 *Arbitration – dispute resolution mechanism*

individuals in their economic and commercial activities, and whether the state could be party to an international commercial arbitration agreement, or not.[30]

Conversely, other opinions in Arab doctrine addressed some criticism[31] of the resolution passed by the General Assembly of the Legal Opinion and Legislation Department at the Conseil d'État, which permitted private-public arbitration in administrative contracts. They pointed out the following two arguments:

First: in the light of the Code of Civil and Commercial Procedures, the general rule in settling disputes is to resort to the judiciary and that the exception is arbitration.[32] Administrative disputes may take place in two channels: the first is through the Conseil d'État courts when the dispute is between any of the public juristic persons and any private person, whether the latter is natural or juristic, and the second is the General Assembly of Legal Opinion and Legislation Department at the Conseil d'État, where the dispute is between two public juristic persons, to resolve the latter dispute by a binding opinion.[33] The Code of Civil and Commercial Procedures No. 13 of 1968 provides another route for private law disputes, through civil and commercial courts, which is different form the legal system enacted by the Conseil d'État Law No. 47/1972 for administrative disputes. Thus, the arbitration system provided for in the Code of Civil and Commercial Procedures Code as a means of dispute settlement cannot be adopted in administrative contracts as they are administrative disputes.[34] Further, this opinion considers private-public

---

30 Mohamed A.M. Ismail, *Globalization and New International Public Works Agreements*, Routledge 2011; Al-Sayed Al-Habib Maloush, member of the International Arbitration Committee at the International Chamber of Commerce, The latest developments in the field of international arbitration in Tunisia, Cairo and Alexandria Conference on International Arbitration, Cairo 11–15 October 1992; Dr. Mohammed Maged Mahmoud, Arbitrability in administrative contracts, Kuwait Conference for International Commercial Arbitration, 1997, in Arabic, 129; Samia Rashed, *Arbitration in Private International Relations*, Dar Al Nahda Al Arabia 1984, in Arabic, 330.

31 In Arab doctrine see Mohamed Kamal Mounir, Arbitration in administrative contracts, 1991, 339 et seq, 1 *Administrative Law Journal* 337, in Arabic; Mohammed Maged Mahmoud, Administrative contracts and the international arbitration clause*Administrative Sciences Journal*, 1993, 35, 1, in Arabic.

32 Those controversial views were adopted by some scholars before the promulgation of the Arbitration Act in 1994. After the promulgation of the Arbitration Act in 1994, one may start arbitration proceedings if one has either an arbitration clause or one relies on an investment treaty. If it is private-public arbitration concerning an administrative contract, the concerned minister's consent is required pursuant to the amendment of the Arbitration Act in 1997.

33 Article 66/d of the Conseil d'État law promulgated by Law No. 47/1972.

34 It is important to add that Article (3) of the Conseil d'État Law, states as follows: '... The procedures provided for in this law shall be applied, as well as the provisions of the Code of Civil procedures where this law is silent, until a law is promulgated in relation to the procedures pertinent to the judicial section.' Thus, the Code of Civil Procedures is applicable if there is no applicable provision in the Conseil d'État law.

Arbitration – dispute resolution mechanism 213

arbitration as an exception of the general constitutional and legislative principles which stipulate that disputes normally must be referred to litigation.[35] Second: Given the fact that dispute resolution between litigants by way of arbitration is exceptional from the general principles which stipulate that disputes must be referred to litigation, therefore, private-public arbitration should be accessed only if there is an explicit legislative provision permitting private-public arbitration.[36]

Other opinions[37] assure the permissibility of the state or any of its public juristic persons being party to an arbitration agreement, as the situation differs in Egyptian law when it is compared to French Civil Code. The latter code prohibits public law persons, as a general principle, from concluding arbitration agreements.[38] The accession by Egypt to the international conventions[39] permits the settlement of disputes arising in relation to investments, by various arbitral mechanisms, in addition to the access to the International Centre for Settlement of Investment Disputes (ICSID) pursuant to Law No. 90/1971, which is part of Egypt's internal legislation.[40] In terms of private-public arbitration, the Egyptian government cannot argue that public law persons are not eligible to conclude arbitration agreements, as this runs counter to states' international undertakings.[41]

---

35 Mohamed A.M. Ismail, *Globalization and New International Public Works Agreements*, Routledge 2011 55–6.
36 This is the situation in Article 2060 of the French civil code.
37 Mohammed Maged Mahmoud, Administrative contracts and the international arbitration clause, *Administrative Sciences Journal*, 1993, 35, 1, in Arabic; Samia Rashed, *Arbitration in Private International Relations*, Dar Al Nahda Al Arabia 1984, in Arabic, 331.
38 See Article 2060 of the French civil code.
39 Law No. 43/1974 on Arab and Foreign Capital Investment and Free Zones, as it involves four options of arbitration, three of which are international and the fourth is domestic. Article 8 stipulates that 'Investment disputes relating to this law shall be settled in the way which was agreed with the investor, or within the valid treaties between the Arab Republic of Egypt and the Investor's country, or within the Convention for the Settlement for Investment Disputes between the State and Nationals of Other States which the Arab Republic of Egypt has ratified pursuant to law no. 90 of 1971, where it is applicable. Disputes may be settled by arbitration, and an arbitration tribunal may be constituted by a member for each of the disputing parties, and a third presiding arbitrator thus shall be nominated by the two selected members. The presiding arbitrator may be nominated by the Supreme Council for Judicial Authorities and selected among counsellor from the judicial authority in Egypt, if the two nominated arbitrators failed to nominate the presiding arbitrator within 30 days from the nomination of the second arbitrator who is nominated by the disputing parties.' This Law No. 43/1974 was annulled by Article 2 of the promulgation articles of the previous Investment Law No. 230 of 1989.
40 An international treaty is valid legislation in Egypt and Arab countries, after ratification by the states' parliaments. For instance, see the Egyptian constitution of 1971, Article 151; and Egyptian constitution of 2014, Article 151; the constitution of the Kingdom of Bahrain, Article 37; the constitution of Kuwait, Article 70; the constitution of Syria, Article 75/6; the constitution of Oman, Article 76; the constitution of Qatar, Article 143.
41 Samia Rashed, *Arbitration in Private International Relations*, Dar Al Nahda Al Arabia 1984, in Arabic, 331.

214 *Arbitration – dispute resolution mechanism*

Finally, the General Assembly for the Legal Opinion and Legislation Department, of the Egyptian Conseil d'État, held that private-public arbitration in general is permissible, stating no differences between domestic arbitration and international arbitration. Given the absence of a special legislation regulating arbitration in contract disputes, where the administrative body is a party, whether civil or administrative contracts, it is imperative to refer to the arbitration general conditions and procedures provided for in the Code of Civil and Commercial Procedures, which do not contradict the nature of administrative relations of the state.[42]

The International Chamber of Commerce (ICC) in 1990 issued an award confirming arbitrability of administrative contracts, pursuant to Article 10/11 of the Conseil d'État Law No. 47 of 1972 and Article 172 of the Egyptian constitution of 1971.[43]

1994–1996

The Egyptian Arbitration Act 27/1994 was promulgated and Article 1, before amendment, stipulated that private-public arbitration is permissible.[44]

The matter of permissibility of private-public arbitration was resubmitted to the General Assembly[45] in 1996, in a contract concluded between the Supreme Council for Antiquities, a public juristic person, and a British company. The dispute between the parties concerned the complementary works to the coordination works of the Nubian Antiquities Museum landscape in Aswan. The contract was submitted to the Second Committee of the Opinion Department at the Conseil d'État for review. Upon reviewing the contract, the Second Committee of the Opinion Department was of the view to omit Article 16 from the first contract, and Article 22 of the second contract, as they contained a provision to resolve any disputes that might arise from the two contracts by way of private-public arbitration before the Cairo Regional Centre for International Commercial Arbitration (CRCICA) on the ground that this dispute falls within the Conseil d'État courts' exclusive jurisdiction.

---

42 Mohamed A.M. Ismail, *Globalization and New International Public Works Agreements*, Routledge 2011, 425–426; Mohammed Maged Mahmoud, Administrative contracts and the international arbitration clause, *Administrative Sciences Journal*, 1193, 35, 1, in Arabic.

43 Jean-Jacques Arnaldez, Yves Derains, and Dominique Hascher, *Collection of ICC arbitral awards*, vol. 3, Kluwer Law International, 75, case No. 6162 of 1990. This award highlights the approach of the international legal community and international arbitral tribunals to the problem of private-public arbitration in Egypt.

44 Article 1 of the Arbitration Act 1994 (before amendment in 1997) pointed out that: '... the provisions of the present law shall apply to every arbitration between parties of the public law or private law, notwithstanding the nature of the legal relations subject of dispute in case such arbitration is taking place in Egypt or if it is an international commercial arbitration taking place abroad, where the parties thereof agree on the present law as the governing law.'

45 The author was honored to participate in the General Assembly deliberations, which were held at the Conseil d'État in Cairo on 18 December 1996.

The Second Committee discovered that the opinion that it was going to adopt agrees with the two rulings issued by the Conseil d'État courts on 1990, which do not permit private-public arbitration. Yet, this opinion disagrees with that reached by the General Assembly for the Legal Opinion and Legislation Departments in its legal opinion issued in the hearings of 17 May 1989 and 7 February 1993, where it concluded the permissibility of private-public arbitration in administrative contracts. Pursuant to the provision of Article 66/2 of the Conseil d'État law the Second Committee referred the matter to the General Assembly for jurisdiction in case it discovered a disagreement with a previous legal opinion issued by the Assembly. The issue was submitted to the General Assembly for the Legal Opinion and Legislation Departments in its hearing held on 18 December 1996.

In the legal opinion of 1996 the General Assembly raised the question of democracy and rules applicable to delegation of powers in administrative law. The General Assembly pointed out in its reasoning that the ministers are delegated by the nation to run the public utilities and, consequently, public juristic entities cannot re-delegate arbitrators instead of the Conseil d'État courts for the settlement of disputes of the administrative contracts. There is an assumption in administrative law in Egypt that delegated persons cannot re-delegate any other person or authority, consequently, if a minister has delegated the power given to him by the nation to run public utilities, he cannot re-delegate arbitrators any power and escape the national administrative court's jurisdiction (Law No. 42 of 1967 for the delegation of powers). The General Assembly rejected private-public arbitration in administrative contracts, as private-public arbitration in the views of the Assembly is contrary to constitutional law principles in particular the right to litigate through national litigation and the above-mentioned administrative law principles. The Assembly stipulated that an explicit legislative provision permitting private-public arbitration is required.

The same subject was submitted to the Cairo Court of Appeal[46] (commercial circuit no. 63) when the Supreme Council for Antiquities (Plaintiff) filed a lawsuit on 12 November 1996 against the British company (defendant) requesting the following: to nullify the arbitral award number 66/1995 passed in the session of 20 October 1992 and consider it as null and void, and to bind the defendant to pay the judicial expenses and fees. The arbitral tribunal decided in its arbitral award to bind the Supreme Council for Antiquities to pay the British company for a total amount of EGP 474,452, and further to pay the company for the distance of 70 meters of insulation works in the amount of EGP 659.26 on the basis of EGP 9.418 per meter, and delay interest at the rate of 5% for the amounts delayed as of 8 November 1995 until final payment of the delayed amount.

---

46 See Cairo Court of Appeals (circuit 63 commercial) in appeal No. 64/113 judicial year (unpublished).

216　*Arbitration – dispute resolution mechanism*

The reason behind claiming the nullification of the arbitration clause, by the plaintiff, is that the contract subject to dispute is an administrative contract and may not be subject to arbitration as per the provision of Article 10 of the Conseil d'État Law No. 47/1972. The plaintiff added that arbitration may not be resorted to in administrative contracts pursuant to Article 11 of the Arbitration Act 1994, where reconciliation is ruled out.

The court rejected the case and bound the plaintiff to pay the litigation fees. The court pointed out that Article 1 of the Arbitration Act 1994 (before amendment) provides that arbitration between public persons and private persons is permissible regardless to the legal nature of the transaction and whether it is public law or private law transaction.[47] The court adopted the rule that stipulates that 'no discretion in the existence of legislative provision' to confirm that Article 1 of the arbitration Act is conclusive and clear text that permits private-public arbitration. The court added that the legislature permits agreement on arbitration even if a party thereto is a public juristic person and notwithstanding the nature of the legal relation subject to dispute.

The court concluded that Article 1 of the Arbitration Act 1994 is applicable, after giving priority to the provisions of the valid international conventions in Egypt, whereby such provisions apply to every international commercial arbitration taking place in Egypt, whether one of its parties is a public or private legal person.

The court alluded to the report of the joint committee made up of the Constitutional and Legislative Affairs Committee and the Bureau of the Economic Affairs Committee in Parliament on the Arbitration Act 1994, which is conclusive in disclosing the legislature's intention from the phrasing of Article 1 of the said law. It stated that the Committee amended Article 1

> to encompass wider scope than the scope of enforceability of the law provisions, taking into account the provisions of the valid conventions in Egypt, the Committee regulated the enforceability of the provisions of the law on every arbitration conducted in Egypt whether any of its parties is a public or a private law person and notwithstanding the legal relation subject of dispute whether it is public law or private law relation.

The court pointed out that the foregoing agrees with the legislative policy behind the Arbitration Act 1994, which is consistent with the state's aim to create a conducive environment for investment and to attract Foreign Direct

---

47 The court had not dealt with the relation between Article 1 of the Arbitration Act 27/1994 and Article 10 of the Conseil d'État law as it must deal with jurisdiction from a commercial court perspective. Conversely, the Conseil d'État judicial organs are more concerned with the application of Article 10 of the Conseil d'État law and its real interpretation, as it is more relevant to their jurisdiction and as the Conseil d'État is tasked with safeguarding public interests.

Investments (FDI). The court added that it is meaningless to argue that the provision of Article 10 of the Conseil d'État Law No. 47/1972 has vested the Conseil d'État exclusively the jurisdiction to resolve disputes arising from administrative contracts, because the legislative policy of the Conseil d'État law is to draw the line between the jurisdiction of the Conseil d'État courts on the one hand and that of the ordinary civil courts on the other, and not to prohibit resorting to private-public arbitration in administrative contract related disputes.

The court elaborated that it is groundless to make a challenge by claiming that Article 172 of the 1971 constitution might be interpreted to prohibit private-public arbitration in administrative contracts, as this article aims to elicit the functions of the Conseil d'État as part of the judicial power in Egypt. The court alluded to the different positions taken by the Egyptian and French legislatures in this regard, and added that the contract has been concluded, providing for an arbitration clause. During the arbitration hearings, no argument was made to the effect of nullifying the arbitration clause in administrative contracts; yet, that same argument was later articulated by the Supreme Council for Antiquities during the Appeal Court sessions, which is against the mandatory stipulation of *bona fide* principle as a general principle in both civil and administrative contracts.[48]

Finally, the court concluded that the Arbitration Act 27/1994 permits private-public arbitration in administrative contracts.

1997 and after: legislative amendment by law 9/1997 to Article 1 of the Arbitration Act 1994

A second clause was added to Article 1 of the Arbitration Act 27/1994 as follows:

> In all events it is permissible to agree on arbitration in disputes arising from administrative contracts upon the approval of the competent minister or his pro tempore involving public legal persons and no delegation is permissible in this regard.

Article 2 provides that the present law amendment has to be published in the Egyptian Official Gazette, provided it enters into force as of the day following the date of publication.[49] The scope of application of this law is limited to

---

48 In the Egyptian and Arab legal systems, any contractual provision cannot be considered as null and void without an express legislative provision or if it is against a legislative mandatory rule which is a matter of public policy.

49 Pursuant to Article 188 of the 1971 constitution, legislation is valid after one month following publication in the Official Gazette, unless otherwise stated in the new promulgated legislation. The same constitutional stipulation exists in Article 225 of the 2014 Egyptian constitution; Article 122 of the Kingdom of Bahrain constitution; Article 178 of the constitution of Kuwait; Article 74 of the constitution of Oman; Article 142 of the constitution of Qatar; and Article 129 of the Iraqi constitution. The Iraqi constitution stipulates that legislation is valid from the date of publication unless otherwise stipulated in the new legislation.

218 *Arbitration – dispute resolution mechanism*

administrative contracts, which suggests that private-public arbitration in administrative contracts requires the consent of the concerned minister, conversely, private-public arbitration in any other dispute that is not an administrative contract dispute does not require the consent of the concerned minister. This amendment to the Arbitration Act that was promulgated in 1997 concerns only arbitration in administrative contracts, between the state and any private person, as the latter contracts are one of the significant bilateral acts exercised by the state and in many cases these contracts contain large amounts of public funds.

The explanatory memorandum pointed out that as administrative contracts are of special necessity to the economy, it was viewed to include legislative amendment to Article 1 of the Arbitration Act to explicitly provide for the permissibility of private-public arbitration in disputes arising from administrative contracts, and to specify the competent authority which grants consent to start private-public arbitration in these contracts.

It is clear from the legislative amendment and practice that the minister's consent must be given before starting arbitration proceedings not before drafting the arbitration agreement in each contract.[50]

The definition of public juristic persons that are considered the administrative bodies of the state does not include state-owned companies.[51] Public juristic persons are subject to the legislative stipulations of entering into private-public arbitration in the Egyptian legal system; meanwhile, state-owned companies are not subject to those stipulations to start arbitration.

Assessment to the Egyptian Arbitration Act as amended in 1997

1. The concerned minister's consent in administrative contracts is a legislative stipulation by the Egyptian legislature to protect public interests and public funds as the administrative contract concerns public interests and it uses public funds to achieve public interests. After long judicial debate about whether private-public arbitration is permissible or not, it is clear that the Egyptian legislature is adopting a new legislative policy that aims to protect public interests as it is the main target of administrative contracts and aims to protect public funds which the nation spends on administrative contracts. The legislative amendment in 1997 shows the interaction between arbitration law and practice in the Egyptian legal system on the one hand, and the

---

50 The minister cannot grant the consent before drafting the arbitration agreements in each contract because some contracts are signed by the president of the public corporation. Pursuant to the Egyptian public corporation's Law No. 61 of 1963, the president of the public corporation, not the minister, is the legal representative for the public corporation in litigation and in relations with third party. The president for the public corporations can sign the contracts and, if a dispute arises, consent may be granted from the minister to start arbitration proceedings.

51 Mohamed A.M. Ismail, *International Construction Contracts Arbitration*, Al Halabi Publishing 2003, 31, in Arabic.

Arbitration – dispute resolution mechanism 219

promotion of administrative law principles on the other if the dispute concerns an administrative contract that falls within the scope of application of the amendment in 1997.

2. There are legislative loopholes in the provisions of this law resulting from the incongruity between certain articles of this law and the substantive nature of private-public disputes in general, and administrative contracts in particular.

It could be inferred from the provision of Article 39 that the governing law[52] applicable to the subject of dispute is elected by the disputants (parties' choice) and the arbitral tribunal applies the substantive rules independent of the rules pertinent to conflict of laws (*Renvoi* is excluded),[53] unless otherwise agreed. The Article then specifies the *modus operandi* of designating the applicable rules in case of absence of choice by the disputing parties. This eventually gives rise to the likelihood of applying a law other than the national law when hearing a dispute where a party thereto is a public juristic person. From the legal perspectives of the administrative judiciary in Egypt, this is a violation of the administrative contract substantive theory[54] as it might be in conflict with the nature of public law contracts which aim to achieve public interests and it might

---

52 Article 1 of the Arbitration Act 1994 permits arbitration in administrative contracts, and Article 39 of the same Act provides that:

   a. The arbitral tribunal shall apply the rules agreed upon by the parties to arbitration to the subject-matter of dispute. In cases where it is agreed to apply the law of a specific state, the substantive rules thereof shall be applied exclusive of the rules pertinent to the conflict of laws, unless otherwise agreed.

   b. In cases where the parties fail to agree on the governing legal rules to be applied to the subject-matter of dispute, the arbitral tribunal shall apply the substantive rules in the law, viewed thereby as the most closely connected to the dispute.

   c. The arbitral tribunal shall, upon deciding on the merits of dispute, observe the terms and conditions of the contract subject to dispute as well as the applicable use and practices in this kind of transaction.

   The arbitral tribunal may, in cases where the parties to arbitration explicitly agree to delegate its powers as *amiable compositeur*, decide on the merits of dispute on the basis of the prerequisites of the rules of justice and equity without being limited by the provisions of law.

53 The same principle exists in English case law, see Lord Wright's judgment in: *Vita Food Products V. Unus Shipping*, [1939] UK HL.

54 The General Assembly Opinion in 1993 pointed out that private-public arbitration is permitted in administrative contracts and this is on condition that arbitration must not violate the substantive theory stipulations of the administrative contracts. The aim of the administrative contract concerns public interests. The substantive theory of the administrative contract requires that the contracting state is not equal with the private person, so the state can achieve public interests through containing the administrative contract excessive clauses. The concepts of state sovereignty and public interests, as they are connected to the administrative contract, mean that the administrative contract may not accept foreign law as an applicable law.

220 *Arbitration – dispute resolution mechanism*

also conflict with a state's sovereignty.[55]Applying foreign law to private-public arbitration disputes contradicts the nature of private-public disputes whether it is an administrative contracts dispute or otherwise.

3. It may be argued if the application of a foreign law to private-public arbitration conflicts with democracy and public expectations. The public usually expect the application of national law, as private-public arbitration deals with disputes relating to public interests and public funds. The application of foreign law may lead to findings by arbitral tribunals that are contrary to the national courts' findings and contrary to the public expectations. In private-public arbitration, it is difficult to predict what arbitrators are going to apply to the merits of the dispute. This may violate the expectations of the public which conflicts, in some cases, with the principle of democracy.

4. The additional clause of Law No. 9/1997 concluded by stipulating the prohibition of delegation of this function vested in the competent minister or in the person acting in lieu thereof, to any authority. This prohibition aims to protect public interests and indicates that the legislature was adopting and implementing the legal opinion issued by the General Assembly[56] where it opined that no delegation may be granted over another delegation, as public juristic persons are delegated from the nation in managing public utilities. Henceforth, they may not re-delegate this authority to others. This codification of this judicial principle that was established by the General Assembly shows the interaction between administrative law principles and Arbitration Act provisions in the Egyptian legal system.

Private-public arbitration and government acts

Egyptian constitutions starting from the 1971 constitution, Article 172, and till the current constitution of 2014, stipulate that the Conseil d'État is the sole judicial organ that is competent with a judicial review upon the administration's administrative acts, whether unilateral decrees or bilateral administrative contracts. Thus, administration decrees are not arbitrable in the Egyptian legal system. If the administration decrees are connected with administrative contracts, the legal effect of illegality of decrees is arbitrable as it is connected to administrative contracts. For instance, if the administration issued a decree to unilaterally terminate a contract, *La résiliation administrative*, with forfeiture of the performance bond of the contractor, the financial consequences of the decree are arbitrable to compensate the contractor against the state. The role of

---

55 The legal opinion of the General Assembly for Legal Opinion and Legislation Departments previously mentioned, 10 March 1993.
56 See the legal opinion of the Assembly on 18 December 1996.

the arbitral tribunal is confined to award compensation to cover the financial consequences.

Through decades, the Conseil d'État jurisprudence[57] has illustrated the theory of administrative decrees that are connected to administrative contracts, and administrative decrees that are not connected to administrative contracts. In all cases, the scope of arbitration is limited to the financial and legal consequences resulting from those administrative decrees. A judicial review to administrative decrees, without a contract, cannot be exercised by the arbitral tribunal. In the Egyptian constitutional and legislative systems, judicial review by the Conseil d'État is one of the democracy guarantees. Thus, the judicial review of state acts is stipulated by the 1971 constitution (Article 172), the 2012 constitution (Article 174), and the 2014 constitution (Article 190). The Conseil d'État is the sole judicial organ that exercises the constitutional principle of legality, on the one hand through exercising a judicial review of the legality of administrative decrees. On the other hand, the Supreme Constitutional Court in Egypt exercises a judicial review upon the constitutionality of legislation and regulations, as stipulated in Articles 191 to 195 of the 2014 constitutions.

PPP disputes' resolution in international organizations practice: potential for disputes[58]

In PPP contracts, the potential for disputes among the parties is high. The imperative to avoid such disputes and maintain working relationships over the lifetime of a project is even greater than in a typical contract situation. How do existing PPPs deal with dispute prevention in the PPP contract structure?

In the countries where PPP is well developed, standardized and often mandatory forms of contracts have been developed for these projects. Often, there are different mandatory forms depending on the sector or nature of the project. The contracts can be extremely complex and detailed. There is little opportunity for negotiation of core terms. Whilst principles of equity may be applied to disputes in certain jurisdictions, there remains uncertainty of outcome. The aim of the draftsman in the availability-based PPP is to provide for the same dispute resolution process in each contract in the project, with only some minor differences, to avoid any contradictory decisions on the same issues. In availability-based PPPs

---

57 Soliman El Tamawy, *The General Theory of Administrative Decrees, Comparative Study*, Dar El Fikr El Araby 2017; and see also: Hamdy Yassin Okasha, *The Encyclopedia of the Administrative Decrees in the Conseil d'État Jurisprudence*, 2010, three volumes.

58 The Dispute Resolution Board Foundation, Fostering common sense dispute resolution worldwide, UNECE publication, Publication date: April 2017, Guidance on the Use of Dispute Boards in Public Private Partnership (PPP) Projects, www.unece.org/fileadmin/DAM/ceci/documents/2018/PPP/Forum/Documents/White_Paper_Guidance_on_the_Use_of_Dispute_Boards_in_PPP_Projects.pdf, last accessed on 5 October 2018.

222 *Arbitration – dispute resolution mechanism*

most of these standardized dispute resolution provisions have been drafted in anticipation of the public authority initiating a dispute with the SPV first and the SPV then initiating the same dispute with its sub-contractors, usually with some attempt at requiring them to be heard or dealt with together. In fact, experience shows that the bulk of disputes in such PPPs start with the sub-contractors as they feel the effect of a dispute through cash flow. For example, in a case where deductions for non-availability are applied by a public authority against the payment due to the SPV, the SPV will pass these down to its sub-contractor by deducting them from sums that would otherwise be due to them. It will therefore usually be the sub-contractor that starts the dispute process against the SPV as its payer, not the public authority or the SPV.

There are Dispute Boards written into certain PPPs. Some of these are, in fact, panels of individuals, technical, financial, and legal, who can be called upon to deal with disputes when they arise. These Dispute Boards or panels are what we describe as *ad hoc* Dispute Boards. Because of their temporary nature and restricted scope to the dispute in question, they do not fulfill any dispute avoidance functions.

Special difficulties relating to private-public arbitration in Egypt

There are some special difficulties in private-public arbitration practice in Egypt such as First, the requirement of the concerned minister's consent in particular contracts such as PPPs and BOT/BOOT agreements as this requirement aims at safeguarding public interests.[59] Second, can arbitrators in private-public arbitration act as *amiable compositure*? Does the application of rules, which are different from the national laws, to private-public arbitration disputes contradict public law principles and the concept of public interests as one of the main concepts of public law? The following parts of this section deal with those difficulties as an attempt to clarify whether those difficulties in private-public arbitration are compatible with public law principles. The concept of public interests is the main concept behind state contracts, whether civil or administrative contracts, and private-public arbitration is a fundamental mechanism that aims at protecting public interest through protecting public funds and minimizing government's loss in the arbitral process. Through decades, the

---

59 The role of investment treaties is important to PPPs as it was pointed out: 'In particular, international investment treaties (commonly referred to as "bilateral investment treaties" (BITs) or "international investment agreements" (IIAs)) impose rules on governments regarding how those governments treat foreign shareholders and foreign-owned investments. Additionally, these international investment treaties also commonly include provisions allowing foreign investors in contracting parties to the PPP to sue their host governments through arbitration (commonly referred to as investor-state dispute settlement (ISDS)). That arbitration may be conducted with little, if any, transparency, and can take place in another country, and/or another language, limiting the public's ability to understand, much less participate in, the proceedings.' PPPs and ISDS: A Risky Combination, Brooke Guven, legal researcher at the Columbia Center on Sustainable Investment (CCSI) and Lise Johnson, Head, Investment Law and Policy at CCSI, posted on 24 May 2018.

Arbitration – dispute resolution mechanism   223

Egyptian government paid considerable amounts of compensation in private-public arbitration whether in international commercial arbitration disputes[60] or international investment arbitration disputes.[61]

Private-public arbitration in PPPs and BOT/BOOT agreements

Are PPPs and BOT/BOOT (Build-Operate-Transfer/Build-Own-Operate-Transfer) contracts and their various types subject to the legislative stipulation enacted in Law No. 9/1997, which requires the concerned minister's consent before recourse to arbitration, as the minister's consent is a safeguard to achieve public interests?

It is suggested that after the promulgation of the PPP law in Egypt, Law No. 67/2010, PPPs are not considered administrative contracts, whether they are purely commercial or of hybrid nature. This includes all PPP contracts as per the provision of Article 1 of the promulgation articles of the PPP law (Law No. 67/2010), which provides that PPP contracts are not subject to the state procurement law and its executive regulations, the Public Utilities' Concession Law No. 129/1947, and the Natural Resources' Concession Law No. 61/1958. The enactment of Egyptian PPP Law 67/ 2010 on PPPs takes such arrangements between the public sector and private actors away from administrative law in both substantive and procedural terms. The treatment of PPPs as commercial contracts has been met with controversy[62] as one of the main consequences is their exclusion from the jurisdiction of the Conseil d'État courts system. In addition, the PPP contracts are not subject to competitive tendering, objectivity in partner selection, and transparency requirements for their awards. PPPs as a contractual pattern suggest that the private-public arbitration shall increase in the forthcoming years. In addition, considerable debate has arisen about the legal nature of BOT/BOOT agreements and whether they are commercial contracts or public contracts. One argument considers BOT/BOOT agreements to be

---

60 For instance, ICC arbitration *SPP v. Egypt*, which started as an ICC arbitration and ended with an ICSID award in May 1992 in the (ICSID case No. ARB/84/3).

61 For instance, *Waguih Elie Siag and Clorinda Vecchi v. Arab Republic of Egypt*, (ICSID case No. ARB/05/15), available at: https://investmentpolicy.unctad.org/investment-dispute-settlement/cases/206/siag-v-egypt, last seen 2 November 2019.

62 Some Egyptian scholars consider PPP contracts as an administrative contract, see: Ragab Mahmoud, *Public-Private Partnership Contracts*, Dar El Nahda El Arabia 2007, in Arabic and *Partnership Contracts between Public and Private Sectors* Dar El Nahda El Arabia 2010, in Arabic. Some other authorities consider new types of state transactions such as BOT and PPP contracts as commercial contracts, see: Hani Sarie El Din, *Legal and Contractual Arrangements for Infrastructure Projects Financed by Private Sector*, Dar El Nahda El Arabia 2001, in Arabic, *Legal and Contractual Regime for BOT* No 177 El Ahram El Eqtisadi Book 2002, in Arabic; Mohamed A.M. Ismail, *Globalization and New International Public Works Agreements in Developing Countries, An Analytical Perspective*, Routledge 2011, and for the same author see: *International Infrastructure Agreements and PPPs in Developing Countries: Substantive Principles, with Special Reference to Arab and Latin American Countries, EPPPL*, Lexxion 2011.

224 Arbitration – dispute resolution mechanism

administrative contracts as they were subject to previous state procurement law No. 89 of 1998. Doctrine[63] considers BOT/BOOT contracts to be commercial transactions and not administrative or public contracts, despite the fact that both types of contracts were subject to the previous State Procurement Law No. 89 of 1998. The substantive clauses of BOT/BOOT agreements are commercial clauses and not excessive clauses that are known in administrative contracts law and practice. Thus, PPP, BOT/BOOT contracts are not administrative contracts, nor do they require the concerned minister's consent to start arbitration proceedings[64]. It is suggested that a legislative reform is needed to extend the requirement of the concerned minister's consent to all state contracts whether they are administrative contracts or private law (civil or commercial) contracts. In the latter case, and if there is a legislative provision stipulating the requirement of the minister's consent in all state contracts, PPPs and BOT/BOOT agreements' disputes will require the concerned minister's consent before stating private-public arbitration. The integration of public law principles with private-public arbitration to cover all state contracts is required to safeguard public interests and public funds.

The situation in other MENA countries

The Saudi Arbitration Act 2012

Article 10/2 of the Saudi Arbitration Act 2012 provides that arbitration is not permitted for public juristic entities without the consent of the prime minster, unless there is a legislative provision permits arbitration. This prohibition applies to all public juristic entities disputes whether contractual (public or private) or otherwise.

The Qatar Arbitration Act 2017

Article 2/2 of the Qatari Arbitration Act 2017 provides that arbitration in administrative contracts' dispute is subject to the prime minister's consent or any authority delegated by him. This impliedly means that civil and/or commercial law contracts' disputes are not subject to the prime minister's consent.

---

63 Mohamed A.M. Ismail, *Globalization and New International Public Works Agreements*, Routledge, 2011, 15–19; and for the same author see: *Legal Globalization and PPPs Egypt*, EPPPL, Lexxion 2010, 54; *International Infrastructure Agreements and PPPs in Developing Countries: Substantive Principles, with special reference to Arab and Latin American Countries*, EPPPL, Lexxion 2011, 147–59; and *International Construction Contracts Arbitration*, Al Halabi Publishing, 2003; and see also: Hani Sarie El Din, *Legal and Contractual Arrangements for Infrastructure Projects Financed by Private Sector*, Dar El Nahda El Arabia 2001, in Arabic; and by the same author: *Legal and Contractual Regime for BOT*, No. 177, El Ahram El Eqtisadi Book 2002, in Arabic.
64 Hani Sarie El Din, *Legal and Contractual Arrangements for Infrastructure Projects Financed by Private Sector*, Dar El Nahda El Arabia 2001, in Arabic; and by the same author: *Legal and Contractual Regime for BOT*, No. 177, El Ahram El Eqtisadi Book, 2002, in Arabic.

The Egyptian PPP law provides that the PPP contract shall be subject to the provisions of the Egyptian law. Any contrary agreement shall be deemed to be null and void. This means that this legislative provision is a mandatory rule in the Egyptian legal system.

After the approval of the Supreme Committee for PPP Affairs, it may be agreed to resolve disputes resulting from the PPP contract through arbitration, or any other non-judicial means of dispute resolution according to what was stipulated in the PPP contract.[65]

The PPP Jordanian law[66] provides that partnership contracts shall be governed by Jordanian law. The parties to the partnership project contract may agree to settle the disputes pertaining to the partnership project contract by alternative disputes resolution methods.

The Moroccan PPP law does not provide for specific provisions. The parties to the contract are free to decide the applicable law. Provision is left to the liberty of the parties who may foresee conciliation procedure, conventional mediation, arbitration or judicial settlement (Article 27).[67]

Can arbitrators in private-public arbitration act as *amiable compositeur*?[68]

Article 39/d of the Egyptian Arbitration Act provides that: the arbitral tribunal may, in cases where the parties of arbitration explicitly agree to delegate their powers as *amiable compositeur*, decide on the merits of dispute on the basis of the prerequisites of the rules of justice and equity without being limited by the provisions of law.[69]

In the light of administrative contracts' stipulations, and the substantive nature of these contracts, which reject the application of foreign law to it, it is difficult to accept in the Egyptian legal system, that arbitrators can act as *amiable compositeur*. The administrative law principles that aim at safeguarding public interests[70] require the necessity of applying national legislation and

---

65 The Egyptian PPP law, Article 35.

66 Jordanian PPP law, Article 16.

67 Moroccan PPP law pointed out that: '*La loi ne prévoit pas de dispositions spécifiques. Les parties au contrat sont libres de décider du droit applicable. Disposition laissée à la liberté des parties qui peuvent prévoir une procédure de conciliation, de médiation conventionnelle, d'arbitrage ou judiciaire (L.art.27).*'

68 See 'Amiable Composition and Ex Aequo et Bono' in Gary B. Born, *International Commercial Arbitration*, 2nd edn, vol. II, International Arbitration Procedures, Kluwer Law Intl 2014, 2770.

69 The same Article, with the same number 39/4, exists in the Omani Arbitration Act, 1997.

70 It is concluded from the previous legal opinions of the General Assembly for Legal Opinion and Legislation that permissibility of private-public arbitration in administrative contracts should not contradict with these contracts' substantive theory which implies that the national law of the contracting state should apply. (See the previously mentioned legal opinion of 10 March 1993).

226 *Arbitration – dispute resolution mechanism*

national regulatory framework to private-public arbitration whether the subject matter of the dispute is an administrative contract or not. In the case of the administrative contracts, administrative contracts are directly connected with public interests and public funds; consequently, *amiable compositeur* may not apply to the contracting state in private-public arbitration, which directly violates the substantive theory of the administrative contracts. This view applies to all kind of private-public arbitration whether the subject matter of the dispute is an administrative contract or not. Applying laws different from national laws, in the view of most Arab countries,[71] violates public interests, and is contrary to the aims of the administrative law. In many cases, it may contradict with the public expectations as the findings of the arbitral tribunal may contradict with the basic principle of public law. Article 39/d of the Egyptian Arbitration Act is not a mandatory rule; consequently, it is not a matter of public policy. It is not obligatory, therefore, for the state to follow it.

Settlement of project company disputes with third parties

If the project company is committed to providing services to the public or operates publicly available infrastructure facilities, the contracting administrative authority may require the company in the PPP contract to establish simple and effective mechanisms for settling claims submitted by users of the infrastructure facility or the services it provides.

The project company and its shareholders shall be free to choose appropriate mechanisms for the settlement of disputes arising between them.

The project company shall be free to agree on appropriate mechanisms for settling disputes between it and the suppliers, contractors, or suppliers and others dealing with them.

71 See the General Assembly opinions in 1989 and 1993.

Conclusions

PPP contracts are new contractual techniques in the MENA countries that represent a remarkable step towards achieving Sustainable Development Goals and the UN 2030 Agenda. PPP techniques underscore the crucial topic of how PPPs can achieve Sustainable Development Goals in the light of the international organs' practice and how MENA governments limited their role and relinquished the role of the employer in favor of being a regulator and supervisor of infrastructure and public utilities projects. State intervention is limited to the minimum and this is evident through analyzing the trajectory of PPP legislation and regulation in the MENA countries. MENA governments' role is consistent with the leading schools in economy like the Chicago School as this role is confined to the legislation and regulation of PPP techniques.

A significant regulatory trend that has emerged as a result of the strategic role of the private sector and its long-term engagement in delivering infrastructure and public services reflects on the legal treatment of risk distribution between the public and private sectors within PPPs and, in particular, the allocation and pricing of construction or project risk, which is related to design problems, building cost overruns, and project delays; financial risk, which is related to variability in interest rates, exchange rates, and other factors affecting financing costs; performance risk, which is related to the availability of an asset and the continuity and quality of the relevant service provision; demand risk, which is related to the on-going need for the relevant public services; and residual value risk, which is related to the future market price of an asset. Risk transfer from the public sector to the private sector has a significant influence on whether a PPP is a more efficient and cost-effective alternative to public investment and publicly funded provision of services.[1]

Despite the fact that the PPP framework in some other countries needs reform, it is a rising contractual technique in the legal and commercial sphere in MENA countries.It is appropriate to refer to the following conclusions and recommendations achieved through this study:

---

1 Christopher Bovis, *The European Procurement & Public Private Partnership Law Review*, Vol. 14, No. 1, 1/2019, Lexxion, p. 1.

228   *Conclusions*

1. MENA constitutions currently are not adopting specific static economic ideology whether socialist or free market economy. It opens the door to the elections whether parliamentary or presidential to determine the right economic dynamic ideology for each presidential or parliamentary term. Therefore, there is no constitutional ban at present in MENA countries' constitutions for the state to enter into PPP contracts with the private sector whether local or international.

2. There is a '*décalage*' between practice and legislation as practice recognizes PPP contracts as a legal and economic fact before the PPP legislation is promulgated in most MENA countries.

3. Due to the liberalization of the MENA countries' constitutions, in particular the Egyptian constitutional system in 2007 and the following constitutions until present, there were rapid legislative and regulatory changes that permitted BOT/BOOT techniques and currently PPP legislation was promulgated in Egypt in 2010, Kuwait in 2014, Jordan in 2014, Morocco in 2014, Dubai in 2015, and Tunisia in 2015. It is worth noting that currently the Kingdom of Bahrain is preparing a very promising PPP draft law, which contains both procedural and substantive legislative frameworks for PPP techniques.

4. In the light of the economic and political approach of MENA countries' constitutions, the state role in PPP contracts is confined to its basic roles as a regulator or supervisor, with some exceptions to this basic rule. The state's basic function and role was illustrated by Adam Smith's theories.[2] The limits of state intervention to the contractual process is different from PPP contract to another as there is no fixed rule or principle but the rule is subject to the PPP contract and party autonomy. PPPs are considered a 'bespoke' pattern of contractual arrangements between a state and private partner which differs from contract to contract.

5. In the light of the economic and political approach of MENA countries' constitutions, the state intervention is confined to the minimum whether through mandatory rules in legislation or through regulations and policies. This approach in PPP techniques is consistent with the basic theories of Chicago School as a leading economist school.[3] State intervention in infrastructure projects and public utilities' management is limited compared with the same role of the state in traditional concessions and traditional administrative contracts.

6. The influence of the cultural and legal globalization is clear upon MENA countries' constitutions, legislation, regulatory frameworks, and contractual patterns. The influence of the Anglo-American jurisdictions upon MENA countries' legal systems which are civil law legal systems is significant. The French system was influenced by English law in adopting PPP techniques

2 Adam Smith, *The Wealth of Nations*, Wordsworth Classics of World Literature 2012.
3 Adam Smith, *The Wealth of Nations*, Wordsworth Classics of World Literature 2012.

and France issued the 2004 decree to regulate PPPs and in 2008 a new PPP law was promulgated in France for the same purpose. It is worth noting that MENA countries have been significantly influenced by the UK jurisdictions in PPP legislation, regulation, and contractual patterns.

7. The new substantive provisions in the PPP legislation in the MENA countries in addition to the new contractual provisions in the PPP contracts in the same countries represent a genuine innovation in state contracts in the MENA region. This genuine innovation reflects MENA states' new role as they relinquished their traditional role as an employer and become a regulator who tends to reduce states' intervention to the minimum in states' contracts. MENA states, while adopting PPP techniques, have liberalized the contractual process in state contracts from the traditional exorbitant clauses that exist in traditional concessions and in administrative contracts in general.

8. PPPs as new contractual techniques clearly represent new ideologies to be adopted in the field of liberalization and modernization of the concept of '*Le Contrat Administratif.*' Further, the new legislation in the MENA countries liberalizing public utilities' concessions such as PPPs and BOOT is of fundamental importance in this transitional period when administrative contracts' legal nature are changing to be commercial contracts or contracts of a *dual*/hybrid nature in the light of the new substantive clauses in PPP contracts.

9. States are still playing the role of supervisor, legislature, and regulator in the light of the increasing trend of liberalization of infrastructure and public utilities' projects. In the MENA countries, where culture is a dynamic value changing from one country to another and from time to time, governments represent the nation in managing and operating public utilities. This concept of representation of the nation by the governments exists in the MENA countries' constitutions and is clear in Tunisia's constitution. Thus, despite the flow of the Anglo-American legal culture to Arab countries, states still maintain their national identity by keeping some of their sovereignty through the administrative contract penalties that still exist, to some extent, despite the new legal nature of the PPP contracts.

10. It is of great significance to developing states when promulgating PPP legislation to treat these transactions as private and commercial transactions. The French Conseil d'État trend considering PPPs as administrative contracts is applicable in the French legal system where the surrounding culture and atmosphere are encouraging IFDI even if there are penalties in the PPP agreements. When considering the same situation in developing countries, the analogy seems difficult, particularly regarding states' unilateral powers upon exercising some exorbitant clauses such as *La Résiliation Administrative* to the contract by the state. These excessive powers exercised by developing states are dangerous to foreign investors, particularly when bureaucracy, corruption and, to some extent, *male fide* host state represent unpredictability to foreign investor when the state exercises its unilateral

230   *Conclusions*

powers. Thus, it is recommended for MENA countries when promulgating PPP legislation to liberalize the latter transactions from the '*Le Contrat Administratif*' stipulations and constraints as the French legal system trend may not be useful for developing states that are trying to increase IFDI in the field of infrastructure sectors and public utilities' services.

11. It is important to ensure that risk allocation and pricing are sufficiently attractive to international project financiers. Reduced oil revenues are not just impacting the government cashflows, but also local banks' capital reserves and, therefore, liquidity significantly. However, this does not mean that the government should pay more. Rather, it should have a greater focus on *value-for-money*. For example, the requirement to provide a performance bond for the life of any project does not provide *value-for-money* and is simply an added cost (approximately 1–2% of the capital costs of the project per annum) with no benefit to a genuine PPP, where the amount of any compensation on termination payable by the public authority typically only exceeds the performance bond value between years 18–20. During this period of time, the performance bond provides very little additional protection but comes at a significant cost. Instead, reliance on set-off rights would be a better *value-for-money* and more 'affordable' solution to the contracting parties.

12. PPP legislative and regulatory frameworks are fundamental pillars and determining factors in any legal system that can be described as incentives to attract and increase the inward of Foreign Direct Investments (FDI) on the legislative side and on the governmental policies' side. There is a direct link between the existence of an advanced PPP legislative and regulatory frameworks on one hand and the increase of the inward of FDI and the improvement of life of the ordinary citizens in Arab countries on the other.

13. Effective e-procurement can provide a wide variety of benefits including more efficiency and savings for governments and businesses. The potential cost savings are massive, as stated by the European Commission. In Italy alone, e-procurement systems cut over €3 billion in costs. An on-line bidding system does not fully exist in MENA countries; however, using technology in award procedures is growing as it is one of the tools of the current legal globalization phenomenon in MENA countries. It is suggested that using a fully automated system in on-line bidding is one of the guarantees to achieve best practices in award procedures particularly maintaining objectivity, integrity, and avoiding corruption.

14. The causality between the proper public procurement system on PPPs and the significant improvement of public services is clear as new technologies are subjected to achieve public interests through adopting new PPPs patterns. The new award evaluation criteria and innovation in award procedures in PPPs in the MENA countries are significant factors behind the improvement of public services and enhancing the life of ordinary citizens in MENA countries.

Conclusions 231

15. It is suggested that in PPP legislation in the MENA countries, award procedures should insist upon using technologies that are friendly to the environment. There is a significant progress in environment legislation and polices in the MENA region countries in recent decades and PPP techniques should be subjected to achieve MENA governments targets for environment protection.

16. The quality and effectiveness of the PPP procurement system in MENA countries is clear. The OECD MAPS are of special significance as, in most cases, PPP Arab legislation has implemented OECD principles in award procedures. An extensive review of the legislative and regulatory frameworks in MENA countries as well as World Bank Bench Marking Report on PPP Procurement 2017, was conducted to identify whether Arab legislation and regulations have implemented the internationally accepted good practices or not.

17. According to the OECD Recommendation of the Council on Public Procurement, Arab states should ensure that procurement officials meet high professional standards for knowledge, practical implementation and integrity by providing a dedicated and regularly updated set of tools, for example, sufficient staff in terms of numbers and skills, recognition of public procurement as a specific profession, certification and regular trainings, integrity standards for public procurement officials, and the existence of a unit or team analyzing public procurement information and monitoring the performance of the public procurement system.

18. A fundamental question arises regarding Articles 8 and 9 of the Kuwaiti PPP legislation of 2014: can executive regulations stipulate or impose new award procedures' rules that do not exist in the Kuwaiti PPP legislation of 2014? Is this a matter of unconstitutionality pursuant to the Kuwaiti constitution? Executive regulations may provide details, and procedures only within the legislative framework stipulated in the Kuwaiti PPP legislation. For instance: can executive regulations stipulate award evaluation criteria which is not existing in legislation? Can executive regulations add to the award evaluation criteria that are stipulated in the legislation?[4] The question of unconstitutionality remains unanswered!

19. PPP arbitration is one of the most important types of private-public arbitration. Harmonizing private-public arbitration and legislation constraints in MENA countries is a crucial question that arises in the international legal arena, particularly in PPP law and practice.

20. The legal globalization phenomenon is a fundamental factor behind the flow of the legal culture from Anglo-American jurisdictions into Egypt and Arab civil law legal systems, and the rise of private-public arbitration. Egyptian constitutions have not prohibited arbitration in principle but have

---

4 See M.A.E. Bana, *The Judicial Review Upon the Constitutionality of Regulations*, Dar El Nahdah El Arabia 1992.

232   *Conclusions*

stipulated certain legislative stipulations relating to judiciary exclusive jurisdiction. Egyptian constitutions, nowadays, are designed to promote positive
and effective participation of the private sector in economic life, which has
a direct impact on the increase and development of private-public arbitration. The constitutional amendments of 2007 in Egypt and currently all
MENA countries' constitutions did not adopt specific economic ideology.
This is a liberal trend that is consistent with the constitutions of many
developed nations. One may refer to the French experience, when President
Valéry Giscard d'Estaing adopted free market economy policies, and then
after a certain period and due to some domestic changes, President François
Mitterrand changed to socialist policies. Again, France is adopting free
market economy polices during the validity of the same constitution of
1958. In the USA, the economic policies adopted before the economic
crisis of 2008 are different from those adopted after the crisis during the
validity of the same constitution. It is clear that not only legislation affects
private-public arbitration but also polices directly affect private-public arbitration in Arab states and affect various contractual patterns. Further, they
directly affect inward of FDI to developing states. As a result, with regards
this vision, the 2014 constitution in Egypt has not adopted a static economic ideology, but it has adopted a dynamic ideology to promote, encourage and increase private-public arbitration. However, the same previous
constitutional provisions concerning jurisdiction of the Conseil d'État do
exist in the 2014 constitution (Article 190), in addition to the constitutional rights of litigation of each individual (Article 97). The right of litigation is not confined to courts, as the real interpretation to this right is that
any litigant may start either litigation or arbitration proceedings. Constitutional rights and principles in Egypt are not contrary to private-public arbitration, whether in previous constitutions or in the current constitution of
2014. Private-public arbitration is a form of justice. There was no explicit
prohibition to private-public arbitration in Egypt before 1997 but the various interpretations of the 1971 constitution and legislation created controversial views.

21. The French influence upon the Egyptian legal system in constitutional
    ideology is clear, as well as the influence on legislation and jurisprudence,
    particularly Article 2060 of the French civil code, which influenced Egyp-
    tian Conseil d'État decisions in private-public arbitration. Moreover, the
    Egyptian legislature in Law No. 9/1997, which stipulates the concerned
    minister's consent, was influenced by the general prohibition of private-
    public arbitration in Article 2060 of the French civil code. This prohibition
    as a general rule was transferred from Egypt to some MENA countries'
    arbitration legislation.

22. The minister's consent in Egypt and the prime minister's consent in Saudi
    Arabia and Qatar legislation are legislative stipulations to ensure that pri-
    vate-public arbitration as a governance mechanism does not compromise
    the public interests. However, it is suggested that the arbitral process needs

Conclusions 233

further liberalized steps, particularly if the consent of the administration is required to start arbitration. In practice, the state signs an arbitration clause with a foreign investor and afterwards, if a dispute arises, the administration refuses to grant consent. In some cases, in practice, states tend to withhold the process. The situation is difficult if the investor is not protected by a certain international instrument such as a Bilateral Investment Treaty (BIT). It is also suggested that legislative amendment is needed to ensure that the administration does not unreasonably withhold consent at the time of concluding the arbitration agreement. It is acceptable that the administration can withhold consent if the aim is to protect public interests; however, *mala fide* practice is a matter of judicial review by the Conseil d'État and MENA countries' courts. The Conseil d'État in Egypt, as a leading judicial power in the MENA region, is tasked with creating a sensible balance between safeguarding public interests on the one hand and protecting private liberties on the other. In practice, it was confirmed that the legislature in Article 1 of the Egyptian Arbitration Act has not provided a penalty through a legislative provision such as nullification of the arbitration clause, if either party to the dispute fails to obtain the consent of the minister.[5] In addition, pursuant to administrative law principles, the plaintiff must prove that the minister is *mala fide*.[6]

23. The concerned minister's consent as a legislative stipulation to start private-public arbitration in administrative contracts is not applicable to private companies in private-private arbitration, as the latter are not public juristic persons. The same vision applies to state-owned companies, as the latter are not public juristic persons in the Egyptian legal system; consequently, a party can start arbitration against a state-owned company without exercising the legislative requirement of the concerned minister's consent. In the Egyptian legal system, arbitration against state-owned companies is private-private arbitration and not private-public arbitration, as it is arbitration against a private juristic person and not a public juristic person. The same vision applies to private companies, whether state-owned or not, even if they are exercising a public function. This legal approach applies to state-owned companies in all MENA countries.

24. The administration's consent (whether the minister or the prime minister) is a legislative stipulation required for both domestic and international arbitrations. However, contract-based arbitration requires the administration's consent, whilst treaty-based arbitration does not require the administration's consent. The foreign investor is covered by an international instrument,

---

5 See the *ad-hoc* Aarbitration case enrolled under number 464/2006 at CRCICA, session 2 July 2006.

6 The Supreme Administrative Court, Appeal 1129/37judicial year, 15/2/1994, the Technical Bureau in the year (39) and the Supreme Administrative Court, Appeal 462/36 judicial year, 9 October 1994, Technical Bureau in the year (40).

234   *Conclusions*

such as the ICSID Convention and a BIT. An international instrument is part of MENA countries' legislation after ratification by parliament. If the host state has signed and ratified the 1965 ICSID convention, and a BIT, it cannot deny the ICSID tribunal's jurisdiction. There are no grounds for the host state to deny jurisdiction and to allege that there is no consent from the administration of the host state to start arbitration.

25. In the MENA countries' legal systems, it is illegal to consider an arbitration clause as null and void when there is no clear legislative provision stipulating expressly the nullity of the arbitration agreement. The national courts cannot consider a contractual provision as null and void without an explicit legislative provision. Further, the legislative stipulation for the administration to grant consent to start private-public arbitration in administrative contracts is addressed to the public juristic person to grant permission and not to the private person[7] to obtain the permission. Thus, in MENA arbitration acts that stipulate the necessity of the administration's consent to private-public arbitration, it is suggested to add a provision to these arbitration acts to provide that the arbitration clause is null and void if there is no consent granted from the administration. Otherwise, the arbitral award is not subject to challenge for the nullity of the arbitration clause.

26. Constitutional and legislative stipulations show that the threshold of protection granted to foreign investors in Egypt is greater than the protection granted to domestic investors. Consequently, foreign investors may rely on the ICSID Convention or a BIT to start private-public arbitration proceedings against a host state, while a domestic investor cannot start arbitration against the state or a public juristic person, without an arbitration agreement, as the domestic investor is not covered either by the ICSID Convention or a BIT. Thus, international private-public arbitration has great significance in this context. This high threshold of protection granted to foreign investors may raise constitutional concerns regarding the principle of equality before the law as a constitutional principle existing in the MENA constitutions.[8] The suggested approach to this problem is to include in the MENA investment laws a legislative provision that a domestic investor can recourse to domestic or international arbitration if the foreign investor has the option to recourse to arbitration and both domestic and foreign investors are on an equal legal position.

27. Rules and principles developed by arbitral tribunals in trans-border private-public arbitration, so-called *lex mercatoria publica*, constitute a proper legal system apart from domestic or international law. Those rules and principles

---

7 See the *ad-hoc* Aarbitration case enrolled under number 464/2006 at CRCICA, 2 July 2006.

8 The Constitution of Egypt 1971 (Article 40), and also the 2014 Constitution (Article 53). See in Arab countries for the constitution of the Kingdom of Bahrain (Article 18); the constitution of Kuwait (Article7); the constitution of Morocco, (Article 5); the constitution of Qatar (Article 35). All Arab constitutions contain similar provision for equality before the law.

developed by arbitral tribunals in international practice should be compatible with public law and public interests' constraints. Private-public arbitration in the MENA countries tries to achieve a balance between protecting public interests and providing a suitable threshold of protection to investors to increase the inflow of FDI to the MENA countries.

28. It is worth noting that setting up a dispute board at project agreement level is needed allowing the key sub-contractor(s), such as the design and build sub-contractor to attend meetings and make any relevant observations; but with no contractual compulsion under the sub-contract.

29. The use of standing dispute boards in PPPs, both concession and availability-based, would assist in the effective management of these projects and resolution of key friction points over their lifetime. The lifetime of the Dispute Board should extend beyond the design and construction phase to include the operational phase. Where it is not considered economic or practicable to have a board over the whole of the operational period, it is recommended to have the board in place as a minimum for the first five years of operations. Board members should have appropriate and relevant experience in PPP. Such experience could include, for example, knowledge and understanding of the PPP process and how it is funded. Experience and knowledge in the economic environment of the country and the sector or area of public services in question is also desirable.

30. It is important to refer to the fact that many Arab countries are underway to promulgate new PPPs legislation. The Kingdom of Bahrain is I the process of promulgating new PPP legislation to encourage the Inflow of Foreign Direct Investments (IFDI) to various economic sectors, and to subject PPP techniques to achieve the Sustainable Developments Goals towards the implementation of the 2030 economic vision of the Kingdom of Bahrain.

31. Unlike English common law jurisdictions, MENA countries' judicial systems do not follow judicial precedents. However, the Egyptian Conseil d'État has a coherent judicial precedents' system since 1946 issued and developed by the Appeal Administrative Court, the General Assembly for Legal Opinion and Legislation, and since 1955 by the Supreme Administrative Court. In practice, and as there is no written administrative law in the MENA countries until present, the Egyptian Conseil d'État lower courts rely on previous judgments issued by the higher courts at the Egyptian Conseil d'État. Legal departments rely on the principles established by the General Assembly for Legal Opinion and Legislation. The Egyptian Conseil d'État is the founder of the administrative law and administrative contracts' principles in the MENA countries. The Egyptian Conseil d'État decisions are considered the main source of administrative contracts in the region.

32. It is still controversial in some Arab countries whether PPP techniques in their current forms are administrative or commercial contracts. In the light of Article 1 of the promulgation articles of the Egyptian PPP legislation, PPP contracts are not subject to state procurement law, public utilities' concession law, and natural resources' concession law. Most of the substantive

236 *Conclusions*

clauses of the PPP contracts in their current form in MENA countries stipulte that the legal nature of PPP contracts is a private law commercial contract or at least of a *dual*/hybrid nature contract that is not at any circumstances an administrative contract. It is clear that PPP contracts in MENA countries, in the light of PPP legislation, are not traditional administrative contracts or traditional concessions. They have a new legal nature that is consistent with the pulse and dynamics of the new role of state in the MENA region and the increasing role of the private sector in economic life. PPP contracts have this legal nature due to the new substantive contractual clauses, new types of agreements, new contractual techniques, and new legislative steps to maintain financial equilibrium to protect foreign investors. Today, civil law legal systems and MENA countries have begun a new era in the field of states' infrastructure projects and public utilities' services in the light of these new contractual mechanisms, which are a result of the legal globalization phenomenon.

33. It is worth noting that a 'bespoke' form of contracts is required to be prepared by MENA governments as a template containing main contractual clauses and not all contractual clauses open the door for party autonomy of the contracting parties and enable them to express their contractual rights.

References

Abdel Azim, Dr Abdessalaam Hameed, 1989. *The Effect of the Prince Theory on the Performance of Administrative Contracts.* N.p.

Abdel Badie, Dr Mohamed Salah, 1993. The Power of the Authority to Terminate Administrative Contract. PhD, Faculty of Law, Ain Shams University, Cairo.

Abdel Baki, Abdel Fatah, 1984. *The Encyclopedia of Egyptian Civil Law, Contract and Unilateral Acts Theory, a Comparative Study with Islamic Doctrine.* N.p.

Abdel Kader, Nariman, 1996. *Arbitration Agreement Pursuant to Arbitration Act No. 27 of 1994.* Cairo: Dar El Nahda El Arabia.

Abdel Latif, Abla, 1990. *The Assignment Theory in Administrative Law.* N.p.

Abdelbaqy, A., 1984. Encyclopedia of Egyptian Civil Law – Theory of Contract and Unilateral Will, an In-depth and Comparative Study on Islamic jurisprudence.

Abdel-Qader, N., 1996. *Arbitration Agreement under the Arbitration Law 27/1994,* 1st edn.

Abdelwahab, Mohamed Salah, 2005. *Globalization Influence upon Various Areas of Law, Cultural Globalization and Public Policy: Exclusion of Foreign Law in the Global Village,* Law and Sociology, 8 edn. Oxford: Oxford University Press.

Abdel-Wahab, Mohamed Salah, 2006. *Cultural Globalization and Public Policy: Exclusion of Foreign Law in the Global Village,* Law and Sociology, 8 edn. Michael Freeman. Oxford: Oxford University Press.

Abul'enein, M.M., 1987. *Legislative Deviation and the Oversight on Its Constitutionality.*

Akitoby, Bernardin, Hemming, Richard and Schwartz, Gerd, 2007. *Public Investment and Public-Private Partnerships.* Washington, DC: International Monetary Fund.

Al Bana, Atef, 1984. *Administrative Contracts.* N.p.

Al Bana, Atef, 1992. *El Wassit in Administrative Law.* Cairo: N.p.

Al Sharkawi, Soad, 1993. *Constitution Liberalization and the Egyptian Constitution of 1971.* Cairo: Dar Al Nahda Al Arabia.

Al Tamawy, Soliman, 1991. *The General Principles of Administrative Contracts,* 5th edn. N.p.

Al-Sawy, A., 2010. *Al Wagiz in Arbitration,* 3rd edn. N.p.

Al-Sharqawy, A.M., 1950. *Civil and Commercial Procedures Law.* N.p.

Al-Tehewi, M., 1994. Arbitration Agreement and Its Rules in Arbitration Law and Civil Procedures Law. PhD thesis, Cairo University.

Al-Sanhoury, A.-R., 1989. *Al-Waseet of the Civil code, Part VII, Work and Employment Contracts,* 2nd edn, vol. 1. N.p.

Amin, M.S., 1992. A Brief Study on the Notion of Administrative Contracts and the Provisions of Their Conclusion.

238 References

Arrowsmith, S., 2014. *The Law of Public and Utilities Procurement*, 3rd edn, vol. 1. London: Sweet and Maxwell, 597–604.

Auby, Jean-Marie and Bon, Pierre, 1995a. *Droit administratif des biens*, 5eme edn. Paris: Dalloz.

Auby, J.-P. and Bon, P., 1955b. *Droit administratif des biens*, 3rd edn. Paris: Dalloz.

Badawi, Sarwat, 1954. *Le Fait du prince dans les contrats administratifs*. Paris: L.G.D.J.

Badawi, Sarwat, 1994. *The General Theory of Administrative Law*, 5th edn. Cairo: Dar El Nahda El Arabia.

Badawi, Sarwat, 2007. *Hierarchies of Administrative Decrees and the Illegality Principle*. Cairo: Dar El Nahda El Arabia.

Badawy, Sarwat, 1985. *Administrative Law*. Cairo: Dar El Nahda El Arabia.

Badawy, Sarwat, 1991. *General Theory of Administrative Contracts*. Cairo: Dar El Nahda El Arabia.

Badawy, Sarwat, 1994. *General Theory of Administrative Contracts*. Cairo: Dar El Nahda El Arabia.

Badran, Mohamed, n.d. ADR for Administrative Dispute in Egyptian Administrative Law. Unpublished paper.

Bana, M.A.E., 1992. *The Judicial Review upon the Constitutionality of Regulations*. Cairo: Dar El Nahdah El Arabia.

Barral, Welber and Haas, Adam, 2007. Public-Private Partnership (PPP) in Brazil. *The International Lawyer (Fall), Int'l Law*, 41, 957.

Bateson, David, 1997. New China BOOT Regulations. ICLR, 14, Part I.

Beale, Hugh, 2008. *Chitty on Contracts*, 30th edn. London: Sweet and Maxwell.

Bererri, M., 1995. *International Commercial Arbitration*. Cairo: Darul Nahda Al-Arabia.

Blackaby, N., Partasides, C., Redfern, A. and Hunter, M., 2009. *International Arbitration*, 5th edn. Oxford: Oxford University Press and 6th edn, Oxford University Press 2014.

Born, G., 2012. *International Arbitration*. London and The Netherlands: Kluwer Law International.

Born, G., 2013. *International Arbitration and Forum Selection Agreements*, 4th edn. London and The Netherlands: Kluwer Law International.

Born, G., 2014. *International Commercial Arbitration*, 2nd edn. London and The Netherlands: Kluwer Law International.

Bovis, Christopher, 2006. *EC Public Procurement: Case Law and Regulation*. Oxford University Press.

Brard, Yves, 1985. *Droit administrative des biens et de la fonction publique*. Paris: Presses Universitaires de France.

Brard, Yves, 1994 [1985]. *Droit administratif des biens et de la fonction publique*. Paris: Dalloz [1er edn: Unive].

Brekoulakis, Stavros and Devaney, Margaret, 2017. Public-Private Arbitration and the Public Interest under English Law. *Modern Law Review, M.L.R.*, 80(1), 22–56.

Bruner, Phillipe Lane, 1995. Force Majeure under International Law and International Construction Contract Model Forms. Vol. 12 (April), ICLR.

Budina, Nina, Brixi, Hana Polackova and Irwin, Timothy, 2007. Public-Private Partnerships, in the New EU Member States, Managing Fiscal Risks. The World Bank Working Paper No. 114.

Bull, Benedicte and McNeill, Desmond, 2006. *Development Issues in Global governance, Public–Private Partnerships* and *Market Multilateralism*. London: Routledge.

Bunni, Nael G., 1997a. *The FIDIC Forms of Contract*, 2nd edn. Oxford: Blackwell.

Bunni, Nael G., 1997b. *The FIDIC Form of Contracts*, 2nd edn. Oxford: Blackwell.

Bunni, Nael G., 2005. *The FIDIC Forms of Contract*, 3rd edn. Oxford: Blackwell.

Cartlidge, Duncan, 2006. *Public Private Partnerships in Construction*. London: Taylor & Francis.

Ceruti, Marco, 2017. Sustainable Development and Smart Technological Innovation within PPPs: The Strategic Use of Public Procurement. *European Procurement & Public Private Partnership Law Review*, E.P.P.P.L.R., 12(2), 183–191.

Chabanol, Daniel and Jouquelet, Jean-Pierre, 1994. *Marches publics de travaux*, 2nd edn. Paris: Editions du Moniteur.

Chapus, R., *Droit Administratif Général*, 8 edn, vol. 2. Paris: Montchrestien.

Chapus, Rene, 1995. *Droit Administrative General*, 5eme edn, tome 2. Paris: Montchrestien.

Chen, John C., 1995. Force Majeure in Construction Contracts, Taiwan. ICLR, Part 2 (April).

Clérment, Jacques and Richer, Daniel, 1989. *Les Marches publics de travaux des collectivites territoriales*, 2nd edn. Paris: Economica.

Clément, Jacques and Richer, Daniel, 1993. *Les Marchés publics de travaux des collectivités Territoriales*, 2nd edn. Paris: Economica.

Cook, Jacques, 2008. Contract Format and Contract Drafting/Financing. Modern Enhancements for PPP Concession Agreements. *The Construction Lawyer*, 24(Fall).

Craig, Laurence, Park, William W. and Paulsson, Jan, 1985. *International Chamber of Commerce Arbitration*. Paris: ICC Publishing.

Craig, W.L., Park, W.W. and Paulsson, J., 2000. *International Chamber of Commerce Arbitration*, 3rd edn. New York: Oceana Publications.

Creed, Adrian, 2016. N Dubai's New PPP Law. *Construction Law Journal, Const. L. J.*, 32(7), 808–810.

Davidson, Nestor M. and Malloy, Robin Paul (eds), 2009. *Affordable Housing and Public–Private Partnerships*. Farnham: Ashgate.

de Barros, Monteira and Vidigal, Cecilia, 2009. PPPs in Brazil. *Informa; International Construction Law Review*, 26(Part 2), 180–181.

De Cazalet, Bruno, 2017. The Expected Benefit of CIS PPP Model Law. *International Business Law Journal, I.B.L.J.*, 2, 97–114.

De Laubadere, Andre, Moderne, Franck and Delvolve, Pierre, 1983. *Traité de contrats administratifs*, 2nd edn, vol. 1. Paris: L.G.D.J.

De Laubadere, Andre, Moderne, Franck and Delvolve, Pierre, 1983–1984. *Traite des contrats administratifs*, 2eme edn, 2 tomes. Paris: L.G.DJ.

de Laubadère, A., Venezia, J.-C. and Gaudemet, Y., *Traité de droit administratif*, 10th edn, tome 2. Paris: Librairie Générale de Droit et de Jurisprudence.

De Richoufftz, Philippe, 2015. The Moroccan PPP Contract. *International Business Law Journal, I.B.L.J.*, 5, 389–398.

Dolzer, R. and Schreuer, C., 2008. *Principles of International Investment Law*. Oxford: Oxford University Press and 2nd edn, OUP 2012.

Dufau, Jean, 1988a. *Le droit des travaux publics*, tome 1. Paris: Editions du Moniteur.

Dufau, Jean, 1988b. *Le droit des travaux publics*, tome 1. Paris: Editions du Moniteur.

Duguit, Le"on 1927. Trait£ de droit constitutionnel, 8 tomes. Paris: Cujas.

Eerily, Mokhtar, 1995. *International Commercial Arbitration*. Cairo: N.p.

240 References

Egyptian Conseil d'Etat, 1996. Administrative Contracts by the Egyptian State Council in 40 Years: Collection of Supreme Administrative Court Judgments and Legal Opinions from the General Assembly for Legal Opinion (Fatwa) and Legislation.

Egyptian Ministry of Finance, 2009. Update on the National Program for Public Private partnership, PPP Central Unit. June: 6. See: www.mof.gov.eg (accessed 31 July 2010).

El Attar, F., 1955. Les Marches de travaux publics. Thesis, Paris.

El Howeidy, El Sallal Gom'a, 1994. The Power of the Authority to Terminate Unilaterally the Administrative Contract. Masters thesis, Tanta University, Egypt.

El Sanhoury, Abdel Razek, 1984. The *General Theory of obligations, Part 3: Expiry of Obligations*, N.p.

El Tamawy, Soliman, 1966. *The General Theory of Administrative Decrees*, 3rd edn. N.p.

El'oyoony, T., 1987. The Criterion of an Administrative Contract. PhD thesis, Ain Shams University.

Elgamal, H.A., 1979. Legal System for the Sanctions in Public Construction Contracts. PhD thesis, Ein Shams University.

Elhelw, M.R., 1994. *Administrative Law*. N.p.

El-Kholy, A., 1993. The Engineer's Unique Dual role, Recent Development in Arab Law. Paper presented at the conference on the latest development in international construction contracts, Cairo, CRCICA, April.

Elsharqawy, S., 1995. *Administrative Contracts*. Cairo: Dar El Nahda El Arabia.

Fahmy, O.H., 1993. *General Provisions of Administrative Contracts*. N.p.

Fayyad, Abdel Meguid, 1974. *The Theory of Penaltiesin Administrative Contracts. Faculty of Law*. Cairo: Ain Shams University.

Fekry, Fathy, 1994. *Lectures on Administrative Contracts*. N.p.

Fiszbein, Ariel and Lowden, Pamela, 1999. *Working Together for a Change, Government, Business, and Civil Partnerships for Poverty Reduction in Latin America and the Caribbean*. Washington, DC: The World Bank.

Fouchard, Philippe, Gaillard, Emmanuel and Goldman, Berthold, 1999. *Traite" de l'arbitrage commercial international*. Paris: Litec.

Ga'afar, M.A.Q., 1985. *A Guide to Public Law. Principles and Sources of Administrative Law*. Cairo: Dar El Nahda El Arabia.

Ga'far, Anas, 1995. *The Theory of Unforeseen Physical Difficulties in Civil Works contracting, a Study of the Key Economic and Legal Aspects*. Cairo: Shalakany Law Firm Publications.

Gad Nassar, Gaber, 2002. *BOOT Agreements and the Modernization of Concession agreements, a Criticism to the Traditional Theory of Concession Agreements*. Cairo: Dar El Nahda El Arabia.

Hamilton, Geoffrey, 2009. FDI, the Global Crisis and Sustainable Recovery. Working Paper for Public Private Partnerships and FDI as a Means of Securing a Sustainable Recovery. Paper submitted to the Fourth Columbia International Investment Conference, Vale Columbia Center, Columbia Law School, 5-6 November. New York; Columbia University.

Hanafi, Said and El Dardiry, Khaled, 2010. PPPs in Egypt. ICLR, 27, Part 4 (October).

Hani Arafat Subhi Hamdan, Legal System for Public-Private Partnership Contracts, Comparative study, Dar Al Nahda Al arabia, 2016–2017 (in Arabic).

Hani Sarie El Din, 2002. Legal and Contractual Regime for BOOT, El Ahram El Eqtisadi book, No. 177.

References 241

Hani Sarie El Dine, 2001. *Legal and Contractual Arrangements for Infrastructure Projects Financed by Private Sector.* Cairo: Dar El Nahda El Arabia.

Harper, Malcolm, 2000. *Public Services through Private Enterprise.* London: Intermediate Technology Publications.

Hartlev, K. and Liljenbol, M.W., 2013. Changes to Existing Contracts under the EU Public Procurement Rules and the Drafting of Review Clauses to Avoid the Need for a New Tender. *P.P.L.R.*, 22, 51–73.

Helmy, O., 1993. Criterion for Distinguishing Administrative Contracts.

Helmy Fahmy, Omar, 1993. *Effects of Administrative Contract.* N.p.

Indraratna, A.D.V. de S. and Ranasinghe, Athula, 2006. *Public-Private Sector Partnership in Economic Development: A Case for Sri Lanka.* Colombo: Sri Lanka Economic Association.

The International Bank for Reconstruction and Development, 2009. *The World Bank, Attracting Investors to, African Public-Private Partnerships, A Project Preparation Guide.* Washington, DC.

Ismail, Mohamed A.M., 1996. Appointing the Arbitral Tribunal in Multi-Party Arbitration. Paper presented to the Conference on Arbitration in FIDIC Agreements held by CRCTCA in May 1996 at Nile Hilton Hotel, Cairo.

Ismail, Mohamed A.M., 2003. *International Public Works Agreements Arbitration.* Beirut: El Halabi Publishing (in Arabic).

Ismail, Mohamed A.M., 2009. Globalization and Liquidated Damages in the International Public Works Agreements, an Analytical Perspective for the Penalty of Delay Clause in Infrastructure Agreements. *International Construction Law Review*, 26(Part 4), 506–518. Informa.

Ismail, Mohamed A.M., 2010a. Globalization and Contract Price in International Public Works Agreements in the Egyptian State Procurement Law: New Trends. *The International Construction Law Review*, 27, Part 1, January, Informa.

Ismail, Mohamed A.M., 2010b. Globalization and Contractual Regime in International Public Works Agreements in Egypt. *ICLR*, 27, Part III, July, Informa.

Ismail, Mohamed A.M., 2010c. Legal Globalization and PPPs in Egypt: An Analytical and Comparative Perspective on the Current Legislative and Judicial Modifications to and Enhancements of the Administrative Contractual Regime on PPP Transactions. *The European Public Private Partnership Law Review*, 1, (March), Berlin, Lexxion.

Ismail, Mohamed A.M., 2010d. *Public Economic Law and the New International Administrative Contract.* Beirut: El Halabi Publishing (in Arabic).

Ismail, Mohamed A.M., 2011. *Globalization and New International Public Works Agreements in Developing Countries: An Analytical Perspective.* Abingdon: Routledge [Ashgate Publishing].

Ismail, Mohamed A.M., 2013. *International Investment Arbitration, Lessons from Developments in the MENA Region.* Abingdon: Routledge [Ashgate Publishing].

Ismail, Mohamed A.M., Innovation in Public Procurements in the Egyptian PPP Legislation (With Reference to PPP Legislation in Dubai and Kuwait). Public contracting and Innovation, Lessons across borders, Gabriella M. Racca, Christopher R. Yukins, 2019, Bruylant, 567.

Jarrosson, Charles, 1987. *La Notion d'arbitrage.* Paris: L.G.D.J.

Jarvin, S. and Derains, Y., 1990a. *Collection of ICC Arbitral Awards 1974–1985.* London and The Netherlands: ICC Publishing/Kluwer.

Jarvin, Sigvard and Derains, Yves, 1990b. *Collection of ICC Arbitral awards, 1974–1985.* London and The Netherlands: Kluwer Law International.

242 References

Jarvin, Sigvard, Derains, Yves and Arnaldez, Jean-Jacques, 1994. *Collection of ICC Arbitral Awards 1986–1990*. London and The Netherlands: Kluwer Law International.

Jones, Douglas, 1995. Force Majeure in Australian Construction Law. ICLR. Part 2 (April).

Kadiki, Khaled, 1979. Contrats internationaux de travaux publics et de developpement en Liby, tome 1. Thesis, Dijon.

Kamel Leila, Mohamed, 1969. *Principles of Administrative Law*. N.p.

Leboulonger, Philippe, 1985. *Les contrats entre etats et entreprises privees etrangers*. Paris: Economica.

Mahmoud, M.M., 1993. Administrative Contracts and International Arbitration Clause. *Administrative Sciences Journal*, 35.

Mazin, Antoine, 2017. Dealing with Political Risk in PPP Infrastructure Projects: Legal Recommendations Based on Recent Cases. *International Business Law Journal, I.B.L.J.*, 3, 189–202.

McKendrick, Ewan, 1995. *Force Majeure and Frustration of Contract*, 2nd edn. London: Informa.

Mert, Ayşem and Pattberg, Philipp, 2018. How Do Climate Change and Energy-Related Partnerships Impact Innovation and Technology Transfer? Some Lessons for the Implementation of the UN Sustainable Development Goals. In *The Cambridge Handbook of Public-Private partnerships, Intellectual Property Governence, and Sustainble Development*, ed. Margaret Chon, Pedro Roffe and Ahmed Abdel-Latif. Cambridge: Cambridge University Press: 289–305.

Mistelis, Loukas and Kioll, Stefan, 2003. *Comparative International Commercial Arbitration*. London: Kluwer Law International.

Mohamed, Said Amin, 1991. *General Principles for the Performance of Administrative Contracts*. Cairo: N.p.

Mohmoud, R., 2007. *Participation Agreements, (PPP)*. Cairo: Dar El Nahda El Arabia.

Morand-Deviller, J., *Cours de Droit Adminstratif*, 4th edn. Paris: Montchrestien.

OECD, Public-Private Partnerships in the Middle East and North Africa. Private Sector Development Handbook, A Handbook for Policy Makers, OECD Publications.

Panadès-Estruch, Laura, 2019. Assessing Public-private Partnership Law and Regulation in the Cayman Islands: Opening Gateways or Closing Loopholes? *Public Procurement Law Review, P.P.L.R.*, 3, 108–119.

Poulsen, S.T., 2012. The Possibilities of Amending a Public Contract without a New Competitive Tendering Procedure under EU Law. *P.P.L.R.*, 21, 167–187.

PPPs and ISDS, A Risky Combination, Brooke Guven, Legal Researcher at the Columbia Center on Sustainable Investment (CCSI) and Lise Johnson, Head, Investment Law and Policy at CCSI, posted on 24 May, 2018.

Rashed, Samia, 1984. *Arbitration Agreement*, vol. I. Cairo: N.p.

Raslaan, Anwar Ahmed, 1994. *Administrative Law*. Cairo: Dar El Nahda El Arabia.

Raslan, Anwar Ahmed, 1980 [1948]. The Theory of Unforeseen Physical Difficulties. *Journal of Law and Economy*, 3 and 4, 1980.

Raslan, Anwar Ahmed, 1994. *Administrative Law*. N.p.

Redfern, Alan and Hunter, Martin, 1991. *International Commercial Arbitration*, 2nd edn. London: Sweet and Maxwell.

Redfern, Allan and Hunter, Martin, 1999. *International Commercial Arbitration*, 3rd edn. London: Sweet and Maxwell.

Redfern, Alan and Hunter, Martin, 2004. *Law and Practice of International Commercial Arbitration*, 4th edn. London: Sweet and Maxwell.

Redfern, Alan, Hunter, Martin, Blackaby, Nigel and Partasides, Constantine, 2009. *Redfern and Hunter on International Arbitration*, 5th edn. Oxford: Oxford University Press and OUP, 6th edn, 2014.

Richer, Lauent, 1991. *Les Contrats Administratifs*. Paris: Dalloz.

Richer, Lauent, 1995a. *Droit des Contrats Administratifs*. Paris: L.G.D.J.

Richer, Lauent, 1995b. *Droit des Contrats Administratifs*. Paris: L.G.D.J.

Richer, Laurent, 2019. *Droit des Contrats Administratife*, 11th edn. Paris: L.G.D.J.

Rivero, J. and Waline, J., 1994. *Droit Administratif*, 15th edn. Paris: Dalloz.

Sachs, Jeffrey D., 2005. *The End of Poverty*. London: Penguin Books.

Sachs, Jeffrey D., 2008. *Common Wealth*. London: Penguin Books.

Sadeq, H., *Law Applicable to International Commercial Contracts*. N. p.

Said, Aly, 2006. *Principle of Not Executing Contract*. N.p.

Sarie Eldin, Hani, 1996. *Consortia Agreements in the International Construction Industry*. London: Kluwer Law International.

Sarie-Eldin, Hani, 2001. *The Legal and Contractual Regime for Infrastructure Projects Financed by the Private Sector*. Cairo: Dar Al Nahda Al Arabia (in Arabic).

Sauvant, Karl P., 2008. The FDI Recession Has Begun. Columbia FDI Perspectives, No. 1, 22 (November). Vale Columbia Center on Sustainable International Investment, Columbia University.

Shaaban, Ahmed Ramadan, 2016. *Negotiations to Conclude Public-Private Partnership Contract and Responsibility Resulting from the Breach of It in the Egyptian Legal System*. Dar Al Nahda Al Arabia (in Arabic).

Smith, Katie, 2019. A Risk Worth Taking? Practical Application of the Law on Contract Modifications in the Context of PPP Accommodation Projects. *Public Procurement Law Review, P.P.L.R.*, 1, 16–25.

Snowdon, B., 2007. *Globalisation, Development and Transition*. Cheltenham: Edward Elgar.

Southard, Katharine, 2010. U.S. Electric Utilities: The First Public-Private Partnerships? *Cont. L.J.*, 395(Winter), 395–410.

Stanley, Jeremiah, 1995. Insurability of Force Majeure Events in Construction Contracts. ICLR, Part 2 (April).

Stein, Stephen, 1994. Build, Operate, Transfer (BOT) -A Re-Evaluation. ICLR II, Part II.

Stiglitz, J.E., 2004. *Globalization and Its Discontents*. New York: W.W. Norton & Company.

Stiglitz, Joseph, 2007. *Making Globalization Work*. New York: W.W. Norton & Company.

Sugg, J., 2008. Interim Relief and International Commercial Arbitration in North Carolina: Where We are and Where We Should Be Looking. *Campbell Law Review*, 30, 389.

Treitel, G.H., 1988. *Remedies for Breach of Contract: A Comparative Account*. Oxford: Clarendon Press.

Treitel, G.H., 1994. *Frustration and Force Majeure*. London: Sweet and Maxwell.

United Nations Economic Commission for Europe, 2008. Guidebook on Promoting Good Governance in Public-Private Partnership.

Vadi, V., 2013. *Cultural Heritage in International Investment Law and Arbitration*. Cambridge: Cambridge University Press.

244 References

Vedel, G. and Delvolvé, P., 1992. *Droit Administratif*, 12th edn. Paris: Presses Universitaires de France.

Venezia, Jean-Claude and Gaudement, Yves, 1995. *Traité de droit administratif*, 10th edn. Paris: L.G.DJ.

Villa, Leonardo and Duarte, Jesus, 2005. Concessionary Public Schools in BOGOTA: An Innovation in School Management in Colombia. In *Private Education and Public Policy in Latin America*, ed. Laurence Wolff, Juan Carlos Navarro and Pablo Gonzalez. Washington, D.C.: Preal.

Westring Arlandabonan, Gosta, 1997. Swedish Experiment in Selecting a BOT Contractor Using Public Procedures. ICLR 14, Part I.

Wiwatpattarakul, Pronchai, n.d. A Critical Examination of the Concept of Force Majeure at Thai Law and Its Impact in the Context of Construction Contracts. ICLR 1.

Yehia, A.W., 1987. *Obligation Stipulations at Egyptian Civil Law*. Cairo: Dar El Nahda El Arabia.

Yossry, A., 1991. *Provisions of the Principles in French Administrative Judiciary*. Alexandria: Monsha'at El Mareef.

Youssef, Sharif, 2017. The New Regulatory Framework for PPPs in Egypt: A Pro Investment Step? *International Construction Law Review, I.C.L. Rev.*, 34(4), 406–429 (overnance, and).

Zapatrina, Irina, 2016. Sustainable Development Goals for Developing Economies and Public-Private Partnership. *European Procurement & Public Private Partnership Law Review, E.P.P.P.L.R.*, 11(1), 39–45.

Zatezalo-Falator, Milica, 2010. Public Private Partnerships in France, State Guarantees Support the Congested Pipeline. *Columbia Journal of International Law*. (Spring). Available at: www.cjel.net/online/16_l-zatezalofalatar/ (accessed 31 July 2011). LexisNexis.

Index

absolute justice 195
accountability 11, 108, 137, 138, 157
accountancy practices 14
adaptability 177
Administrative Contract (*Le Contrat Administratif*): arbitration 219n54; and BOOT transactions 79; conclusions on 229–230; constitutional frameworks 33, 35; definition 26; and legal globalization ix, x–xi; principles in MENA countries 57–76; substantive mechanisms 159, 160, 161; substantive theory of states' contracts 39–56
administrative contracts: arbitration 204, 207n9, 210–212, 217, 218, 223–224, 226; conclusions on 228, 229, 235–236; international dynamics of PPPs 145; substantive mechanisms 181, 193; substantive theory of states' contracts 39–56
Administrative Judiciary Court, Egypt 49n21, 53–54
administrative supply contracts 48–50, 53, 54
advertisements of projects 111, 113, 115, 116, 117, 124, 125, 130
ADWEA IWPP 21, 121
affordability benchmarks 15
African Development Bank 103
airports and civil aviation 3, 73–74, 78, 79
Alexandria Water Company 46
Algayerova, Olga 143
Algeria 25, 31, 32, 33, 104–105
amendments of contract 51, 90–91, 113, 120, 127, 158–202
amiable compositeur 203, 222, 225–226
Anglo-American legal culture 35, 229, 231
Appeal Administrative Court (Egypt): administrative contracts 39, 42, 48–49,

54–55, 57, 60, 75; concession contracts 65, 66, 68–69
Arab Spring x, 108
arbitration: administrative contracts 11n30; Egypt 27; international arbitral awards 185–187; Kuwait 86, 88; legal globalization 35; Morocco 127; substantive mechanisms 160, 174, 175, 203–226, 231–235
Argentina 36
asset disposals 83–84
asset ownership 164
asset security 91, 102, 162, 167
asset transfers 168, 176, 180
assignment of PPP contracts 85, 167
auctions 85
audit 83, 96
austerity 14
Australia 12–13
availability fees 7
availability-based PPPs 7–8, 177, 178, 179–180
Awqaf and *Al-Ahram* case 210–211

bad faith 59, 229
Bahrain: bidding processes 109n10; constitutional frameworks 31, 32, 37; development of PPP 19, 21, 105, 161, 228, 235
bank prudential regulations 3
bargaining power, inequality of 35, 50, 55, 62, 75, 145
benchmarking 15
Benchmarking PPPs Procurement Report (World Bank) xi, 3n8, 5n18, 77n1, 92n28, 108, 124, 152, 153–154, 231
bespoke contracts 181, 228, 236
bid bonds 119, 120n47, 123, 134, 165

246 *Index*

bid evaluation: Dubai 123; Egypt 110, 111, 112–113; international standards 153, 230; Jordan 129–131, 132; Kuwait 91, 114, 116–121; Morocco 125; *see also* procurement processes
bidding processes 82, 109–110; *see also* tendering processes
bilateral investment treaties (BITs) 222n59, 233, 234
Birmingham 136
blended finance 7
BOOT (Build, Own, Operate and Transfer) 73–74, 78, 79, 80, 229
BOT (Build, Operate and Transfer) ix, 38, 78, 89
BOT/BOOT (Build, Operate, Transfer/ Build, Own, Operate and Transfer) 31, 33, 37, 79–80, 222, 223–224, 228
Brazil 33, 35–36
breach of contract 10, 173, 181–182; *see also* arbitration
bribery 137; *see also* corruption
British colonies 24–25
Bull, Benedicte 2n4

Cairo Court of Appeal 215
Cairo Regional Centre for International Commercial Arbitration (CRCICA) 214
Cambridge Economic Policy Associates (CEPA) 12
Canada 137, 155
cancellation of tender process 133
capacity building 11, 85
cassation courts 182
causality links (*lien de causalité*) 181–182, 183
change of circumstances '*l'imprevision*' *see* unforeseen circumstances ('*l'imprevision*')
Chicago School xi, 3–4, 34, 35, 77, 104, 227
circular economy 135–137
city-level partnerships 136
civil codes: and administrative contracts 41–44, 46, 47; arbitration 210, 212; conclusions on 232; *force majeure* 182, 184; history of 25, 26; traditional concession contracts 72–73; unforeseen circumstances 182, 184, 193–194
civil contracts 51–54, 55, 68
civil courts 27, 48, 49, 50, 208, 212, 217
civil law ix, 27, 33–38, 57n1, 68, 72, 145, 152
climate change 10, 136n68, 148, 150

collaborative cultures 178
commercial contracts 51–54, 68, 79n5, 235
commercial courts 48, 49, 50, 208, 212
Commission de Partenariat Public-Privé (Morocco) 102–103
common law systems 27, 35n20, 36, 60, 152
compensation payments: arbitration 220–221; difficulty of performing obligation 187–193; Kuwait 91; Morocco 126; Prince Theory 191, 192; substantive mechanisms 163, 170, 174, 183, 188–193; termination of contract rights 230; unforeseen circumstances 194–198; unforeseen physical difficulties 198–200
Competition Committee (Kuwait) 95, 114, 115, 117, 120
competitive dialogue 110, 126, 154–155
competitive tender processes 13, 15; *see also* tendering processes
competitiveness: and confidentiality 110–111, 124; dialogue processes 110, 126, 154–155; direct contracting (without tendering) 123–124; international standards 153; as justification for PPPs 3, 4; Kuwait 114; limitations on freedom of competitor projects 63; monopolies 63, 68, 71; procurement processes 106; in sole bidder situations 120, 133, 153, 156–157; and value for money evaluations 18
concept proposals 114–115
concession contracts: Administrative Contract Theory 62–63, 65; administrative contracts 46, 48, 49, 50–51, 54; conclusions on 235–236; Egypt 46, 48, 49, 50–51, 54, 78–79, 80, 81; identifiable risks 178, 179–180, 181; Public Utilities' Concession Contract 65–66; state role 228; substantive mechanisms 158, 159–160; traditional concession contracts 65–70
concession PPPs 8–9, 10, 47, 179
conciliation procedures 127, 175, 225
confidentiality 110, 111, 124, 132, 166
Conseil d'État, Egyptian: administrative contracts 41–42, 45, 47–51, 53–54, 57; arbitration 205–221, 223, 232, 233–234; constitutional frameworks 30, 31; establishment of 46; excessive clauses (*clauses exorbitantes*) 60, 63–64; *force*

majeure 184–185; history of 26, 27; influence on all MENA countries 57; judicial precedent 235; judicial review role 37; on pre-qualification committees 112; Prince Theory 191, 193; traditional concession contracts 66, 70n33; unforseen circumstances 194, 196, 198; unforseen physical difficulties 199

consortia 91, 112, 130, 131, 132

constitutional frameworks 29–38, 69–70, 73, 78, 105, 156, 228, 229, 232

continuity 2, 73, 100, 111, 127, 129, 163, 183, 201–202, 227

contract law (private law) 41–42

contract price 159–161, 190, 192, 193, 197, 200, 230

contract templates 94, 236

contractual clauses 66–67, 74, 80

corruption 4, 11, 137–138, 143, 151, 229, 230

cost-benefit analyses 14, 128

counter-parties 173

cultural globalization viii–ix, 25, 27, 28, 33, 34–35, 155, 204, 228–229; *see also* legal globalization

currency fluctuations 141, 161, 190, 196, 197

De Laubadere, Professor 192

Deauville Partnership Transition Fund 103–104

debt, grace periods 44

default 10, 44, 50

demand risk 2, 6, 227

deposit forfeiture 35

desalination 89n18

destabilization of the contract's economies 193–198

development agencies 7

dialogue processes 110, 126, 154–155

digital economy 142; *see also* e-procurement

direct contracting (without tendering) 123–124, 157

direct joint management of the public service 64–65

Direction générale des partenariats public-privé (DGPPP), Tunisia 103–104

discretion 43, 45

discrimination 4, 107, 126, 139, 147

Dispute Boards 222, 235

disputes: administrative contracts 48, 49, 53, 55, 56; Appeal Administrative Court (Egypt) 48, 49; availability-based PPP 8;

constitutional frameworks 30; contractual obligations 163; dispute resolution processes 13, 174–175, 203–226; Dubai 127; excessive clauses (*clauses exorbitantes*) 63–64; investment policy-making 139; Kuwait 86, 88; main substantive mechanisms of PPP contracts in MENA countries 174–175; traditional concession contracts 67, 72; *see also* arbitration

dual judicial systems 25–26, 37

dual/hybrid nature contracts viii, 229, 236

Dubai: amendments of contract 159n2, 201; civil law 152; codification of PPP legislation 105; constitutional frameworks 33, 36; development of PPP 21–23, 105, 228; direct contracting (without tendering) 123–124, 157; financial equilibrium maintenance 160; innovation in PPP award procedures 121–124, 152–153

Duche case 199

duration of contracts: Egypt 74, 80; Kuwait 82–83, 88, 91; Morocco 102; substantive mechanisms 162, 171, 179–180; traditional concession contracts 70–72

dynamic economic ideologies x, 29, 30–32, 105, 228, 232

e-commerce 107

economic crisis 2008-9 2–3, 20, 21

economic effectiveness 10

economic growth 4, 136, 138, 139, 144, 150, 151

ecosystems 150

Egypt: administrative contracts 39–44, 46–56; amendments of contract 201; arbitration 203, 204, 205–221, 222–224, 225–226, 231–232, 233–234; civil law 152; competitive dialogue 154; constitutional frameworks 29–31, 32–38, 205–206, 208, 210, 228, 232, 234; contract price amendments 159n2; development of PPP 78–82, 105, 109, 228; dispute resolution processes 174; financial equilibrium maintenance 160; *force majeure* 182, 184; innovation in PPP award procedures 108–113, 152–153; institutional frameworks 81–82; legal framework for PPP 81–82; legal system 25, 26–28; legislative reform and the Administrative Contract 73–74;

248   *Index*

overview of PPP in 19–20; Prince Theory 188–189; project companies 165–166; supervision and evaluation of projects 172–173; unforseen circumstances 193–194; *see also* Conseil d'État, Egyptian

Egyptian Court of Cassation 182

electricity sector: circular economy 137; Dubai 23, 121, 123; Egypt 73–74, 78, 79, 81; IWPP law (Kuwait) 89n18; Morocco 99

end users: balancing interests of 11, 180; changing demands of 176, 177; contracts with concessionaire 73; end user payments 8, 13, 46–47, 63, 65–66, 74, 80, 101–102, 180; equality principles 112, 169

energy sector 3, 81, 99, 150

English legal system influence 71n36, 183, 228–229

environmental concerns 135–137, 145–149, 150–151, 155, 173, 231; *see also* sustainability

e-procurement 151, 156, 230

equal opportunity practices 110, 112, 124, 131, 140, 145, 147

equality of contracting parties principle 35, 50, 55, 62, 75, 145, 180

equality principles 112, 124, 149, 169

equity 1, 10, 17, 143, 219, 221, 225

EU Circular Economy Package 136

European Investment Bank 103

exceptional prerogative clauses 62–63

excessive/exorbitant clauses (*clauses exorbitantes*) 26n51, 27, 31, 35, 37, 40, 54, 56–58, 75–76, 160, 229

Executive Privatization Commission (EPC), Jordan 96

export of labor 141

expressions of interest 115–116, 130, 166

expropriation 62, 164, 176

extensions of contract 44, 88, 171

failed PPPs 2–3

feasibility studies: Egypt 74, 80; Jordan 97, 98, 128–129; Kuwait 85, 94, 114, 115; Unsolicited Proposals 83; value for money 12

fees 6, 7, 8, 13, 63, 65, 87, 99, 163, 166, 177, 215–216; *see also* end user payments

financial equilibrium 159–160, 170, 181, 187–202, 236

financial risk 2, 11, 227

fines 50, 61, 191; *see also* penalty terms

Finland 136

food security 149

force majeure 42–43, 73, 127–128, 162, 181–187, 196, 201

foreign contractors 73, 74, 80, 83, 92, 155

Foreign Direct Investment (FDI): Bahrain 161; creating the best environment for 74, 105, 111–112, 140, 229–230; Egypt 33–34, 35–36, 38, 80, 81, 108; Inflow of Foreign Direct Investments (IFDI) x, 33, 35–36, 229, 235; innovation in PPP award procedures 138–139; international dynamics of PPPs 142

foreign investors 111, 229, 233–234

fortuitous events 42–43

France 45, 51–54, 59, 229, 232

free markets 3–4, 29, 32, 34–35, 228, 232

free movement of goods and services 4

French colonies 24–25

French Conseil d'État: administrative contracts 45, 46, 48, 51–54, 57, 64, 65, 229; excessive clauses (*clauses exorbitantes*) 59–60; *force majeure* 183, 184; influence on Egyptian Conseil d'État 27; Prince Theory 188, 192; unforeseen circumstances 194; unforeseen physical difficulties 199

French legal system influence: and administrative contracts 40–41, 45; administrative contracts 51–54, 228–229; arbitration 207, 209, 213; conclusions on 232; development of MENA legal systems 25–26, 27, 29–30, 31, 33, 35; French Napoleonic codes 25, 26, 28, 31; Morocco 101, 102; traditional concession contracts 73

frustration of contract 183

G20 Guiding Principles for Global Investment Policymaking 138–139

gas sector 32, 79, 81

gender equality 145, 148, 149

General Assembly for Legal Opinion *Fatwa* and Legislation, Egypt 41, 48, 50, 51, 54–55, 67n27, 69, 78, 188–189, 190, 193, 196, 197, 199, 206n7, 207n10, 208, 209, 210–211, 212, 214, 215, 219n54, 235

geographical scope of research 18–24

global partnership 150

globalization *see* cultural globalization; legal globalization

Index 249

grace periods 44
Green Book on the British Government Guidance on Appraisal and Evaluation, HM Treasury, 2018 12
grievance mechanisms 88, 121, 134
Guide to Public Private Partnership in Dubai 121n54
Gulf Cooperation Council (GCC) 21

Hamilton, Geoffrey 137, 155
health and safety 173
'held harmless' 9
Higher Committee (Kuwait) 84, 85, 88, 92–93, 115–116, 118, 120
hospitals 6, 81, 102
housing 81
human dignity 147, 148
human rights 145, 147, 148–149

impact measurement 18
impediments to performance of PPP contracts 181–202
indicative presumptions 64
industrial symbiosis 136
inequality 147–148, 150
Inflow of Foreign Direct Investments (IFDI) x, 33, 35–36, 229, 235
infrastructure policies 10
infrastructure projects 1–2, 4, 87, 89, 96, 99, 144, 180, 227, 229
institutional frameworks: Egypt 81–82; Jordan 97–98; Kuwait 82, 83–86, 87–88, 92–96; Morocco 102–103; Tunisia 103–104
insurance 162
interest costs 15
interface agreements 9
international arbitral awards 185–187
International Bank for Reconstruction and Development 5n22
International Centre for Settlement of Investment Disputes (ICSID) 204, 213, 234
International Chamber of Commerce (ICC) 214
International Conference of Financing for Development 2n4
International Finance Corporation 103
international investment agreements (IIAs) 222n59
International Public Works Agreements 33
international state contracts 35
international treaties 213n40

internationalization viii–ix
investment policy-making 138–139
investment treaties 222n59, 233
invitation for qualification 116, 117, 131
invitations to tender 130, 131, 133
IWPP law (Kuwait) 21, 89n18, 121

Jacquin case 65n23
job creation 140, 141, 144
joint jurisdictions 49–50
joint liability 9; *see also* risk; sub-contracting
joint stock companies 83, 84, 88, 89, 90, 94
Jordan: arbitration 225; constitutional frameworks 33, 36; development of PPP 78, 96–98, 105, 228; dispute resolution processes 174–175; innovation in PPP award procedures 128–135; institutional frameworks 97–98
Jordan Investment Commission 129
judicial precedent 42, 235
judicial review role 37, 221
jurisdiction 45, 48–50, 52–54, 58n2, 63–64

Keynes, John Maynard 4
Kuwait: amendments of contract 159n2, 201; civil law 152; constitutional frameworks 31–32, 33, 36, 37, 156, 231; development of PPP 78, 82–96, 105, 228; financial equilibrium maintenance 160; innovation in PPP award procedures 113–121, 152–153, 156; institutional frameworks 82, 83–86, 87–88, 92–96; legal system 25; overview of PPP in 22, 23–24
Kuwait Authority for Partnership Projects (KAPP) 87–88, 89, 93–94, 95

laissez-faire economics 4
land leases 91
land values 83, 88
Latin America 33–34, 35–36
leases 91
'least cost' risk allocations 15
legal globalization viii–ix, 25, 27, 28, 33, 155, 156, 159, 181, 204, 228–229, 230, 231, 236
Legal Opinion and Legislation Department (Kuwait) 95–96
Legal Opinion *Fatwa* Department *see* General Assembly for Legal Opinion *Fatwa* and Legislation, Egypt

250 *Index*

legality principle 37
Legislative Affairs Committee (Egyptian Parliament) 48
lenders: balancing citizens' and investors' rights 11; risk sharing 13–14, 178–179; step-in rights 10; typical contract frameworks 10
lex mercatoria publica 234–235
liability 9, 66–67, 177, 181–182; *see also* risk
liberalism 35
liberalization 3, 105, 107, 111, 160, 181, 228, 229, 232
libertarian economics 4
Libya 25, 185–187
licences and permits 70–72, 98, 129, 162, 176, 180
liens 83
local suppliers 169–170
lock-in periods 91
long-term contracts 1, 2–3, 5–6, 70–72, 80, 144, 161, 176, 179–180
Lyon 136

Maamoura Company for Housing and Development 59
mandatory clauses 101–102, 174, 228
Marxist ideology 30, 31, 34, 205n4
McNeill, Desmond 2n4
media advertisements of projects 111, 113, 115, 116, 117, 124, 125, 130
mediation 127, 175, 225
methane 136n68
methodology 24
metro projects 21, 121
Millennium Development Goals 145
minimal intervention (state) 34–35, 77, 104, 227, 229
Mixed Courts, Egypt 46–47, 68
modification of contract 120, 127, 135, 170, 187–193, 200–201; *see also* amendments of contract
monetarist economics 3–4
monitoring 20, 62, 82, 84, 86, 93, 127, 155, 162, 172, 231
monopolies 63, 68, 71
Morocco: amendments of contract 201; arbitration 225; constitutional frameworks 31, 32, 33, 36; development of PPP 78, 98–103, 105, 228; dispute resolution processes 175; financial equilibrium maintenance 160; innovation in PPP award procedures 124–128;

institutional frameworks 102–103; legal system 25
mortgages 83, 88
motorways 98–99, 100
Mubadala Development Company 21
multidisciplinary approaches 144
multilateral banks 7
multinational corporations 140
multi-party interfaces 177–178

Nasser, President 30
National Audit Office, UK (NAO) 12, 16–17
nationalization 30
natural resources: BOOT (Build, Own, Operate and Transfer) 73; circular economy 135–137; constitutional frameworks 32–33, 36, 69–70; Egypt 79; Sustainable Developments Goals (SDGs) 146, 147–148, 235; traditional concession contracts 68
Net Present Social Value (NPSV) 14
New Cairo Wastewater Treatment Plant 20
New Public Economics 35–36
New Urban Communities Authority (NUCA) 20
New York convention (arbitration) 204
non-administrative contracts 40
nondisclosure agreements 124
non-discrimination 4, 107, 126, 139, 147
non-negotiable conditions 111, 113, 135
Nubian Antiquities Museum 214

obligation, sources of 41–42, 43, 60, 62, 145, 178
obligations, difficulty in performing 187–193
obligations, freedom from 62
obligations, impossibility of executing 181–187
occupancy rights 63
OECD (Organization for Economic Co-operation and Development): on corruption 137–138; *Dedicated Public-Private Partnership Units: A Survey of Institutional and Governance Structure* 15n35; international PPP standards i, 81, 92n28, 103–104; OECD MAPS xi, 4n17, 92n28, 107n4, 108, 124, 151, 152, 231; *Public-Private Partnerships in the Middle East and North Africa, A Handbook for Policy Makers* 1n1, 2n5, 3n7, 78n4, 79n7, 82n10, 102n56;

Index 251

Recommendation of the Council on Principles for Public Governance of Public- Private Partnerships 13n33, 16n36; Recommendations on Public Procurement 124, 151, 153, 154–155, 231

'off the balance sheet,' PPP projects can be 14

Office of Government Commerce (OGC), UK 18, 106

oil 5, 22, 32, 38, 79, 81, 230

Olive case 42

Oman 21, 22, 31, 32

one bidder situations 120, 133, 153, 156–157

on-line bidding 151, 156, 230

open tendering 125, 126

Operationalising PPPs in Tunisia project 103–104

optimism bias 14

Ottoman Empire 25

outcomes 18

output measurement 179, 180

output specifications 7–8, 179

overrunning projects 12–13

pacta sunt servanda 46–47, 66, 68n30, 184

parallelism of legal rules 208

Partnerships Technical Bureau (PTB), Kuwait 82, 84, 85–86, 93–94

party autonomy 46, 47, 57, 77, 210, 228, 236

'pass-through' 8, 10, 177

'Paulabeuf' case 60

penalty terms 35, 50, 55, 61, 62, 102, 173, 229

People First PPPs 10–11, 136, 143

performance bonds 35, 123, 163, 165, 220, 230

performance monitoring 86, 171, 178; *see also* monitoring

performance risk 2, 227

permits and licences 70–72, 98, 129, 162, 176, 180

'Peuaraya' case 60

pilot projects 20, 103

police 62

political risk 3, 6, 81, 170, 176

pollution, designing out 135–137

Port Fouad Fishery 55–56

ports 73–74, 78, 79, 80, 98–99, 100

post-qualification processes 117

poverty 4, 145, 146, 147, 148, 149, 151

PPIAF 77n1

PPP (Public Private Partnerships): availability-based PPP 7–8; concession PPPs 8–9; definition 1–7; People First PPPs 10–11; typical contract frameworks 9–10

PPP Central Unit (PPPCU), Egypt 19, 80–82, 109–110, 111, 151, 165

PPP Reference Guide 6

PPP Unit/*Commission de Partenariat Public-Privé* (Morocco) 102–103

pre-assessments 13, 125, 126

pre-procurement processes, codified 122

pre-qualification committees (Egypt) 109–110, 112–113

pre-qualification processes 109–113, 123, 125, 126, 130–132

primary bonds 165

Prince Theory 181, 187–193

private assets 91

private law versus public law and state contracts 39–44, 47–48, 50, 51–54, 55–56, 58, 68

privileges granted solely to the authority 62

procurement law 36, 37

procurement processes 106–141; Dubai 121–124; Egypt 108–113; and infrastructure development 4; international standards 92, 152–157, 230; Jordan 128–135; Kuwait 89, 113–121; Morocco 124–128; People First PPPs 11; Tunisia 104; typical contract frameworks 9–10; and value for money evaluations 13

profit ceilings 71–72

prohibitions of PPPs 32, 38

project companies 7, 83, 89, 91, 165–166, 168, 226; *see also* Special Purpose Vehicles (SPVs)

property seizures 63

public interest: administrative contracts 50, 51, 55, 56, 66, 76; amendments of contract 170; arbitration 205, 226; in public contracts 31, 135; in public procurement processes 111, 128

public juristic persons 39–40, 42, 50, 54, 55, 56, 100, 110, 123, 210, 213, 218, 234

public law 39–44, 47–48, 50, 51–54, 55–56, 57–65, 100

Public Private Partnership Unit, Jordan 97–98

public property sale agreements 53

public services contracts 14, 52, 227

252 *Index*

public utilities 45, 65, 66, 71, 73, 76, 81, 229, 235
Public Utilities' Concession Contract 65–66
public works contracts 45, 48, 49, 50, 54, 99, 155, 187–188
public-sector comparator calculations 14–15

Qatar 21–23, 224, 232–233
quality assurance 127, 162, 171, 172
quasi-PPPs 21, 121
Quran 25

railways 3, 78
rankings (international financial institutions) ix
reference projects 15
regulatory clauses 66–67, 74, 80
regulatory risk 6
relative weight selection criteria 113
renegotiations 13, 127
renewal of contract 173–174
rent values 83, 86
Renvoi 219
reporting 20, 98, 127, 163, 166, 172; *see also* monitoring; supervision of projects
rescission of contract 35
residual value risk 2
resilience 10, 144, 177
restricted procedures methods 126
revolution 2011 x, 108
right of establishment 4
Rio Earth Summit 2n4, 147
risk: allocation in PPP contracts 6, 127, 135, 175, 178, 181, 227, 230; and the benefits of PPP 2; contractual obligations 162; and corruption 138; costing 14; dynamic nature of 175; identifiable risks in PPPs 175–181; infrastructure projects 144; 'least cost' risk allocations 15; 'pass-through' 8, 10, 177; private versus public sector perceptions of 11; profit ceilings 71; risk sharing 15; risk transfer 176, 179, 227; Special Purpose Vehicles (SPVs) 178; sub-contracting 8, 178; sustainability risk 144; typical contract frameworks 9–10; and value for money evaluations 13
Rivet, Mr 42
roads and highways 3, 6, 21, 23, 73–74, 78, 79, 98–99
Romeo, Commissioner 45

Saudi Arabia 21–23, 224, 232–233
schools 6, 81
security rights 167
seizure of property 63, 164
sensitivity analysis 14
service charges 46–47; *see also* end user payments
service fees/availability fees 7, 177
service pricing 80
service provision commitment 168–169
share offers 83, 88, 90
share transfers 167–168
shareholding structures 83, 88, 89–91, 100, 167–168
Sharia'a law 25, 27, 30, 31
short-listing 14; *see also* bid evaluation
site rights 164–165
Smith, Adam viii, xi, 3–4, 29, 34, 35, 228
social costs/benefits 14
social impact 124
Social Return on Investment (SROI) 18
social value 14
socialist economics 228, 232
socialist ideologies 29, 30, 32, 34
socio-economic developments viii, 27, 34, 105, 108, 124, 128, 139–141, 150–151, 230
sole bidders 120, 133, 153, 156–157
sovereignty 68, 211–212, 220, 229
Soviet Union 30
special nature projects 84, 85
Special Purpose Vehicles (SPVs) 7–10, 83, 88, 176, 177, 179, 222; *see also* project companies
specialized ports 73–74, 78, 79, 80
specifications 111, 115–116
sponge fishing 69n31
standard conditions 63, 98
standardized contracts 158, 181; *see also* bespoke contracts
State Audit Bureau (Kuwait) 96
state contracts 39, 51–54
state intervention, minimal 34–35, 77, 104, 227, 229
state power/role viii, 3–4, 31–32, 34, 211, 215, 228; *see also* unilateral powers
static political ideologies 29
'Ste. Des voiliers francais' case 64
step-in rights 10
'Stien' case 60
stipulations and specifications 111, 113, 223, 233–234
strategic investment plans 13

Index 253

sub-contracting 9–10, 176, 178–179, 222, 235
substitution rights 102, 127
Suez Canal ix, 70n34, 78–79, 108
Sunnah 25
supervision of projects 172, 228, 229; *see also* monitoring
Supreme Administrative Court (Egypt) 39, 40–41, 42, 54–55, 58–59, 67, 70–72, 75, 184–185, 190, 194, 195, 196, 198, 199, 208, 235
Supreme Committee for Financial Policy (the Committee), Dubai 21
Supreme Committee for Public Private Partnership Affairs (Egypt) 82, 170, 171, 174, 225
Supreme Constitutional Court, Egypt 37, 56, 59, 221
Supreme Council for Antiquities, Egypt 214, 215
suspension of project 171
sustainability 135–137, 139, 140
Sustainable Developments Goals (SDGs) ix, 2, 4, 10–11, 99, 105, 137–138, 142–151, 227, 235
sustainable financing 11
Sykes-Picot Treaty 24

technological innovations 11, 136–137, 140–141, 148, 155, 230–231
temporary rights of occupancy 63
tendering processes: Dubai 121–124; Egypt 82, 108–113; fixed tender prices 190–191, 193; international standards 13, 151–157; Jordan 97–98, 128–135; Kuwait 84, 85, 91, 94, 113–121; Morocco 101, 124–128
termination of contract 61, 62, 84, 127–128, 163, 174, 180, 183, 191–192, 220–221, 230
'Terrier' case 45
Theis, Mr 42n7
third party dealings 62–63, 173, 175, 181, 194, 226
Third Sector Organizations (TSOs) 17–18
tort 181, 184
trans-border arbitration 234–235
transition arrangements 88
transparency: competitive dialogue 154; and confidentiality 124; direct contracting (without tendering) 124; Egypt 112; international standards 92, 153; investment policy-making 139;

Jordan 132, 133; as justification for PPPs 3, 4; Morocco 100; People First PPPs 11; procurement processes 107; and value for money evaluations 13; zero tolerance for corruption 137–138
Transparency International 137
Treasury, UK 12, 17n39
Tripoli airport 185–187
trust 138
Tunisia: amendments of contract 201; constitutional frameworks 31, 32–33, 36, 229; development of PPP 78, 103–104, 105, 228; financial equilibrium maintenance 160; institutional frameworks 103–104; legal system 25–26
typo errors 43

UAE (United Arab Emirates) 21, 22, 25, 31, 32, 121; *see also* Dubai
UN (United Nations): 2030 Agenda for Sustainable Development 137–138, 142–143, 145–149, 227; increasing role 142–143; international PPP standards 81; Regional Commissions 143; UNCED (United Nations Conference on Environment and Development) 2n4; UNCITRAL (Commission on International Trade Law) 143–145, 204; UNCITRAL Legislative Guide on Privately Financed Infrastructure Projects 77n1; UNCITRAL's PPP legislative guide 143–145; UNCTAD World Investment Report 142; UNCTC (UN Centre for Transnational Corporations) 2n4; UNECA (United Nations Economic Commission for Africa) 143; UNECE (United Nations Economic Commission for Europe) 136–138, 143; UNECE Guidebook on promoting good governance in Public Private Partnership 77n1; *see also* Sustainable Developments Goals (SDGs)
uncommon clauses 57–76; *see also* excessive/exorbitant clauses (*clauses exorbitantes*)
unemployment 140, 148, 150
unforeseen physical difficulties 198–200
unforeseen circumstances (*'l'imprivision'*) 46, 71, 159, 160, 170–171, 181–187, 193–198, 201
unilateral powers: administrative contracts 51, 62, 67, 74, 75–76; arbitration 220–221, 229; constitutional frameworks

254 *Index*

34, 35, 39n1; substantive PPP
  mechanisms 159, 163
Universal Declaration of Human Rights
  147, 148–149
unsolicited proposals 83, 84, 88, 92, 101,
  123, 126
USA 232
usufruct rights 83

value for money: as feature of PPP 1, 5,
  12–18, 140, 153, 230; in procurement
  106, 113, 124, 128–129, 133; and the
  SDGs 144
value for people 1, 11, 143
Vancouver 137, 155

waivers 76, 174
waste, designing out 135–137

water 3, 6, 20, 46, 81, 89n18,
  121, 123, 150
website-based advertisements of projects
  118, 125
whole life costing 18, 106, 122
win-win situations 109, 145
women 10, 145, 149
World Bank: Benchmarking PPPs
  Procurement Report xi, 3n8, 5n18,
  77n1, 92n28, 108, 124, 152, 153–154,
  231; guidance on PPPs 77n1;
  international standards 81, 92n28, 108;
  role in availability-based PPPs 7
World Investment Report 142

Zero Tolerance to Corruption
  137–138, 143